The
Jet-to-Let
Bible

Dominic Farrell

The Jet-to-Let Bible
by Dominic Farrell

© 2006 Lawpack Publishing
   Reprinted 2007

Lawpack Publishing Limited
76–89 Alscot Road
London SE1 3AW

www.lawpack.co.uk

ISBN: 978-1-905261-11-6

Weather data in country studies reproduced by permission of
www.weather.com.

Exclusion of Liability and Disclaimer

Contents

About the author

Dominic Farrell is a full-time property investor in the UK and overseas. He has a degree in Economics and a Masters degree in Business. He attended the Royal Military Academy, Sandhurst, and served as an Infantry Officer in the British Army until retiring to continue with his property investments on a full-time basis.

He is the founder of Bewarethesharks.com – a leading property, economics, investment analysis and investor training company. The business offers training courses for novice and experienced investors seeking the skills and techniques to further their property investment success. Dominic is a prominent speaker at property events and trade shows and his views are sought by the national press and television. He also writes for investment journals and newspapers.

Dominic is the founder of a large international property investment company and is passionate about the opportunities that overseas investments can offer the intelligent investor. In his first book, *The Jet-to-Let Bible*, Dominic draws on his extensive experience, and the many and extremely diverse experiences of his students, and provides a comprehensive framework for successful overseas property investment.

Acknowledgements

I would like to thank everyone who has contributed to this book either directly or indirectly, particularly across our companies where others have shouldered my workload for the last few months. I would particularly like to thank Luke Moore and Alina Shnaidruc for their hard work and enthusiasm in researching and putting together Part 2.

I have drawn the ideas for Part 1 from personal experience and have used material from the many property seminars I give throughout the year to thousands of people in the UK and overseas.

Thanks also to the many property investors, both novice and experienced, I have met through our property investment training company Bewarethesharks.com. I believe that we all learn from each other and the time I have spent with many of our students has been extremely rewarding both personally and professionally and I now count many as personal friends. It's very satisfying that so many of them have now quit the rat race to pursue property investing full time and have reaped the rewards for time spent learning, researching and experiencing.

Without Stephanie none of this would be possible as she has been my right- and left-hand woman for many years as we have journeyed together down the road of property investing. Happy to stay in the background publicly, she is very much at the forefront of our investment and business strategy and is a firm hand on the tiller.

And finally for my Mum, Molly, who many years ago persuaded me that investing, particularly in property, was better than buying expensive cars. How right she was.

Part 1: Introduction

Welcome to *The Jet-to-Let Bible* – your guide to the exciting and profitable world of overseas property investment.

What is the major advantage of jet-to-let? You can be free! Free to decide how to use your time; free to live anywhere in the world; free to spend more time with your family and free to pursue activities which really stimulate and interest you. Most importantly, you are free from answering to anyone else – except yourself. For investors, financial freedom is the main reward at the end of the property investment journey.

This book aims to demystify the process of buying abroad and will provide you with all the tools you need with which to be successful. Whether you are a complete newcomer or an experienced international investor, this book's clear and simple approach will guide you in making your overseas property work for you!

What is your goal? Successful property investors have choice. Some carry on working for other people, some start their own businesses and some 'retire'. Whichever path you choose, the key factor is that a successful investor makes decisions based on his wants and needs and not on economic necessity. Whatever your aim is, whether it's to be totally financially free or to give yourself a lucrative second income, *The Jet-to-Let Bible* is essential reading.

So, what makes this book different from all the others on this subject? Well, for a start, it's not a disguised travel guide with a few 'tips' thrown in for the sake of credibility and it's not just pages of common sense which will leave you feeling cheated. Instead, it's a unique guide to every aspect of the buying process which you can use to get ahead of less savvy investors and leave them floundering at the departure gate. As the old saying goes, forewarned is forearmed, so the book's well-researched chapters will give you all the information you need to invest with confidence.

Why should you invest in property abroad? Property is an effective money-making investment and overseas property investment is particularly popular. Chapter 1 outlines this through the analysis of supply and demand, economics, and how these factors affect the domestic and international property markets. The phenomenon of jet-to-let and the reasons for its prolific growth are also examined in some detail.

Opportunity cost, return on investment and using other people's money is the subject of the second chapter. These key investor concepts will change your approach to property investment and the level of profits you can earn. They will also adjust your thinking when you are considering the best way to get the highest return on investment. Just by using simple principles, you can make money without investing much of your own.

The most difficult question is where to start investing. Chapter 3 shows how to use a 'top-down approach' to property investment so that you can maximise your profits. The most popular types of location may seem obvious (beaches, waterfronts, exclusive city neighbourhoods, etc.) but it's important to understand the reasons for their profitability. Money makes the world go round, so why not go round the world and make some too?

Chapter 4 focuses on strategy and looks at how goal-setting, reviewing and a 'big-picture' approach will ultimately lead to success. It looks at the different types of investors and shows you how to play to your strengths while keeping a realistic approach to your investment. Using the technique of investor profiling will also make the process of property investment a lot clearer.

Number-crunching and the financial considerations of jet-to-let form the body of chapter 5. Many novice investors don't take into account the costs associated with purchasing a property and then letting it out on a commercial basis. Cash flow is king and this chapter outlines the techniques used by professional investors to ensure maximum profitability.

Property development, renovation projects and 'off-plan' packages are examined in the following chapter, with information on how to use and improve your negotiating skills to get the best deal. All the jet-to-let strategies available are examined so that you can choose the best one to suit you.

Vital to any investment is an understanding of risk. How to plan, to control and mitigate (i.e. hedge against) any potential problems is fundamental to your investment success. Risk takes many forms and is examined in detail in chapter 7. We also show how a risk management matrix can assist you in formulating a robust risk management plan.

Everything that you need to know before signing on the dotted line is dealt with in chapter 8. There is also crucial information on whom to buy from, and the risks involved in buying in another currency. We then look at contracts as well as the potential pitfalls that await the ill-prepared when investing overseas.

So, you've looked into buying your property, prepared yourself to negotiate the best price, have overcome the potential hurdles with ease but something's missing: people! Chapter 9 shows you how to find tenants for your property, whether short- or long-term, and from across a multitude of different markets. There are some useful tips to ensure that your property is never empty, and that the people paying to stay there will be happy to come back again and again.

The final chapter outlines the necessity of having a checklist when researching and analysing where to invest. The book includes a list of the factors you should consider before embarking on the jet-to-let journey and shows you how to apply your own criteria to this analysis so that you can get the most out of your future overseas property investments.

Now, let's go back to the question of where to start. In Part 2 of the book, there is a reference section which has information on 20 locations across four continents detailing everything from the climate to currency, from politics to property, using the most up-to-date data. These outline some of the most popular and up-and-coming jet-to-let destinations at the moment. They also provide you with a framework for research so that you can compile your own information for other destinations.

Finally, in the Appendices, the book aims to add the last pieces of the puzzle to your overseas property investment jigsaw. It includes a list of UK holidaymakers' top destinations, low-cost airline routes, retirement destinations, economic facts, exchange rates and transaction costs. These facts and figures will make it easier for you to plan your overseas investments and make *The Jet-to-Let Bible* your new best friend!

CHAPTER 1

Why invest in property and why jet-to-let?

The advantages of investing in property

If I asked you why you wanted to invest in property, you probably would say that you want to make money and subsequently obtain financial freedom. Numerous people have written about the advantages of property investment over the years and, needless to say, the main attraction is the possibility of getting high returns from a relatively small investment, but let's explore some of the other factors that make property investment so appealing.

1. It's easy to understand

Unlike stocks and shares, property is a lot easier to understand. Share prices move for many reasons, some of which are purely psychological or even influenced by computer trading programs, and myths abound in the UK that you must have a good knowledge of stocks and shares in order to profit from share trading. However, for the average person in the street, the most effective way to gain exposure to the markets is by using a stockbroker. The commissions you pay for trading are effectively the fee for the broker's professional services, his years of experience and training, plus a contribution to his costs, such as salaries, marketing and insurance.

Alternatively, you can train yourself. There are some great books written on the subject and training courses are also a popular way to fast-track your knowledge, but, in my view, it takes years to achieve the level of knowledge and experience with which to successfully trade in the markets.

Property, on the other hand, is something with which we are all familiar and use 24 hours a day. We all understand what a bedroom is and know what amenities we need. The advantage of property investment is that we already have the basic knowledge to start with, so all we need to do is add a few investor concepts and we're ready to go!

2. It's an asset which won't go out of fashion

We all have a basic need for shelter. So, unlike stocks, shares, bonds, or even lottery tickets, we need property in order to survive. It's as basic as food and water and will never go out of date.

3. Property is in demand for many reasons, not just for investment

We all contribute to the demand for property and whether we buy or rent, we still need somewhere to live. Equally, businesses demand property in order to operate. Whether residential or commercial, the demand for property is generated and sustained by our very existence.

4. Property can be leveraged to achieve huge returns on investment

What is meant by 'leverage'? Here are a couple of definitions:

> 'Using someone else's money to purchase property.'

> 'Using resources in such a way that the potential outcome is magnified.'

The benefits of using leverage can be substantial. I will return to this key investor concept in the next chapter.

5. Property can be purchased 'below market value'

It can be argued that stock markets operate a more efficient market than property markets, as the price of individual shares reflects all the information available in the market. 'Market-makers' also provide a ready market for the buying and selling of shares and this makes them highly liquid. With the press of a button you can sell your entire portfolio and realise your cash. In contrast, property is illiquid, which means that you generally cannot sell quickly at the prevailing market price.

This illiquidity works as both a strength and a weakness. It's a strength because property markets are less volatile than stock markets as property investment is a 'get rich slowly' activity. However, the disadvantage is that it takes time to market and sell a property and there is no guarantee that someone else will want it at the time you want to sell it or at the price you would like.

This is where we arrive at the concept of buying 'below market value'. There is no such thing as a national property market – it's just a series of regional and local markets. Within these markets it's impossible for every participant to have all the knowledge and information available, which means that it's not efficient. Some of the participants have more information than others and may use special marketing activities to gain a competitive advantage. Maybe the following picture from your local newspaper looks familiar?

Just take a look under the classified section for examples in your area.

The nature of the property market means that one party may be a 'forced seller' and the asset (i.e. the property) can be bought for less than its expected price on the open market. After all, for the seller, desperate times call for desperate measures. Buying below market value is a strategy pursued by many property investors, and after refinancing allows the investor to own the property with little or none of his own cash invested.

6. Property consistently rises in value

Whether you invest in property in the UK or overseas, one thing is for certain – good things come to those who wait. For most things it's an old cliché, but in property investment it holds true. If you hold property for the long term, you will have an appreciating asset that pays handsome rewards through both income and capital growth.

If you look at the average house price in the UK, the upward trend (represented by the thick black line) of house prices is unmistakable.

Average house price in the UK 1990–2005

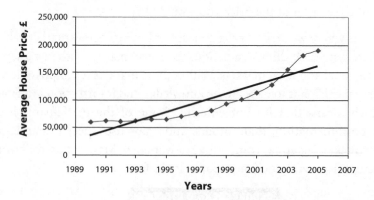

(Source: Department for Communities and Local Government)

This trend isn't specific to the UK and has been repeated in many of the countries that are examined in the case studies at the back of the book. Here is data from the Spanish Ministerio di Vivienda to illustrate the point:

Average house price in Spain 1990–2005

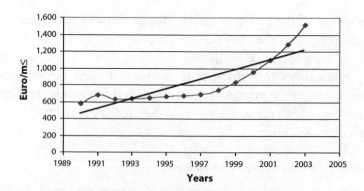

(Source: Ministerio di Vivienda)

While there may be peaks and troughs along the way, long-term returns on property consistently show a steady rise.

These are just a few of the reasons why you should invest in property. Now, let's turn our attention to the overseas residential and lettings market, which is exciting, expanding and has a wealth of benefits that are presently lacking in the UK.

Why should you invest overseas?

A recent survey of 4,000 people showed that 47 per cent of the 18–29 age group plans to buy overseas, with 64 per cent of those being first-time buyers. 81 per cent of this new generation will let out their overseas property when they are not there.

40 per cent of all Britons plan to buy abroad. Why? If we were lying on a psychiatrist's couch and he asked us this question, our immediate answers might be the following:

- Financial gain
- Sunshine
- Pension
- Travel
- Income
- Holidays
- Prosperity
- Family
- Affordability
- Portfolio diversification
- The UK market stalling
- The UK exodus
- Retirement
- Lifestyle

- Opportunity
- Economic expansion
- New Europe (the countries which acceded to the European Union (EU) on 1 May 2004)

These quick-fire words help to explain the phenomenon of jet-to-let. It's no exaggeration to use the word phenomenon – you only need to visit property exhibitions up and down the country to notice the proliferation of companies selling overseas properties.

The usual suspects of Spain, Portugal, France, Italy, Canada and the US (mainly Florida) are well represented, but new kids have arrived on the block and some are giving the traditional investment countries a run for their money. These 'new' investment locations are diverse in terms of economics, geography, politics, history and risk, and include:

- Bulgaria
- Cape Verde
- Caribbean
- Croatia
- Cyprus
- Dubai
- Germany
- Greece
- Malta
- Morocco
- Romania
- Turkey
- Eastern European 8: Czech Republic, Estonia, Hungary, Latvia, Lithuania, Poland, Slovakia and Slovenia

A third group of countries are emerging, mainly in Central and South America and Asia, and these are:

- Argentina
- Brazil
- China
- India (Goa)
- Honduras
- Panama
- South Africa
- Thailand
- Venezuela

In short, there are three distinct groups of countries which make up the jet-to-let market:

- Traditional
- New European, Middle East and North Africa
- Emerging worldwide

Where you invest will be determined by your goals, tolerance to risk, and desirability. Another important factor is due diligence, which encompasses all of the research that you will do when you are considering investing in a specific region.

You will no doubt have taken one look at the countries listed and said to yourself, 'yes, no, no, maybe', etc. My aim with this book is for you to be able to say 'yes' or 'no' based on fact and reason, rather than any preconceived ideas or distance.

The reasons behind the growth of jet-to-let

There are many reasons why jet-to-let has taken off in the last couple of years, if you will forgive the pun.

1. Stagnation in the UK property market

Property investors have seen substantial returns from the UK property market over the last seven years, but times are changing. It would have been possible for a blindfolded monkey with three darts and a map of the UK to have prospered in the strong bull property market of recent years. The ethics of proving this entrepreneurial monkey's success may be questionable, but it's clear that prices have risen all over the UK, from Dover to Darlington and from Liverpool to Leicester.

Why? Property prices are determined by a number of economic factors which include interest rates, the accessibility of finance, employment levels and growth in real incomes. These are discussed further in later sections of the book.

In November 2003, the Bank of England's Monetary Policy Committee (MPC), which has an independent remit to set interest rates, raised rates for the first time in nearly four years by 25 basis points or 0.25 per cent. It can be argued that this, with other interest rate rises, was the catalyst for the cooling of the UK property market.

2. Affordability in the UK

Property prices in the UK are stretched when measured against the traditional yardstick of earnings. In essence, wages have not kept pace with the explosive growth in house prices, hence affordability (or the lack of it), particularly for first-time buyers, is contributing to a stalling UK market.

The 'house prices to earnings' ratio (HPE) is an important measure of the value of the UK property market as a whole. This ratio is very simple to understand.

If the average wage in the UK is £20,000 and the average property value is £100,000, then:

£100,000 ÷ £20,000 = 5.

Therefore, in this scenario, the HPE ratio is 5.

It's relatively straightforward to show how an increase in property prices or a rise in average wages reduces or increases the HPE, as follows:

Average wages increase to £25,000 per annum while property prices remain stable at £100,000, so:

£100,000 ÷ £25,000 = 4 and the HPE ratio is 4.

As wages rise, property becomes more affordable, but the problem we face presently in the UK is that the ratio of property prices to wages is too high and affordability is stretched. The ratio at present is 5.84 (*source: Nationwide*) up from 4.77 three years ago, while the long-term trend over 25 years is below four.

So now, in terms of affordability, investors are looking overseas where the cost of entering the market is lower, and where they can get a bigger bang for their buck.

3. Falling yields in the UK property market

Another method which can be used to measure the value of a property market is to look at the relationship between prices and rents. Firstly, gross yield can be defined as:

'The annual income received on a property, expressed as a percentage of its capital value.'

Example

So, a property worth £100,000 which rents at £6,500 per year has a gross yield of:

£6,500 ÷ £100,000 x 100 = 6.5%

If the value rises by 30% and rents remain static, then:

£6,500 ÷ £130,000 x 100 = 5%

The gross yield or income return from that property declines and becomes a less attractive option for new entrants into the market. This is another factor that pushes buyers to look at other markets for greater returns.

4. The substitution effect

Property investors who have been accustomed to strong returns have started looking overseas for the same factors which propelled the UK market to historical highs. These factors are falling interest rates, economic growth and accessible finance.

Therefore, property investors have begun substituting two-up-two-downs in Hull for new-build apartments in Poland, Slovakia and Hungary or villas with pools in Cyprus and Florida.

They are seeking countries with a strong economic and political outlook, such as accession to the EU and the adoption of the euro currency. Outside of Europe, general economic and political stability are the main pulling factors for investors.

5. Property market cycles

All markets move in cycles with key points being:

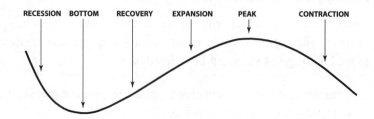

RECESSION BOTTOM RECOVERY EXPANSION PEAK CONTRACTION

You can see from the diagram above how property markets work. In fact, all markets work in the same way. After a recession, or falling market, a bottom is reached. One stock market strategy is 'bottom fishing', where investors buy shares which have fallen in value, because it's thought that they will not fall any further but start to rise. The same principles can be applied to the property market and Germany is a present day example of this approach.

The UK property market was in recession throughout the early 1990s and bottomed in 1995. After a period of recovery and then considerable expansion from the late 1990s through to mid 2004 where it peaked, it then went into a period of contraction for 16 months until the end of 2005 (according to data from Hometrack).

It's because of the cyclical nature of property markets that we have substitution effects. As the UK market was peaking, savvy investors were already looking for the next market which was in a different stage of the property market cycle.

6. Liberalisation of overseas political, economic and financial institutions

The Berlin Wall was erected on 13 August 1961 and became the physical embodiment of the divide between Western democratic market economies and Communism. I lived in West Berlin from 1988 to 1990, and was there at the opening of the crossings between the east and the west of the city on 9 November 1989.

If anyone had told me that within a couple of years of my arrival in Berlin, the Soviet empire would collapse and that property investors, some years later, would be investing in Latvia, Poland and other former Communist countries, I would have questioned their sanity.

Nevertheless, one of the key drivers of the property market in Europe has been the demise of the Soviet Union and the accession to the EU on 1 May 2004 of the former Soviet satellite countries of Poland, Slovakia, Slovenia, Estonia, Lithuania, Latvia, Hungary and the Czech Republic.

What a remarkable turnaround of events! These 'Eastern European 8' have recently attracted considerable investor interest due to the fact that they have had to play catch up with the rest of 'old' Europe.

Property investors have been attracted to these relatively new markets because of:

- EU entry and the benefits of the single market;
- high foreign direct investment leading to economic growth;
- the reform of legal practices;
- falling interest rates;
- euro currency entry;
- the liberalisation of financial markets making housing loans (i.e. mortgages) more readily available; and
- the potential rapid increase in property prices.

Most investor interest to date has been within the capital cities of these countries, as this strategy tends to have less risk than investing in secondary and tertiary cities. Capital cities have a dynamic of their own, a worldwide demand and provide attractive bases for corporations and government departments.

However, as some of the Eastern European 8 capital cities, such as Prague and Budapest, have risen in value, many investors are now looking at the secondary cities (such as Brno and Debrecen respectively) for further growth and diversification.

7. Lifestyle

It was once fashionable to work long hours, commute many miles, talk about how it was killing you and have mad parties, wear red braces and drink champagne a lot. I think people call it the 1980s!

Well, things have changed. Gone are the indulgences of the 'me, me, me' culture and they have been replaced by those pillars of modern society – quality time and work–life balance. We live in an era where leisure and free time are again very important.

Jet-to-letters have realised this and have invested in what I term 'live-and-let' property. Unlike investments in the Eastern European 8, which tend to be let out to long-term tenants as in the UK, 'live-and-letters' invest in sunshine destinations or ski resorts.

Traditional locations, such as Spain, Italy and Portugal, have now been joined by Cyprus, Florida, Greece and the Caribbean as destinations for an investment which is as much to do with lifestyle as business.

Investors in these destinations use the property for themselves, their friends and family and then let the property for the time they are not there. In countries which have an all-year-round warm climate, the return on a well-marketed property can be amazing.

Lifestyle investments will continue to grow as we become wealthier and demand more leisure time and, particularly living in the UK, we need a bit of welcome sunshine or time on the piste!

8. Entrepreneurial opportunity and the global village

An increasing number of investors are looking overseas for greater returns because the world is simply a smaller place. Travel, communications and technology advances mean that most overseas investors have travelled outside of their respective countries and have realised that distance should not be a barrier to a sound investment opportunity.

Anyone who lives in London and has travelled to the Lake District on a Friday evening will understand that it can be quicker to get to Spain for the weekend. Until the advent of 'Easy-Rail' or 'Ryan-Track', it will ironically remain cheaper to get to Andalucía than Ambleside!

9. Superior financial returns

Property investors have driven the jet-to-let phenomenon because they recognise that all markets have cycles, and that investing in countries which have strong political and economic reasons for future growth will provide them with superior returns.

Example

Luke has £100,000 cash to invest and decides to invest in a market which is growing by 3% per annum for 5 years.

After 5 years his return (excluding income) is £115,927 – a profit before tax of £15,927.

Alina invests the same amount of cash in a market which is growing by 10% per annum for 5 years.

After 5 years her return (excluding income) is £161,051 – a profit before tax of £61,051.

Alina makes £45,124 more than Luke by investing in a market which is at a different stage of the property market cycle, revealing some alarming differences in the performance of property markets around the world.

Before making an investment in a particular city or locality, an investor must look at how the national market is performing and at what stage it is in the cycle.

1997–2005 world property price growth

Hong Kong	−44%
Japan	−28%
Germany	Nil
UK	155%

Spain	171%
Ireland	196%
South Africa	263%

(Source: The Economist)

A property investor who had invested in South Africa would be more content after eight years than someone who had picked Japan or Hong Kong.

With all of these factors considered, it's very clear that not all jet-to-let locations are equal. It's not a homogeneous market and because of this, the importance of research and analysis when deciding on where to invest is hard to overstate.

Why invest in jet-to-let? Overseas property markets at different stages in the cycle promise and can deliver better returns than those predicted to occur in the UK. Demand, opportunities and potential for profit exist in abundance, so perhaps the question should be rephrased to 'why not?'

Key points summary

- Property as an investment is easy to understand
- It's an asset which will not go out of fashion
- We need property in order to live
- Property can be leveraged to achieve massive returns
- Property can be purchased below market value
- Property consistently rises in value over time
- The jet-to-let phenomenon has many causes:
  - A cooling of the UK market
  - Affordability in the UK for new entrants into the market
  - Falling yields in UK residential property
  - The substitution effect
  - Property market cycles

- Liberalisation of overseas political, economic and financial institutions
- Lifestyle
- Entrepreneurship and the global village
- Superior financial returns

CHAPTER 2

Key concepts to unlock investment success

There are various key concepts that must be understood before you can improve your chances of jet-to-let investment success. This chapter explores these concepts in detail using examples to illustrate how they can be applied to your future overseas property ventures.

Opportunity cost, return on investment and using other people's money ('gearing')

What is opportunity cost?

Opportunity cost is an extremely important concept. There are numerous definitions to be found in the many texts on economic theory. The definition is usually in the first few pages of the book as it's not just the cornerstone of economics, but it also forms the basis of property investment. It underpins everything and as long as you adhere to its principles you will be a successful property investor.

 Opportunity cost is the true cost of what you have given up in order to get something else.

In other words, it's the 'foregone alternative'.

I'll give a couple of examples to illustrate this crucial concept:

1. John, Collette and their two children go on holiday for two weeks in the summer to Spain. John is self-employed and in a two-week period would normally earn £2,000 as an accountant. The opportunity cost for him in financial terms of holidaying is £2,000 because he would have earned that amount if he had stayed at home. So, if the cost of the holiday was also £2,000, then the true cost of the holiday is actually £4,000.

    Collette is employed, but has the option to trade holiday for pay. She chooses her holiday which, like the above example, has an economic cost.

2. A 'big-picture' moment if I may: The UK government has a finite amount of resources, which are raised through taxes and borrowing. It has to make choices on how to spend the limited resources that it has available. For every hospital it builds, it has to forego a school and for every tank it manufactures, there is less money to spend on roads.

Clearly this last example is not as simple in practice, as budgets are set and resources distributed accordingly, but the principle still stands. In order to get something, we have to give something else up and that something else is the true cost or 'opportunity cost'.

Opportunity cost and savings

Jane and Peter, unlike Collette and John, have decided to focus on their savings rather than go away on holiday. They compare accounts and see that Jane's bank pays 5% interest on her cash while Peter's 2%.

Both accrue interest, but Jane receives more than double that of Peter. In terms of opportunity cost, Peter has lost 3% by not making the right investment choice.

If both investors have £10,000 in the bank, after one year and before tax Jane will have £10,500 and Peter will have £10,200 – a difference of £300 and an opportunity cost loss for Peter!

If you start thinking in this way, your financial circumstances will change for the better. Even if you just ensure that your cash is in an account which makes your money work as hard as possible for you, then you are on the road to an investor's mindset.

So, why not start right now? Put down this book and check what interest you are receiving on any savings that you have. Check out the highest paying interest account via the internet or the weekend press and move your money so that it works better for you.

 Check out whether the rate is just a promotion or is only applicable in the short term. Go with the company which has a track record of long-term sustainable market leading rates.

Opportunity cost and jet-to-let

In chapter 1, I looked at world property price growth from 1997 to 2005. Here is the table again to refresh your memory:

Hong Kong	–44%
Japan	–28%
Germany	Nil
UK	155%
Spain	171%
Ireland	196%
South Africa	263%

In terms of opportunity cost, the losses made in Japan are greater than 28 per cent because the property investor could have invested in South Africa instead!

While this is of no comfort to the owner of an apartment in Tokyo or Osaka, the effective opportunity loss is 263 per cent + 28 per cent = 291 per cent. This could quite easily be referred to as the 'blimey' factor, especially when we look at in terms of cash!

So, in the table, what would a £100,000 house be worth today if you had paid cash in 1997?

Property Market	Purchase Price 1997	House Price Inflation (HPI)	Market Value 2005
Hong Kong	£100,000	−44%	£56,000
Japan	£100,000	−28%	£72,000
Germany	£100,000	Nil*	£100,000
UK	£100,000	+155%	£255,000
Spain	£100,000	+171%	£271,000
Ireland	£100,000	+196%	£296,000
South Africa	£100,000	+263%	£363,000

* In real terms, when accounting for the erosion of buying power through inflation, the investor has made a real loss in Germany, although in monetary terms he still has £100,000. Sadly, his £100,000 is worth a lot less than it was eight years ago, when he could have gone to the movies, caught a bus home and still had change for fish and chips out of a fiver!

The figures in this table clearly illustrate the concept of opportunity cost.

House Price Inflation (HPI) 1997–2005

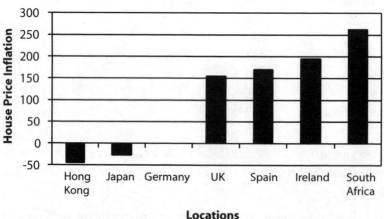

 A successful investor weighs up all the alternatives before making a decision.

Now the figures, as they stand, speak volumes – the House Price Inflation (HPI) figure is effectively our return on investment (ROI).

Return on investment

 Return on investment (ROI) is the total profit expressed as a percentage of the amount of cash initially invested.

Example

If I had invested £100,000 in a house in the UK in 1997 and sold it in 2005, according to the table above I would have made a profit (before income, costs and tax) of £155,000.

So, profit = £155,000 and cash invested = £100,000.

ROI is profit/cash invested x 100, which in this case is £155,000 ÷ £100,000 x 100 = 155%

We will return to this important investor ratio in chapter 5.

The concept of opportunity cost really kicks in when you add in leverage or gearing.

 Gearing is 'borrowing funds to increase buying power'.

Most people who own a property have a mortgage – it's the most common example of gearing or borrowing. If a property is worth £100,000 and you have a deposit of £10,000, the borrowed mortgage of £90,000 allows you to increase your buying power. In other words, you can buy a £100,000 property for only £10,000 with gearing or borrowing other people's money (i.e. the bank's).

Loan to value

Loan to value (LTV) is the ratio of the loan to the price of the property, and is usually expressed as a percentage.

Example

If I borrow £90,000 from the bank to purchase a property worth £100,000, the LTV is £90,000 ÷ £100,000 x 100 = 90%.

High gearing and low gearing

When an investor has a 90 per cent LTV mortgage, he is considered to be highly geared. In other words, his borrowings are high. If the same investor has a mortgage of only 30 per cent of the price of the property, he is considered to have low gearing as his borrowings represent a relatively small percentage of the property's price.

 Another term for borrowing or gearing is 'leverage' and this term is often used in the US or outside of the UK.

There are many differing views about gearing. Some people believe that gearing and risk go hand in hand; the higher the gearing, the greater the risk and the lower the gearing, the lower the risk. Personally, I don't go along with this simple view – risk has many faces, including opportunity risk.

Why not? Well, we are trying to maximise the ROI (i.e. the return on the cash that we have invested in a project). If we look back at the example of Jane and Peter, Jane has maximised the ROI by receiving five per cent interest from the bank. Peter has not maximised his return, and his cash is not working as hard for him as Jane's.

How does high gearing increase my ROI?

Example

Jane bought a property in Spain for £100,000 in 1997 with a 10% deposit. She borrowed £90,000 from the bank, which gave her an LTV of 90%.

Peter also bought a property at the same time and for the same price next door. He obtained a mortgage at 50% LTV.

They both sold their properties in 2005 at an increased value of 171%.

For simplicity, we are ignoring costs, taxes and income.

The gearing effect

The ROI is calculated as follows:

Jane's case

Selling price – purchase price = gross profit

ROI = gross profit ÷ cash invested x 100

So, £271,000 – £100,000 = £171,000

£171,000 ÷ £10,000 x 100 = 1710%

Peter's case

£271,000 – £100,000 = £171,000

£171,000 ÷ £50,000 x 100 = 342%

In the example above, Jane's ROI is five times that of Peter's due to gearing. Her money has worked harder.

Now, what if the following happened:

They both started with £50,000 seed capital and instead of investing in one property, Jane actually invested in 5. At 90% LTV, Jane has 5 deposits of £10,000 each. So, Jane can now borrow £450,000 at 90% LTV and buy 5 properties.

In 1997, Jane's portfolio was valued at £500,000.

She sells all 5 properties in 2005 at a portfolio selling price of £1,355,000.

Her profit before tax is £855,000.

Although the ROI has not changed in percentage terms, the amount of money Jane has made has gone through the roof.

Peter versus Jane

The investors started with the same capital and invested in the same properties.

> Peter's gearing was low and he made a 342% ROI amounting to £171,000.
>
> Jane's gearing was high and she made 1710% ROI amounting to £855,000.

This example illustrates the power of gearing in rising markets and the massive gains that an investor can make if he targets the right markets.

As with all things, there are drawbacks with gearing and it may not be suitable for everyone.

Drawbacks

1. Cash flow risk

Jane has five mortgages to cover and will pay a greater monthly repayment than Peter. In this example, with an interest-only mortgage at five per cent per annum, Jane has to find £1,875 per month[1]. Peter has to pay only £208 per month[2]. In most cases overseas, however, repayment mortgages are the standard and capital also has to be repaid each month, increasing the burden on Jane.

 Have a contingency fund for voids (i.e. times when your property is empty and isn't generating any income to cover your costs). Even in the sunniest locations, it's important to have money put away for a rainy day!

[1] Jane has borrowed £450,000 with an interest rate at five per cent. The annual repayment on an interest-only mortgage is calculated in this way:

Borrowed amount x interest rate ÷ 100.

Therefore, in this example it will be:

£450,000 x 5 ÷ 100 = £22,500 and because it's the annual figure, Jane will be liable to pay £1,875 per month (£22,500 ÷ 12).

[2] Peter has borrowed £50,000 with an interest rate at five per cent. His monthly repayment figure is calculated in the same way as in the example with Jane.

2. Financial risk

If property prices fall, Jane has greater exposure to losses. If prices fall by just ten per cent to £90,000 per property, Jane's initial capital is wiped out. Her £100,000 properties are now worth only what she has borrowed from the bank (she has borrowed £450,000, which is the same as £90,000 per property multiplied by five). In the case of Peter, he still has £40,000 of capital remaining – he has invested £50,000, so when property prices fall by £10,000 he still has £40,000.

To gear or not to gear?

The merits, or otherwise, of gearing can be debated until the cows come home, but if you are serious about making money through property investment, you have no choice. It's financially unwise to invest cash and the most successful investors understand the concept of OPM – 'other people's money'.

It's an inefficient use of capital to have it all tied up in one or two assets. By using the principle of OPM – in this case, the bank – a savvy investor can magnify the effect of his available resources.

The simple case of Jane highlights the greater returns associated with gearing, but also identifies the increased risk.

Note: Property investment is not just for Christmas, but for the long term. Risk is proportionate to time. An investor who wants to make a quick return has a higher exposure to risk than one with a ten-year view or longer – proving that patience is indeed a virtue.

 Always plan for rises in the rate of interest you pay on a mortgage. You want to know the likely effect on your cash flow and at what rate of interest you will have financial difficulties.

You should now feel more comfortable with the key concepts of opportunity cost, ROI and gearing. These are the core basics, so you may find it useful to go back over this chapter as I detail jet-to-let economics and the 'top down' approach to overseas property investment next.

Key points summary

- Opportunity cost is the cornerstone of all investing.

- Borrowing money increases buying power and is known as 'gearing' or 'leverage'.

- Gearing has many advantages and in rising markets can be a potent tool.

- Gearing also has disadvantages in terms of cash flow risk and financial risk in falling markets.

CHAPTER 3

The 'top down' approach to property investment

This chapter aims to demystify the economic principles which drive worldwide property markets, helping you to learn and understand how a country's economy ultimately determines the success of property as an investment and over what timeframe this occurs.

By the end of this chapter you will have a good understanding of how economic growth, interest rates and inflation affect property markets. You will also learn how to apply that knowledge in order to find countries, regions and localities which have the right investment conditions to support rising property prices and rents.

The top down method of jet-to-let

A top down approach starts with the concept of 'the world's your oyster' and, through research, finishes with you identifying a specific property in a specific postcode. The top down approach to jet-to-let looks like this:

- The world
- A continent
- A country
- A region

- A county
- A city/town
- A locality
- A postcode
- A property

Don't be daunted by the prospect of starting with the world and then narrowing it down to an individual property. By following the template in chapter 10 you will ensure that you have considered all the salient points.

How to spot an overseas property hotspot

Personal preferences for a country, its culture and cuisine should be left completely to one side, as only the investment potential of a particular country, region and locality is of any great significance at this stage.

What is a 'jet-to-let hotspot'?

Here are two definitions:

1. A jet-to-let hotspot is created when demand for property exceeds the available supply and prices are pushed higher, above the international average, by those wanting to buy.

2. A jet-to-let hotspot is a country, region or city where economic factors are combining to increase long-term wealth, which will have a direct, positive effect on property prices and rents.

These definitions encapsulate the key drivers of world property prices:

1. Supply and demand
2. Multiplier effects
3. Sentiment or 'the crowd'

What determines the price of property?

Before embarking on an analysis of hotspots and how they are created, you must first examine why property prices rise and fall and what factors are at play.

1. Supply and demand

In order for you to understand why professional investors decide to choose one country over another, you must understand thoroughly the relationship between supply, demand and price. The table below provides a summary of the relationship and how a change in supply or demand moves price.

Supply	Demand	Price
Static	Increases	Rises
Static	Decreases	Falls
Increases	Static	Falls
Decreases	Static	Rises

As you can appreciate, there are many permutations and not all goods behave the way we would expect; for instance, some goods may see an increase in demand after a price hike because they will appeal to the elite. However, normal goods follow a similar pattern to the illustration above.

Ideally, investors want demand to increase for both property and rental accommodation, with both prices and rents rising together. They also don't want any more properties built after they have invested – ever. If demand continues and there is no more supply, then prices will continue to rise and they will be in profit. This is the essence of jet-to-let and property investing in general.

 Look to invest in areas where demand is increasing, there is a limited supply of property and where supply is not likely to expand sufficiently to absorb new buyers.

The degree to which supply or demand can change due to a change in price is referred to by economists as 'elasticity'. If the percentage change in supply or demand is greater than the change in price, then goods can be called 'price elastic'. If it's less, then they are 'price inelastic'.

 Investors should seek out areas where the supply of property is price inelastic. So as prices rise, the supply of property cannot expand sufficiently to match the increase in demand and so prices continue to be squeezed upwards.

Where do I find areas of inelastic supply?

- Beaches and waterfronts are perfect examples of this concept of 'inelastic supply'. No matter how much demand increases and developers are tempted to build more properties to meet that demand, they cannot because the land is finite. A beach is a beach and cannot be replicated inland.

- Prime city centre or exclusive areas – Manhattan is a small island with very large skyscrapers. More properties cannot be built easily so prices rise to absorb increasing demand.

- Properties which have spectacular views will always be in demand and again they cannot be replicated easily.

- Properties on golf courses and around marinas usually attract and maintain a premium to the market.

- Properties which are located in national parks and areas of outstanding beauty.

- Properties which have a historical interest or are listed due to their architectural importance for the nation.

Scarcity, exclusivity and inelastic supply are a jet-to-letter's dream come true.

2. The multiplier effect

A multiplier effect occurs when an increase in investment spending by governments, corporations and international bodies, such as the European Union (EU), causes an increase in jobs, wealth and prosperity.

How does it work? A large motor vehicle manufacturing plant opens in a city in Eastern Europe, recruits a workforce of unemployed people and, after training, employs them in making and selling cars. Their weekly pay goes from £20 on state benefits to £120 on a working wage. They have more money to spend on goods and services and, as a result, the local economy strengthens. In addition, the plant requires supplies, transport, energy, security staff, maintenance, etc. – the very fact that the plant is in existence creates jobs to service it.

So, the initial increase in investment multiplies itself through the local economy, which increases wealth and drives up property prices.

The diagram below illustrates the circular nature of the multiplier effect and how investment funds multiply through the local economy.

The popularity of jet-to-let in Eastern Europe is due in part to an increase in the number of these multiplier effects. The base level of property prices in Eastern Europe was a lot lower than the equivalent properties in 'old' Europe. The recent rises in prices have readdressed some of these differences, particularly in Prague and Budapest, but the gap is still very wide in some places.

As outside investment continues, multiplier effects will have a significant and positive influence on wealth, prosperity and property prices.

3. Sentiment or 'the crowd'

There is a subtle difference between a change in tastes and fashion, and expectations and sentiment. The latter drive all financial markets. Expectations that a property market will rise leads to a 'wall of money' effect where demand for property rises in anticipation, or the probability, that the market will rise and profits will be healthy. The UK property market, as well as overseas markets such as the US, Australia and Ireland, have been through this effect in the last five years.

The media, emerging markets and a self-fulfilling prophecy

The 'dot com' bubble of the late 1990s is a great example of a self-fulfilling prophecy. Speculators noted that share prices were rising dramatically and invested in dot com shares in anticipation of further price rises. Companies floated on the stock market at very large market capitalisations (i.e. the value of the company) based on the future potential for products and profits rather than on current value. Speculators didn't invest in dot com shares because of any analysis of intrinsic value; they just expected future profits and/or rising share prices.

However, instead of massive profits there was a meltdown and the psychological scars are still there today. The media, which reported the rise of the market, was now reporting the bloodbath and as fear replaced greed the meltdown was encouraged by speculators selling shares. The crash became a self-fulfilling prophecy of the opposite kind.

All markets, whether stocks, currency, commodities or property, exhibit similar characteristics. When profits and losses are the outcome of trading activities, fear and greed will always be prevalent in the market.

As a jet-to-let property investor, you must be careful not to be caught up in the hype, often generated in the media, regarding certain overseas property markets. Look very carefully at the intrinsic value of what you are investing in and not at the crowd who are propelling prices even higher.

 Remember that one day you will wish to sell your property for profit, so you will need someone who wants to buy it from you.

The factors which affect supply and demand

Now, let's look at the factors that drive demand for property and those which affect the supply of property. As a top down investor, you will be looking for countries which have sound economic reasons for investment: economic growth, a high level of foreign direct investment (FDI), strong employment, low inflation and low interest rates. Regions and localities are then identified where the supply and demand relationship of property, combined with multiplier effects, creates favourable conditions for property investors.

1. Demand

Here are the key factors which increase the demand for property:

a. FDI and economic growth

b. Interest rates

c. Real incomes and wealth

d. Employment

e. Inflation

f. Regional factors

g. Local factors

h. Special events

i. Tastes and fashions

a. FDI and economic growth

Investment from other countries or multi-national corporations can have a profoundly positive effect on a country's economy. Firstly, FDI leads to greater overall wealth, or economic growth, through multiplier effects. It's as if the cash reprints itself many times over and is respent.

But what is economic growth? It simply means that as a society or economy we are becoming wealthier. The term GDP (meaning 'gross domestic product') refers to the value of a country's annual output of goods and services. It's everything we produce – what we spend in the shops, investments, government spending, changes in stocks and exports minus imports. It's what we are worth as a country.

It's extremely important for countries to grow national worth in order to increase the living standards of their people. So governments make a great play on the economic growth figures as they drive future prosperity.

You may also come across another measure of wealth, which I think it's important to cover – GDP per capita as an indicator of wealth per person. As the name suggests, this is a measure of the wealth of a country divided by the number of people. Clearly an annually increasing figure is favourable as it simply means that the population is generally becoming wealthier. More on economic growth can be found in the Appendices.

b. Interest rates

There tends to be an inverse relationship between interest rates and property prices. This means that as interest rates fall, property prices rise and when interest rates rise, property prices cool and can also fall. There are a number of reasons why this happens, but the key ones are as follows:

- **Affordability.** As interest rates fall, prospective buyers have more disposable income because mortgage payments take less of their monthly income. At relatively low rates of interest, more buyers can afford to purchase a property.

  The opposite is also true. As mortgages get more expensive and take a bigger slice of our income, the number of potential buyers declines as property becomes less affordable.

- **Greater profits.** As interest rates fall, more investors are attracted into the marketplace as the difference between what you can receive in rents and what you must pay out in mortgage costs gets larger. This is one factor which explains the explosive growth in UK buy-to-let. From the mid 1990s mortgage products, designed specifically for the buy-to-let market with long-dated terms, interest-only payments and flexible loan to values made the profit per month attractive, particularly in relation to the amount of capital or deposit investors had to find.

- **Expectations.** An expectation of further rate rises or falls has an effect just as powerful as an actual movement in rates.

 Investigate countries where there is a falling interest rate environment and where interest rates are likely to remain low for some time.

c. Real incomes and wealth

The demand for property increases as we become wealthier. One of the key supports of a rising property market is the growth in real incomes. 'Real' income is what we really have after we have taken inflation into account.

Example

David's pay increase this year is 5%, while inflation is 2%. In real terms, his pay has risen by only 3% because his living expenses, as measured by the level of inflation, are up 2%.

5% – the level of inflation (2%) = growth in real income of 3%.

One of the most attractive factors for investors is the potential for growth in real incomes as a result of EU membership. This drives the demand for property and has a very positive effect on prices.

d. Employment

High levels of employment support property markets. Clearly the more people who work, the greater the number of potential buyers – it's that simple. So, the jet-to-letter is interested in researching countries where high levels of sustainable employment can be found.

It would be useful here to make a distinction between national and local employment. Generally, when economies are growing, employment opportunities increase and the headline unemployment number will fall. However, this is a national average so it's important to still examine the employment rate in the local area where you are considering investing. For example, in Italy in the last quarter of 2005, the jobless rate was 4.5 per cent in the north, 6.7 per cent in central Italy, while in the south there was a sharp decline to 14.2 per cent. You will also find similar patterns in many of the Eastern European countries, where employment opportunities are mainly found in the capital city and large secondary cities.

So, when you are researching your potential property investment you should be attracted to countries and then regions where there is strong growth in employment. This is particularly important if you are letting to the local indigenous population or corporations on long-term tenancies. This is less of an issue with holiday letting.

Unemployment associated with the decline of specific industries is known as 'structural unemployment'. It takes a long time for localities to recover from the loss of a large employer, such as coal mines, steel works, car making and shipbuilding yards. Many former Communist countries are slowly getting to grips with reorganising their economies and industries.

e. Inflation

We hear a lot about inflation in the press and on the television, but how does it affect property investors? Inflation can be defined as a 'sustained rise in prices'. It has two main drivers: costs and demand.

- **Costs.** When a company experiences a rise in any part of its cost base, such as wages, rents, interest payments on loans and raw materials, it has the option to pass on the increased costs to the customer in the form of higher prices. The extent to which it can do this will depend on the sensitivity of the consumer to a rise in the price of its products and the availability of substitutes. Inflation caused as a result of an increase in costs is known as 'cost-push'. In property markets, prices can be driven higher by increasing land prices, taxation and the rising cost of cement, bricks and labour.

- **Demand.** As UK property investors and home buyers, we have experienced one of the greatest examples of 'demand-pull' inflation in recent years, right on our doorstep. UK property prices have been pulled up by an insatiable appetite for property since the latter part of the 1990s, associated with falling interest rates, the liberalisation of the financial services industry and a strong economic environment of high employment, low inflation and a growing economy.

These two components of inflation are worth bearing in mind, particularly when you read or learn of any demand or cost factor in your jet-to-let country of focus, which may lead to a rise in property prices.

Inflation has an impact in two other ways:

- **Interest rates policy.** Firstly, most sophisticated economies target inflation as one of their key economic concerns. Countries, such as the UK, and international organisations, such as the EU, have adopted a target rate which the central banks must aim for through their monetary policy.

  If inflation is rising, then it's likely that interest rates will have to rise in order to maintain the target rate of inflation set by the government. Depending on the economic environment, central banks – such as the Bank of England, the Federal Reserve in the United States and the European Central Bank – will make statements which, in effect, forewarn of any interest rate movements. They signal whether their intention is to raise, lower or maintain a neutral rate.

  So, inflation is important because it affects interest rates, which, in turn, affect your mortgage costs. It's also a useful factor to consider if you are offered the option of a fixed-rate mortgage.

  If you think interest rates have peaked, then maybe you will choose a variable rate product. If you think that interest rates must rise much further in order to control the level of inflation, then maybe a short-term fixed-rate mortgage may be the preferred option for you.

- **The value of money.** Secondly, inflation erodes the value of money. If I bought a jet-to-let apartment for £100,000 with an £80,000 mortgage in local currency and inflation was running at 20 per cent per annum, then the property after two years will have risen by 40 per cent (as well as everything else in the economy). More importantly, the value of the £80,000 debt will have been eroded. If this continues, then the debt, in local currency, will become negligible over time. This is what has happened in the UK during the post-war years. How many of our parents bought properties for £1,000 or less and now sit on a pile measured in £100,000s? That's inflation!

f. Regional factors

After you have examined the bigger picture of macro-economic factors (i.e. economic growth and employment), you need to focus on specific regions – regions where there are special factors which a property investor will identify as having a positive effect on the market.

- **Regional aid.** A popular investment strategy is to look for turnaround situations where regions, cities and localities are given an economic boost through regional aid. This aid takes many forms, including the provision of grants from regional or central government or from international bodies such as the EU.

  The EU classifies regions in a number of ways, but I want to highlight EU Objective 1 status, which provides financial support to regions where the income per person is at or below 75 per cent of the EU average.

  Why is this important for property investors? Well, we have seen that economic growth and a rise in income (GDP) per person is an important step in increasing wealth through investment and jobs. The injection of funds tends to multiply itself and creates a positive economic effect. Increasing wealth and prosperity drives property markets as new workers require homes, existing workers upgrade their homes and corporations seek accommodation for migrant workers attracted by the new opportunities and, in some cases, tax breaks.

  Many of these Objective 1 regions start from a lower base than other areas – clearly at least 75 per cent below. So, investors who follow the money speculate that the increased investment in infrastructure, particularly transport, training and jobs will eventually push property prices higher.

  The regions where the GDP per head is at or below 75 per cent of the EU average are widespread and in some cases surprising. I have reproduced in the Appendices the most up-to-date list available from the EU in order to give you a flavour for the regions involved.

- **The Easyjet and Ryanair effect.** For the sake of balance, I am using the two most popular no-frills airlines to illustrate the economic benefits of low-cost carriers. The positive effect of low-cost carriers entering a market is a factor to consider when making an investment, particularly flights to destinations which you wish to target for short lettings.

I recently flew from John Lennon Airport in Liverpool for a business meeting in Màlaga, Spain. I left my home north of Liverpool early in the morning and drove the few kilometres to the airport. I then dropped my car off, jumped on the plane and was in Màlaga in just over a couple of hours. It was cheaper and just as quick as getting the train from Liverpool Lime Street Station to London Euston.

The frequency, reliability and cost of this sort of airline is revolutionising air travel and the destinations they fly to are receiving an economic boost, whether through holidaymakers in Spain or stag parties in Prague.

This is not just a British effect and a glance at the routes of many of these low-cost European carriers will have a much larger European and, in some cases, worldwide effect.

A word of caution: You must consider the impact on your chosen area of focus if a low-cost carrier pulls out of a particular route! The airlines appear to be announcing new routes every week so you will need to look at their websites for the very latest news or you can keep up to date by looking at my property investment news blog at http://blog.bewaresharks.com.

 Check whether the airlines stop flying to a destination out of season. It might be difficult to let the property if there are no flights!

- **New airports.** Allied to that, clearly the establishment and even the upgrading of an airport is an important factor which will have a positive effect on demand for property.

Try to look at investment properties within two hours' driving distance of the local international airport. The last thing a prospective tenant wants is a four-hour drive on arrival.

 Check that your property is not directly beneath a flight path as this would be a constant source of annoyance to the occupants!

- **New marinas.** Property prices can be sky high around established and well-maintained marinas, so look out for areas where new marinas are planned, invest off-plan early and buy the best properties in terms of size and view.

  People who own boats usually have money and like to spend it. This 'spending effect' will attract the type and quality of service that wealthier people demand from restaurants and hairdressers to shops and property. This will make your property even more desirable and place it in a segment of the market which is robust, whatever stage we are at in the economic cycle.

- **New golf courses.** Like jet-to-let, golf is also a phenomenon. Golfers are a breed apart. You see them out on the courses come hail, rain and snow. Golfers enjoy the challenge and occasion of playing on different courses and will travel in order to do so.

  Winter golf breaks are now very popular and attract a considerable following in Spain, Portugal, Florida and Morocco. Other countries have cottoned on, such as Cyprus and Bulgaria, which have advanced plans to increase the number and variety of courses on offer. This is great news for the short-term letter in sunshine destinations as golf extends the season. A lot of Mediterranean destinations close down in the winter and rely on the summertime rush for revenue, although there is a growing market for long-term winter rentals from Scandinavians, Britons and Germans fleeing the freezing cold and rain at home.

  But golf is a great winter-season activity. Playing in a Mediterranean country, for instance, at 19°C in winter is surely a more pleasurable experience than 2°C in the howling rain in the UK.

  So, should you buy a property on the golf course? In short, it depends on why you are buying the property. Properties on golf courses come at a premium. To illustrate the point, I recently bought an off-plan villa one minute's walk from an extensive, clean beach, close to a lovely, unspoilt local village. The international airport is a 15-minute taxi ride and the plot is not under the path of aircraft. The properties are presently front line, but in time the very expensive land in front will be built on, making my property look comparatively less expensive and therefore very marketable in the resale market.

I've invested in this area because an international standard golf course with five-star leisure facilities was to be built just four kilometres from the site. I paid about £1,325 to £1,500 sterling per square metre. To compare, properties on the new golf course were recently being offered off-plan at around £3,000 plus per square metre. I believe that being on the beach and close to the golf course has more advantages than being on the golf course and close to the beach.

- **New skiing facilities.** I would probably group skiers with golfers and risk the wrath of both communities because they appear to have a few things in common:

    - A passion for their sporting pursuit

    - Willingness to travel

    - Willingness to spend

    - The sports are sociable and involve other people

    - There is often an annual event

Investing in quality ski chalets in popular locations has proven to be a sound investment for many in terms of both capital growth and income. Properties in France, Switzerland, Austria, the United States, Canada and elsewhere have provided very good financial returns for their owners. Additionally, the investors have used the facilities themselves for holidays, thus enjoying their investment as a live-and-let.

Many investors are now attracted to emerging ski destinations in the hope that history will repeat itself. Many are buying in areas of Bulgaria, such as Bansko and Borovetz, which are undergoing significant change, even bidding for the Winter Olympics. Before you rush off and pile in, stand back and ask yourself a few common sense questions:

- What makes a good skiing resort?

- Will the average skier be attracted by low-cost destinations?

- Will they be prised away from Chamonix and Val d'Isère for Bansko and Borovetz?

- How long is the season?

- How competitive are the hotels?

- What is the transport like?

- Is the après-ski good?

- Are there alternative amenities for non-skiers?

There is no doubt that a quality property in a quality skiing area will make a sound investment over the long term. But all properties and locations are not equal and a lot of research and knowledge of this market is necessary before committing hard cash, particularly if you're not a skier yourself and you don't know what the market wants.

 If you don't know, ask. Don't try to guess the needs and wants of a market you are unfamiliar with.

Patterns are emerging

Can you see a pattern emerging?

We have two very distinctive jet-to-let strategies – short-term leisure-orientated markets and traditional long-term tenancy arrangements similar to the traditional buy-to-let model. The present jet-to-let boom can be broken down to:

- sunshine and ski; and

- urban buy-to-let on contracts akin to, but not legally the same as, UK assured shorthold tenancy (AST) arrangements.

g. Local factors

What is the difference between regional and local factors? I would suggest that the difference is in effect. I believe that an event such as the Olympic Games in London in 2012 will have a national, regional and local effect. All three pillars should be supported. However, a good local school will have a much smaller impact, but will support property prices for family dwellings in a locality.

Local factors which affect property prices and rental demand are as follows:

- Crime
- Antisocial behaviour
- Transport links
- Electricity pylons
- Mobile phone masts
- Undesirable shops
- Takeaways and smells
- Traffic noise
- Aircraft noise
- Trains
- Flooding
- Water shortages
- Acceptance of foreign nationals
- Oil refineries
- Gas works
- Nuclear power stations

It's worth noting that local factors are extremely important when considering the market you are trying to target for your jet-to-let strategy. The points I have listed are equally relevant whether you are investing in Slovenia, Slovakia or South Africa.

It's important to visit the local areas at different times of the day and also at night. If it's a hot and sunny destination, what's it like in the winter when it's raining? We all know from personal experience that areas change according to the time of the day and whether it's midweek or the weekend. Check your locality out thoroughly and you will not get any unpleasant surprises.

Top down

When you are taking a top down approach to property investment, do reduce in scale from the international level, through to the national, then regional and then finally the local level. The issues become more detailed at the lower level, but they are no less important than the overall political or economic situation in a country.

h. Special events

The Olympic Games, Commonwealth Games, Channel Tunnel, European Capital of Culture and other special events have a direct effect on property prices through the regeneration effect that many of these projects create.

When researching special events overseas, look for improvements in the regional and local infrastructure, such as roads, rail, airports and jobs. The jobs have to be real and sustainable for their creation to have any effect on the local property market. Part-time fast-food outlet type jobs are not what you are looking for as a property investor!

Also, investigate what use any special event buildings will be put to after the event, such as a technology park, business park or shopping mall.

i. Tastes and fashions

A change in tastes and fashions can have a dramatic effect on the demand for property. The most obvious example of this effect has been the transformation of Spain due to the introduction of the package holiday. Mass tourism has created not just a demand for air travel and hotel rooms, but also a demand for private apartments and villas as both holidaymakers and retirees flock to the Costas.

It became very fashionable from the early 1970s for the masses to holiday abroad and Spain was (and still is) the number one destination for British holidaymakers. However, fashions change and as we become wealthier, air travel becomes more accessible and as a society we become more adventurous.

I was fortunate enough to be taken by my parents to Honolulu, Hawaii in 1982 for a family holiday. At the time it seemed a long way away, and my friends were very impressed, particularly as the cult programme of the day was 'Magnum', which beamed exotic Hawaiian landscapes and lifestyles into our homes once a week. We stayed on Oahu Island and throughout the whole holiday we met only one other British family. 24 years later, British and other Europeans take holidays all over the world as a matter of routine – from Australia to Zanzibar. Distance is not a problem.

We really do live in a 'global village' and as such a property investor should not restrict his investments to countries which are just around the corner. Psychologically this may be appealing, but if you have a more profitable opportunity with a six-hour flight, rather than a two-hour flight, then why not take advantage of it?

If you can catch this change in taste and invest at the correct time, you will receive a very rewarding return on your investment. You only have to look at the growth figures for South Africa, Bulgaria and Dubai over the last few years to see good examples of this principle.

2. Supply

We have looked extensively at the factors influencing demand and now we turn our attention to the supply of property on the other side of the equation.

How many times have you heard the term 'housing shortage' in relation to UK property? And it's not just in this country. Supply is struggling to keep up with the growth in the population due to birth rates, immigration and social changes in society.

A hundred years ago, and even less in many countries, one-parent families were an exception and traditional marriage was the norm. Now, the stereotypical married couple with 2.4 children are not the only demographic group that buy and rent property and this has led to a surge in the number of households requiring accommodation. Contributing factors include an ever-increasing divorce rate, a growing student population and an increased desire for independence (especially amongst university graduates, who have grown used to living away from their parents).

You don't need to be an economist to work out that where there is limited supply of property, there is greater potential for higher than average price rises, as the excess demand cannot be satisfied by building more properties – remember inelastic supply?

There are a number of factors which affect the supply of property and the list below highlights just a few:

a. Property prices

b. International and regional price differences

c. Availability of land

d. Planning regulations

e. Special status areas

a. Property prices

Property developers are in the business of making money and it's this profit motive that increases the supply of property when prices rise. Property developers have more incentive either to develop land which is already banked or to buy land with the intention of developing it. 'Banked' land is simply land which has been purchased with the view to developing it at some time in the future and as such is referred to as if it's held in a bank. So, in a rising market developers have the incentive to increase supply.

The opposite is also true. Why, if you are sitting on land that you purchased a year ago with a view to development, would you wish to start digging while property prices fall by ten per cent per annum?

The fact that property developers increase supply when prices rise results in prices being dampened due to the long production process. It dampens prices because decisions are made today about future demand based on present demand. For example, if the projections are wrong on a two-year build and demand falls in the meantime, then a surplus of supply will prevail. Multiply this across many developers in the region and suddenly there is a real problem.

But why would this be the case? Surely the developers understand demand, interest rates and the economy? Yes, they do, in the main, but no-one has control over other factors such as:

1. Fear and greed. Developers want market share, growth and profits.

2. Tastes, fashions, expectations and sentiment. What happens when the next hotspot appears on the horizon? If the market is driven by relatively cheap property, what happens when another market appears with even cheaper property? Simple – the market shifts and in doing so prices fall as supply exceeds demand. This is an important point to remember if you are drawn to a particular investment country because you perceive it to be cheap. What happens to the price of your two-bedroom off-plan apartment when the market shifts?

b. International and regional price differences – the 'ripple effect'

A ripple effect is both a supply side and demand side issue. When property prices become expensive relative to incomes in a particular area, then new buyers purchase in the next cheaper postcode or district, but close enough to still take advantage of the attractions of their preferred, more expensive first choice.

The attraction may be proximity to family, landscape, transport, work or leisure, but eventually prices will rise in this new area as well due to the ripple effect. As properties become more expensive, new buyers demand properties further out from the earlier centre of activity causing prices to rise in these areas.

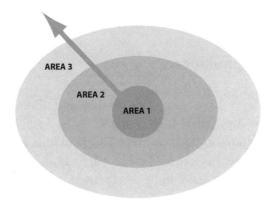

The simple diagram above represents the ripple effect of rising prices as new buyers are forced out of area 1 and so purchase in area 2, and eventually area 2 becomes unaffordable for new entrants, who then buy in area 3. This effect also works on the supply side.

We can all remember the strapline 'the next Spain' with reference to some of the newer emerging markets. I have personally heard this in relation to locations as varied as Cyprus, Croatia, Montenegro and Bulgaria, but I am sure you can name some others.

These markets have opened up thanks to the success of countries like Spain. Governments and private companies have seen the benefits of tourism and property and have entered the market.

The ripple effect is such that prices in these newer markets look attractive when compared to Spain, but very quickly make up a lot of ground as demand increases. The ripple effect is not just local or regional, it's international.

c. Availability of land

The supply of property is clearly affected by the availability of land, but not all land is equal in terms of development. Many areas around the globe prohibit development in certain areas, whether for agricultural, economic, military, political or density reasons.

Generally, islands have a limited area in which to develop, particularly along the coast and on the beach. Cities have similar issues so the land shortage is normally resolved or compensated for by the use of high-rise buildings.

d. Planning regulations

How many times have you been abroad and thought, 'They're just throwing them up', when there appears to be very little in terms of planning regulations in the local area? This is an important issue to grasp. There are many areas overseas where they have built very quickly and have regretted it ever since. Build in haste, repent at leisure.

As an investor, you need to identify areas where there are strong local planning regulations and where there are limitations on what can be built. You want this for two reasons:

1. **Limited supply of new builds.** Remember that when you come to resell an investment property, your greatest competition is from

developers and not others in the resale market. This is because developers generally offer very good incentives in order to sell properties quickly. You may get:

- cashback, equivalent to say five per cent of the purchase price;
- your deposit or part deposit paid;
- a guaranteed rental scheme;
- a free furniture pack;
- your legal or survey fees paid;
- the stamp duty and other taxes paid;
- landscaped gardens with water features;
- a shared equity scheme;
- a part exchange; or
- a free parking space.

OK, some of these incentives are presently only available in the UK, but watch this space – overseas markets are catching up fast!

Now, I return to the concept that underpins this whole chapter. You should look for areas where supply is limited for whatever reason as resale and rentals will be dependent on it. If not, you need a competitive advantage or such a 'wow' factor that people will ignore all of the other properties. However, this is hard to achieve and it generally requires a large investment. For the vast majority of investments you should look for it to have a view, be close to a beach, have a ski lift, local amenities and good transport links (airports, trains, trams, underground, buses), be convenient for the city centre and have job opportunities, which can all fit under the heading of location.

2. **The area has to be appealing.** I'm not just talking about the holiday market here, but also any area where you are considering investing. You don't even have to venture overseas to see some hideous examples of so called 'town planning'. There are many examples in the UK, and I am sure you know one or two in your own region. Strong planning regulations ensure that your second line idyllic three-bedroom villa doesn't have a 30-storey hotel built in front of it.

e. Special status areas – World Heritage Sites, national parks, conservation zones and historical areas of importance

The supply of property is generally restricted in areas which have been designated as having a special status, such as national parks, conservation areas and historical sites. The scarcity value of properties which are located in these areas should not be underestimated.

To bring the point closer to home, the Lake District National Park in the UK is an area of outstanding beauty and is rightly protected. In this particular area you cannot build properties that are out of keeping and in order to maintain the essence of what the area wants, you cannot build too many. After all, scarcity, desirability and demand feature largely when one considers properties in special status areas.

Key points summary

- Think 'top down'.

- Property prices are driven by demand, supply, multiplier effects and sentiment.

- Invest in areas where demand is increasing and there is limited supply of property, like beaches, waterfronts, marinas, city centres, exclusive areas, great views and national parks.

- Think location, particularly in relation to transport links for the long-term rental market.

- Look at the larger economy or macro-economy such as FDI, interest rates, employment, inflation, and then drill down.

- Look for areas which are on the rise as a result of investment in jobs, training and infrastructure.

- Choose your property investment with a specific target market in mind.

- Remember that other factors such as low-cost airlines, new airports, marinas, golf, special events and tastes and fashions have a direct influence on demand, supply and prices.

- Be alert to the effect of expectations and sentiment and how strong shifts in either one can have a significant impact on property prices.

- Try not to be fearful of missing out on the 'deal of a lifetime' which you may be offered at some stage in the future. Likewise, don't be consumed by greed and allow rational decisions to be overtaken by avarice.

- Don't confuse perceived value with intrinsic value – remember the dot com bubble?

- Look at both the demand side and the supply side of your intended property investment market.

- Think scarcity, limited supply and exclusivity. Who will rent this property from you and who will eventually buy it from you when you come to sell?

CHAPTER 4

The pathway to success

'Strategy is not the consequence of planning, but the opposite: its starting point.' Henry Mintzberg

Having an effective strategy is synonymous with being successful. It may seem a daunting process at first, but don't be deterred; with a strategy tailored to you, your jet-to-let investments will prove successful.

But where do you start? We are presented with masses of material in newsagents but the problem is which one to pick up. France? Spain? North Korea? Even our newspapers, particularly at the weekend, are crammed with deals, discounts and cashback offers tempting us to invest.

We are bombarded by salespeople telling us that their location and product is better than anyone else's. You only have to wander down the aisles of the many property exhibitions to see this for yourself. You can invest in properties all over the world and can have a portfolio on which the sun never sets!

I personally think that these shows are a good way of finding everything from property, furniture and finance to industry experts giving advice through seminars on many aspects of property investment, all under one roof. I might be biased, as my companies do exhibit at these shows, but I would challenge anyone to show me a quicker and more efficient way in which to quiz, question or interrogate some of the leading companies dealing with the jet-to-let market and property investment in general.

So, use the shows to gather intelligence, but don't invest in anything without a lot of research and due diligence afterwards, and when you are content and have made a decision, then buy. No self-respecting company will pressure you into parting with cash on the day so leave your cheque book and credit cards at home!

 Visit the country and site in which you are looking to invest before signing any contract.

Define your strategy

Whatever you are planning, defining a strategy has to be the first task. You have to forget about detail and how you will achieve it, and concentrate on the result.

Strategy dictates the why, when, where and how of property investment and is the key driver of your jet-to-let property investment plan. It's essentially a 'big picture' exercise which lacks detail deliberately, deals only in results and is a systematic plan to achieve specific objectives. As a result, you need to set yourself specific objectives or goals and there are lots of tools and techniques available to assist you – on the internet, in books and on personal development courses.

Strategy is a crucial first step for the novice property investor and something that an experienced investor monitors and reviews in light of his performance. Leading on from this, a strategy is not something that is set in stone. An investor should never be unwilling to make changes. That said, if it's not broken, don't fix it!

Investing in property is a business and as such you should apply business techniques. Throughout this book, I am producing a framework which will assist you to be a successful jet-to-let investor. It's no coincidence that many of the concepts we use are also tried and tested business principles.

To be a successful property investor you need a vision and a strategy. Whether it's a £4 billion international business or a jet-to-let investment apartment in Warsaw or Crete, the success or failure of the operation will be determined by the same factors:

- Research and analysis
- Demand for the product
- Cash flow and finance
- Seizing opportunities

 If you have a partner, bring him on board with your vision.

Setting goals

The process of goal-setting allows you to have greater control over your future. Research has found that people who set goals for themselves are more likely to:

- concentrate and focus;
- have greater self-confidence and belief;
- achieve more;
- be happier and more content with life; and
- suffer less stress and anxiety.

Consider what you want to achieve

This is also referred to as a mission statement and acts as a long-term driver for all of your other goals. An investor goal might be 'to invest in property in order to accumulate £3 million of profits and retire at the age of 50 in 2026.'

SMART goals

This is a great way to assess what you want to achieve from five different angles. Whether you are planning long- or short-term goals, you want every goal to be a SMART one:

1. Specific
2. Measurable
3. Action-oriented and achievable
4. Realistic and rewarding
5. Timed

1. Specific

You want the goal to be specific, rather than vague; for example, 'to achieve £3 million in equity in overseas property'. It's also important that you write your goals down.

2. Measurable

Identify the means by which you will measure each goal. How will you know when you have reached it? In the example above, the first measurable point is £500,000 followed by £1 million of equity. By now you will be into your stride so you could set the next measurable points as £2 million and £3 million respectively.

3. Action-oriented and achievable

Describe your goals using action verbs. What will you do step by step to reach your goal? Set goals which are challenging but not unrealistically high. Once you are there, set your sights higher if this fits in with your revised goals and continue onwards and upwards.

4. Realistic and rewarding

Write down reasons why the successful outcome of your efforts is so important to you and create a strong mental picture of that outcome. Ensure that your goals are realistic and achievable and imagine how it will feel when you have accomplished your goal. There will be times when you hit hurdles, find it difficult and wish to give up and stick to the daytime job. Well, don't. You've come this far after all. Re-read your reasons for the goal in the first place, recharge the batteries, discuss your goals with a friend to make them even more real, and then get back on track.

5. Timed

Determine deadlines for each of your goals. Deadlines can be flexible and adjusted as needed, but deadlines that specify time limits help to keep you focused and moving. So, back to the example above, you now have 'to achieve £3 million in equity in overseas property in five years' time in order to quit the rat race'.

From this simple statement you can now make your plan with the £500,000, £1 million, £2 million and £3 million points as measurable targets within specific timeframes. This set of sub-goals will keep you on track and give you cause for celebration and assurance when you hit each of these targets. For example:

- £500,000 within two years

- £1 million within three years

- £2 million within four years

- £3 million within five years

When setting your goals, bear in mind the following:

- What skills you need in order to achieve your goal.

- What information and knowledge you need.

- Who can help?

- What resources you need.

- What challenges can hinder your success.

- Are you making any assumptions and if so, what are they?

- Is there a better way of doing it?

- Has the situation changed since you formulated your plan?

Plan, review and revise

You can plan, plan and plan, but once you begin with lawyers, financiers, developers, agents, insurance brokers, letting agents and other players in the market, you often have to change the plan quickly and adapt before you can continue. Flexibility and determination are essential.

After a period of time, say six months, review your plan to see if you are on track to achieving your ultimate goal. If not, revise the plan again, take action and continue the process.

'However beautiful the strategy, you should occasionally look at the results.' Winston Churchill

Here is a five-step plan for achieving your goals:

1. Write a mission statement of what you want to achieve.
2. Write a plan with targets to accomplish your goal.
3. Visualise and feel yourself achieving the goal.
4. Review progress, revise plan, adapt, improvise, and then
5. Attack!

Formulating your strategy

You have looked at the importance of goal-setting to focus the mind on what you want to achieve from your jet-to-let property investments. Once your goals are determined, you can then proceed to formulate a strategy from which a plan will materialise.

Research, knowledge and the will to do something with it are key determinants of successful property investing. Gather as much useful information as you can albeit in the form of property investment seminars and training, books, magazines, exhibitions or just speak to people who may know a little bit more than you. The internet has also quickly become the tool of choice for a lot of people, but unless the information comes from an independent source (as in someone that isn't trying to sell you something), then treat it with caution.

Look into joining property networking organisations with the opportunity to speak with like-minded people, some of whom will have been through the process of investing in overseas property many times.

Find time to process the information so that you can sort out the wheat from the chaff. Keep the good, relevant and factual material and, from experience, I would suggest that many of the glossy, expensive marketing brochures are a bit wide of the mark for investors.

Armed with your cutting edge information you then need to shift your focus and look at the factor that has the most influence on how you proceed – you.

Investor profiling

Investor or psychological profiling could fill a book in its own right and is something that I feel strongly about. Many of us forget that we have different goals and ambitions and different tolerances to risk. There is no 'one size fits all' property investment strategy.

> **Example**
>
> John and Ann are neighbours. John is 26, has spare cash and wants to invest. Ann is 55, has spare cash and wants to invest. John has no dependants and Ann has one child still at school. John works in the City and Ann is a housewife. John likes a fast lifestyle and Ann likes to take things a bit slower and hasn't been one to act quickly at any stage in her life. John by nature is a risk-taker and Ann is instinctively cautious. John wants to retire at 40 and Ann wants to supplement her pension at 60.

So, would you suggest that they follow the same jet-to-let investment strategy?

This is the essence of investor profiling. It matches you to an investment strategy which is based on your behavioural characteristics and preferences and no-one else's. We are all different and as such we require tailor-made strategies.

I read hundreds of investor profiles a year and can now instinctively look at summary charts and know what strategy fits that particular person. It's not an exact science, but it's interesting how accurate it is. So which type of investor are you?

I have devised a number of investor categories to illustrate the point. There are, however, many very good and well-researched models of profiling which you can find on the internet or in good bookshops. My examples are as follows:

1. The 'entrepreneur investor'

The entrepreneur investor is focused, hasn't much time, wants the information presented succinctly and will make a quick decision based on numbers. He isn't interested in the detail, only the potential profit, risk and any spin-off opportunities which may arise.

2. The 'analyst investor'

The analyst will want the most detailed information and will scrutinise every last detail. He deals in facts and not hyperbole. Numbers, numbers and numbers will determine whether an investment is a starter or not. However, once he has completed the analysis, he will make a decision.

3. The 'laid-back investor'

With a laid-back attitude to property investment, this investor type is often hard-working and very much career- and family-orientated. He tends to believe that once a property investment is made it will look after itself, and that a good job is the best way to make money.

4. The 'impulsive investor'

This type of investor follows the latest hotspots and may have properties scattered around the country or globe. The latest investment fashion is his game. He would consider looking at beach villas in Iceland if that was the latest trend. This type of investor can be classified as a crowd follower and lacks any detailed strategy or idea of his intended goals.

5. The 'information junky investor'

This type of investor cannot get enough information. He will read the shelves of WH Smith bare, listen to others who have been successful and turn up at all the property industry events. He will continue to want more and more information before making a decision. Sometimes he will often miss opportunities, but is confident in his own ability that he will invest successfully after covering all the bases.

But the question remains whether he will ever make the final step.

There are more, but the key point is that you have to sit down and really think through how your own personality, temperament and tolerance to risk fit in with a property investment strategy.

Decide on your strengths

Investor profiling can help you decide on your strengths. If you are good with planning and detail and getting your hands dirty, why not contemplate a project renovating or refurbishing a property for profit. Places such as inland Spain, Crete, Cyprus, Italy and other Mediterranean countries offer many opportunities for such a strategy. It's not without difficulties, but what is?

If you are not the hands-on type or your work and family preclude regular trips to meet your project manager, then you may wish to consider a new-build or off-plan property. Both options allow good returns, although the latter is less demanding on time and resources.

If you find it easier making decisions with other people, then get a partner on board in order to discuss options. Make sure it's someone who has different strengths and complements your skills.

If the thought of investing off-plan in Latvia or Lithuania gives you sleepless nights because you are naturally more conservative in your approach, then don't do it. Choose a more established, tried and tested market more suitable to your profile and tolerance to risk.

Work to your strengths, not your weaknesses. You know yourself better than anyone else, so working to your strengths shouldn't be difficult. Do what you feel comfortable doing and it will work for you.

Define your market

Once you have defined yourself, your strengths, weaknesses and goals, you are now ready to look at where to invest.

To define your market, you have to use all the information which you have collected about various markets to formulate an investment strategy which you are comfortable with and which will fulfil your long-term goals. An example of a strategy is as follows:

> To buy a villa in a country with an all-year-round climate, no more than a three-hour flight away, to use for the family and let it out to cover its costs.'

This particular strategy would rule out Bulgaria, Cyprus, Florida, the Caribbean, Turkey and South Africa and it narrows your focus to countries such as France, Italy, Spain and a few others.

Here you have narrowed your market down significantly to match your goals. You can then collect information about the options you have in order to make a more detailed assessment of where to invest.

I live in Liverpool and don't want to travel too far to an airport and would like cheap flights available most days of the week. As a budget airline flies to Màlaga every day, Spain would probably make its way to the top of my list.

Define where you want to focus

So, based on my previous analysis, I will now focus all my energies, research and time into looking for property in an area no more than two hours from Màlaga Airport.

OK, I know it appears a bit too simple, but after a considerable amount of research and taking time to decide on what you want from your investment property, you should at least have narrowed your choice down to one or two countries.

It's by focusing all of your time and energies in mastering a particular subject that you get the best perspective on it. If you are a UK buy-to-let investor, then be the master of your particular area of investment. Know your market inside out and be the specialist, because it's by specialising that you will gain an edge over everyone else looking to do the same thing as you.

Identify, prioritise and implement strategy

For some people this is the most difficult phase because they have to do something; it requires *action*. They conduct the research, they analyse themselves, set realistic goals, formulate a strategy, get focused and then quit! What a waste of time and effort.

I'm not underestimating how difficult it is for a novice investor to take the first step, but when you embark on a journey and the end is in sight you have to give it one determined push.

Having taken action, the strategy is implemented and you are now on the way to making a fortune. You can sit back, relax and wait for the money to roll in, but don't rest on your laurels!

Monitor performance and review strategy

Whatever you invest in, it's important to monitor your performance, particularly in terms of the opportunity cost of your strategy.

Many UK property investors, including myself, have been successful in the UK market for a number of years. However, as interest rate rises began to bite in the UK from November 2003, many investors reviewed their strategy, looked at all of the opportunities available, and decided to adopt a jet-to-let strategy to take advantage of markets which were in a different stage of the economic and property market cycle.

This review is important, because by continually looking at the performance of your portfolio in relation to the goals you have set, you will be able to make the necessary adjustments to ensure that you remain on target. You cannot step back, cross your fingers and hope that everything will turn out as planned.

Strategy is where it all starts

Once you have defined your strategy, everything else will flow from there. By following the system outlined in this chapter, you will gain a level of confidence and faith in your ability to formulate a plan.

Once your plan is in place, you can confidently seize the opportunities that overseas property investment has to offer. I don't think there are many better ways to make substantial returns on your capital this year, next year and beyond.

Key points summary

- Successful property investment begins with a sound strategy, based on your profile and goals.

STRATEGY

GOALS:

- Visualise your goals.

- Set SMART goals:
  S pecific
  M easurable
  A ction-oriented and Achievable
  R ealistic
  T imed

- Write down what you want to achieve.

- Don't fail to plan!

ACTION:

- Define a strategy that suits you.

- Use investment profiling:
  What type of investor are you?
  Consider your strengths
  Define your market
  Choose an area of focus
  Implement your strategy

- Monitor performance and don't be scared to alter *your* strategy to suit the circumstances.

CHAPTER 5

The financial considerations of jet-to-let

'Even though work stops, expenses run on.' Cato the Elder

You have to approach property investing as you would any other business. You still have customers, costs, revenue, assets, suppliers, debtors (hopefully not too many), short-term creditors, possibly staff and premises, marketing and accounts.

As owning property is the same as owning a business, you need to use business techniques to ensure that you:

- remain in business and don't go bust – cash flow is king;

- make a profit;

- expand the business; and

- add value to the business giving you the potential at some stage in the future to sell it.

If you have holiday lets overseas, you need to consider how you will fill your properties and this means you need a marketing strategy.

Now it's time for some maths. OK, don't all cheer at once, but think of it like this: without understanding the numbers, how will you know if you're making a profit or if crisis is looming? Not many of us like dealing with figures but getting to grips with them now will save you a lot of frustration in the future.

Costs

The word 'costs' crops up many times in this book because costs, particularly when they are increasing, can be your undoing. Costs are your enemy. This may sound a little dramatic, but you really do need to have them at the top of your agenda when considering jet-to-let. There are many potential pitfalls with property investment, but none are greater than runaway costs and negative cash flow.

Investor financial tools

I'm now going to introduce some key property investor financial tools which you would do well to use when assessing a potential jet-to-let investment. The chapters on strategy and economics explain the concepts of top down investing, ensuring that you find the very best areas in which to make your investments. The tools here are designed to help *after* you know where you will be putting your money. This sort of financial analysis is critical for ensuring that the investment is viable and stacks up.

I'm going to look at the following:

1. Transaction costs

2. Operating cost statement

3. Property wealth check statement

4. Yield

5. Return on investment (ROI)

6. Return on equity (ROE)

7. Revaluation model for portfolio expansion

8. Capital growth

1. Transaction (or acquisition) costs

After you have done all of your research and put together a strategy, you will be ready to invest in a jet-to-let property.

The property you are interested in has a price of £100,000 and you arrange for finance at 80 per cent loan to value (LTV). All you have to find is 20 per cent in the form of a £20,000 deposit – right? I'm afraid that this is wishful thinking.

There are costs associated with buying property and these costs are broadly similar the world over. Some of the costs to consider are as follows:

- Legal fees

- Survey costs or valuation

- Mortgage arrangement fee

- Stamp duty and/or local taxes

- Other costs, such as estate agency fees (in some countries) and finder's fees (can be for an individual or company which has done the leg work on your behalf and sourced the property for you)

These are known as 'transaction costs'. So, it's possible that the £100,000 figure may increase quite a bit, but it's up to you to find out by how much before you commit. A summary of transaction costs of the countries we feature in *The Jet-to-Let Bible* can be found in the country studies.

Transaction costs vary from country to country, but it's worth noting that the costs in emerging markets are far less than those in the more traditional ones. For example, for investors with a short-term strategy of selling off-plan properties on completion, it would be wise to target countries where the transaction costs are low, so that they don't form a disproportionate percentage of the overall profit.

2. Operating cost statement

Your operating cost statement details all of the costs involved in running your property. It's generally calculated on an annual basis, but can be monthly. The costs of owning and operating a rental property, regardless of its geographical location, are as follows:

- Mortgage or other finance repayments

- Insurance – contents, buildings and public liability

- Maintenance – repairs, fixtures, fittings, white goods, swimming pools, etc.

- Service or management charges

- Letting agency fees

- Marketing for holiday homes including brochures, website and membership fees of third party advertisers

- Changeover charges for holiday lets – linen, welcome pack, cleaning, etc.

- Personal expenses – flights, hotels, car hire when inspecting your property, etc.

Therefore, all of these expenses need to be factored in to your operating cost statement. Let's have a look at these in a bit more detail.

Mortgage costs

A worked example

Tony and Cherie have invested in a property which costs £200,000 (before transaction costs). It's estimated that they will be able to rent the property for £14,000 per annum. They obtain a mortgage at 80% LTV, which is £160,000, and put down a deposit of £40,000.

a. Interest-only mortgages

An interest-only mortgage means that each mortgage payment that you make just pays off the interest on your loan. At the end of the mortgage term, you will have to repay the loan from other sources of finance, perhaps from the sale of the property or other investment vehicle.

Let's say that the interest-only mortgage is for a 25-year term at an interest rate today of 4%, so what is their annual repayment to the bank? After some short calculations, we find that the repayment figure is £6,400 per annum or £533.33 per month. To refresh your memory, it's calculated in this way:

Borrowed amount x interest rate ÷ 100 = yearly repayment figure

£160,000 x 4 ÷ 100 = £6,400 per year or £533.33 per month

b. Interest and capital repayment mortgage

With an interest and capital repayment mortgage, each payment you make pays the interest and a proportion of the capital. Therefore, at the end of the term you own the property without any debts.

This type of mortgage is more common in overseas markets. However, the annual repayment to the bank is higher than with an interest-only mortgage. Using the same example and performing some calculations, we find a repayment figure of £10,134 per annum or £844.54 per month.

Please note that the formula for calculating a repayment figure on an interest and capital repayment mortgage is complicated. You can find mortgage calculator tools on the internet, which will perform the necessary calculations for you.

Your costs are very different depending on which type of mortgage you are able to secure. One of the attractions of overseas markets is that many of them have fairly rigid and, what are by UK standards, quite dated financial services industries. The liberalisation of these services will lead to a growth in the affordability, attractiveness and accessibility of property which we have seen in the UK, Ireland and Spain in recent years. This is one of the main factors which is attracting investors now in anticipation of easier finance and the positive effect that it will have on property prices.

Annual operating cost statement for Tony and Cherie

Total rental income (gross)	£14,000
Operating costs:	
• Mortgage payments (repayment mortgage)	£10,134

• Insurance	£400
• Maintenance*	£300
• Letting fees	£1,400
• Personal	£500
Total costs	**£12,734**
Before tax cash flow (which is total rental revenue minus total costs)	**£1,266**

* They have made a 'provision' for maintenance of £300. The term provision means that they are setting aside £300 as a contingency fund for maintenance. Although at present there may be no maintenance outstanding, experience suggests that there will be some throughout the year. If there is not, then Tony and Cherie have an extra £300 for their profit or contingency fund. They would also make a provision for void periods or at the very least be aware that their property may have periods when there is no-one occupying the building.

 It's important that you account for higher interest rates when you do your figures. What if interest rates rise by 0.5 per cent this year? How will it affect your cash flow? This is known as a sensitivity analysis and will alert you early to any potential cash flow issues you may have in the future.

Contingency fund

Before we leave the subject of operating costs, I would like to emphasise the importance of building a contingency fund which you can call on when needed. The idea of a contingency fund is that you never know if and when you might need it, but when a problem arises you will be grateful that you have funds immediately available. Apart from adding cash from another source to such a fund, you could channel any revenue which you had earmarked for voids, maintenance or repairs which is not spent in the year to the fund.

3. Property wealth check statement

Companies would call a property wealth check statement a balance sheet, which shows your net worth on a particular day. It lists your assets (i.e. what you own), your liabilities (i.e. what you owe) and what capital or equity you may have accumulated. I'm only considering the property part of wealth here, so here's an example for Tony and Cherie:

Assets		Liabilities and capital	
Property 1 value	£180,000	Mortgage 1	£100,000
Property 2 value	£190,000	Mortgage 2	£100,000
Property 3 value	£200,000	Mortgage 3	£160,000
Cash in bank from property business	£10,000		
Inventory:			
Furniture			
White goods			
Miscellaneous items	£30,000		
		Equity	**£250,000**
Total assets	**£610,000**	**Total liabilities and capital**	**£610,000**

As you can see from the statement, Tony and Cherie already own two other properties which have seen some good equity growth. You can see why a statement such as this is also known as a balance sheet as your total assets must equate to or balance with what you owe and the equity you have invested.

You may find a statement such as this and a business plan with an estimated operating cost statement a useful addition to the standard mortgage application forms you send to your bank. The criteria that banks use around the world vary greatly. Some don't carry out credit scoring and the sort of checks we are used to in the UK. Some banks or brokers may not be influenced in their decision to grant you a loan; others may. As I have said throughout the book, you have to find ways and methods to stack the odds in your favour and something like this can only help by demonstrating to the bank your solid understanding of the financial aspects of your investment.

4. Yield

Yield is a term and calculation which is used across the industry – at home and abroad. What does it mean? A great deal is made of yield figures by many individuals and companies, but in reality it tells you nothing. You can't even compare potential investments to gauge which may be the better by using yield alone. What I am referring to here is gross yield.

a. Gross yield

A definition of gross yield is as follows:

> The annual income, before costs, from a property expressed as a percentage of its total purchase price.'

So, in the case of Tony and Cherie's recent acquisition, the total purchase price of the property is £200,000 plus the transaction costs, which will add a notional cost of five per cent.

Total purchase costs = £200,000 + 5% = £210,000

We know that the gross revenue or rent is £14,000

So, the gross yield is £14,000 ÷ £210,000 x 100 = 6.66%

Many companies advertising gross yield returns don't take into account the transaction costs in the calculation. By doing this, it artificially raises the attractiveness of the investment in terms of gross yield. I'm not suggesting that this is a deliberate ploy by companies and I'm sure that in some cases it's not; I'm just saying that it happens. Check which figure is being used.

So, if we didn't add in transaction costs what would the gross yield figure be?

£14,000 ÷ £200,000 x 100 = 7%

Forget gross yield. Here's why:

> You have 2 properties both costing £100,000. In both cases you have a gross yield of 7%, which is a rent of £7,000 per annum.
>
> In Country A the transaction costs add 7% to the purchase price whereas in Country B the transaction costs are 3%.
>
> In Country A the interest rate on the mortgage is 5% and in Country B it's 4%. Property taxes in Country A are £400 per annum and in the second almost negligible. Management charges in Country A are £1,000 per annum and in Country B £400. Insurance is £500 per annum in A, and £200 in B.

Costs	Country A	Country B
Mortgage (interest only)*	£5,000	£4,000
Property taxes	£400	£100
Management charge	£1,000	£400
Insurance	£500	£200
Total costs before provisions	£6,900	£,4,700
Income	£7,000	£7,000
Profit before provisions and tax	£100	£2,300

> * In most cases overseas mortgages would be interest and capital repayment so this figure would be higher, but I have used interest only to keep the calculations simple.

On the surface, the gross yield made these two investments look similar in terms of income. However, when you look at the detail of the respective costs, the picture is very different.

 Get down into the detail before you invest in any overseas property.

b. Net yield

Net yield is the same as gross yield except we take costs into account. So, in the case above, we would calculate the net yield as:

> Country A: £100 net income ÷ £107,000 total cost (includes 7% transaction costs) x 100 = 0.09% net yield
>
> Country B: £2,300 net income ÷ £103,000 total cost (includes 3% transaction costs) x 100 = 2.23% net yield

I've spent some time smashing the myth of gross yield because I think it's important that you concentrate just as much on the potential costs as you do on the income and possible capital gain.

Remember costs are your enemy – better the devil you know!

5. Return on investment

By return on investment (ROI), I mean the return you receive on the capital that you have invested – not the bank's money, but your money. In property investment you are aiming to commit as little or even none of your own cash. Why?

Because if you're investing in an asset which is producing income and is exposed to the potential for capital growth and you have none of your own cash in it, in simple terms the returns are free and you are on to a winner.

So, what does the ROI equation look like? Well, let's look at a geared off-plan scenario where we sell the property on completion.

> You purchase a property for £100,000 and after 2 years of 10% growth per annum it's worth £121,000 (£100,000 x 10% = £110,000 for the first year, then £110,000 x 10% = £121,000 for the second). The deposit of 20% when you bought the property was £20,000.
>
> The increase in property value over 2 years is £21,000 (£121,000 – £100,000 = £21,000).
>
> Gross ROI = £21,000 (increase in value) ÷ £20,000 deposit (excluding costs) x 100 = 105%

Be aware that this percentage return would be reduced depending on the level of transaction costs. For example, if transaction costs were two per cent, then the ROI would be:

£21,000 ÷ (£20,000 + £2,000 costs) = 95.5%

This is a useful example to remember when comparing alternative investments in different countries which have very different transaction costs. Clearly the higher the costs, the less will be your return on cash invested – all other things being equal.

Invest as little of your own cash as possible

By investing as little cash as possible, you drive up the ROI. Take the example above. If you had invested half as much deposit, which would be £11,000, then the ROI is equal to:

191% (£21,000 ÷ £11,000 x 100 = 191%)

As part of your jet-to-let strategy you should consider how you can maximise your ROI.

6. Return on equity

Your return on equity (ROE) is the same simple equation as the one you used for ROI but with the added factor of time. When you invest in a property you start at 0 in terms of time. So, you invest today and your ROI is X per cent. After a period of time, say five years, the ROI changes because the property is likely to have risen in value. At this stage, you have equity in your property. Here is a simple example:

You invest in a property which costs £100,000. The rental net of costs is £3,000 per annum. The mortgage is 80% LTV, which is £80,000.

You have £20,000 invested in this property. The net rental return is £3,000, so the gross ROI is:

£3,000 ÷ £20,000 x 100 = 15%

This is better than any bank deposit rate I know and the property is also subject to capital gains if the market continues to rise. Let's assume that it does and continues to do so for five years at ten per cent per annum cumulatively and that the net rent rises cumulatively by two per cent per annum.

> After 5 years, your net rental income is £3,312 and the property value is £161,051.
>
> The ROE after 5 years would be:
>
> £3,312 ÷ (capital growth of £61,051 + £20,000 deposit) x 100,
>
> which is a total equity figure of £81,051.
>
> ROE = 4.1%

What you have here is a dramatic reduction on the return on the equity tied up in this property. The ROE reduces as a property increases in value. Your investment becomes less efficient in terms of *opportunity cost.*

In this example, your return has fallen from 15 per cent to 4.1 per cent.

Opportunity cost – the investor's mantra for success

We looked at opportunity cost in some detail in chapter 2 and now we have the perfect opportunity to demonstrate its power for the investor.

Let's assume that even after five years in the country in which you have made your investment, the LTV offered on a mortgage remains at 80 per cent. However, you are able to refinance as financial services have evolved. This means that you can remortgage the property at the new valuation, thus releasing some of the equity you have tied up.

Equity release in the UK has been one of the main factors behind the recent consumer boom and also one of the drivers of UK buy-to-let and overseas jet-to-let markets.

So, you can remortgage your property for £161,000. You have an 80 per cent LTV mortgage meaning that the bank will now loan you £128,800 on the new valuation. Your previous mortgage is for £80,000 so you release £48,800 (which is calculated by subtracting £80,000 from £128,800). We'll come back to this figure.

Critically, the amount of equity you now have tied up in the property is:

£32,200 (= £161,000 – £128,800).

£3,312 ÷ £32,200 x 100 = 10.3%

Note: Unless the interest rate has fallen, your mortgage payments will increase and this will affect the percentage return, but the key to this is what you now do with the £48,800 released equity! You need to put it to work to ensure that you are earning more than the loan is costing you.

To summarise, the astute investor ensures that he has crunched the numbers before he commits to an investment. He checks out the costs against the rental income and isn't fooled by such concepts as gross yield. He understands that gross yield is used by marketers trying to sell property.

The astute investor also knows that he should invest as little of his own money as possible to drive the ROI into the clouds. As the property increases in value over time and rents cannot keep pace, then the ROI, or more accurately the ROE, over time declines and makes the investment less efficient. In other words, your equity is not working as hard as it can do.

You then need to refinance and extract as much of your equity as you can to continue the battle elsewhere with additional property investments.

7. The revaluation model

By continually revaluing your jet-to-let portfolio, you're providing further ammunition in the form of cash to grow your portfolio. So, back to the example: you may be paying more in interest payments because you now have a bigger loan, but it's relatively small change when you consider what else you can do with the cash.

You now have £48,800 to re-invest. The £48,800 can now be used to invest off-plan, for instance, to take advantage of the gearing effect. It can be used to invest in a property fund or used with others as part of a syndicate. It can be used to buy property or land.

You now have the world at your feet because you have the funds to move in any direction you like. This is the key to successful investing. Don't leave cash or equity tied up when opportunity cost tells you that it could be working harder elsewhere!

Portfolio diversification

An additional benefit of releasing equity to help finance new property investments is that it diversifies your portfolio. It spreads your risk across more properties and leaves you less vulnerable, and with more to offer. There is less risk owning ten properties than one, as your eggs aren't all in one basket, so to speak. If you have one house which doesn't have any tenants for a year, it's not much of a financial problem as the other nine properties will contribute to the costs. If you have one property and it's empty for a year, you have a problem!

8. Capital growth

Many jet-to-let investors are attracted to markets by the prospect of strong and sustained capital growth. Many of the countries we examine in the country studies at the back of the book are experiencing fundamental economic and political change. It's an exciting time for many in these countries and also for those of us with investments there. These markets offer exciting and real opportunities for investors and many have seized the chance with both hands. If you do careful research and follow the principles of this book, you too will be able to share in this vibrant and growing overseas property market.

Financial return

A financial return is the combination of income and capital growth. We have to look at the two aspects of a return in tandem.

A couple of years ago, I had a debate with another investor who had a strategy of negative cash flow, because he said that the capital growth would compensate for any monthly losses he incurred. In other words, growth was so strong that it was worth taking a hit on the cash flow. At the time I said that I thought it was a severely flawed strategy and I would never recommend such a view.

Well, since then, capital growth in the UK has slowed and stagnated, for now, and interest rates have risen from historical lows, thus pushing investors like him further into the red. He can't say he was never warned!

Don't just count on capital growth in jet-to-let markets. Undoubtedly, many of the markets we cover in this book will enjoy sustained growth over the coming years. Countries which we haven't yet covered in the book will come to the fore in 2007 and others in 2008 and 2009.

So, don't be swayed by just capital growth; your property investment also has to be cash flow positive!

Key points summary

- Property investment the world over is about numbers, getting them right and making profits. You don't need a degree in economics or mathematics to conduct a financial analysis – a pen and paper will do!

- Your costs are your enemy. Understand them, control them and don't under any circumstances allow them to undermine or destroy your jet-to-let business aspirations.

- Use the financial tools of this chapter, with the broader economic and risk aspects we look at elsewhere, to form a complete picture of the investment potential of individual properties in particular countries.

- Forget gross yield – it's only used by people trying to sell you something. Look at your true cash flow, which is net yield, to ensure your success.

- Review your investments over time and consider revaluing the properties in order to release capital for further expansion.

- Transaction costs must be taken into account when investing in property. When you buy and sell property you incur costs which you must factor in to any projections of cash flow or capital gain.

- Do estimate your operating costs. Check the validity of the claims by the agent or developer about rental values, and then do your cash flow projection.

- Conduct a sensitivity analysis and factor in any potential rises in the rate of interest paid on your mortgage to forewarn of any potential cash flow issue in the future.

- Consider the benefits of an interest-only mortgage if it's available or when it becomes available in the future.

- Remember not to be fixated with capital growth. Check on the income and cash flow before committing.

- Think maximum profits, think opportunity cost.

CHAPTER 6

Jet- to-let property investment strategies

Earlier, we spent some time looking at the relationship between goal-setting and developing a property investment strategy that works for you. I want to avoid offering prescribed 'this is the way to do it' advice based on my own goals and personality because everyone's goals, ambitions and personalities are different.

Instead, you will find a framework so that you can develop your own thoughts, a series of options for you to think about, and hopefully the confidence and knowledge to step up to the challenge.

We will now consider and explore in more detail some of the strategies open to you as a jet-to-let property investor. The list is not exhaustive, but it covers the main areas which you should think about before deciding where to focus and includes:

- property development;
- jet-to-sell renovation projects; and
- off-plan investing.

Property development

If you want to invest overseas and become a property developer, you will construct or refurbish single or multiple properties with the intention of selling them for a profit.

If you are in a good market where demand is strong and prices are rising, then the option to develop is attractive. But before you get carried away, there are a few things to consider.

1. Partners

It's possible to enter an overseas market as a foreigner and develop, market and sell property, but this is easier in some markets than others.

Ideally, you need a partner who is from the country in which you wish to develop and preferably someone who has a bit of clout, as the doors that open for a local will in some cases be closed to you. The opportunities to buy good development land or buy out small developers who are in difficulty will present themselves more often with a local partner.

As with all things jet-to-let, choose your partner carefully as you have to trust him 100 per cent. Property developing involves large sums of money and requires clear decision making and the ability to live with a high degree of risk.

If it's possible, an introduction via a mutual third party is the perfect start, but how many people are in that position? This is why I am a great believer in networking and meeting people. Who knows who you will meet at a networking event?

On one of my courses last year, we had two very experienced property developers from Spain fly in for the weekend. They sat through the course, asked some excellent questions and then stayed for the networking drinks afterwards. We had a chat and I was impressed with everything they were telling me about their operations in Spain.

They are developing 400 villas on the Costa Blanca, but need a specialist consultant to advise on accessibility issues. The market for property that provides for those with mobility problems is growing. How often have you been to a hotel or villa and wondered just how on earth anyone in a wheelchair could get around?

Anyway, within 24 hours we had put them in touch with a member of our property investor community who was an expert in accessible property and had previously advised on some of our developments. He flew out a few weeks later to provide consultancy services.

So, get out and about. Opportunities will always arise if you make yourself available, but if no-one knows who you are, it's more difficult.

2. Cultural practices

You have probably seen the advertisements on TV for a major retail bank promoting its view that it's 'the world's local bank'. The adverts highlight cultural differences around the world. Making eye contact, the giving and receiving of gifts, greeting one another and many other activities have different meanings, messages and interpretations across cultures. You are not going to pick these things up overnight and, again, a local partner is invaluable in steering you through a potential minefield.

3. Legal advice

 Don't confuse what is taken to be normal with what is actually legal.

In some countries it's not uncommon for people to make payments in order to secure a more favourable business position. In the UK we would call it a bribe. It's illegal in the UK and is also against the law in most foreign countries, although in some it's 'culturally acceptable' and sometimes necessary to get anywhere in business. However, don't fall into this trap.

Normal practice and legal practice should not be confused and a good English-speaking lawyer needs to be on your team to ensure that at all stages you remain within the law.

Additionally, your lawyer will be able to draw up any legal contracts that you require, conduct searches on any companies you deal with and carry out any due diligence and checks on any land you may purchase. The robust Land Registry system of the UK is replicated only in a few of the jet-to-let investment areas, and title or ownership of land can be contentious.

You cannot hope to cut through the mist of bureaucracy and red tape without the support of a good local lawyer.

Your lawyer should ideally be recommended by someone you know, such as your business partner, or you can ask the local British Embassy, High Commission or Consulate for their list of recommended English-speaking lawyers.

4. Finance

The big question is where do you get the money from? You will need to use finance or possibly raise cash via some form of offering.

You can raise cash from other investors to finance the development for either a fixed return or for a percentage of the profit. They will require security, a return commensurate with the risk and a detailed investment appraisal.

However, it's not easy finding investors. To pull it off, you will need a good track record, a persuasive personality and a sound business plan!

Alternatively, you can leverage against your portfolio in the UK. This means that if you have investment properties which have significant equity accrued over a number of years, you can use them.

You can also form a syndicate with a group of friends, family or other like-minded individuals. This involves a legal contract setting out the terms and conditions of the syndicate, the management of it and how each of you will take your money out at the end (i.e. an exit plan).

Finally, you have the banks both in the UK and overseas. Many UK banks will not lend for overseas development projects unless you are a big player with a strong track record, but many overseas banks will lend for development projects. Your relationship with your bank is one of the key factors which will determine whether you are successful.

Returning to that local partner again; if your partner is a successful businessperson with an identifiable track record built over a number of years, who already has a relationship with a bank, it will be a lot easier raising funds.

5. Tax and currency controls

Check out the tax situation in the country in which you wish to develop. How big a slice of the profit will the government take in the form of Corporation Tax? Is there a Wealth Tax (i.e. an annual tax based on your overall wealth usually expressed as a percentage) and if so, will you have to pay it? What other taxes are there? What effect does VAT have and how much can you claim back? Is there any form of currency control? How do you get your money out? Make sure that you get all these answers before you start, and the best way to do this is to pay for advice from an accountant and/or lawyer.

6. Contractors

A contractor is someone who actually does the work and constructs the project. You present your development in the form of a competitive tender to a number of contractors with a detailed specification and timeline. The contractors will study the proposals and make an offer.

a. Costs

Your research will give you a clear idea of what the going rate is for new-build properties in a particular area. This is normally expressed in terms of pounds per square metre (or whatever the local currency is).

Example

If your construction costs are £600 per square metre and a house is 150 square metres internally, then the cost to build the house is £90,000.

If the land itself costs £90,000, then the total cost of the house is £180,000.

Let's add in a notional 10% VAT cost on land and building costs at £18,000 and a contribution to other costs, such as sales and marketing, of £18,000, then the overall cost to the developer for this property will be £216,000.

Depending on the country and location, it will probably be sold for between £260,000 and £280,000.

It's also possible that the land may cost a fraction of what I have proposed if it was purchased sometime earlier or if a change of use of that land (e.g. from agricultural to residential) has occurred. I will cover this later in the chapter.

b. Economies of scale

In the example you will have noticed that I put a figure of £18,000 onto the cost of the property in order to cover some additional costs. This contribution will go towards any fixed costs you have, such as staff, offices, motor vehicles and insurance. It doesn't matter how many houses are built – these costs will stay constant.

Other costs associated with sales, marketing, seminars and exhibitions are variable, because if you didn't have developments to sell, then you wouldn't have these costs. But, in essence, your costs won't be much different whether you market ten properties or 100. The key point is that with 100 units these costs are spread over ten times as many properties, thus reducing the costs per unit significantly.

7. New-build versus refurbishment

There is absolutely no reason why you couldn't have a new-build plan running in parallel with, and in support of, refurbishment projects. We will come back to both types of investment a little later.

8. Critical mass

It's easier and more cost effective to sell three development projects than one, as we observed earlier (see above). How can this be true? What about all those costs I was talking about earlier?

Certainly, some of the marketing costs such as brochures will be greater but, on the whole, it takes the same marketing effort to target the buyer whether you have one development of 100 units or three developments of 33 units.

However, what you have with three developments is choice for the buyer or investor. In marketing speak, as a developer you have a 'product mix' as preferably the locations and pricing points will be different. You are offering the client, who may have taken a special trip from another country to view your sites, options. Remember that for the customer, choice is happiness.

If you have one option and your client dismisses it because of any factor, then you are up the creek without a paddle, have incurred costs in terms of marketing, time and resources and your buyer will go to someone else who has the product that he wants.

9. The package

Investors and home buyers are looking for a package – a turnkey solution where all the hassle of buying overseas is taken away from them. They want a top quality product, delivered on time with you taking care of everything from furniture to insurance.

Developers now compete, not just on price and quality, but also on the finance, after-sales and property management that they can offer to the client.

So, if you are considering developing overseas, take into account the non-property ways in which you can compete in the marketplace and thereby create a competitive advantage over your rivals. One way is to produce a package which reflects the wishes and aspirations of your clients.

10. Sales and marketing

Often overlooked in the rush to develop, sales and marketing will be the main factor in determining whether you are a success or failure in overseas property development.

a. Exit strategy

I haven't covered exit strategy yet in this book and now is probably a good time to introduce the topic. By 'exit strategy' I mean the route by which your profit becomes real. The end result of developing property, whether on a small or large scale, is the successful sale and the realisation of profit.

The biggest risk is not the planning authorities, the construction, the finance or any legal anomalies, but the exit. All of the other issues can be hedged, mitigated against, and if your business planning has been meticulous, there should not be any major surprises.

b. Marketing and selling property

In order to reduce their risk, developers sell properties off-plan, take deposits from their client and exchange contracts. The developer will be in a sounder financial position by selling more properties before the land has been cleared and a foundation laid.

Before you decide to develop in an overseas market you have to be very clear to whom you are going to market and through which sales channels. I would not rely on local estate agents, as this route tends to be slow, and in my view relatively passive.

Routes to market:

- A professional sales and marketing team
- Website
- Marketing materials
- Property exhibitions
- Property marketing companies
- Sales agents
- Property investment clubs/associations/syndicates in the UK
- Editorial features for highly targeted newspapers and magazines

What about putting a few adverts in the Sunday newspapers or one of those glossy magazines? Personally, I'm not a great fan of general print advertising. It's about bangs for your buck. The very large companies have very large marketing budgets because the cost is spread across so many properties, as we looked at earlier.

On a smaller scale, I don't think the effect justifies the expense. You have to do a considerable amount of it to get a return. I also think that the industry has moved away from general print advertising onto the internet.

I would, however, consider advertising in specific, subscription-based property investment magazines where you know that the reader fits the profile of your targeted market.

11. After-sales and customer service

Often underestimated, the after-sales process is both time and manpower intensive. You neglect it at your peril. The post-sale work occurs once a verbal agreement has been reached to sell a property.

I want to highlight this, as I know of UK-based investors embarking on developing overseas who have given no consideration to the after-sales process.

The process of selling a property goes something like this:

> Sales and marketing activities = Sale

A sale involves:

- Receipts of money and paperwork
- Contracts
- The mortgage application process
- Choice of tiles, kitchens, upgrades
- Furniture packs
- Takeover of the property
- Takeover procedures
- Snagging
- Property management
- Many questions about all of the above

And this takes a strong, well-trained customer services team.

12. The client

I have left the client until last because he is the most important external factor in your business plan as an overseas property developer. Without clients you have no business.

One satisfied client is worth five prospective clients. A satisfied client will come back and buy more and will do your advertising for you by telling friends who will also buy. For many people, word-of-mouth is a deciding factor when parting with cash, so a satisfied client is your best marketing tool.

I think points 1 to 12 above will give you some food for thought and will make you ask the right questions of others as well as yourself before you embark on what is possibly the highest risk/reward strategy that I cover in this book.

Jet-to-sell renovation projects

I think that a key contributor to the jet-to-sell phenomenon has been the proliferation of TV programmes dedicated to the subject of people leaving the UK for a better life overseas, which may say more about modern Britain than the countries people are moving to. Anyway, the exodus is clearly underway.

Property developers and investors are aware of this and are also following the exodus, not to emigrate, but to buy the derelicts before the ex-pats arrive and, after renovation, selling them to this growing market. There is also an indigenous market in many countries, but it's the foreign market that most of these renovation projects are aimed at.

I call this 'jet-to-sell' and it's becoming increasingly common. To put it simply, you take an overseas property which is run down; you do it up and then sell it on for a profit. This strategy is very popular both in the UK and overseas for a number of reasons:

- You expect to purchase the property at a good development price. In other words, you have calculated that after the cost of renovation and selling you will make a decent profit.

- If it has been there for a while and the owners don't wish to develop it themselves, they may be open to an offer. In many cases overseas, property may well have been left to the family and no-one has actually thought about selling it until you make an offer.

- There is a growing market of Europeans, not just the British, who want the cottage in the country, or the villa in the mountains, lifestyle and are willing to pay a good price for the property of their dreams.

- You are not in competition with the big developers, who can often have a competitive advantage by offering a package which makes it difficult to operate on a level playing field. We are dealing here with a bespoke product.

- You can use this strategy in any market, not just the idyllic rural house one, but also in cities and towns throughout the world. It's presently a popular strategy in many cities in Eastern Europe.

By renovating multiple properties, you can achieve economies of scale, just as we looked at in the previous section on property developing. Your costs are then spread over a number of projects and you will also get a better deal from the contractor.

The main disadvantage, however, is that the barriers to others entering this market are low. You literally have to buy a house and do it up. If others, particularly entrepreneurial locals, see that you are doing well, then they may be tempted to set up in direct competition.

So, what should you do? You must have a competitive advantage with your product (i.e. your renovation project) and you need to have something which is a bit different from the competition; for example, the quality of your construction, the finishes, the personal service you offer or the after-sales care.

Business principles

The same business principles which we looked at in the developer section are also applicable with jet-to-sell, but you will need a clear business plan before proceeding. Whether it's one property or 100 you are still developing property and as such the principles are the same, albeit on a different scale.

For success in jet-to-sell you need to consider some crucial factors:

- You must not alienate your market by over-personalising a property. Keep it neutral so the buyer can put his own stamp on it. You must bear in mind that it's not your dream home, so if you like red walls with green ceilings, think again!

- With jet-to-sell, your property is likely to be old, so don't try to make it look like the new-build further down the road. Your competitive advantage is that it's old, has character and is very different to the other properties in the area. Let that work in your favour, so make sure that any renovation work is in keeping with the feel, charm and character of the property.

 Check with the local authorities during your research regarding what the restrictions may be on renovating properties in the area. You may find, for instance, that the regulations are different inside a village than on the outskirts. As always, find out before you commit.

Make a profit

Don't lose sight of the principal aim of the venture, which is to make a profit. The three factors which determine your profit are:

1. Purchase price
2. Costs
3. Selling price

Your aim is to minimise the purchase price and costs and maximise the selling price. It seems obvious, but you only have to watch the property renovation shows on TV to see how often people forget!

1. Purchase price

Achieving a realistic purchase price in order to make the jet-to-sell project profitable is your first task. Before you negotiate on a potential project, you must have a very clear idea of how much it will cost you to renovate and then add 20 per cent as a contingency. Estimate other costs and then you will have a good idea of your ceiling price. Simple planning such as this will reduce your risk.

Some people love negotiating and others hate it, but negotiation skills are what you need in order to secure the right price to make your project profitable. If you are particularly shy and loathe negotiating, rope in someone else who is particularly adept in the art.

 Remember to work to your strengths, not your weaknesses, and if necessary, bring in someone who is a more skilled negotiator. This person may be a family member, friend or a joint venture partner or may even be someone you pay to act on your behalf.

Don't allow any difficulty you have with negotiating hold you back. However, where do you start?

A negotiating checklist

- **Be prepared.** Make sure that you have conducted a considerable amount of research and know:
    - the costs of other comparable properties in a similar state in the area;
    - the renovation costs;
    - the background of the vendor;
    - how long the property has been on the market for;
    - why it's being sold; and
    - any legal, boundary and title issues.
- **Anticipate.** By being prepared and analysing all the information, you now know what you want from the negotiation. You also have to anticipate what the vendor wants from the negotiation. Taking it one stage further, you also have to anticipate what he thinks you want from the negotiation!

There is an overused term called 'win/win', which means that both parties are successful at the conclusion of a negotiation, and this should be your outcome. Just be careful that when he is second-guessing what you want from the negotiation that he doesn't think you are really wealthy and, as a result, he believes that he can charge you a premium for what may be a very profitable renovation project.

- **Build trust.** There is nothing wrong with a good old-fashioned lunch! Moreover, you will find in many countries that it's the normal way to conduct business. The business lunch is a proven concept throughout the world and one which is invaluable in building mutual trust.

- **Listen.** It's important to listen to what the other party has to say and to take his facial expressions and other forms of non-verbal communication into account. As a listener, you are gathering intelligence that can help you discover which of the other party's needs must be met before an agreement can take place.

- **Analyse.** You have conducted thorough research and know your best-case and worst-case scenarios. Best case you think will be £X, worst case it will be £Y. You cannot go beyond £Y because the project then carries significant risk which may result in failure.

- **Act.** You want to be closer to £X than to £Y in order to increase profitability and reduce risk. You may have to compromise, but don't be so quick to do it. Don't get emotional but remain objective and business-like. You can always walk away, but don't give the other party that impression – you are trying to build trust. If you agree a price within your range (£X to £Y), that's fantastic. If you don't, smile, shake hands and walk away. Don't under any circumstances pay more than your profit margins will allow.

  You then have to look for other options inside your budget, but don't be surprised if the vendor comes back with a revised offer a day or two later – perhaps after another lunch!

If you are entering an overseas market for the first time, you may need the services of an estate agent or property sourcing service – see chapter 8 for more information.

2. Costs

The favoured phrase in the property world is 'location, location, location', but as a jet-to-sell developer you must control your 'costs, costs, costs'. These will become your biggest concern and even with the most meticulous planning there will be surprises. Remember that you are dealing with old properties.

Your first task will be to produce a schedule of what works need to be carried out. You may want to instruct an architect and/or building surveyor depending on the level of work, the state of the building or if you want to create a particular feature, extension or modification.

You will need to ensure that what you are doing is within local planning regulations (which the architect can advise on) and then invite bids for the work from three contractors, based on the plan produced by your architect or building surveyor. This may be in the form of a schedule of works. There are many ways to do this and the example below shows you one way of how to do it.

The important thing is to agree a fixed price and it has to be in writing. A written schedule is important because both parties have it to refer to in case of any disagreements or misunderstandings. It's a document which is unambiguous, sets out what you are paying for and also protects the contractor's interests.

You will also have to consider the best language to use for the document; do take legal advice before doing anything. There is no point having it in English if the extent of the contractor's response is 'sí' or 'OK' and if he nods at everything you say.

You will find that some contractors will not put a figure against each item on your schedule, but will quote for the overall job. This doesn't matter. The schedule specifies the tasks and the standards and as such allows you to compare each contractor on an equal footing.

 Make sure that you see examples of the quality of work carried out by any local contractors as a guideline before you proceed.

Extract of a schedule of works

Job 1

Task: Replace all damaged windows with wooden framed double-glazed units which comply with current regulations.

Comment: The windows should be as close as possible to the original in appearance.

Job 2

Task: Create an en-suite bathroom in the main bedroom. It is to have a shower cubicle (900mm x 900mm), a shower with mixer, basin and pedestal and a top flushing toilet. A window is to be created on the external wall and glazed.

Comment: Tiling and flooring to be advised. We will supply it and, as a result, it should not be costed other than for labour.

Job 3

Task: The interior walls are to be painted with magnolia emulsion.

Comment: Three coats standard.

Mission creep

 Mission creep is the expansion of a project beyond its original goals.

There is a danger with every project to do 'just a little bit more' or to plump for more expensive materials after the costs of the original project has been outlined. But you are almost certain to fail in your profit projections if you allow the project to expand and/or if you lose control of your budget. The only time when you need to be really ruthless, unbending, aggressive and forthright is in the control of your costs!

Contingency fund

You will probably not be dealing with minor 'cosmetically challenged' properties, but ones where a substantial amount of work is required. Your costing will be as accurate as circumstances allow, but with older properties you just don't know what problems may arise as plaster is ripped off the walls, services such as water and electricity are connected and pipes are laid. With all of this to think about, a minimum 20 per cent of the overall costing needs to be factored into your budget.

3. Selling price

If you buy at a reasonable price and keep within the budget for the project, you have a very good chance of making a tidy profit.

Ultimately, the price at which you sell the property will be a key factor and one which is unfortunately out of your control. Why? Well, who says anyone wants to buy it at the price you wish to sell it?

Many people embark on the jet-to-sell route to instant wealth without considering who the buyer is for their property. Forgetting that this is 50 per cent of the jet-to-sell equation, they will have to settle for less than they would have hoped.

Liquidity risk

One of the risks associated with this jet-to-sell strategy is that once the work has been completed and you have expended time and energy on producing the finished product, you may not be able to sell it!

Liquidity risk is the time it takes to turn your developed property into cash. There are many reasons why you might not be able to sell:

- Rising interest rates
- Falling prices or an unrealistically high asking price
- Change in tastes and fashions
- Change in the character of the village (are they hostile to foreigners?)
- A natural event, outside of your control, such as a flood or landslide
- The oversupply of property in general
- New taxes
- New laws

- You have not appealed to a broad enough market
- Bad location
- Poor quality finishes
- Poor marketing
- An unfavourable news item – such as a town planning corruption scandal

These are just a few of the more obvious factors that come to mind.

You also need to consider that if you have financed the project through a loan, then the longer it takes to sell your property, the smaller your profit will be, as interest payments and other costs mount up. So, you must ensure that the property you deliver is finished to the highest quality that your budget will allow and that its location is unquestionable.

You can sell a second-rate property in a first-rate location a lot quicker than a first-rate property in a second-rate location.

Most potential purchasers will consider the location of your property first, before the quality of the property, so do use this to your advantage.

Off-plan investing

There has been an explosion of interest in recent years in off-plan property investment. This involves purchasing a property which has not yet been built and has been chosen from an architect's plans or perhaps an artist's impression of the site. You may have floor plans and impressions of what the rooms will look like, but little more.

You will sign a contract which states that the property will be delivered to you in a set amount of time (e.g. two years) to a certain specification and lays out the terms and conditions of the sale. The signed contract is binding and effectively states that you will buy and the developer will sell.

What are the advantages of buying off-plan?

The magic of gearing

As a property investor you want your cash to be working as hard as possible on your behalf. One of the best ways to achieve this is through gearing, which we looked at in chapter 2.

The advantage of off-plan investing is the degree to which you can gear, or leverage, your investment. Generally, you only have to deposit with the developer a fraction of the overall cost of the property. In the UK, it's presently about ten per cent, while overseas it varies greatly from country to country.

> **Example**
>
> Let's say that you purchase an off-plan apartment for completion in 2 years' time. The price of the apartment in sterling is £100,000 and the developer requires you to pay a deposit of 20% (£20,000) and then nothing else until completion.
>
> The property market in this country is growing by 10% per annum. So, in 2 years' time the property will be valued at £121,000.
>
> Now, you have only put in 20% or £20,000, so your return on that cash or your return on investment (ROI) is a whopping:
>
> £21,000 ÷ £20,000 x 100 = 105% (gross).

However, you also need to look at the other side of the coin, which a lot of books on the subject, seminars and sales literature either don't mention or gloss over. What if prices fall by ten per cent per annum over two years?

> The property purchased for £100,000 is now worth only £81,000 on completion in 2 years' time, which is a loss as follows:
>
> £20,000 – £19,000 = £1,000
>
> A loss of 95% (£19,000 ÷ £20,000 x 100 = 95%), before costs.

In this example, you will almost be wiped out!

Gearing works very well, whether the property market is rising or falling, by magnifying movements in the underlying price. It's a rising market strategy, so don't buy off-plan geared investments in markets which you think are falling or are about to fall. It is, however, a very powerful investor strategy which, if used correctly, can make your bank balances rise quickly and substantially.

 Only invest off-plan if you expect the property market to rise over the timeframe of your investment.

No tenants

When investing off-plan, if you are aiming to sell before completion, you have the additional benefit of not having to find and manage tenants. If you have ever had trouble with a tenant, you may consider this factor as a major bonus.

Once an off-plan project is completed you have three options:

1. Sell

2. Let

3. Live-and-let

1. Sell

You must check with your lawyer that you have a fully assignable contract which allows you to sell the property (or more accurately to sell your contract) at any time. This is very important, as you may wish to sell for personal or financial reasons of which you were not aware at the time of purchase. Don't be tied in to contracts which prevent you from exiting at a time of your own choosing.

Trading contracts

Some off-plan investors deliberately sell their contracts prior to completion to gain a competitive advantage, as they don't want to be lost in a potential crowd of other sellers on completion. This is particularly relevant if there are a lot of investor buyers in your chosen development.

Others sell before completion because they have adopted a strategy of trading contracts. They treat the contract almost like a stock market traded option or future, selling it as its price rises, parallel to the rise in the price of the underlying asset, which is the property being constructed.

Some manage this successfully and others don't. Of all the strategies we will cover in this book, this one carries the highest risk in terms of the result or outcome. You have to know what you are doing and have a proven route to market. You must always be in a position to financially complete given the illiquid nature of property.

If the development has been predominantly sold to investors who have no intention of letting the property, you may find it difficult to sell on completion as the competition and available supply will be fierce. Stack the odds in your favour for a sale and think as a developer.

I repeatedly use the term 'competitive advantage' and you will have guessed that I am a fan of stacking the odds in my favour by doing something a bit different. Let's get back to the example we used earlier:

> After 2 years your property is worth £121,000 and you want to sell. There are also 15 other owners with similar properties in terms of size, position and view.

Whether the property is in a sunshine destination, ski resort or city, the same principles will apply.

Presently, you have made £21,000, or have you? No. You have costs that need to be taken into consideration before you can arrive at a figure for (before tax) profit:

> Legal fees: let's say £1,000 in total for both transactions of buying and selling.

> Purchase taxes such as stamp duty, Transfer Taxes, other local or country specific taxes: let's say £2,000.

> Estate agents' fees can be very high in some countries, but I will use 3% in this example: £3,630.

Other expenses: £1,000

So you have total expenses of £7,630.

£21,000 – £7,630 = £13,370 before tax, which represents a healthy 63.66% ROI.

Given the psychology of the crowd I should imagine that the vast majority of sellers would now offer their properties for sale somewhere between £121,000 and £129,950. You will have to gauge the market at the time. Look to see what the 'going rate' is, which generally will be determined by the prices of any new phases in the development and by the strength of the overall market.

If the range is somewhere between £121,000 and £129,950, then you don't have enough profit to compete on price without giving it all away in costs, which is not what investing is about.

You must stand out from the rest of the sellers, so you should offer an incentive to a buyer. Allocate a percentage of your profit for incentives; for example:

- Cashback on completion of £2,000.

- A furniture pack of £3,000.

- Pay the buyer's legal fees of £1,000.

- A prize of £1,000 for the successful estate agent who sells your property (check the legality of such a prize with your lawyer in the market in which you are investing).

I'm not suggesting that you do all four, but what I am suggesting is that you do something to make your offer stand out from the crowd. If you keep your expectations modest, then you are more likely to receive a pleasant surprise than a nasty one.

2. Let

This carries less risk than the 'sell' option because of the issues we have just looked at. You will be in a similar situation to the seller, chasing tenants rather than buyers, but you haven't got the bigger issue of trying to sell under a particular time constraint, even if it's only psychological.

If your property stands out from the crowd in terms of presentation or price (or both), and you have instructed a professional lettings company with a reputation for finding quality tenants, then you will be in a strong position and can look forward to years of rental income and capital growth.

One of the major advantages with this strategy is that if you are creative, you can take most of your original deposit out by refinancing. Yet again, situations differ depending on where you are investing, your own personal circumstances and the banks, so you will have to take specific professional advice.

There are differences between overseas countries and the UK in the availability of mortgage finance. In the UK you can get mortgage finance based on the value of the property, but in some countries it can be based on the price you actually paid. So in the case above, you could apply for a mortgage based on today's value of £121,000 and not the price in the contract of £100,000. In this case at, say, 85 per cent LTV, you would receive a loan from the bank of £102,850.

You can see immediately that you would have more than your initial deposit and some paid back, effectively making it a so-called 'no money down' transaction. To clarify, you originally had £20,000 deposit for a property priced at £100,000. After capital growth and a higher LTV (80 per cent increased to 85 per cent) now available on the market, the bank gives you £102,850 based on the increased value. This effectively means that you take your original cash deposit out and use the accrued equity or capital gain as your 15 per cent contribution required by the bank. You can then use your £20,000 for further property investments.

A second advantage of letting your property is that you are treating the business as an investment and you are not speculating solely on price rises to provide a capital gain. With a sell strategy, whether by trading the contract or selling on completion, you are speculating that the market will rise. There is absolutely nothing wrong with this and many property investors have made and continue to make significant profits doing so.

Property is a long-term investment

Property is a long-term investment and if you treat it as such, you will undoubtedly achieve your financial goals. Property prices rise over time due to the factors we looked at earlier in the book. There may be short-term price fluctuations, but the medium- to long-term trend is up.

Warren Buffett, probably one of the most successful investors of this present era, says, 'My favourite timeframe for holding a stock is forever'. He is well known for not having thrown himself and his investment fund into the dot com bubble of the 1990s. He resisted the temptation to follow fashion and, in some quarters, was ridiculed. Buffett has survived and prospered while others have fallen, as the great bubble burst in 2000.

Buffett selects solid, well-managed companies with strong businesses he understands and then buys the shares. His philosophy is that if his research is correct and he has bought great companies, then he doesn't need to sell.

This way of thinking has a parallel in property markets and in particular jet-to-let. Every year there appears to be a new fashion, a new hotspot and a 'dead cert' for making money. Buffett knew better when it came to the fashion of the stock market. He realised that the technology companies with huge valuations could not justify those valuations assigned to them by the market. There was a lot of hype and very little substance.

I would advise all investors to conduct a Warren Buffett-style investigation into markets in which they are considering investing. Ask yourself the key questions:

- Is there really a rental demand for this type of property in this area and from whom?

- Is the market sustainable?

- Will it be affected by any newer markets where prices are cheaper?

- Is it a passing fad?

If the answers to your questions support your view that the market is strong for the right reasons, then holding for the long term, à la Warren Buffett, would seem to be a sensible and profitable strategy.

There are further considerations you must bear in mind when letting property which I will cover in chapter 9.

3. 'Live-and-let'

There has been a sea change in people's attitudes to work and their aspirations for more free time and leisure time. The brash, 1980s 'show me the money' philosophy has given way to a more considered, thoughtful and lifestyle-orientated view of work in the 21st century.

I enjoy our investors' meetings, as it seems the primary motivation of many of our students is to quit the rat race, and we discuss the many ways they might achieve this. They are seeking to control their own time and not be reliant on anyone or any organisation for financial support.

Many students, after leaving our courses, very quickly quit their daytime jobs and use property investing as a means to achieving a better quality of life. Some have taken considerable personal risk by giving up well-paid careers, but they have used the drive and tenacity they already possess to accelerate their new careers in property.

As a result, many have invested in lifestyle property investments in addition to the mainstream UK buy-to-let and buy-to-sell. I call a lifestyle investment a 'live-and-let'. By this I mean that you invest in a property which you use yourself for holidays and short breaks, but you let it out to receive an income when you are not using the property yourself.

Unlike the other strategies, which are generic and can be applied to any jet-to-let market, the live-and-let idea is found mostly in countries which have good, all-year-round climates. Skiing resorts have been a proven success for many following the live-and-let strategy, as they can be equally attractive as a holiday destination in the summer.

Often you will find that your break-even point (i.e. where your income and expenses balance) is surprisingly low. Given the level of rent many overseas properties can command, it often only takes a good run during the high season to cover many of your costs.

All the evidence suggests that this is a growing proportion of the jet-to-let market and the savvy investor will look to countries which have an all-year-round appeal in order to maximise his own enjoyment as well as the rental income.

Off-plan property checklist

As I pointed out earlier, many investors have made a great deal of money from investing off-plan and reaping the benefits of gearing in a rising market. I would contend that in the past there has been less risk associated with UK off-plan, as the due diligence that you are able to do here is in many cases superior to that overseas.

The risk now in UK off-plan is that at the time of going to press in May 2006, the market is stagnating and, at the very best, is estimated to grow this year and next by about four per cent. As this is an average, clearly some locations will do particularly badly, which suggests a very high-risk off-plan investment.

1. **Check out the developer**, which is easier in some countries than others (see below for pointers on how to do this).

    -   Get your lawyer to check out the development company.

    -   What is his reputation like locally?

    -   Does he have a reputation in the UK? If so, what do people say?

    -   Are there any news stories concerning the company?

    -   What other developments has the company completed?

    -   Can you have a look around at previous developments on a visit?

    -   What is the reputation of the construction company?

    -   Are the company's employees qualified? In other words, are the key skills of electrics, gas, water and general plumbing conducted by qualified tradespeople?

    -   Get a good independent local lawyer who understands property and ideally is a property investor himself.

2. **Check out the property**

    -   Does the developer have a legal right to the land and therefore the legal right to sell a property?

    -   Is your deposit safe? What safeguards do you have?

    -   What guarantees does the legal system afford the buyer?

- Is the contract fully assignable, i.e. can you sell it on to another buyer before completion?

- Do you have to pay the developer a fee to reassign the contract? If so, how much?

- Does the development have the appropriate planning permission?

- What guarantees are there for the construction?

- What are the development plans for the area?

- If there is available land adjacent to the site, what is the plan for that land? Get your lawyer to double-check what you are told by the developer or sales agent with the planning authorities.

- Check the plans relating to the site, the position of your property and the sizes and dimensions quoted.

- Do the sizes and dimensions match those given to you in the price list?

- Particularly, what are the sizes of any balconies and are they included or excluded from the dimensions of the property? Do the listed measurements in metres squared include purely internal built areas or do they include covered verandas or a share of communal areas in the case of apartments?

- Is parking included or excluded? If it's included, ensure that it states so in the contract.

- Visit the site with the plans and check the position of the sun if you have been promised a particular sunrise, sunset, sun in the morning, afternoon, etc.

- Are the detailed specifications of what you get for your money in the contract, such as white goods, tiling, air conditioning units, heating, swimming pool, etc.? Whatever you have been promised needs to be in the contract.

- Are the responsibilities of the developer in the contract, such as the delivery date, any penalties for late delivery, insurances, etc.?

- Is the contract in English or two languages and for legal purposes which has precedence in case of a dispute?

- If you are buying an apartment, what will be the service charge and what does it cover?

- What is the structure of the management company?

- What about the residents/owners' association?

- How many of the properties have been sold to investors?

- Do you know the ratio of those holding to selling?

Developer discounts

Those of you who have been involved in property investing for some time will be aware of the many marketing 'hooks' used by development companies and their agents to sell you properties.

The discount is a hook which is being used excessively these days and it's losing a lot of credibility in the industry. Firstly, you can get a genuine discount off a property at certain times of the year, particularly through public-quoted companies which may want to strengthen their accounting position. You may also get a genuine discount if you buy multiple properties or a complete development from a developer. By selling you the development outright, the developer foregoes a lot of costs, such as interest on loans, sales and marketing, staff, exhibitions and the like, so the discount can be offered in a straightforward way.

Apart from these situations, however, to give a genuine discount, the developer has to give you a slice of his profit. If the 15 per cent quoted discount is truly genuine, then the developer is giving away 15 per cent of his profits. Few companies are willing to give away their profit so readily.

One industry trick is to inflate the market value of properties in order to discount them back. In order to ascertain the fair price, do some research and look for comparable property in a similar location taking into account any special terms you may have, such as finance. If you are not able to do this, as distance may be an issue, then commission an independent valuation from a local, independent valuer. I also know investors who commission UK-based surveyors and pay a fee to have them fly to their chosen jet-to-let property investment to conduct a valuation.

Always be careful of internet research as sometimes it can be misleading. Some agents and developers deliberately advertise property that has already been sold, maybe two years ago at prices appropriate at the time. When you come across such a good deal and pick up the phone to ask for more details, you are told that unfortunately it's now sold, but they have other properties you may be interested in. This is another industry hook to be aware of, so conduct your research on the ground yourself or through a valuer to whom you pay a fee.

How tempting is the proposition that for simply signing a piece of paper (reservation contract) and leaving a deposit you will get an instant 15 per cent profit?

> Property price = £200,000
>
> Discounted price = £170,000
>
> Instant equity profit = £30,000

If this is so good, why isn't everyone doing it? Well, everyone is not doing it. Clearly some people are, and best of luck to them, but you do have to think through the logic of a developer giving away a very large slice of his profits. If he keeps doing it, then he will not be in business very long!

A word of caution: It's only fair to point out that property valuation is not a science and I have seen valuations conducted on the same property by up to four different valuers where the range in price was about 25 per cent.

Land investing: the Las Vegas of property investment

You may have seen advertisements in newspapers and magazines from companies offering land investment opportunities – it appears to be a growing trend as more companies enter the market. This is also happening overseas and many novice investors are investing in companies which buy land and then sit on it. These companies are doing one of the following two things:

1. Land banking

This is where you buy land at today's prices and 'bank' the land by allowing it to remain unused, with a view to selling it later at a higher price or developing the land for profit. This is a good, sensible strategy in any market and a good long-term strategy even when markets are flat or falling. Land is land and has a good solid value, particularly in prime or up-and-coming areas.

2. Speculative land banking

This is where you buy land in the hope that at some stage in the future you will be able to develop that land or sell it for a profit after it has been 'rezoned'.

When you buy it, the land may be zoned for agricultural use only. Therefore, you cannot use it other than for grazing sheep or growing crops. It's a speculative investment because you are hoping that at some stage in the future you may be able to develop the land if and when the area is rezoned.

Zoning

Zoning outlines the uses of land for residential, office, industrial, agricultural and other uses and also stipulates the type and density of what can be built. If you can buy land when the zoning is for agricultural use and then two years later that land is rezoned to residential, you win the jackpot.

Example

1000m² of agricultural land purchased in country X for £10,000.

Due to a change in planning policy, which could be for many reasons, your land now falls into a zone which has been re-classified for residential use. Overnight, because of what you can now build on that land, the price shoots up to £60,000.

It's like winning the jackpot at Las Vegas! So, why isn't everyone running out and doing it when it appears to be a 'no-brainer'? Well, maybe it's not. As with any form of investment, research and due diligence are the watch words.

'Gambling promises the poor what property performs for the rich – something for nothing.' George Bernard Shaw

There are a lot of companies in the market which have good intentions, are well managed and explain in detail the risks associated with speculative land investment. They are professional companies with a track record and they will still be around in the years ahead.

Then there are the others, who will make a quick buck on the back of Mr and Mrs Smith who don't fully understand the speculative nature of what they are getting themselves into, particularly where the advertising and the contract are in a foreign language. This may be a bit harsh, but this is an area of the property investment world where some of the marketing literature beggars belief.

I again come back to research, due diligence and professional advisors. Don't be put off the idea of investing in land by what you read here. My aim is not to dissuade you, but to persuade you to cut through the hype and look at the facts. Speak with professional advisors in the country you have chosen and look at the history of rezoning, timeframes, what the locals are buying, where the locals are buying and ask the sort of questions which make people feel uncomfortable. You have the right because it's your money and it's your future.

Key points summary

The jet-to-let property developer's checklist can be used to formulate a plan and provides the key components that you will need to understand and have in place to be successful:

1. Partners

2. Cultural practices

3. Legal

4. Finance

5. Tax and currency controls

6. Contractors

7. New-build versus refurbishment

8. Critical mass

9. The package

10. Sales and marketing

11. After-sales

12. The client

Other points:

- Remember that the people assisting you are a critical factor and they will have a positive or negative impact on your performance.

- Don't confuse what is seen as normal with what is legal.

- Have a clear and well-defined strategy that deals with the entry, the administration and the exit from your investment.

- Understand your risk and how to control and manage its potential effect.

- Make profits – it's allowed to be fun as well.

- Use the negotiating checklist.

- Keep control of your costs, as if your life depended on it.

- Buy off-plan only in rising markets.

- Property investing has the highest risk when you treat it as a speculative short-term punt.

- Property is a medium- to long-term investment and should not be regarded as a 'get rich quick' scheme.

- Use the off-plan checklist to assist with your planning.

- Beware of discounts. Has the price been artificially increased so it can be discounted back to a more realistic figure?

- Investing in quality land can be a very profitable business.

- Speculating that land may be rezoned is simply that – speculating – and it carries potentially high risks or rewards.

CHAPTER 7

Understanding risk

Risk is the chance that events will not turn out as expected. Our approach to risk is determined by many factors, but the main influence is clearly our character, personality or profile. We are all very different and as such will not tolerate risk uniformly. Some people avoid risk while others get a real thrill from it.

What determines your attitude to risk in investment terms?

- Age
- Upbringing
- Family
- Past experiences
- Future expectations
- Goals
- Overall wealth

Risk and reward

The correlation or relationship between these two Jekyll and Hyde terms can best be illustrated by the chart below:

RISK

REWARD

You will note that higher risk is associated with potentially higher rewards and lower risk attracts lower rewards. The savvy investor strikes a happy medium and spreads his exposure to risk and reward with a combination of investments. This is known as a portfolio approach, which can be defined as 'minimising risks while maximising returns through diversification'.

Your approach to risk is personal and is highlighted through investor profiling – see chapter 4 for more information on how to analyse your approach to risk.

In my company we ask our clients to complete an online questionnaire which takes about 15 minutes to complete and is overseen by a behavioural psychologist. The questions have been designed to assist with identifying patterns in a person's behaviour which will ultimately help identify his tolerance to risk. Determining an investor's behavioural pattern and how he responds to risk enables us to devise an appropriate property investment strategy.

Remember that risk and reward go hand in hand. In fact, replace the word reward with 'opportunity' because this reflects more accurately the reality you face.

The reality is that one day soon you will be faced with an opportunity. It may be in the form of land purchase in Mauritius, off-plan in Morocco or in a syndicated joint venture project in Moscow. Whatever it is, you will be faced with an opportunity and opportunities generally carry a risk to your capital. It's how you deal with opportunities which will determine your success as a jet-to-let investor.

It's by thorough research, analysis, planning and hedging that you mitigate risk. In life we face risks and learn to deal with them on a daily basis. So why can't we do that with property investing? Well, we can.

There are a number of potential risks involved with jet-to-let investing which I call 'total risk'. It includes everything from just being in the property market, to a tenant falling down the stairs and suing you.

Just a cursory glance at the total risk diagram above illustrates that I'm considering everything. Let's have a look at the risks you must look out for and the questions you must ask yourself when considering jet-to-let or property investment in general.

Risk checklist

- **Political risk**

    - Is the government of the country you are investing in stable or on the brink of a revolution?

    - Are there any factors which may contribute to that government becoming unstable?

    - If it becomes unstable, what might the implications be for foreign investors?

    - Would a future government confiscate land and property or other assets held in the country?

- **Opportunity risk**

    - Are you missing a great financial opportunity by not investing in overseas property?

- Are you investing in the wrong country or property for your strategy?

- Is your equity working as hard as possible for you now that your investment properties have increased in value?

- **Market risk**

  - Will the market crash or stagnate?

  - Will other markets crash and have a knock-on effect in your market? In other words, is your market dependent on others, such as Spain and the UK?

- **Liquidity risk**

  - How quickly can you turn your overseas property into ready cash?

  - How strong is the resale market?

  - Is there likely to be an oversupply of property in your chosen market and region?

  - Will demand be sufficient in relation to supply, to maintain or even increase prices?

  - Will a buyer purchase this property from you at the price you want?

- **Business risk**

  - Is there a strong rental market for your property? Is it for holiday lets or longer-term tenancies?

  - Is the demand from foreigners or locals?

  - If foreigner-demand dries up, can the locals afford to rent your property?

  - What are the local health and safety and legislative requirements for letting property?

  - How easy is it to evict tenants?

  - What are the squatting laws in your chosen country?

- **Legal risk**

  - Is your lawyer independent?

- Does your contract favour the developer?

- Is your contract fully assignable?

- What protection do you have as a foreign investor?

- What historically has happened with regard to legislation concerning foreign investors, property rights, title deeds and enforced nationalisation of private property?

- What title guarantees are there?

- How robust is the law relating to property ownership?

- **Financial risk**

  - What if you cannot get a mortgage on completion?

  - If you can't, how much money will you lose? What does the contract commit you to?

  - Can you make your monthly payments with ease?

  - What about currency risk?

  - In what currency should you have your mortgage?

  - In what currency should your rental income be advertised?

  - Can you cover voids and for how long?

  - What if interest rates rise; can you still cover your operating costs?

  - What is your break-even point if interest rates rise (i.e. at what rate does your revenue match your costs)?

  - What will happen to your income after the rental guarantee expires? Will you get the same net yield renting independently?

  - Have you got the best mortgage product available?

  - Are there any hidden costs that you have not accounted for?

  - What is the tax situation in your chosen jet-to-let country?

  - Does it have a double-taxation treaty with the UK or will you effectively pay tax twice?

  - Is there a Wealth Tax and will you have to pay it?

  - What if you lose your job?

- **Environmental risk**
    - What if there is a natural disaster? Do you have all your eggs in one basket?
    - Has your property been built on contaminated land?
    - What other buildings are being built near your property and what is their purpose?

- **Geographical risk**
    - Is your property in an earthquake zone?
    - Is your property in a hurricane zone?
    - Is your property in an area prone to flooding?
    - Is your property underneath a pylon line or is there a mobile telephone mast nearby?
    - Will a motorway be built in front of your property?

- **Management risk**
    - Do you trust the management and lettings companies?
    - Will they find suitable tenants for your property?
    - Will they ensure that the property is well maintained?
    - Will they be competent with regard to current legislation?
    - If you have a holiday let, can you be sure that when they say the property is empty, that it truly is and is not being sub-let without your knowledge?

- **Corruption risk**
    - Has your property been built illegally due to corruption in the local planning office or mayor's office? What are the consequences?
    - Will you be asked for money at any stage as a 'backhander'?

- **Tastes and fashions**
    - What will happen when the next cheap hotspot arrives on the scene?
    - What happens if your location becomes unfashionable?

Ask the questions

Often jet-to-let investors overlook some of the most basic due diligence questions in their rush to secure the deal. You must make a thorough analysis of the risks as well as remembering the potential rewards before you sign any paperwork or part with any money.

This chapter is designed to arm you with the relevant questions to ask both yourself and the agent or developer. Its aim is to make you stop and think before you leap into the unknown. Those investors who get the answers to all of their questions before they buy are generally successful. This is my purpose here, to assist you in becoming a successful overseas property investor by highlighting some of the issues which may deflect you from that goal.

Firstly, you have to understand that there are risks you can do something about and others that you cannot. It's difficult to hedge for international events such as war or bird flu.

A useful management tool is my risk management matrix, which is a straightforward way of making your risk strategy concrete. I've listed a few risk factors and examples in the table below to get you started.

Risk management matrix

Risk Number 1

Risk: Financial: what if interest rates rise?

Action you can take now:

a. Ensure that the property in which you invest has solid rental potential which is well in excess of your costs at the present level of interest rates.

b. Conduct a sensitivity analysis of your revenue and costs and determine your break-even point.

c. Check economic events. If you have a euro mortgage, look out for the press releases of the European Central Bank and the minutes of its meetings which may forewarn of any changes and the longer-term outlook.

d. Join a free property investment newsletter which will give you advance notice of any changes and possible changes in interest rates.

e. Create a contingency fund.

Remark:

You have invested using a euro mortgage and are relatively content that interest rates, historically, have remained low and that volatility (i.e. the frequency of movements up and down) is also low.

Risk Number 2

Risk: Geographical: your property is in an earthquake zone.

Action you can take now:

a. Ensure that you have comprehensive insurance which covers the risk.

b. Check that the construction of your property conforms to the latest building regulations with respect to earthquakes.

Remark:

a. Get a quote for a policy to cover the rebuild cost of the property.

b. If you are renting the property, enquire about contents and public liability insurance, which you will need anyway.

Risk Number 3

Risk: Opportunity: are you investing in the best possible country and location?

Action you can take now:

a. Conduct thorough research and analysis. Don't invest in the first thing that crops up – you will not miss out on anything by being methodical with your investigations.

b. Gain knowledge by reading this book, attending seminars and exhibitions and meeting with other property investors.

c. Investigate options for yourself and use the knowledge you have acquired to make your own decisions on what is right for you.

Remark:

You are content that you have researched sufficiently to invest in an area which is suitable for you, your tolerance to risk and your goals.

Risk Number 4

Risk: Market: what if the market crashes?

Action you can take now:

a. You have a long-term view of property investing and as such you are not overly concerned.

b. You have other investments which are not correlated to this particular property market, such as property in the UK, a large stock market portfolio, bonds and cash.

Remark:

a. You have portfolio and asset diversification, so you are not too concerned about any one market or asset ruining your life.

b. There is nothing you can do to stop the market crashing.

Risk Number 5

Risk: Liquidity: what if you cannot sell your off-plan property on completion?

Action you can take now:

a. Consider your exit strategy before you buy and not after choosing your investment property.

b. Research the robustness of the resale market, the transaction costs and the supply side factors, such as the number of new-build properties.

c. Ensure that the property you purchase has unique features which will make it stand out from the crowd.

d. Do a lot of research!

Remark:

a. Before committing, research, research and research.

b. Also research the rental market because if you are forced to complete on the property, you may have to rent it to cover your costs.

c.   Understand that some markets carry higher liquidity risk than others.

d.   Be aware that the worst-case scenario means that you have to complete on the property or walk away losing your deposits (depending on the contract).

This matrix is a useful tool to consolidate your thoughts and concerns, to think through consequences and outcomes and to check that you have thought about all the potential downsides of your investment. The most successful entrepreneurs and investors are those who think not one, not two, but three steps ahead. This level of thinking is what you must strive for, and tools such as this one will force you to write things down and think through the solutions.

The ultimate aim is that you are so conditioned to think about the pitfalls, that eventually you don't need to write your thoughts down as your reactions become instinctive.

As a jet-to-let property investor, you need to be so tuned in to the issues, factors, markets and yourself that very quickly you know what is right for you. Then, when investment opportunities arise, you can make a rapid assessment and act quickly before the opportunity passes by.

Fortunately, there are a lot of professional companies offering advice and investment services in the jet-to-let market that will have your interests at the top of their agenda too. Their ethos is such that the customer is right and that a happy customer is the best advert that they can possibly have. They are in the marketplace as suppliers for the long term, not just a few months.

However, not all sellers in this marketplace operate in the same way. In particular, there has been an explosion of one-man-bands on the internet and there are plenty of opportunists who will be here today and gone tomorrow – with your cash.

My advice is to stick to established companies with a reputable track record of delivery and customer service, whom you can meet in their offices and who will be more than delighted to let you speak to previous clients.

Failure happens to people who don't plan; success is for those who have spent time formulating strategy, plans and taking advice from professionals.

Key points summary

- Risk is all around us. Control it or it will control you.

- You control risk with education, knowledge and experience.

- Determine what level of risk is acceptable for you, your partner and your family.

- There is no such thing as a 'risk-free investment'.

- Have a portfolio approach, mixing low-, medium- and high-risk opportunities according to your goals and acceptance of risk.

- Embrace risk, for it always comes with an opportunity.

- Use the risk checklist and risk management matrix to formulate a strong and considered risk plan.

CHAPTER 8

Buying your property – the process and potential pitfalls

This chapter explains the usual buying process for a jet-to-let property and what to look out for when you are navigating your way through the plethora of salespeople, advisors and paperwork. However, this process is not the same in all of the locations that we feature. There are always differences in the detail, but the approach, procedures and potential pitfalls are similar.

I'm going to take you through the following:

- Selecting your jet-to-let investment property

- Selecting advisors

- Financing your investment

- Buying the property

- Taxation

Selecting your jet-to-let investment property

Throughout the book I've described the top down approach to property investment and I've also put it in context with strategy, finance and risk, so you should know by now that you should be directed towards a particular country, region and property because it represents a sound investment opportunity, not because you perceive it to be cheap.

A bottom up approach is where an investor buys simply because of price and his perception of value. My advice would be to avoid this approach and to look for properties that have true investment potential.

'There is scarcely anything in the world that some man cannot make a little worse, and sell a little more cheaply. The person who buys on price alone is this man's lawful prey.' John Ruskin

Who should you buy a property from?

There are a number of sources:

1. UK estate agents
2. Local agents based in your chosen market or country
3. Direct from the developer
4. Large property agents
5. Direct from the vendor (seller)
6. Auctions
7. Property finders

There are pros and cons to each of the above methods.

1. UK estate agents

You only have to walk down your local high street to see the growing number of UK estate agents selling overseas property. These companies have rightly spotted an opportunity, as the growth in jet-to-let has made it profitable to have a UK high-street presence.

These companies work with larger organisations which pay them a commission for sales. UK estate agents tend to get a bad press, some deserved, some not, but generally most know what they are doing – at least in their own country. I'm not sure whether a high-street agency is the best place for an international property investor to look, but it will not hurt to visit a few during your research phase.

2. Local estate agents

The first thing you have to remember about all estate agents is that they make their money by selling property! They are not friendly, charming, witty companions who have your best interests at heart. On the whole, they represent the interests of the vendor or developer and they are interested mainly in their commission.

Remembering this and their motives will enable you to better assess the validity of their advice. Having said this, the comprehensive knowledge of many of these agents is their main strength. Tap in to this local knowledge and have your list of questions written down in preparation for your meeting. Get them to show you around and learn as much as you can.

Warning: Although many jet-to-let countries are perfectly safe, it's prudent not to go out alone in a car with someone you have just met. Take your partner and ensure that the estate agent is 'bona fide' and that he is who he says he is. Ensure that someone else knows where you are going and whom you are going with.

Also, check to see if the agency is a member of any local group or professional body, such as a national association of estate agents.

3. Direct from the developer

If you have conducted your research and know exactly where you want to invest, then why not buy direct from the developer. Whether you go through an agent or not, if you are purchasing an off-plan property, you will eventually find yourself with the developer picking fixtures, fittings and tiles and possibly arranging mortgages.

Before doing so, make sure that the developer can provide the services that you expect. A complete turnkey package is the desire of many property investors, but some developers are high on promises and low on delivery and they don't have the customer services support that many busy property investors require.

4. Large property agents

Property agents differ from estate agents in that they are generally organisations which promote properties from multiple countries on behalf of developers. Some of these companies have huge marketing budgets and appear to be very good at what they do, which is selling property. They are effectively a channel between you and a number of overseas developers who rely on these agents to sell for them. They are a good starting point if you have not yet decided on your chosen country as they should have staff who are familiar with a number of different overseas investment markets and they will be able to offer advice which may assist you with narrowing down the options.

In most cases, you will not get a better price for the property by dealing direct, and reputable agents will provide many professional support services that make investing overseas easier to manage. The companies to look for are those with a reputation for customer service and added value, which provide a complete turnkey solution.

5. Direct from the vendor

Often you can pick up some very good resale property through classified advertisements or on the internet. Standard due diligence research and investigations apply, but you have the opportunity of dealing direct with the person who is selling the property. The first point to note is that by not dealing through an estate agent, the vendor is saving a significant amount of money in fees which clearly vary from country to country. You would expect this to be reflected in the asking price; if it's not, then it's a good starting point for the negotiations. Secondly, by dealing with the vendor, you will be able to assess the reasons for sale, how quickly he wants to move, how long the property has been on the market and all the other questions you need to ask in order to assess the level at which to pitch your opening offer.

6. Auctions

In some countries you can buy property through auctions. This is a specialist subject and I would draw your attention to Lawpack's *Buying Bargains at Property Auctions* by Howard Goodie. Although Howard's book is aimed specifically at the UK market and UK auctions, he has very successfully conveyed the process, due diligence and the do's and don'ts of property auctions, which are similar the world over.

7. Property finders

Some property finders provide a good service, particularly for very busy people who don't have the time to jump on a plane for a few weekends to source property.

However, all property finders are not equal. There are some opportunists in the market who know very little about property, investing, overseas markets and the process of jet-to-let. They have spotted a money-making opportunity, have attended property investment courses and specific seminars and copied the materials and then presented them as their own. These cowboys are to be avoided at all costs, so always do your research.

There are, however, some very reputable companies which source property all over the world for clients. They have offices, staff and reputations to maintain. After you have read this book and followed its principles, you will be able to find these companies for yourself.

Selecting advisors

You want advisors who have your best interests at heart. Although they are paid, they should be wise and worldly enough to realise that your success is their success and your failure is theirs. You should consider the following when selecting advisors:

- **Legal advisor.** Whether you are buying a single property, multiple properties or developing from scratch, your closest ally should be your lawyer. The research you conduct in order to find a top quality, independent English-speaking lawyer is worth every hour and the fees you pay for quality will be justly rewarded later.

- **Financial advisor.** A good financial advisor is worth his weight in gold. He can suggest a variety of ways in which to finance your investment, have the contacts to offer sometimes unorthodox solutions for funding and will take a holistic view of all your financial affairs, which allows him to put your jet-to-let aspirations into context. You would be best served following a recommendation from someone whose judgement you trust and who has had protracted dealings with the advisor over a number of years.

- **Accountant.** HM Revenue & Customs tax you on your worldwide assets and income, so you will need an experienced UK qualified accountant to help with your tax return. If you have an overseas company or you are investing in multiple properties, then an English-speaking accountant in your chosen country is also required. The two of them need to consult with each other to make sure your affairs run smoothly and keep both tax authorities content.

- **Specialist tax consultant.** If you are investing substantial amounts of cash overseas in jet-to-let property, potentially in many different markets, then you will require the expertise of an international tax specialist to ensure that you are doing it in the most tax-efficient manner. Should you buy properties in your own name, joint names, in your children's names, through a trust, through a UK limited company, an offshore company or a local company? What are the benefits of changing your domicile? What are the benefits of spending most of the year overseas? The answers to these important questions will vary considerably depending on your personal circumstances, so bespoke advice is imperative. Your accountant should be able to recommend a specialist tax consultant, the property investment company you may be investing with may have one, or any of the big accountancy firms will be able to assist.

- **Currency broker.** It's inefficient to transfer large sums of money via high-street retail banks as you can receive a very poor rate of exchange. The use of specialist currency brokers will often result in a much more favourable rate, which can amount to the cost of a family holiday when transferring large sums. Choose a large well-known foreign exchange company, such as Travelex.

- **Architect/surveyor/valuer.** If you are considering renovating old property or developing, then you will need a good team of property professionals starting with an architect and a surveyor.

- **Insurance broker.** One of the methods of limiting risk is to insure against possible events, such as fire, theft, earthquakes and being sued by your tenants or holidaymakers. A good insurance broker can supply policies which cover most eventualities. Please don't ignore insurance; you will regret it if the occasion arises where you need it.

Financing your investment

The amount of finance you require will vary considerably depending on the investment strategy that you have adopted. The options of developing land and buying an off-plan apartment in Budapest require two very different levels of funding. In this particular section, I focus more on the financing of individual or multiple units rather than developing.

This section is not a substitute for sound professional advice from someone who is authorised to give that advice, such as a financial advisor or mortgage broker. As we all have different goals, varying degrees of financial commitment and tolerance to risk, you should consult with a professional advisor to work out a specific, personalised financial plan for your overseas property investments.

Investors can finance their property investments using:

1. Cash

2. UK equity release

3. Overseas mortgage, in a choice of currencies

4. Syndicates

1. Cash

Cash-rich investors use their funds to invest in property. They don't wish to mortgage their properties and are not concerned about the lack of gearing or leverage. Be aware that in some countries, such as Turkey and Romania, you cannot get a mortgage, so cash is the only option.

2. UK equity release

One of the drivers of the jet-to-let boom has been the buoyant UK property market. Home owners and buy-to-let landlords are using the equity in their UK properties to finance an overseas property investment strategy. The process is fairly straightforward and involves taking either a further advance on an existing mortgage or a complete remortgage with possibly another provider and better terms. The advantages of this course of action are as follows:

- Set-up costs in the UK are relatively inexpensive if you remain with the same lender.

- You have been through the process before so it should be easy to understand, plus the documents are in English. Also, you don't need to leave the country to set up the mortgage.

- If your loan is in sterling and the repayments of that loan are from a sterling account, then you will not be exposed to currency risk.

- UK interest rates are presently lower than some jet-to-let destinations.

- You can borrow interest only, which is a significant advantage as many foreign mortgages are interest and capital repayment, thus reducing your ability to maximise cash flow.

- You can get a better loan to value (LTV) mortgage in the UK, particularly if you are using your home (which is also known as your 'principal private residence' (PPR) for taxation purposes) as security. If you can borrow up to 95 per cent of the valuation of your home at say five per cent interest, your monthly cash flow and costs of borrowing may be substantially less than the alternative product in your jet-to-let country.

3. Overseas mortgage

The liberalisation of local mortgage markets is one of the drivers of property prices, as we have experienced in the UK, Ireland and Spain over the last five to ten years. The liberalisation of the Danish mortgage market in 2005 was responsible for a boom in property which saw prices rise by up to 50 per cent in parts of Copenhagen and over 20 per cent nationally.

The introduction of UK-style interest only mortgages has provided a significant boost to an already strong market.

As money becomes easier to obtain and payments are reduced through lower interest rates, new liquidity in the market increases the demand for property and prices rise. This effect is even more marked where supply lags significantly behind the change in demand as was also evident in Denmark.

Overseas mortgages tend to be based on the same principles that we have in the UK. They are loans secured on the price of a property. Some points to note are as follows:

- They are generally repayment mortgages.

- LTV rates can be low.

- The timeframe of the mortgage can be as little as ten years.

- Check if there are any redemption penalties for early repayment – they may be high or may not exist.

- Check on the arrangement costs/fees and whether any taxes have to be paid to the government.

- You may need to travel to the country to apply and receive the loan in person.

- You are exposed to currency risk through fluctuations in the exchange rate.

- Your suitability will generally be assessed on your income and ability to repay the loan, not on assets and potential rent.

'A bank is a place that will lend you money if you can prove that you don't need it.' Bob Hope

4. Syndicates

A quick search on the internet came up with a lot of different, contrasting views of what constituted a syndicate:

- A loose affiliation of gangsters in charge of organised criminal activities.

- A group of individuals who have formed a joint venture to undertake a project they would have been unable to complete individually.

- A combination of people or firms formed to accomplish a business venture of mutual interest by pooling resources.

- A news agency that sells features or articles or photographs, etc. to newspapers for simultaneous publication.

- A group of individuals who come together to purchase a property.

My advice would be to stay away from the first of these unless you want to trade 30 years of bliss on some sun-drenched Mediterranean island for time at Wormwood Scrubs.

A syndicate is about pooling resources. There are companies which offer syndicated funds where an investor buys into various property investment opportunities. Many jet-to-let investors may be attracted to this option in the future as the rules concerning self-invested personal pension schemes (SIPPS) are made more widely available through the media and financial services providers, and the benefits of investing through tax-efficient funds are understood.

However, in its simplest form, a syndicate is a group of friends, family members, business colleagues or other investors who invest collectively in property. In some cases, the arrangement is formalised with a syndicate agreement, which is in effect a contract.

It's wise to have a syndicate agreement drawn up by a lawyer as it will prevent any misunderstandings or disputes later. The terms and conditions are important and should specify a timeframe and exit strategy for the investment and under what circumstances members can leave and new members join. You should collectively instruct a lawyer to draft the agreement. This may sound a bit formal for many considering investing with friends, but if you want to keep your friends, then this is a good course of action.

The advantages of a private syndicate are clear:

- Risk diversification, as the risks are shared across the syndicate.

- Accessible investing – you can invest with a smaller capital sum.

- A mixture of investor profiles, knowledge and experience should prove a positive combination (the sum being greater than the parts).

- Spreading the workload of managing overseas property investments.

- It can be fun.

There are also disadvantages:

- You dilute your returns between other members of the syndicate.

- You may disagree with other members on the direction and strategy of the syndicate.

Only you will know whether this type of investment method will work for you, but if you are short on start-up capital, this is a good way to get started.

Currency risk

One of the major differences between jet-to-let and property investing in the UK is currency risk. I have chosen to discuss currencies in this section as opposed to the chapters on understanding risk or even economics because it's highly relevant to the buying process and raising finance. You must ask yourself the following:

- Do I take a mortgage in sterling for my house priced in euros?

- Do I make staged payments from sterling to euros, for instance, at the exchange rate on the day?

- What if sterling strengthens/weakens against the US dollar/euro or the currency with which I am working?

There are charts in the Appendices section which illustrate the volatility of many of the currencies referred to in this book. Without doubt, not having a currency strategy in some of these markets could result in financial loss, while planning will definitely produce strong currency profits as we will see below.

Fortunately, you have professionals in your team of advisors who will be able to work with you to determine the most appropriate currency strategy to fit your property investing timetable.

But what can happen? Here are a few examples:

> Simon and Jane have decided to buy a property in Florida outright for cash as they wish to retire and live out their days in the sun. They had an offer accepted on a house for $300,000 in December 2004.

Five-year GBP v US dollar currency chart

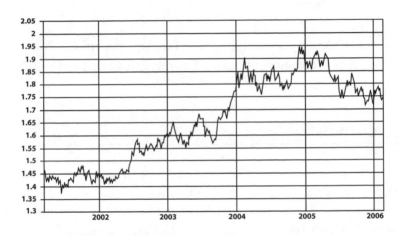

If you take a look at the five-year chart, which shows the relationship between GBP or pounds sterling and the US dollar, you will see that Simon and Jane had the offer accepted on the house when sterling was at a high of £1 = $1.95. If they had made the purchase there and then, they could have rightly claimed to have 'called the top' or 'the bottom' of the currency market, depending on which side of the Atlantic you live.

So, why is this such a clever thing? Well, Simon and Jane were using sterling funds to make the purchase, so a $300,000 house at an exchange rate of $1.95 to £1 means they will have to find £153,846 before transactions costs ($300,000 ÷ $1.95 = £153,846) = good deal.

> For various reasons it takes almost a full year to finalise the transaction and they eventually complete just before Christmas 2005.

The exchange rate has now changed quite dramatically. It has fallen from $1.95 when they had their offer agreed to stand at $1.73 at the time of completion in December 2005. The dollar has strengthened by just over 12% over the year, which means that instead of having to find £153,846 for the property, they now have to find £173,410 – a huge difference of £19,564. If Simon and Jane don't have the extra £20,000, then they will be unable to complete the purchase.

This is why it's imperative to consider the effect that changes in exchange rates have on your jet-to-let strategy. Some currencies are less stable than others and their movements can be more dramatic than the one we have seen over the year between sterling and the US dollar.

Currency fluctuations can be used to your advantage. In the example above, if Simon and Jane had completed in December 2004, they could have sold in December 2005 at a profit of £20,000, with no house price inflation (HPI). Alternatively, they could have fixed the exchange rate at the high of $1.95 through the services of a currency broker.

 Speak to a currency broker about how to manage risk when investing in overseas property.

Mortgage

Let's continue with the example of Simon and Jane to illustrate the currency effect of holding your debt in one currency or another.

The transaction for Simon and Jane was completed speedily and they managed to purchase their property for $300,000 in December 2004 at £1 = $1.95. Instead of paying cash, they obtained a mortgage at 80% LTV.

Deposit = $60,000

Mortgage = $240,000

In this example I'm excluding all transaction costs.

So, in sterling terms, the deposit has 'cost' £30,769, which is $60,000 divided by the exchange rate of $1.95.

The mortgage is a mortgage, simple as that, but to pay that mortgage back at the December 2004 rate would cost £123,076. I'm assuming that Simon and Jane don't have any US dollar income or savings.

> One year later: Simon and Jane have had a fantastic year in the US, but due to a family issue in the UK, they are now moving back. It's unlikely that they will be able to return to the US for some time and will need to release some cash to fund the purchase of a new house.

In this example, we are only interested in currency effects, so we will again eliminate transaction costs and any capital gains or losses from the equation.

> They sell their house for $300,000, but the exchange rate is now $1.73 dollars to the British pound.

> They owe the bank $240,000, which they pay off, and they are then left with the $60,000 deposit, which when converted back into sterling is now worth £34,682. They have 'made' money on the deposit in terms of the exchange rate. The original deposit was £30,769, so the difference between £34,682 and £30,769 is £3,913.

But what if Simon and Jane had funded the property purchase in the US using a sterling equity release strategy which we looked at on page 134 (i.e. by releasing funds from a UK property in order to use them overseas)? Would it change anything by having the debt in sterling?

Well, again we will assume an 80 per cent LTV mortgage. The big difference now is that the debt on the US house is held in sterling.

So, in December 2004, $240,000 = £123,076, which is the value of the new mortgage they have with their UK bank.

But in December 2005, with the new exchange rate, the sterling value of their mortgage is £138,728 – a difference of £15,652.

If Simon and Jane had to redeem or pay off the mortgage tomorrow based on the sale of the property, the mortgage element of it would convert back into sterling and be worth £138,728. They only owe the bank in the UK £123,076 so, in simple currency terms, they have made £15,652 on the movement in the exchange rate.

This is great, but it could equally go the other way. What if they had bought at $1.73 to £1 and then either the US dollar had weakened or sterling had strengthened? In this case, the revenue from their sale in the US would not be enough to pay off the mortgage in the UK.

The subject of currency risk is very important and is easily overlooked by inexperienced overseas investors. As investors, we want to limit the risk and one way of doing this is to take professional advice.

What to look for in a currency broker

- Shop around, as rates can vary considerably from day to day.

- Use a well-known company in the currency business. The company should have a strong track record and at least three years of audited accounts.

- Stay away from 'one-man-bands'. You will be placing large sums with your broker so it's important to know that this is safe.

- Make sure that the person you are speaking to on the telephone is a trained currency dealer and not the administrative person in the office.

- Discuss your investment strategy, your timeframes, your cash flow and what you are trying to achieve in order to get the best advice.

- Most property investment companies and sales agents will have a preferred partner whom they will recommend to clients. You are not under any obligation to use that company and you may wish to shop around instead.

What might a currency broker recommend?

You will be offered a number of options depending on what you want to achieve with your currency strategy:

- **Spot contracts.** The broker simply buys the currency in the market today for delivery in a couple of days. He buys it on the spot. It's the real time currency price at the time.

- **Fixed-term forward contract.** You agree an exchange rate today for delivery at some stage in the future. This can be generally fixed for up to two years in advance for a small deposit, generally five per cent of the sum you will be exchanging. The advantage is that if the rate is particularly strong, such as the example we used earlier with the US dollar, you can agree to fix the rate of $1.95 for up to two years. The rate is guaranteed regardless of what is happening in the market.

- **Forward time option contract.** This is similar to a fixed-term forward contract, but it has more flexibility. The exchange rate is fixed but the currency can be transferred at any point within a fixed period and not at a fixed time. A deposit is required to secure the rate and final payment is made when the full foreign currency transfer is required.

  A forward time option contract is useful if an exact date for the transfer of foreign currency is unknown, but you want a fixed exchange rate because it's favourable. The best example is if you are investing in a property overseas and the completion date is unknown.

- **Limit orders.** If you are moving substantial amounts of cash, you may wish to get a better rate than is currently available in the market. This option assumes that you have time before the funds have to be transferred, allowing the broker to wait for the better rate.

- **Stops.** You agree in advance the minimum acceptable rate you want. If the market falls, a buy or sell order is automatically actioned providing a safety net in volatile markets.

My aim with this section was to make you aware that currency movements can have a major impact on your jet-to-let strategy. Currency doesn't only affect the sterling price of any property you buy and sell, but also whether any debt secured on that property will rise or fall in value in line with exchange rates.

So, the questions you need to ask yourself are:

- What is my currency strategy?

- In what currency should I hold my mortgage debt?

Before I leave the subject of currency risk, I want to mention devaluation. Devaluation refers to a sharp reduction in the value of a currency and can be used as a tool of government economic policy. This is important to remember when dealing with emerging markets as some may be affected. For example, in recent years devaluations have occurred in Argentina, Thailand, Mexico, Czech Republic and other countries.

There are often complex political, macro-economic and indeed speculative reasons why currencies fall sharply. For completeness I wanted to highlight this issue as it's something you can discuss with your currency broker.

 Choose your professional advisors carefully. Don't go with one rather than another because he is cheaper. If you have to pay a little more for the best, then get the best.

Buying the property

Most of what is covered under this heading has been covered elsewhere in the book, but I think it's useful to summarise, in the form of a checklist, the process you go through to purchase your investment property.

Buying process checklist

- Define yourself and your goals.
- Research, research, research.
- Discuss your options with property companies.
- Visit your country of choice and development sites.
- Establish your team of professional advisors.
- Decide which property (or properties) you wish to purchase.
- Consult professional advisors regarding the legalities, finance and the building. In particular, establish at this stage who should own the

property you are buying. Should it be as an individual, partnership, in children's names, limited company, trust, etc.? This is an important question to ask your professional advisors and is the specialist area of an international tax advisor.

- Seek an independent valuation on the property (you will usually need to pay for this).

- Negotiate on the price of extras. (If there is a lot of demand and limited supply, don't be too hopeful.)

- Agree the price (after the independent valuation).

- Take legal advice about the terms of any reservation contract you are to sign. Does this mean that you are committed to buying the property? How long does the reservation period last? Don't sign a document in a foreign language. You will have to pay a small fee on signing the reservation contract.

- Your lawyer will check the legality of the transaction to ascertain if there are any outstanding debts on the land/property, whether the vendor has the legal right to sell, any town planning authority regulations which may affect you and all other appropriate issues relevant in your chosen country.

- Arrange your mortgage (where applicable) in principle.

- Full contracts will be issued and should be scrutinised by yourself and your lawyer. Make changes which you and your lawyer think are appropriate in order to safeguard your interests. This is why you should instruct an independent lawyer and not the vendor's 'in-house' lawyer.

- Open an account with a currency broker.

- Sign the contract and pay the deposit via your currency broker. In some countries the contract has to be signed in front of a notary in person or by someone appointed by you, using a Power of Attorney.

- Pay any taxes and purchasing fees which are due.

- Make staged payments (where applicable) according to the terms of the contract or draw your mortgage and the bank will then supervise the release of the staged payments to the developer.

- Choose fixtures, fittings, tiles, kitchen, etc.

- Review the progress of construction (where applicable).

- Prepare your lettings marketing strategy and/or instruct agents.

- Complete and pay the remainder of the price either by mortgage or by cash.

- Arrange insurance for buildings, contents and also for public liability if you are letting.

- Check for 'snaggings' and have them resolved by the developer. As with any new-build property, there will always be minor issues of finish which need to be addressed, such as light switches, appliances, doors and any other features which have not been completed to your satisfaction. In some cases, a lawyer may stipulate in a contract that up to five per cent of the completion monies may be held back until the snaggings have been addressed.

Legal considerations

I'm a great believer in paying professionals a fee to advise me on matters where their expertise is greater than mine. No person is so worldly as to be an expert in everything. Certainly, when considering such weighty matters as tax and law, it's good to get it right.

The legal systems of many of the jet-to-let countries are so different, it's imperative that specific local advice is obtained from a lawyer who is an expert in the laws of the relevant country.

The lawyer

Your lawyer has a number of critical tasks to perform on your behalf. He is in charge of due diligence and therefore must be good at what he does. Don't try to save pennies on the quality of legal advice you get. In short, your lawyer should:

- Check out the development company.

- Conduct searches on the land, adjacent land, planning, the building, and any debts encumbered on the land/property.

- Analyse and make recommendations concerning the contract.

- Advise you on your legal rights and safeguards.

- Advise on appropriate accounts in which to make your deposits.

- Advise on setting up local bank accounts.

- Advise where appropriate on forming a limited company.

How to find a good lawyer

A firm recommendation from someone you trust is the best course of action, but this isn't always possible. The Law Society of England and Wales has a searchable database on their website at www.lawsociety.org.uk, which you may find useful.

Embassies and consulates

Some British embassies and consulates can provide you by fax or by email with a list of English-speaking lawyers in their areas of responsibility. During my research, only one embassy in Eastern Europe could not help.

 Don't choose your lawyer from the telephone directory! Just because they can afford to advertise, it doesn't mean that they are worth using!

The contract

Most of the horror stories I come across involve the contract signed by the client. These tales are not confined to any one country, any one developer or any one lawyer. This issue is common in all countries.

Just to clarify, a contract or sales purchase agreement is a document which sets out the terms and conditions of the sale and the responsibilities of both the vendor and the purchaser, all of which are legally binding on both parties.

When you are reviewing the contract or sale purchase agreement, consider the following:

- Get an independent lawyer to advise you.

- Check that the price for the property is what you agreed (discrepancies do happen).

- Check the payment terms – do they match what you have agreed?

- Check that the specifications you expect, such as doors, windows, tiles and the level of quality, are in the contract.

- Ensure that it contains any verbal agreements you had with the sales consultant, particularly if he has given you any extras as part of the negotiation, such as white goods or granite work surfaces.

- Check whether parking is included or excluded.

- If you intend to sell before completion or wish to keep your options open, then the contract has to be assignable. In other words, you must be able to reassign (effectively sell) the property at any stage to another buyer and release your cash so that you can exit the investment. Is there a fee to pay for reassignment and if so, how much will it cost? If the fee is significantly above what you would consider reasonable, why is it so?

- Check the completion date for off-plan property. What penalties are there for late delivery? Your lawyer will be able to advise you on what penalties are appropriate in the country in which you are investing.

- Does it specify in the contract that you cannot let the property? Are there restrictions on the use of the property?

- Are there any guarantees in the contract concerning the quality and standard of the work? For how long after completion will the developer make good any defects free of charge?

- If there are taxes to be paid ensure that the responsibilities are clearly written in the contract.

I cannot emphasise how important it is to use a lawyer independent from the developer. I am amazed at how sensible people leave their brains behind at the airport terminal when flying overseas to purchase a property. Please keep yours in your head and treat the overseas property purchase with more due diligence than you would when investing in the UK.

Power of Attorney

Power of Attorney authorises an individual to act on behalf of someone else. I have found it very useful to give Power of Attorney to my lawyer, who represents me and who acts on my behalf on matters which I have stipulated in a written document. By giving Power of Attorney to someone else, you are in effect giving him the power to sign documents as if he were you. This is the essence of the power. It has to be written and very specific, but you will find it convenient and a useful time saver and for most busy jet-to-let investors it's a must.

Notaries

In many European countries a notary is a civil servant who checks the title deeds and records sales agreements. The notary's role is not to advise either party, but to authenticate. A simple definition for a notary would be 'a person authorised to certify a document'.

To conclude this section, there are not many things that can go wrong when buying property overseas when the buyer has conducted thorough research and due diligence. The one area where it can go badly wrong is the legal process, particularly with regard to the content and wording of the contract. Some people switch off at the contract stage because they wrongly think that the hard work is behind them – it's not. This is the stage to move up a gear and to ensure, with the help of your lawyer, that your interests are well cared for.

Taxation

'But in this world nothing can be said to be certain, except death and taxes.' Benjamin Franklin

The question of taxation can be complex and is best covered by experts in the field. Tax is specific to an individual set of circumstances and it changes over time and with new legislation. What is certain is that we all want to minimise, within the law, the amount of tax we pay.

I'm a great believer in paying quality professionals for quality advice. I'm not a lawyer, nor an accountant, nor an architect, nor an international tax specialist, but I employ very good examples of each as part of my team of professionals. If you are serious about adopting a jet-to-let property investment strategy, you need to do the same.

You need your 'home' and 'away' team – a group of advisors in the UK as well as in the countries in which you wish to specialise. Your international tax specialist becomes the referee between the advice you receive from your accountant in the UK and that which you receive overseas. He will then co-ordinate and produce particular tax advice according to your circumstances.

Advice such as this is not cheap and can cost the price of a very good family holiday and more if the situation is complicated. In fairness, the fees of tax specialists and accountants are normally saved, with some left over, by the results of their advice.

Myth buster 1: HM Revenue & Customs tax you on your worldwide income and assets. The fact that a particular overseas country may have zero taxes doesn't mean that you don't have a tax liability in the UK. This is a myth that novice jet-to-let investors sometimes fail to realise believing that, by having their investments offshore, they will be outside the reach of UK taxation – this is not so. However, you can legitimately minimise the amount of tax you pay.

Myth buster 2: Holiday lettings overseas don't have the same tax treatment as holiday lettings in the UK. Additionally, the favourable treatment of UK holiday rental properties in terms of business asset taper relief is not applicable on overseas properties.

Checklist – questions to ask your accountant and tax advisor

- What should be the ownership structure of my investment property?

- Who should receive the income from the property I am buying?

- What are the advantages and disadvantages of forming a UK or foreign limited company in which to hold the property?

- Why are 'residence' and 'domicile' important considerations for tax purposes and what is right for me, given my personal circumstances?

- How can I plan for a Capital Gains Tax liability?

- What planning should I consider for Inheritance Tax?

- What use are trusts?

A good advisor will cover all of these points as a matter of course when you have your first meeting. He will gather all of the facts of your case and work out a specific plan relevant to your circumstances.

Key points summary

- Invest with well-known and reputable companies and avoid the one/two-man-bands that flood your email account with so-called 'deals'.

- Select your team of advisors carefully, based on recommendations. If you cannot get recommendations, try other sources such as British embassies abroad.

- Think about the best method to finance your jet-to-let investment and get good advice. Think through what currency you should have for your mortgage.

- Consult with your currency broker to determine the best strategy for your overseas investment plan.

- Use the buying process checklist as an aide-memoire which will help you map out the sequence of events and ensure that you are thinking three steps ahead.

- Ensure that the contract is fair and contains any verbal agreements you may have made and that it's scrutinised by your independent lawyer.

- Arrange your tax affairs before you purchase. Discuss, in particular, who should own the property (or properties) and who should receive the income.

- Finally, don't be daunted by what you have read here or in other parts of the book. I have deliberately set out to highlight all of the potential pitfalls and tricks to ensure that you don't have to learn from your mistakes, but can have the benefit of learning from others. If you follow my advice, particularly with regard to forming a team of advisors, then the buying process will be straightforward as your team work on your behalf.

Jet-to-let and all overseas investment, for whatever purpose, is fun, profitable and will provide you with the financial security you are looking for – but, as with all adventures, careful planning and good advice will make the journey smoother.

CHAPTER 9

Marketing and letting your investment property

The majority of jet-to-let investors have a long-term view of their investments and wish to let out their property to gain an income, while at the same time watching it grow in value. There are two distinct types of jet-to-let approaches to renting:

- Long-term tenancies

- Holiday and short-term lets

Long-term tenancies

I'm making a bold assumption that if you have an apartment in Warsaw, Prague, Budapest or even Bucharest, you will not be managing the tenancy yourself. Maybe you are, but for the majority of jet-to-let investors, it makes more sense to outsource this requirement to a local agent.

What do agents do for their money?

- Find the tenants and screen them to determine suitability. Screening varies significantly from country to country.

- Prepare the letting contract in accordance with local laws.

- Advise on whether the market expects furnished or unfurnished properties. They will also produce an inventory of contents where required.

- Arrange viewings and meet potential tenants.

- Manage the tenant, the property and any issues on your behalf.

- Inspect the property ensuring that the tenant hasn't knocked down an interior wall or extended the living room without telling you or the planning authorities.

- Collect the rent! If the tenant is late in paying, then the agent should have tried and tested procedures to pursue payment on your behalf.

- Prepare regular statements of account. This is effectively your profit and loss statement. This includes payments out for such things as emergency repairs and payments to you for rental income.

- Process the paperwork.

- Have up-to-date knowledge of the current tenancy regulations and health and safety legislation.

Their fees vary depending on the level of service you require, but make sure that you enquire the cost before you commit to anything.

What should you look for in a letting agent?

- Do you trust them? I know it sounds a bit old fashioned, but sometimes even after a lot of analysis, your gut feeling and instinct will normally guide your decision.

- Size isn't everything. Choose agents who specialise in the type of property you wish to let.

- Are they members of a professional association?

- How do they handle your money? What safeguards do you have if they go bust? Do they have insurance?

You have to ensure that the local agents know what they are doing as they are the custodians of your investment on a daily basis. Overseas tenancy contracts can be for extended periods, way beyond the six-month initial contracts we have in the UK. Getting the right tenant in the first place and then having them effectively and efficiently managed is critical.

Holiday and short-term lets

Investment in holiday homes, holiday villas and holiday lets is becoming very popular thanks to programmes such as 'A Place in the Sun' and changes in our attitudes to work and leisure. As we have become wealthier, through economic growth and the huge equity in our homes, the demand for the second home in the sun or on the slopes has increased significantly.

Add in the jet-to-let concept of treating your property as an investment as well as a haven and there is no surprise that savvy buyers are letting their properties to make them pay their way.

Some holiday markets might only give you 20 weeks or so of revenue, but the cash that you generate on these lettings can be up to four times the monthly rate for standard long-term tenancies.

Marketing your holiday home

In order to reap the rewards and achieve as good a financial return as possible from your investment, it's important that you market your holiday home effectively, because even the most sought-after property will not sell itself. You won't get the right guests if you don't have the right marketing strategy. Effective marketing is the key to success in any business and property is no different.

To be successful, you should consider the type of tenant that you are trying to catch, and then think about where he will search for a property to rent. Below is a guide to the different options available to you for marketing your jet-to-let investment property.

1. Using a lettings agent or a holiday company

If you decide to use a lettings agency, they will market your property and their costs will be included in their fee. Lettings agencies will usually advertise your property in a brochure and/or on the internet featuring a description and possibly a few photographs.

Agency costs vary greatly. Most companies charge between ten and 20 per cent plus VAT, while nationally known agencies, which have brochures on the high street or in places like WH Smith, will charge between 20 and 30 per cent plus VAT. It sounds expensive, but the main advantage of using an agency is exposure.

You are a start-up business and you should look at every opportunity to market and sell your product. Don't dismiss this route because of the commission. If the choice is paying a commission or having an empty property and no income from it, which one would you rather take?

As a start-up, you want as much exposure as possible and this is a good route to building a client base. The guest who books through an agent and enjoys the experience of staying in your property can book directly with you for the following year in order to receive his loyalty discount. This can earn you an extra 15 per cent (if the agency fees are 25 per cent) and you have begun the process of building a customer base.

2. Advertising in newspapers and magazines

There are various forms of print media that you can use to advertise your property, but in order for it to be a success you will need to reach a specific target audience. If, for example, you use newspaper advertising, you will need to think carefully about the kind of customer that would be attracted to your property, and then advertise in the newspaper that he is most likely to read. A lot of print media advertisements fail to reach the desired target audience because they are placed in the wrong paper or magazine.

If your holiday property is targeted at specific groups (e.g. golfers or skiers), then advertise in a specialist magazine. Print advertising is expensive. You will have to look at how much of your budget you are willing to spend on advertising in newspapers, which have a lifespan of about eight hours if they are produced in the morning and even less if they are evening papers. Your 'reach' may be wide, but your impact may disappoint. Print advertising works best if it's sustained over a long period.

3. Using the internet

Internet use has rocketed in the past few years and the amount of business generated via the web is growing daily, with 64 per cent (29 million) of all adults in the UK having internet access either at work or at home (*source: National Statistics*).

Internet advertising offers numerous opportunities which are not possible with conventional marketing techniques and it's also more cost effective. You can show details of your property with photographs and particulars and promote it to a worldwide audience, 24 hours a day, 365 days a year. Your website provides an open book for your potential guests to browse and read at their leisure and as such should be professional, informative and accessible.

Data capture

Data capture is about acquiring the details of prospective customers via your website or another source and storing it for future use when you implement various marketing strategies.

 In the UK, you must conform to the provisions of the Data Protection Act 1998 – details of which can be accessed at the Information Commissioner's Office at www.ico.gov.uk.

Look at your potential competitors on the web, and you will see that they have some form of data capture, whether it's 'sign up for our free newsletter with all the last-minute deals and special offers' or 'register for our free tourist guide to Antarctica'.

This is an important consideration, as the data you capture will form your client base.

Information

Think carefully about how much data and what sort of information you want to capture. Think also about the visitor to your site, who is probably very busy, hasn't much time and doesn't want to give you his inside leg measurement because it's intrusive. If you want information, make it as simple as possible for the other party to supply it.

As a minimum, you want the customer's email address and possibly a contact telephone number. Ideally, you would also want his home address as this gives you three opportunities to send marketing material – electronically, by telephone and by traditional mail through the post. These three methods when combined are powerful drivers of your holiday letting business.

Add value

Add lots of useful information to your website about the country, area, locality and things to do while they are there. Add value to your site and even sell useful products such as guide books which can be arranged on an affiliate basis with the likes of Amazon. You may also wish to sell other relevant products, such as insurance or car hire, on a referral basis, which will contribute to your cash flow.

4. Making the most of other business opportunities

There are many business opportunities which can evolve from holiday lettings; for example, you may wish to offer marketing services to other owners who are letting in return for an agent's fee. If you are going to the trouble and expense of marketing your property, why not do it for others? This could prove to be a lucrative contribution to your cash flow. Additionally, you are building your customer base all the time.

Think laterally about all the places you go regularly where you could possibly promote your holiday home – on company electronic notice boards (intranet) at sports clubs or places where you socialise and in local shops or restaurants.

5. By word-of-mouth

I mentioned word-of-mouth earlier in the book as the most powerful form of advertising, and here's why. It's the most cost-effective way to promote your property and keep your customers returning. Many businesses thrive due to word-of-mouth referrals, and it can be said that it's the most effective way of marketing a business.

What you need to do:

- Identify which of your customers will give you a good reference or testimonial.

- Make sure that your friends and colleagues know about your holiday home and that it's available to let. You should be able to rent your property for the first year simply by promoting it to your circle of friends and family.

Finally, it's important to review your marketing strategy regularly, to ensure that your property continues to generate the greatest possible returns. It's crucial to ask people how they got your details (whether they saw you in the newspaper, on the internet, etc.) in order to see if your various marketing efforts are effective. This marketing audit will help shape your strategy and allow resources to be directed to the most successful channel.

Managing your property

This is often left to the end as it's the least interesting aspect of owning holiday or recreational property. It is, however, incredibly important.

First impressions count and are hard to mend if you get it wrong. If your guests have travelled for many hours to get to your property, the last thing they want is a dirty apartment or villa. By dirty, I don't mean mud and muck everywhere (although it does happen), but just not cleaned to a high enough standard.

The quality, integrity and professionalism of the company managing your property locally are key to your rental success. If you want word-of-mouth advertising and repeat business, then your product has to be first class and that means clean, well maintained and with all the fixtures and fittings in working order.

In addition, the management company should provide you with a detailed report of the condition of the property and recommendations for repairs or replacement of damaged contents, such as the TV, CD player, kettle, etc.

Satisfying your guests

Always over-deliver on your promise. You should make the experience of your guests memorable for all the right reasons. Try to provide a simple welcome pack with all the basics needed for the first night and include a well-researched and up-to-date visitors' guide with everything from the local amenities, restaurants, pubs, water sports and entertainment to practical information such as bus timetables, pharmacies, taxis, doctors and an emergency telephone number if they have a problem with the property.

Leave a note from yourself, as the owner, welcoming the guests to your property and wishing them a very happy holiday. Remind them that they qualify for a discount off their next holiday as valued returning guests.

A customer satisfaction questionnaire

You may want to consider a customer satisfaction questionnaire for guests to complete at the end of their holiday. This is vital customer information which tells you first hand how to improve your product. Again, make it as easy as possible to fill in as many people are put off by things that seem too wordy, especially if they don't benefit from the results.

A visitors' book

A visitors' book is also a great idea. Guests can share their personal experiences and recommend to future guests places, restaurants, beaches, mountains and other useful tips that they have picked up on their holiday. This works really well and can also be an entertaining read, and what better incentive to make sure everything is perfect for your customers?

Checklist: marketing your holiday property

- Do you have a unique selling point (USP)? In other words, why should people stay at your property and not the one next door? Check on the competition.

Here are a few things where you can gain the edge. This may be a part of the property itself or relate to the services you offer:

- Quality of fixtures, fittings and furniture.

- Multiple bathrooms in villas and a bathroom on the ground floor.

- Modern kitchen with good appliances including dishwasher and washing machine/dryer.

- Health club memberships if you have one located nearby.

- The use of local hotel facilities.

- Jacuzzi spa.

- Swimming pool.

- Sauna.

- Maid/daily cleaner.

- Fresh linen and towels.

- Access for disabled guests.

- Flat screen TV, DVD player and DVDs.

- CD player and radio.

- Satellite TV.

- Barbecue.

- Quality garden furniture.

- Landscaped gardens.

- Negotiated discounts at local restaurants, car hire and similar incentives.

- Airport pick-up and drop-off.

- A personal welcome visit by your representative.

- A welcome pack of milk, tea, coffee, water, wine and fruit.

- Get the product right.

- Ensure that your property is spotlessly clean on changeover.

- Ensure that the fabric (both internal and external) of the building is well maintained.

- Think about packaging your product with flights (through a bonded agent), car hire and insurance for those people who don't have the time to do it for themselves.

- Get the price right – the price has to reflect the clients' view of the benefits. If it's too cheap, they will wonder what is wrong with it and if it's too expensive, they will look elsewhere. Do your research and get it right based on comparisons with similar properties. Conduct a competitor analysis to determine what prices and product your competitors are working with.

- Offer last-minute deals or discounts if you have void periods.

- Get your property in front of your customers – the internet is a cheap, cheerful and very effective way to start. Get a website!

- Have flyers produced promoting your property and don't be shy to give them out.

- Get the procedure right. If you are taking bookings yourself by email and/or telephone, respond to the client as soon as possible, otherwise, in the age of the internet, he will book with someone else. If you are not able to do this, consider using an agent.

- Have a standard email response where you just have to fill in the gaps to save time, but be sure to produce this in a way that seems personal to the reader as opposed to the style used for junk mail.

- Issue receipts for payments.

- Ensure that you have a written contract between yourself and your tenant covering issues such as breakages policy, damage, non-arrival, additional guests, etc. Lawpack has a *Holiday Letting Agreement Form* which you may wish to look at.

- Keep detailed records of your income and expenses for your tax return.

Remember that property investment is a business. To succeed in any business you must offer the right product to targeted clients at a price acceptable to them, based on their idea of value and at a cost that makes the venture profitable for you!

Key points summary

Outsource the management of your jet-to-let investment property to a quality agent and management company or you can do it yourself if you have the time, energy and resources.

Successful holiday letting has:

- a quality product;

- in a quality location;

- which is well maintained and managed;

- marketed in a professional manner;

- using multiple routes to market – web, print, voice and word-of-mouth;

- puts the guest first;

- over-delivers; and

- has repeat and referral business.

CHAPTER 10

The jet-to-let checklist

I want to conclude this book by providing you with a jet-to-let checklist, which you may wish to use when you are analysing where to invest overseas. It's designed to help you consider everything when looking for your first or next investment and covers all of the topics we have looked at in this book.

It's a simple checklist so that investors can consider factors relevant to an investment and then make a subjective analysis of the importance of these factors to them. So, please use the checklist to assist you with your research. You also have the research that we have carried out on your behalf which is in the country studies in Part 2 of this book. Compare and contrast alternatives which fit your overall investment strategy.

Simply put a subjective score, between 0 and 10, against each factor on the checklist. If you think gross domestic product (GDP) growth in a particular country is strong and a positive factor, then you would be closer to 10 on the scorecard than 0. Alternatively, if you think that the level of unemployment in a country is very high, then the opposite would prevail. A high and persistent level of unemployment is bad for an economy and its associated property market and would therefore attract a low mark. However, if the situation is moving favourably towards more jobs being created and it's predicted that the rate of unemployment will decline, then this would also have an influence on the score.

Add the scores up at the bottom of the checklist to give you the overall score for your location – the higher the score, the better the potential investment.

Scoring system

0	1	2	3	4	5	6	7	8	9	10

poor   ➤   average   ➤   excellent

The higher the score the better

Factor	Score	Comment
Politics		Is the location politically stable?
Economy		
Economic growth (GDP)		Look at the trend in GDP growth and consensus forecasts.
Interest rates		Look for falling interest rate environments.
Unemployment		Look for falling unemployment.
Inflation		Look for low inflation.
Foreign direct investment (FDI)		Is it increasing or sufficient in order to create wealth and jobs?
Economic outlook		Look for growth with low inflation, low interest rates and growing employment opportunities. This may be as a result of FDI or internal fiscal or monetary measures.
Tourism		
Outlook		Is tourism rising or falling and what is happening to revenue or spend per tourist (this is more important than just the number of arrivals)?
Vulnerability to a change in tastes and fashion		If it is a 'bucket and spade' tourist destination, what will happen when the next one emerges?

Factor	Score	Comment
All-year direct flights		Add an extra mark for the availability of low-cost airlines.
Length of the season (where applicable)		Is there more opportunity to rent? Is there a winter market such as the mass exodus from Scandinavia looking for some light and warmth?
Property market		
Price inflation performance		The past is not necessarily a guide to future performance, but can be helpful in looking at trends, momentum and cycles.
Projected performance		Don't put too much faith in figures produced by marketing companies selling property in countries for which they are providing the house price inflation (HPI) news.
Internal demand for property		This is most important when considering secondary and tertiary cities in growing markets. It's important to note the ratio between property prices and earnings/rents.
External demand for property		This is most important when considering tourist-related investments.
Supply of property		The lower the supply, the higher the score and vice versa. You should be interested in areas which are under-supplied with property relative to the demand.
Property transaction costs		Consider with regard to both buying and selling.
Rental opportunities		Short-term lets for the tourist market and longer-term lets for cities and towns.

Factor	Score	Comment
Resale market – exit strategy	? x 2 =	I would apply a little bit of weighting here, as I believe that this is a really important issue. Apply a weighting of x 2; so whatever your score, just multiply the number by 2.
Annual costs		Look at the comparative data produced in Part 2, which will give you an idea of whether on a comparable basis annual costs are high or low.
Legal processes and title deeds		A strong, robust legal system should score highly. The opposite is also true.
Taxes		Relatively low, middle or high?
Double taxation treaty with the UK or the country in which you live and are domiciled for tax purposes		Yes = 10. No = 0.
Corporation Tax (if applicable)		This information is available in Part 2.
Capital Gains Tax		This information is available in Part 2.
Wealth Tax		Do you have to pay an annual Wealth Tax? This has to be considered as a dent in profits and as such would score accordingly.
Corruption		10 is the least corrupt. 0 is the most corrupt.
Overall risk		Consider the factors discussed in chapter 7: 10 is the least risk, 0 is the greatest risk.
Total score		

The checklist allows you to rate factors according to your wishes, aspirations and needs. I could have produced one of these for each location covered in the book, but as it's subjective, some of my in-built prejudices for or against some of the investment countries would come out.

There is no doubt that there is a gulf between some of the locations featured here in terms of risk, reward and investment potential and this checklist will help you decide which way they rank based on your own criteria.

Importantly, because I have added a very simple scoring schedule to this checklist, it allows you to compare potential investment opportunities. If you produce two lists and the numbers differ dramatically, then you need to analyse why. This in itself is a useful exercise.

Add in your own factors

The list is not exhaustive and there is certainly plenty of room to add in factors which you think are particularly important. The main purpose of the checklist is to be able to compare alternatives and also to provide you with a line-by-line tool for analysis.

I've deliberately avoided producing a weighted checklist because you may rate some factors higher or lower based on your goals, ambitions and tolerance to risk. Make your own weightings – if you think that overall risk is a significant factor and more important to you than some others, weigh it more heavily.

Some extra calculations

After calculating the final score for a particular country, you can produce the same checklist for other countries which interest you. This will enable you to compare final scores and help you to make a decision on where to invest.

Apart from that, you may want to see if a location is an above- or below-average investment. In order to do this, you have to find the mean value of your score. To find this out, divide the final score by 28. Why 28? In the checklist we have 28 factors (27 really, plus the exit strategy which we count twice). Place this mean value on the scoring table and it will show you if the location is above or below the average.

Scoring system

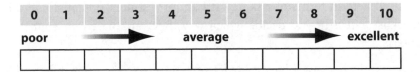

What if you add in your own factors?

If you add in one factor, you divide by 29; two factors, by 30 and so on. If you weigh any factors, let's say by two, then you have to count it as two factors; by three it becomes three factors and so on.

So, 'Exit strategy' in the example above could be given a score of six. In this case, I have weighted that factor by two, so the overall score is 12. But this is represented in the mean value calculation by counting it as two factors with a score of six, rather than one factor with a score of 12. This prevents the result or outcome from being skewed and biased in a disproportionate way.

Use common sense

Quite often the greatest asset you have in making an investment decision is your own common sense. Do the research, do the maths, do your due diligence and then use your abundance of common sense to make the final judgement.

Don't forget that having chosen your country, region and postcode, you then have to look at the individual investment property and examine its operating costs, net yield and return on investment as discussed earlier in the book.

Finally, thank you for taking the time to read this book and I wish you every success with your property investment ventures at home or overseas.

Part 2: Introduction

Part 2 of *The Jet-to-Let Bible* is a reference guide covering 20 countries across four continents. Each section gives an overview of the current political, economic and property market facts to be considered during your top down analysis when seeking the best overseas investment opportunity for you. This reference guide will enable you to quickly sort the wheat from the chaff and direct your more detailed research to specific countries. You can then use the guides as a template for your own in-depth research into each country.

Each country section introduces a historical overview and reasons for investing in that country. I include the country's location, climate, language and currency. I then examine the politics and economic situation, both of which should be considered in the earlier stages of deciding where to invest.

I look at each property market showing the performance, demand and attitudes to buying and renting as well as the impact of tourism. Each country, whether a traditional location for investing overseas (such as Spain, France and Italy) or a fresh new market (the Eastern European 8 or Morocco), has a number of property hotspots. I look in turn at cities, coastal and island locations, countryside and ski destinations. As some of these markets are developing quickly, your own research will reveal new areas which I may not have covered here.

After this is the all-important information on the buying process, outlining how easy or difficult it is to purchase a property in your chosen country. I also list the transaction costs incurred and taxes payable. At the end of each country reference guide, the 'Facts at a glance' list gives details on mortgages and interest rates.

The Appendices include lists and charts that will steer you through the choices open to you for your jet-to-let investments. These include low-cost airline routes, most popular overseas holiday and retirement destinations, and a summary of the economies of each of the 20 countries covered in this section.

This is then followed by a glossary which includes definitions of some of the technical and property industry terms that appear throughout the book.

This reference guide is intended to help you narrow down your search for your ideal jet-to-let property, but it's up to you to conduct the detailed research within each country to find the exact property to suit your investment needs.

Country studies

1. Bulgaria
2. Cyprus (South)
3. Dubai
4. Eastern European 8 (Czech Republic, Estonia, Hungary, Latvia, Lithuania, Poland, Slovakia, Slovenia)
5. USA – Florida
6. France
7. Germany
8. Greece
9. Italy
10. Morocco
11. Portugal
12. Spain
13. Turkey

1. Estonia	5. Czech Republic	9. Bulgaria	13. Italy
2. Latvia	6. Slovakia	10. Greece	14. Spain
3. Lithuania	7. Hungary	11. Germany	15. Portugal
4. Poland	8. Slovenia	12. France	

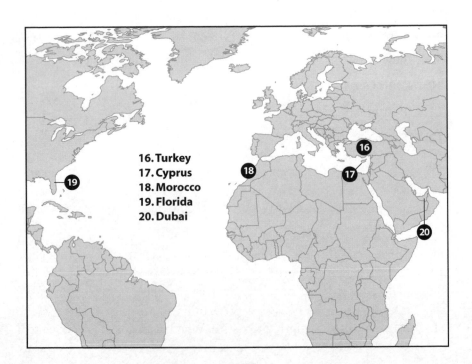

16. Turkey
17. Cyprus
18. Morocco
19. Florida
20. Dubai

Bulgaria

Bulgaria has recently seen a huge boom in property investment and this looks set to continue for a while to come. Thanks to the advent of low-cost flights and the invasion of the bucket-and-spade brigade, suddenly everyone knows where it is.

Why invest in Bulgaria?

The Bulgarian property market is becoming increasingly popular. Demand has been boosted by foreigners, who find Bulgaria a cheap alternative to Spain and Portugal and its anticipated accession to the European Union (EU) in 2007 is expected to continue this trend.

Bulgaria is a clear example of the 'substitution effect' at work. Put simply, a property in Spain or Portugal is being substituted for a property in Bulgaria because the buyer perceives it as a similar product, but at a cheaper price. The buyer believes that the property will give the same level of satisfaction as the Spanish alternative. Whether this is true is open to debate, but the important point is that as long as the buyer believes it to be so, then to all intents and purposes it's true!

The Bulgarian economy is highly dependent on foreign direct investment (FDI). Despite this, Bulgaria's residential property market has failed to attract large-scale foreign investment in comparison with countries such as Poland, Hungary and the Czech Republic.

Even though property prices have risen on average by 25 per cent last year, particularly in Sofia, in the Black Sea beach resorts (Varna, Bourgas, Sunny Beach) and in the ski resorts (Borovets, Bansko), prices are still relatively low by EU standards.

The market is only just starting to approach the conditions that already exist within more developed jet-to-let destinations. The harmonisation of Bulgarian legislation with that of the EU means that the process of buying a property is not too dissimilar to that which exists in other European countries, although, as we will see, there are still some differences that need to be addressed.

The story so far...

The 20th century was difficult for Bulgaria, being on the losing side in both World Wars. After the First World War, Bulgaria was made to pay reparations and lost large areas of land, including its opening to the Aegean Sea. Defeat in the Second World War came at an even higher cost when Soviet troops invaded the country and established a Communist regime making Bulgaria a satellite state of the Soviet Union.

Bulgaria remained under Soviet influence until 1990, when it held its first democratic elections and subsequently adopted a new constitution in 1991. It began the slow process of moving towards democracy and a market economy while fighting the continuing problems of inflation, unemployment, corruption and organised crime.

In the last 15 years Bulgaria has successfully transformed into a market economy and since 2000 has maintained a respectable average economic growth rate of four per cent per annum. Bulgaria joined NATO in 2004 and is expected to join the EU in 2007.

Where is it?

Bulgaria is in south-eastern Europe and occupies the north-eastern part of the Balkan Peninsula. To the north it borders Romania and to the west Serbia and Montenegro and the Former Yugoslav Republic of Macedonia. To the south are Greece and Turkey and to the east is the Black Sea. The coastline is 378km long and the country's total territory is 111,000km².

Bulgaria has a varied landscape. The main mountain ranges include the Balkan and Rhodope mountains. The rest of the country is mostly hilly combined with plateaus, with major plains in the north and the centre of the country.

What is the weather like?

The climate is regarded as one of the country's main attractions with four clear seasons and generally temperate conditions. Summers are hot and dry while winters are cold with snowfalls.

The average temperature in summer (April–September) is 23°C and in winter is 0°C. The average yearly temperature is 10.5°C.

Sofia

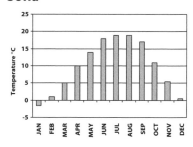

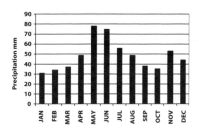

Varna

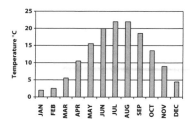

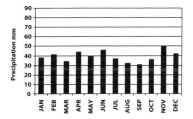

Bansko

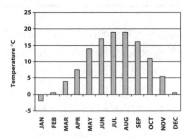
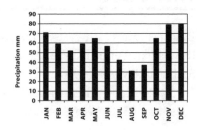

Language

Bulgaria has a population of over 7.4 million consisting mainly of ethnic Bulgarian (84 per cent), with two sizeable minorities, Turks (nine per cent) and Roma (five per cent). The official language is Bulgarian and is spoken by 85 per cent of the population, with the largest ethnic minorities speaking Turkish and Romany. Other spoken languages include English, German, French and Russian.

Currency

The Bulgarian currency is the Lev (BGL) divided into 100 Stotinki.

Politics

Bulgaria is a parliamentary democracy with a separate legislative executive and judiciary. The current coalition government consists of the Bulgarian Socialist Party (BSP), the National Movement Simeon II (NMS) and the Movement for Rights and Freedoms. The President of Bulgaria serves as head of state and is elected for a five-year term. The current President is Georgi Purvanov, who has held the position since 2002 and the current Prime Minister is Sergey Stanishev, who came to power in 2005.

A rocky road to European accession?

Recent elections in Bulgaria have seen a low turnout by the electorate, reflecting a general disaffection with politics. The elections in 2005 failed to find a majority government and the result forced the main parties to form a coalition which if unsuccessful, particularly in reforming the legal system, may result in Brussels postponing the country's accession to the EU.

Economy

The fall of Communism was closely followed by the collapse of the Bulgarian economy. Living standards fell dramatically and it took the country 15 years to regain pre-transition levels. Since then, the economy has moved up a few gears as a result of the reforms and initiatives instigated by the government.

In 1997, the government made an agreement with the International Monetary Fund (IMF) and the World Bank on a plan for economic reform, which included:

- accelerated privatisation of key industries;
- price and trade liberalisation; and
- financial services reforms.

These reforms helped to create the circumstances which led to a fall in inflation from 570 per cent in 1997 to just one per cent in 1998. They also led to increased FDI, improved macro-economic strength and smoothed the way for EU membership, currently scheduled for 2007.

Economic indicators

Economic growth

It's estimated that the economy grew by 5.4 per cent in 2005, compared to

4.3 per cent in the previous year. The gross domestic product (GDP) per capita or income per person increased to €7,500. The Economist Intelligence Unit forecasts a slower growth rate in 2006 at 4.3 per cent.

Growth has consistently been above four per cent over the last five years, which is good news for the economy and also the jet-to-let investor.

Inflation

Inflation reached five per cent in 2005, which was largely due to the surge in fuel prices and other energy costs. Inflation is expected to rise in 2006, due to increases in duty, higher heating and transport costs.

Interest rates

Bulgarian interest rates have halved since 2001 and are now relatively low with the National Bank offering a rate of 2.28 per cent in March 2006.

Unemployment

High unemployment still remains a problem for the economy, but it has been steadily falling since 2001.

Unemployment rate (percentage unemployed)

2000	2001	2002	2003	2004	2005
16.4	19.2	17.8	13.6	11.9	9.9

Source: Eurostat, the Statistical Office of the European Communities

Decreasing long-term unemployment is one of the government's main policies. Unemployment is forecast to be around ten per cent in 2006.

Foreign direct investment (FDI)

The Bulgarian economy is dependent on FDI and in 2004 it accounted for almost 11 per cent of GDP. Bulgaria aims to increase competitiveness and to further liberalise its economy in a determined effort to attract more overseas investment.

The chart below illustrates the growth FDI since 1997. For the property investor this is an important consideration as increasing FDI leads to economic growth, greater wealth through multiplier effects and therefore increases in property prices and rents.

Foreign direct investment in Bulgaria (€ million)

1997	1998	1999	2000	2001	2002	2003	2004	2005
570.2	605.1	866.0	1,103.3	903.4	980.0	1,850.5	2278.2	1,876.0

Source: Bulgarian National Bank

Economic summary

The transformation of the Bulgarian economy from a centrally planned Communist model to one based on the principles of the free market has been a success. Economic growth, with falling unemployment, relatively low inflation and low interest rates, bodes well for the future and EU accession will further enhance the attractiveness of Bulgaria for FDI.

Present levels of FDI indicate that other countries and corporations view Bulgaria as a good long-term economic bet. An analysis of FDI flows by industry makes for interesting reading. FDI in construction has increased from €2.9 million in 1998 to €82 million in 2004. Similarly, FDI in 'property and related renting and business activities' has increased from €38 million in 1998 to €137 million in 2004. Over the same period agriculture has declined and utilities, transport and communication have increased substantially, further emphasising the shift in focus of the Bulgarian economy.

What does this mean for the property investor?

As investors we are looking for multiplier effects and growth in real incomes – the wealth effect which drives property markets. The economic analysis I have conducted here clearly illustrates a country which is modernising, investing and growing and will also clearly benefit economically from entry into the EU and the single market.

So, what is the catch?

Bulgaria faces a number of issues that were suppressed under Communism. Although they are not exclusive to Bulgaria, these problems are significant and threatening to delay its EU accession in 2007. The country is stuck in a cycle of political instability that has seen seven different governments over the last 15 years and this isn't helping to solve the country's problems.

Unemployment

Unemployment has been a persistent issue in Bulgaria since its political and economic transition in 1990. Unemployment is highest in rural and agricultural regions, where 44 per cent of the population lives. The agricultural sector is having difficulties adjusting to the new economic realities and market forces.

Weak judiciary

The Bulgarian judiciary has a reputation for corruption and is still considered weak by the EU. This could hinder accession next year.

Organised crime

Organised crime has long been an issue and the murder of a prominent businessman last year has initiated fresh concerns. The Bulgarian interior minister announced new measures in 2005 aimed at confronting the problem, but the successful prosecution of criminals is rare.

Corruption

Transparency International publishes a yearly Corruption Perception Index (CPI). This measures the perceived degree of corruption as seen by businesspeople and country analysts. The 2005 index ranks Iceland as the cleanest with a score of 9.7 and Bangladesh and Chad joint last in 158th place with a score of 1.7. Bulgaria is ranked joint 55th along with Colombia, Fiji and Seychelles, which each received a score of 4.0. This would suggest Bulgaria has a higher than average level of corruption.

The property market

Off-plan investing in Bulgaria continues to attract intense interest from jet-to-let investors who believe that the country can sustain the sort of growth that has been witnessed in Spain and Florida over the last few years. Only time will tell, but there is no denying the fever which surrounds Bulgarian property.

Tourism

Tourism has thrived with the number of arrivals increasing by 50 per cent over the past three years. This has had a positive impact on the economy. In 2005, tourism revenues were more than €1.8 billion, representing about 11 per cent of GDP.

Tourists came from:

- Greece   (707,000)
- Macedonia   (656,000)
- Serbia and Montenegro   (577,000)
- Germany   (565,000)
- UK   (259,000)
- Russia   (121,000)

Many property investors are backing the potential growth of the Bulgarian tourist sector by investing in properties on the Black Sea coast and in mountain ski resorts. The strategy for most is either to let the property full time to holidaymakers or to live-and-let, using it themselves and letting at other times for income. Others are buying off-plan with the intention to sell on prior to or on completion and to make a profit.

Property hotspots

Sofia

Sofia, the capital of Bulgaria, offers possibly the best risk-adjusted investment opportunity in the country. The Bulgarian government is planning to redevelop the city in line with other European capitals and as FDI continues to flow and corporations set up headquarters in the capital, demand for property as well as rents will increase in the medium to long term.

Sofia is expected to see a significant increase in the number of foreign companies setting up over the next few years due to the many commercial benefits offered to relocating companies such as:

- 15 per cent flat rate Corporation Tax;
- low operating costs, with average monthly salaries below €200 per month;
- a highly educated workforce, particularly in the IT sector;
- access to the European single market.

In addition to office space, these companies require properties for their employees to live in, which is a fact not gone unnoticed by early bird jet-to-let investors. Sofia is also one of the candidates for the 2014 Winter Olympics, which will help the city's self-promotion as it prepares its bid.

Sofia has all the characteristics of a capital and as such the demand for quality rented accommodation among the local population and those who visit the city is strong. Diplomats, corporate clients, airlines and the emerging local middle classes provide a good target market for long-term rentals. A one-bedroom apartment in the capital can be purchased for as little as €45,000, although some of the more spacious apartments with additional bedrooms can be over €110,000. Rental prices are equally varied but are set to increase with property prices, although not at the same rate. Gross yields of between seven and ten per cent are achievable depending on location.

As prices have increased in the more popular districts, investors are following the ripple effect and many analysts are predicting growth in the west and north of the city this year and beyond.

Ski resorts

75 per cent of Bulgaria is covered in mountains and presents a jet-to-let property investor with many opportunities. The slopes and the mountains represent possibly the next best investment potential after Sofia.

The most popular town is **Bansko**, which has recently expanded its ski facilities to the size of a small European resort and is building rapidly to provide accommodation for the anticipated increase in visitor numbers. The resort is in the foothills of the Pirin Mountains and has received significant infrastructure investment, which has included adding new lifts and developing new slopes. The après-ski is also increasingly better catered for with almost 100 restaurants and tavernas to choose from after a day on the slopes. Studio apartments in Bansko can cost just €45,000, and a two-bedroom apartment can cost as little as €100,000 and has good rental prospects with estimated gross yields of 12 per cent per annum. The relatively inexpensive prices are one of the driving forces of the market.

But what happens in the summer? Well, further infrastructure investment is adding a golf course and other sporting facilities with the aim of establishing an all-year-round mountain and ski resort. The area is beautiful and with the development of walking, mountain biking and other activities Bansko is hoping to attract visitors well beyond the traditional skiing season. It remains to be seen whether this strategy and product is compelling enough to attract the number of tourists which are expected.

Other resorts worth researching are **Pamporovo** and **Borovets**, where studio apartments can be found for €42,000. Some predict that the next popular investment destination is going to be the area around **Veliko Tarnovo**, the ancient capital of Bulgaria. Property prices are relatively cheap, but they will be rising in line with expected demand over the coming years.

The Black Sea coast

Seaside visitors accounted for 75 per cent of Bulgaria's tourism revenues in 2004. The Black Sea coastline of 354km of bays and beaches is a target of many jet-to-let property investors and tourists looking for a cheaper alternative to traditional destinations such as Spain. Most resorts along the coast have undergone a major overhaul over the past couple of years and there is now a wide range of hotels and apartment complexes to accommodate the growing number of visitors.

The main resort of **Sunny Beach** has been unfairly likened to the less fashionable seaside resorts in Britain where pie, chips and tattoos are the more memorable features. Sunny Beach is 36km north of Bourgas and 90km to the south of Varna and is the largest holiday destination on the Black Sea. The easterly facing beach is impressive and is eight kilometres long and 30–60m wide. One-bedroom apartments are available from €40,000, while two-bedrooms can be purchased for around €85,000 with the latter having estimated weekly rentals of €430 per week between May and September.

One of the issues of property investing on the Black Sea coast is that the rental season is effectively only five months long. So, in the case of the two-bedroom apartment above, you cannot afford too many voids over the 20-week season if the property is to pay its way.

The second major holiday resort on the coast is **Golden Sands**, which is similar to Sunny Beach, but on a smaller scale. Coastal cities **Varna** and **Bourgas** were top investment destinations in 2004 and 2005 as property prices rose by more than 50 per cent.

Prices vary considerably in Bulgaria and even within a matter of streets apartments can have dramatically different price tags. This isn't unusual in Eastern Europe as modern developments are introduced and prices reflect a demand which is essentially derived from overseas.

As yet the resale market is untested for properties on the coast and in the mountains although anecdotal evidence is suggesting that some investors are finding it difficult to sell or 'flip' their off-plan properties. Only time will tell, but you must look carefully at your exit strategy outside of Sofia and also consider a realistic projection of rental income, given the relatively short season.

The buying process

There are no restrictions when purchasing an apartment. However, foreigners cannot own land and despite the country's expected EU membership in 2007, they will not be able to do so in the near future.

A loophole in the law allows foreigners to purchase land in order to buy a house through a local limited company. The legal and administrative fees for registering a company are about £340–550 on average and a company can own any number of properties. The purchaser is required to use a local lawyer to set up the company, proceed with the transaction and administer it on a permanent basis. Additionally, you must open a company bank account and deposit start-up capital for your new company.

When signing a preliminary contract, the buyer will need to pay ten to 30 per cent of the total purchase price as a deposit. After about a month the buyer pays the remaining purchase price and obtains a title deed.

When buying off-plan the buyer will pay a deposit and then make staged payments. A normal payment schedule would involve a deposit of 30 per cent on exchange of contracts and then staged payments of 30 per cent, another 30 per cent and 10 per cent throughout the construction period.

Staged payments can be part of the negotiations with the developer. For instance, you may be able to negotiate a 30 per cent deposit and then nothing until the completion of the project.

Transaction costs

The transaction costs are as follows:

- **State tax** is two per cent of the purchase price and is similar to stamp duty.

- **Notary fees.** All property dealings in Bulgaria must be done before a notary. Fees are paid on a scale based on the purchase price of the property. The maximum is £1,225, but it should be in the range of £150–250.

- **National Registration Tax** is 0.1 per cent of the purchase price.

- **Estate agents' fees** are three to five per cent and usually include a total for the court fees and the lawyer's fee.

Note: If both buyer and seller agree, it's quite common for a lower declared price to be entered on the contract of sale. This can lessen the Capital Gains Tax liability for the vendor and save the buyer transaction costs.

The only problem with this is that the buyer is then exposed to a greater Capital Gains Tax liability if he sells in the future, particularly if his purchaser is unwilling to follow this local practice. You are strongly advised to consult with an independent lawyer on every aspect of the property purchase. Remember that what is considered the norm may not be in line with the letter of the law.

On average the total fees will amount to eight to ten per cent of the purchase price.

Annual costs

Annual operating costs for property in Bulgaria are considerably lower than in the rest of Europe and include:

- **Real Estate Tax**, equal to 0.15 per cent of the purchase price of the property.

- **Municipal Tax**, approximately 0.5 per cent depending on the area.

Taxes

The major taxation rules for Bulgaria are outlined below:

Income Tax
From January 2005, Income Tax bands range from 10 to 24 per cent.

Tax	Annual income (BGL)
0%	Up to 1,560
10%	1,561–1,800
20%	1,801–3,000
22%	3,001–7,200
24%	7,201 and above

Corporation Tax

The standard rate of Corporation Tax is a flat 15 per cent.

Capital Gains Tax

Capital gains are treated as income and are therefore liable to Income Tax rates.

Summary

Strengths

- Political democracy.

- Fast growing economy.

- Low interest rates.

- Falling unemployment.

- High and growing levels of FDI.

- Growing tourist industry.

- Property prices are cheap compared to the EU standards.

- Bulgaria has one of the least expensive costs of living in Europe.

- Geographical diversity offers a wide choice of properties in cities, on the coast and in the mountains.

- Relatively low taxes, particularly Corporation Tax at 15 per cent.

Weaknesses

- Spare capacity in the hotel industry will absorb a large proportion of the estimated increase in tourism.

- Competition from the many other owners of properties for rentals.

- The segment of the tourist market which visits Bulgaria is low budget/low spend.

- Package tour versus private rentals in a low-budget destination favours the package tour.

- Flying time (four hours).

- Seasonality (five months).

- Relatively high levels of corruption.

- Presence of organised crime.

- Weak judiciary.

- Restrictions on foreign ownership of land.

- Potential title deeds and ownership issues.

- Lack of an indigenous (home-grown) demand on the coast.

- Little second home demand and negligible demand from retirees on the coast.

Opportunities

- EU entry in 2007 (to be confirmed).

- Euro adoption at some stage in the future.

- Developing tourism promises potential investment returns.

- Winter Olympics candidate for 2014.

- The development of Sofia as a major European capital city will have a positive effect on prices and rents.

- EU single market attracting corporations and the creation of jobs.

- Potential opening of no-frills airline routes from UK and other countries.

Threats

- Exit strategy – who will buy your off-plan property when you come to sell?

- Who will rent your property, particularly on the coast?

- Potential for long voids on the coast outside of the five-month season.

- No historical evidence of a resale market on the coast or in the ski resorts.

- Will seasoned skiers choose Bulgaria over France, Austria and North America?

- The oversupply of new-build properties on the coast and a fall in market prices.

Facts at a glance

Geography	
Population (2005 estimate)	7,450,349
Language	Bulgarian
Ethnic groups	Mostly Bulgarian. Minority groups are Turks and Roma
Local currency	Lev divided into 100 Stotinki

Political system	
Political structure	Republic with parliamentary government
President	Georgi Purvanov
Prime Minister	Sergey Stanishev
Main party	Bulgarian Socialist Party (BSP) National Movement Simeon II (NMS)

Economy	
Unemployment rate in 2005	9.9%
Unemployment rate, February 2006	11.5%
Inflation rate in 2005	5.0%

Inflation rate, February 2006	3.0%
Interest rate, March 2006	2.28%
GDP growth in 2005	5.4%
GDP growth forecast for 2006	4.3%
GDP per capita (income per person) in 2005	€7,500

Taxation

Income Tax	10–24%
Corporation Tax	15%
Capital Gains Tax	As per Income Tax

Corruption statistics

Corruption rate	4.0
Corruption rank	55th

Industry and technology

Major industries	Agriculture
	Electricity
	Tourism
	Textiles

The Bulgarian property market

Hotspots	*Capital:* Sofia
	Coastal: Varna, Bourgas, Sunny Beach, Golden Sands
	Ski: Bansko, Pamporovo, Borovets

Property taxes (transactions)

Company registration	£340–550
State tax	2%
Notary fees	Variable. The maximum is £1,225
National Registration Tax	0.1%
Estate agents' fees	No more than 3–5%

Total fees	Average 8–10%

Property taxes (annual)	
Real Estate Tax	0.15%
Municipal Tax	0.5%

Mortgage	
LTV	70%
Term	Up to 20 years
Currency	Euros only
Current interest rate	Approximately 7.0–7.5%

Investor resources

Embassies

British Embassy in Bulgaria

9 Moskovska Street, Sofia

Tel: +359 2933 9222
Fax: +359 2933 9250
Website: www.british-embassy.bg

Bulgarian Embassy in the UK

186–8 Queen's Gate
London SW7 5HL

Tel: 020 7584 9433
Fax: 020 7584 4948
Website: www.bulgarianembassy.org.uk

Useful websites

Bank of Bulgaria

www.bnb.bg

Bulgarian News

www.sofiaecho.com

Invest in Bulgaria
www.investbg.government.bg

National Statistical Institute of Bulgaria
www.nsi.bg/Index_e.htm

Tourism in Bulgaria
www.bulgarian-tourism.com/new/index.htm
www.bulgariatravel.org

Cyprus (South)

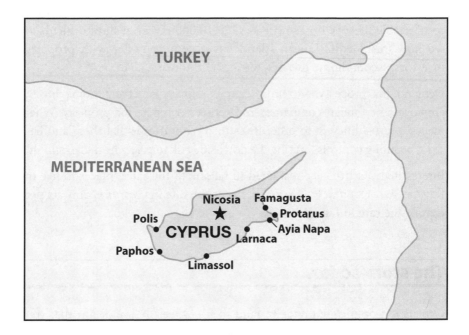

Since gaining full membership of the European Union (EU) in May 2004, Cyprus has attracted a lot of attention from property investors. The fantastic all-year-round summer climate, fine beaches and smart new golf courses on the way has led to a swarm of investors coming to the island over the last couple of years – but what is all the buzz about?

Why invest in Cyprus?

The Cypriot property market has been one of the better performers in the EU during the last three years with growth forecast to continue to be driven by a strong economy, high demand for property and adoption of the euro in January 2008. Added to this is the fact that income returns for some residential properties can reach eight to ten per cent.

Modern Cyprus is politically stable with an advanced economy, very low taxes and a developed infrastructure. It has robust economic growth, with the gross domestic product (GDP) averaging 3.5 per cent over the last five years. The forecast for GDP growth in 2006 is four per cent.

English is widely spoken, you can drive on the left and a couple can live a comfortable lifestyle on as little as CYP 10,000 a year. It's not difficult to see how this Mediterranean island has become popular with property investors, second home owners, retirees and tourists alike.

Demand for property currently exceeds supply as second home buyer, employees of foreign companies and retirees compete for property. What makes Cyprus different to other investment countries is that the island has strict planning controls limiting the downside risk to prices from oversupply.

Interestingly, Cyprus is considered to be one of the safest places to live in Europe. According to EU statistics, the crime rate in Cyprus is only six per cent of the rate in the UK.

The story so far...

Cyprus is a politically divided island so it's especially important that you know its history when considering it as a place for investment.

Since 1974, the island has been divided into the north (Turkish Republic of Northern Cyprus or TRNC) and the south (Republic of Cyprus). The south comprises 68 per cent of the land and is inhabited mostly by Greek Cypriots, and the north is largely populated by Turkish Cypriots and Turkish nationals.

In 1955, the war against British rule was launched by the National Organisation of Cypriot Combatants (EOKA). Three years later, Greek Cypriot leader Archbishop Makarios called for independence and Turkish Cypriots demanded that the island be divided between the Greeks and the Turks. Cyprus eventually gained its status as an independent state in 1960 after Greek and Turkish Cypriots agreed on a constitution and Makarios became the country's first president.

In 1974, the Greek Junta in Athens initiated a coup against the Cypriot government as a reaction to its choice not to unite with Greece. Turkey then used its right to protect the Turkish Cypriot minority and invaded a third of the island, displacing over 200,000 people living on that part of the island. Greek Cypriots were forced to leave the Turkish-controlled north and the Turkish Cypriots were also dislodged from the south. The island was divided into Greek and Turkish areas separated by a UN-occupied buffer zone, called the 'Green Line'. The Turkish Cypriots declared a separate state in 1983, calling it the Turkish Republic of Northern Cyprus (TRNC), which remains unrecognised by the international community except for Turkey.

Despite occasional pressure from the United Nations (UN), Cyprus remains divided. In May 2004, the Republic of Cyprus gained membership of the EU.

This chapter will only discuss property investment in the Republic of Cyprus.

Where is it?

Cyprus is at the eastern end of the Mediterranean, just 65 kilometres from the coast of Turkey, in a location that places the island at a crossroads between Europe, Asia and Africa. The whole of Cyprus has a total area of 9,250km² and 648 km of spectacular coastline.

What is the weather like?

Cyprus enjoys one of the best Mediterranean climates with approximately 340 days of sunshine per year. In general, the island experiences mild wet winters and dry hot summers. The average annual temperature is about 20°C. There is also a short season of snow in the mountains from January to March. During winter, it's possible to sunbathe in the morning and ski in the afternoon.

As Cyprus is a relatively small country, there is little variation in climate from coast to coast. The weather charts therefore apply to the island as a whole.

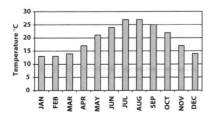
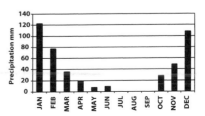

Language

The official languages are Greek and Turkish, spoken by 84 per cent and 13 per cent of the population respectively. Other minority languages include Armenian and Arabic, though with Cyprus being a former British colony, English is widely used as a second language.

Currency

The official currency is the Cyprus Pound (CYP) divided into 100 Cents. The Cyprus Pound is a member of the Exchange Rate Mechanism 2, which is a precursor to adopting the euro with a commitment to adopt the new currency on 1 January 2008.

Politics

The Republic of Cyprus has a democratic presidential system and the main parties are the Communist Progressive Party of Working People (AKEL) and the Conservative Democratic Rally (DISY). Under the 1960 constitution, the President serves as both the head of state and government. Tassos Papadopoulos is the current President of Cyprus and has held this position since 2003, although national elections in May 2006 may change this.

Administratively, Cyprus is divided into six districts and two small coastal enclaves, Akrotiri and Dhekelia, which are British military bases and British territory.

Economy

Since gaining independence in 1960, Cyprus has managed to transform considerably from a small colony into a modern free market economy, with a strong services sector and a highly educated and skilled labour force. Cyprus is categorised as a high-income state and its GDP per capita is a very acceptable 85 per cent of the EU average. Economic growth has been strong and the economy benefits from full employment, low inflation and a stable currency.

Cyprus has effectively refocused its economy from dependence on agriculture to become an advanced international business centre. In 2005, the services sector accounted for 76 per cent of GDP of which tourism revenues accounted for about 13 per cent of GDP.

The island has recently benefited from its accession to the EU as it now has more opportunities to diversify its economy and attract overseas investment.

Economic indicators

Economic growth

Last year Cyprus' economy grew by 3.8 per cent, thanks in part to growing tourism revenues and increasing consumer demand. Furthermore, GDP per capita in 2005 stood at €19,600. The European Commission forecasts strong growth in 2006, which may possibly rise above four per cent.

Inflation

Inflation reached 2.0 per cent in 2005, which is a positive step towards Eurozone entry in 2008. One of the requirements to join is that the rate of inflation should be no more than 1.5 per cent above the average of the three lowest rates within the zone. This target currently stands at 2.6 per cent.

Interest rates

Interest rates in Cyprus were cut by 1.25 per cent in 2005 to 4.25 per cent. Interest rates are one of the most powerful influences on property markets and prices and Cyprus is particularly well placed to take advantage of a falling interest rate environment.

In order to join the euro on 1 January 2008, interest rates have to converge with the European Central Bank. In March 2006, the difference between the two was 1.75 per cent, but the two rates must be the same by the proposed date for the adoption of the euro.

Falling interest rates and convergence will provide a strong boost to the Cypriot property market.

Unemployment

Cyprus has the lowest unemployment rate among the 2004 EU accession countries and one of the lowest rates among the Eurozone member states.

Unemployment rate (percentage unemployed)

2000	2001	2002	2003	2004	2005
5.2	4.4	3.9	4.5	5.2	5.3

Source: Eurostat, the Statistical Office of the European Communities

The labour market is relatively flexible and unemployment is forecast to fall further. Under conditions of almost full employment, foreign workers mainly from Eastern Europe have been encouraged to fill job vacancies and it's estimated that 14 per cent of the workforce is now made up of foreigners.

Foreign direct investment (FDI)

Cyprus is attracting considerable amounts of FDI for a small country with a population of less than a million people. The EU is the main investor with the largest proportion of FDI directed towards trade and financial services.

Foreign direct investment in Cyprus (million US dollars)

	2001	2002	2003
	956	1,060	1,000

Source: www.state.gov

Economic summary

Cyprus is a small economy which is adjusting well to being in the EU.

Reliant on tourism, there are plans to develop the industry to appeal to a broader market. New golf courses are planned all over the island and the construction or enhancement of marinas is taking place in Larnaca, Limassol, Ayia Napa and Paphos.

The Cyprus Tourist Organisation (CTO) considers all of these things to be a great way to bolster the country's credentials as an all-year-round destination, attracting different segments of the tourist market throughout the year. This includes sporting and cultural groups as well as the more traditional tourists. For example, international teams, such as the Great Britain Olympic Athletics team and international football teams, use the excellent sporting facilities for their pre-season training.

The economic situation is excellent, with a growing economy, low inflation and falling interest rates, which should all contribute to an even healthier property market over the medium to long term.

So, what is the catch?

The Cyprus problem

Cyprus has been divided for over 30 years and a solution suitable to all sides to end the partition has still not been agreed. The latest effort to reunite the island was in February 2004. The political parties in Southern and Northern Cyprus began talks on the basis of the Annan Plan, which was put to a vote on both sides. Turkish-Cypriots accepted the plan but the Greek-Cypriots rejected it by a big majority. So, Cyprus remains divided and there have been no additional efforts to restart negotiations between the two sides.

The property market

EU accession had an extremely positive effect on the property market in Cyprus. Pre-accession property prices grew by 10–15 per cent on average and since joining the EU they accelerated to 15 per cent and in some cases 20 per cent per annum. The property market is forecast to remain strong in the next few years due to Cyprus adopting the euro in 2008, the continued strength of the economy, falling interest rates and a lasting demand from retirees and second home buyers.

Cyprus is another jet-to-let location that is benefiting from a substitution effect with Spain and other more mature property markets. Property prices are no longer cheap, but are still around 30 per cent cheaper than prices in Spain, southern France and Italy. Cyprus' main advantage is that it attracts all types of buyers – investors, retirees and families of many different nationalities. Due to the island's strict planning and building regulations, the supply of properties remains limited. This protects the property market from oversupply, which is a risk in some other markets.

The Cyprus property market is also benefiting from the uncertainty in the UK market, which has meant the creation of a substitution effect of UK investors seeking growth and income in a market at a different stage of the property cycle.

UK investors are attracted to Cyprus because they understand the robust English-based legal and banking systems and English is widely spoken. It's almost a home away from home, with popular retail outlets such as Marks and Spencer, Debenhams, Next and others providing services to the large retirement and second home communities.

Tourism

Cyprus has established itself as a well-known tourist destination and every year almost 2.5 million people visit this island, which is three times the country's total population! The British account for over 57 per cent of visitors, while the majority of other arrivals come from Germany, Greece, Russia and Scandinavia.

Tourism is a key source of income for the country and plays a major role in the country's economy. In 2005, tourism revenues were CYP 1,005.7 million (£1,212.5 million), which amounted to 13 per cent of GDP.

The government is implementing new plans with the intention of further increasing the number of visitors. Cyprus already has a highly developed infrastructure, but more new projects are on the way. The two international airports at Larnaca and Paphos are being expanded at a cost of €500m to further increase the capacity to 7.5 million passengers a year. These projects will be completed by 2009.

Property hotspots

When deciding where to invest in Cyprus, one of the most important factors to consider is location. Below is a brief guide to some of the most popular locations for jet-to-let investors.

Paphos

Paphos is situated on the south-west coast of Cyprus, and is a smart Mediterranean coastal town with a year-round holiday business and significant retirement community. The Cypriot government has invested in roads and infrastructure and the opening of Paphos International Airport has had a very positive effect on the district.

In the wider Paphos area, a new marina is planned in the Coral Bay area which will significantly add to the development of the district and is targeted to attract high-spending visitors, which will in turn have a multiplier effect on the local economy. A further boost comes from the announcement of a multi-million-pound mixed-use development made up of residential and commercial property as well as a hospital and university in the Universal district of Paphos town.

Paphos already has three golf courses which add to the year-round appeal of this area. Its popularity with holidaymakers, investors and expatriate residents alike means the area has very good rental and resale markets.

Paphos is a great place to retire as evidenced by the large numbers of people in the UK and the European expatriate communities living there. This community effect provides an ideal exit when selling property for profit as any established community attracts other members of that community and when restricted supply and increasing demand combine, property prices are supported.

The Paphos property market experienced strong growth from 1996 to 2002, when four out of five properties purchased were by foreigners either for living on the island or for investment purposes. Currently property prices in Paphos are on average 20 per cent higher than similar properties on the eastern half of the island. This price differential has led to an increase in demand for properties in the other districts and a levelling of prices in Paphos.

A two-bedroom apartment in Paphos can be purchased for CYP 80,000 and would let during the peak season for upwards of CYP 500 a week depending on the location.

Polis and **Latchi** on the north-west coast are currently attracting a lot of attention as investor areas due to their proximity to the Akamas Peninsula, a protected area of outstanding natural beauty. They were previously small fishing villages, and they now attract those interested in a more rural experience during their time in Cyprus.

Cyprus is experiencing its own 'substitution effect' and with the plans of the Cyprus Tourism Organisation to expand the facilities and golf courses, Larnaca and Famagusta Districts are leading the way for property investors.

Famagusta District

Famagusta District is in eastern Cyprus, less than an hour's drive from Larnaca Airport, well known for its white sandy beaches and turquoise waters. The area is particularly popular among Scandinavians, but as property prices in Paphos have risen in recent years, Famagusta District has become an alternative for retirees and second home owners.

Famagusta town is located in the Turkish Republic of Northern Cyprus (TRNC) and was the administrative centre of the district before 1974. It was also the tourist 'jewel of the Eastern Mediterranean' with long sandy beaches, restaurants and hotels and was the major tourist area on the island of Cyprus. As a result of the division of the island, it's now a ghost town and will form a major part of any negotiation on future reunification. Indeed, many investors have been attracted to this area because of its proximity to Famagusta town and the benefits that can be attained after reunification and the massive multiplier effects which will undoubtedly follow any reconstruction, including the opening up of the port and the regeneration of the tourist industry.

Paralimni is now the administrative centre of Famagusta District and provides a town with all the key industries and services that one would expect in a thriving regional hub. It has a growing international community and many British-run businesses are springing up in property management and lettings, bars, restaurants, car hire and other tourist, property and service industries. The tourist area of Paralimni on the coast is often referred to as Protaras, covering ten kilometres from Kapparis in the north to Konnos Bay in the south, and including the lively, family-friendly resort of Protaras itself. New-build apartments in Paralimni with communal swimming pools start at CYP 55,000 for a one-bedroom rising to CYP 70,000-plus for a two-bedroom apartment depending on location. Rental returns are CYP 300 to CYP 400 a week respectively in the peak season, which runs from June to October, although April, May and November are also popular short-term letting months. In the winter months your market is the long-term renters escaping the UK and North European cold and rain.

Kapparis is very popular with second home owners and is quickly establishing itself as a jet-to-let investment area, due to its close proximity to clean beaches, and plenty of new restaurants and bars as well as benefiting from the short distances to Paralimni, Protaras and Ayia Napa. It's a fast growing area, with property prices reflecting the increasing demand, particularly from Cypriots living in Nicosia looking for a weekend retreat near the beach as well as Europeans looking for a quieter, more relaxed getaway location. A three-bedroom villa in Kapparis would cost from CYP 225,000 or more and could be let out in the peak season for CYP 1,000 a week, while a two-bedroom apartment with communal pool and within walking distance to the beach could be bought from CYP 80,000 and would let for CYP 400–450 per week in the peak season.

The property market in **Protaras** and the rest of Famagusta District is doing extremely well as a clear substitution effect with Paphos is evident. In effect, these areas are playing catch-up with their more successful counterparts and the eastern side of the island has remained relatively undiscovered in terms of retirement and second home ownership until recently. Protaras has some of the most amazing beaches on the island and a family-friendly approach to tourism. It also has an appeal which has led to a growing demand for property from both Cypriots and foreigners.

Ayia Napa is a popular beach resort which lies 40km to the east of Larnaca on the south coast. For a number of years it has received unfavourable press due to the type of visitor it attracted. 'Lager louts' and lots of noise were the headlines. This has changed. The mayoress has led Ayia Napa to substantially clean up its image and it has once again become a holiday destination for families boasting superb beaches and excellent hotels, but it still retains numerous excellent restaurants and exciting nightlife. The resort is extremely popular with UK, European and Cypriot families in the summer and in the winter becomes the home to migrating Scandinavians seeking shelter from the dark and cold days at home.

Property in Ayia Napa represents a solid investment; it has the best sandy beaches in Cyprus, attracts a wide range of nationalities and is moving towards being an all-year-round resort. A new-build two-bedroom apartment would cost from CYP 70,000 and would let for CYP 380–400 in the peak season.

Limassol

Limassol is the second largest town in Cyprus, and is the island's main port, as well as being the centre of the wine industry and a holiday resort. It has been the centre for hundreds of Russian off-shore companies over the years, which has continued to have a positive effect on the local property market. Limassol has a high demand from Russians and Eastern Europeans and as such is the predominant location for their property purchases when looking to invest in Cyprus.

Commercial and residential property prices in Limassol are approximately 15 per cent lower than in other areas of Cyprus, yet the town offers good long-term rental options for commercial and residential properties and short-term letting for holidays during peak seasons.

Limassol has all the attractions of a modern holiday resort which rests comfortably alongside a vibrant business and commercial sector. Its international port welcomes the steady flow of cruise ships that stop off at the island and there is a busy trade in short cruises to the Greek islands.

Larnaca

Larnaca is on the south-east coast and is the location of the island's main international airport. Larnaca, like other Cypriot coastal towns, is divided into an older town centre as well as an unevenly distributed array of modern hotels and restaurants along the waterfront. Its established infrastructure and proximity to the airport and road network make it a very popular choice with both tourists and those seeking a second or retirement home in the sun. Larnaca is a lively town throughout the year and the amenities and facilities here make it an ideal location for retirement.

There are two aspects to Larnaca's property market: one is the development of the main town and the other is the growth of beachside areas on the outskirts.

The satellite villages of **Pervolia**, **Kiti** and **Mazotos** are beginning to attract second home owners, retirees and jet-to-let investors who appreciate the unspoilt natural beauty of the area and the potential for investment and living. The announcement of a new golf course and leisure complex at **Tersefanou**, with local villages and several kilometres of unspoilt, clean and uncrowded beaches, make this one area of Cyprus to keep an eye on for the future. A new two-bedroom apartment in Mazotos would cost from CYP 65,000, while a three-bedroom villa with private pool and sea views in Pervolia would cost from CYP 190,000.

Transaction costs

Foreign individuals are entitled to own one property – a villa, apartment or a piece of land up to 4,012m^2. There are no restrictions on Cypriot companies or individuals. This means that if a non-Cypriot wishes to purchase more then one built property, he must incorporate a company in Cyprus (until 2007 when this law will be reviewed).

The legal system in Cyprus is based on the English legal system. For this reason, the property buying process is very similar to that in the UK. When buying off-plan a reservation deposit is required to reserve the property, after which you receive a sales contract to discuss with your lawyer. Foreigners need to seek the approval of the Council of Ministers to buy, but this is a routine government procedure and permission could almost be regarded as a formality.

When you are ready to exchange contracts, a deposit is paid according to the terms set by the developer and the remaining balance is paid by the time the property is completed. Once the contract is signed and stamped, it's lodged at the Land Registry and the buyer is protected by the law on specific performance, which protects the purchaser's ownership rights until the title deeds are transferred into his name. If you are buying a resale property, exchange of contracts, completion and final payment can happen at the same time.

Total transaction costs are summarised below:

- **Stamp duty** is low and charged at a rate of 0.15 per cent on the first CYP 100,000, and 0.20 per cent above.

- **Legal fees**, including search fees and the application to the Council of Ministers, is approximately one per cent.

- **Mortgage registration costs** are approximately one per cent of the amount secured.

- **Property transfer fees** are payable on receipt of the title deeds, which may be up to two years after completion of the property in order to transfer the ownership into the buyer's name. It's a one-off payment payable to the Land Registry Office. The amount is based on a sliding scale as shown in the table below:

Property value (CYP)	Transfer fee
Up to 50,000	3%
Up to 100,000	5%
Over 100,000	8%

The transfer fees can be substantially reduced if you buy with another person.

On average, the total costs will be approximately five to eight per cent of the purchase price.

Note: For investors looking to sell before the transfer of the title deeds (typically two years after completion), which is perfectly legal, buying costs are reduced significantly to no more than just above two per cent.

Annual costs

Annual operating costs are summarised below:

- **Immovable Property Tax** is based on the property value and is calculated on a sliding scale:

Taxable value (CYP)	Annual tax
Up to 100,000	Nil
100,001–250,000	0.25%
250,001–500,000	0.35%
Over 500,000	0.40%

- **Municipal Tax.** Local authority taxes range from 0.1 to 0.5 per cent per annum to cover refuse collection, sewerage, street lighting, maintenance, etc.

Taxes

One of the major benefits of investing in Cyprus is the low tax regime for both residents and investors. It has the lowest Corporation Tax level in the EU and individual allowances are generous.

Income Tax
Income Tax rates for 2006:

Tax	Annual tax base (CYP)
0%	Up to 10,000
20%	From 10,001 to 15,000
25%	From 15,001 to 20,000
30%	20,001 and more

Corporation Tax
The standard rate of Corporation Tax in Cyprus is ten per cent, which is the lowest in the EU.

Capital Gains Tax
The standard rate of Capital Gains Tax is 20 per cent.

Summary

Strengths

- Political democracy.

- Member of the EU.
- Consistent economic growth.
- Low unemployment and low inflation.
- Strong established tourist industry.
- Strong demand for property for holidays, investment, retirement and expatriate living.
- Established property market, procedures and resale market.
- Advanced UK-based Land Registry system.
- Worldwide appeal.
- No restrictions on foreign ownership.
- Excellent beaches.
- Relatively cheap property prices, compared to EU giants.
- Year-round good climate.
- Low crime rate.
- Low cost of living.
- Very low corporate taxation.
- English-based legal system.
- English-based banking system.
- English widely spoken and they drive on the left!

Weaknesses

- Country split over political divides.
- Competition from hotel industry for rentals.
- Competition from other owners of properties for rentals.
- Flying time from the UK is 4.5 hours.
- Presently no low-cost airlines.

Opportunities

- Euro adoption in 2008.

- Lifestyle investment for 'live and let'.

- Large expat community providing a proven exit strategy.

- Low-cost airlines seeking to open up routes.

- Entrepreneurial culture.

- New golf courses, marinas and casinos.

- VAT will be applied to land in 2007, which will have an inflationary effect on new-build properties.

Threats

- Political divides and instability regarding the outcome.

- Market may overheat.

Facts at a glance

Geography	
Population of the island (estimate)	780,000
Language	Greek, Turkish
Ethnic groups	Greek-Cypriot (99.5%)
Local currency	Cyprus Pound divided into 100 Cents

Political system	
Political structure	Republic with a presidential system
President	Tassos Papadopoulos

Main parties	Progressive Party of Working People (AKEL) Democratic Rally (DISY)

Economy

Unemployment rate in 2005	5.3%
Unemployment rate, February 2006	5.2%
Inflation rate in 2005	2.0%
Inflation rate, March 2006	2.3%
Interest rate, March 2006	4.25%
GDP growth in 2005	3.8%
GDP growth forecast for 2006	4.0%
GDP per capita (income per person) in 2005	€19,600

Taxation

Income Tax	20–30%
Corporation Tax	10%
Capital Gains Tax	20%

Corruption statistics

Corruption rate	5.7
Corruption rank	37th

Industry and technology

Major industries	Textiles Cement Printing and publishing Tourism Business services

The Cypriot property market

The most popular destinations to invest	Paphos, Polis, Larnaca, Pervolia, Mazotos,

Paralimni, Protaras,
Kapparis, Ayia Napa,
Limassol and Nicosia

Property taxes (transactions)

Property Transfer Tax	Sliding scale rate of 3%, 5% and 8%
Stamp duty	Sliding scale rate of 0.15% and 0.20%
Legal fees	1%
Mortgage registration costs	Approximately 1%
Total fees	Average 5–8%

Property taxes (annual)

Immovable Property Tax	Sliding scale rate up to 0.4%
Municipal Tax	0.1–0.5%

Mortgage

LTV	80%
Term	Up to 30 years
Currency	Cyprus Pounds and other currencies
Current interest rate in CYP	Varies between 6.50 and 7.25% Euro mortgages from 4.2% Swiss Franc mortgages from 2%

Investor resources

Embassies

British High Commission in Cyprus

PO Box 21978, 1587 Nicosia

Tel: +357 2286 1100
Fax: +357 2286 1125
Website: www.britishhighcommission.gov.uk

High Commission of Cyprus in the UK

93 Park Street, London W1K 7ET

Tel: 020 7499 8272
Fax: 020 7491 0691
Website: http://cyprus.embassyhomepage.com

Useful websites

Bank of Cyprus
www.centralbank.gov.cy

Invest in Cyprus
www.investincyprus.com

Statistical Service of the Republic of Cyprus
www.mof.gov.cy

Tourism in Cyprus
www.visitcyprus.org.cy
www.kypros.org/Cyprus/tourist.html

Dubai

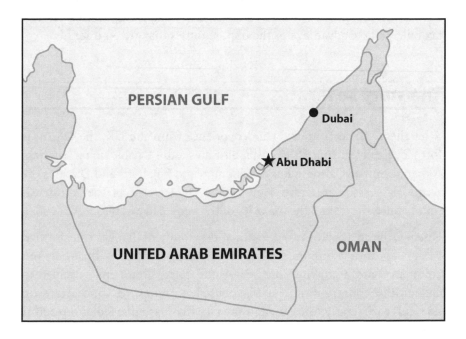

Dubai is the second largest of the seven Persian Gulf states that constitute the United Arab Emirates (UAE). The name Dubai also refers to the modern, highly developed and lively city with a prosperous business centre, high temperatures and coastal resorts that have attracted the wealthy from around the world. Visitor numbers are growing and extremely elaborate property developments look set to further establish Dubai city as a true gem of the Middle East.

Why invest in Dubai?

Dubai offers a virtually crime-free location, modern buildings and many business opportunities. The tax system has been a key incentive for foreign investors. With no Corporation Tax in the selected 'free zones', many overseas companies have chosen Dubai as a country in which to locate and expand their businesses.

In addition to this, the personal tax system in Dubai is extremely favourable for investors. This doesn't mean that the taxman in the UK will not want some of it, but with professional advice you can minimise your tax bill and take advantage of the opportunities that are on offer here.

The story so far...

After the 1971 declaration of independence from the UK, the UAE was formed. The UAE consists of seven emirates (Abu Dhabi, Dubai, Sharjah, Ajman, Umm al-Qaiwain, Ras al-Khaimah and Fujairah) and Dubai is the second largest by area after Abu Dhabi. 80 per cent of the country is uninhabited desert and the majority of the people live in the city of Dubai.

Dubai is the creation of two decades of development that has transformed what was once a minor port into a leading centre of business and commerce and a growing tourist hotspot. The ruling family decided to change the country from an oil-focused economy to concentrate on services, particularly tourism, and the city that has emerged as a result is remarkable.

Development is continuing at rapid pace with approximately 15 per cent of the world's cranes currently located in Dubai, making it the fastest growing city in the world. Each new development is more incredible than the last. The three Palm island developments, The World, and now the $14 billion development known as the Dubai Waterfront are amazing projects. The Waterfront project will be seven times larger than the island of Manhattan and add over 800 kilometres of coastline. The size of this development is difficult to overstate. The many man-made islands dotted with houses and hotels, 70 kilometres of canals, a new city centre and one of the world's tallest buildings will accommodate over 400,000 people in an area over 270 square kilometres. This will be packed with luxury hotels and resorts, including an underwater hotel, as well as shopping centres and entertainment venues.

Dubai offers a fantastic quality of life with modern medical services, excellent schools and outstanding shopping and entertainment facilities. The people at the leading edge of this rapid change describe it as the city where dreams come true. Will this be true for the jet-to-let investor?

Where is it?

The UAE is in the eastern part of the Arabian Peninsula. The country's total area is approximately 82,880km² and its neighbours are Saudi Arabia to the west and south, Qatar to the north and Oman to the east.

The UAE coastline is 1,318km along the southern coast of the Persian Gulf and for about 90km along the Gulf of Oman – an area known as the Al Batinah coast.

What is the weather like?

Dubai is a hotspot for more than property – summer temperatures often exceed 48°C. The climate is subtropical and arid and summers are extremely hot with high humidity near the coast. The temperature generally ranges from 20 to 35°C with an average night-time temperature of 15°C.

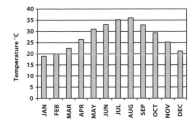
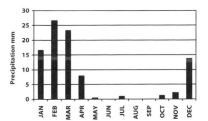

Language

The estimated population of the UAE in 2006 was over 2.6 million of which only about 20 per cent are thought to be UAE citizens. The remaining inhabitants are other Arabs, Iranians, South Asians, East Asians, Europeans and Americans.

The UAE is an Islamic country and its official language is Arabic. English is used as a second language in business. Persian, Hindi and Urdu are also spoken.

Currency

The currency across all of the UAE is the Dirham (AED), which is made up of 100 Fils. The Dirham is pegged to the US dollar at AED 3.671: US $1.

Politics

The UAE is a federation of seven emirates, each of which is ruled by a hereditary monarch. Individual emirates control their own economy and decide what to do with oil revenues, although a substantial amount goes towards the UAE central budget. The current President of the UAE is His Highness Sheikh Khalifa bin Zayed bin Sultan Al Nahayan, who acceded in 2004 and is also the ruler of Abu Dhabi. The Prime Minister and Vice President of the UAE, and ruler of Dubai since 2006, is His Highness Sheikh Mohammed bin Rashid Al Maktoum.

Dubai is similar to other gulf states in that it's dominated politically by ruling families, in this case the Al Maktoums, who hold all of the key positions in the city state's government. The Al Maktoums are largely popular, as Dubai has experienced exceptional prosperity since the 1970s under their rule. This is due not only to the discovery of oil but also to the phenomenal development of recent years.

There are no political parties or voting rights within the UAE, no Income Tax and the standard of living is high.

The UAE has a form of Assembly known as the Federal National Council. (FNC). Steps towards greater democracy have been taken with the announcement that FNC members will be elected.

The UAE was a founding member of the Gulf Co-Operation Council (GCC), created in 1981. Members of the GCC include Saudi Arabia, Kuwait, Bahrain, Qatar and the Sultanate of Oman.

Economy

Historically, the UAE's economy has been largely financed by oil revenues.

To reduce dependence on oil export earnings, the government launched a strategy of economic diversification and, as a result, non-oil sectors now contribute more than 94 per cent of its national income (GDP). Dubai's contribution to the UAE's overall economy is about 29 per cent.

Other strong sectors have been financial services, construction, trade, technology and communications and tourism. The Emirate has established free trade zones to boost investment and more are in the pipeline. Dubai's economy is booming and its current rate of economic growth is among the best in the world.

Tourism

Tourism remains an important economic activity in Dubai and all across the rest of the UAE. The country has made considerable investments by constructing world-class hotels, leisure facilities, restaurants and motorways.

Some 6.2 million tourists visited Dubai in 2005, up about 14 per cent from the previous year. Hotel revenues were almost $9 billion in 2005. Tourism is forecast to continue expanding and Dubai plans to increase arrivals to 15 million by 2010. A new project is planned to expand Dubai's airport capacity to 70 million passengers per year by 2009.

Economic indicators

Economic growth

In 2005, the UAE's economy grew by 6.5 per cent and the GDP per capita was $29,100. Economic growth has been very robust over the last few years and between 2000 and 2005 real GDP averaged a remarkable 7.25 per cent. The Economist Intelligence Unit forecasts growth of 6.4 per cent in 2006. Dubai has now fully established itself as a regional hub for trade and finance.

Interest rates

Short-term interest rates in Dubai currently stand at 4.19 per cent.

Unemployment

According to the Ministry of Labour, the number of unemployed nationals has increased from 8,000 in 1995 to 35,000 in 2005. While the official unemployment rate is zero, the reality is that the rate is considerably higher for UAE nationals.

Inflation

The UAE has managed to keep inflation low in the last couple of years, despite expected rises. The rate of inflation was 4.5 per cent in 2005 and it's forecast to drop slightly in 2006.

Foreign direct investment (FDI)

The UAE government understands the importance of FDI and established free trade zones in an attempt to attract large international businesses. Presently, the UAE (particularly Dubai) is home to many large information technology and media companies such as Microsoft, Compaq, IBM, CNN and Reuters.

Currently, there are 15 'Free Zones' in force in the UAE and 12 more are planned. The UAE Free Zones, which allow 100 per cent foreign ownership and tax exemptions on all company earnings and private income, are home to approximately 5,000 companies.

Foreign direct investment in the UAE (billion US dollars)

2000	2001	2002	2003	2004	2005
0.5	1.2	3.5	4.3	10.0	11.3

Source: Central Bank of the UAE

Economic summary

There is no doubting the huge economic advances made in Dubai over the last five years and the FDI table above is a clear illustration of this. It's an attractive place to do business, fiscal policy (tax) is favourable and the government's free trade zones and grants are attracting big international companies. Dubai has managed strong economic growth with inflation under control. The growth story will continue as the country strives to take a dominant regional lead in information technology, financial services and tourism.

What does this mean for the property investor?

The property market is led by overseas property investors and expatriate workers. Property prices have risen dramatically over the last few years, driven in part by demand and lack of supply and in part by development companies raising prices. At this stage, the jury is out on Dubai for the jet-to-let investor as few investors are selling on the open market (rather than to other investors) so it's difficult to judge how long they take to sell and at what price.

There is no shortage of property in Dubai and the supply side of the price equation is certainly not inelastic. So getting in at the right price is crucial. Picking up a resale cheaply may offer more opportunity for a bargain than buying off-plan. As with all investments, you also need to have a clear exit strategy.

So, what is the catch?

Dubai has relatively few social issues in comparison to its Middle Eastern neighbours. Crime is virtually non-existent and the population is a glowing example of cultural harmony, but there are a few things to bear in mind:

Transport

According to the 2005 Gulf Traffic Survey, only 13 per cent of people using cars or public transport felt safe on the roads. Dubai's public transport system was rated bad or very poor by 74 per cent of users. Of all methods of transport, the abra (water taxi) was the most dependable with almost 86 per cent of users rating them as good or excellent.

Human rights

Labour issues in the construction sector have attracted the interest of human rights groups after workers from India and Pakistan caused $1 million worth of damage in riots in March 2006 in protest about low wages and poor conditions.

Terrorism

Although not presently an issue any investor who keeps an eye on world affairs will understand that Dubai, particularly given its Western leanings, is a possible future terrorist target. Investors must look at all potential risks when investing in any market and have a plan for all eventualities.

The property market

Property investment in Dubai first hit the headlines in 2002 when Sheikh Mohammed issued a decree allowing foreigners to buy freehold property in the country. Since then, prices in this new market have risen sharply, doubling in just three years.

One factor which has supported the property market in Dubai is the country's acceptance of other cultures. Dubai is one of the most popular overseas locations for expats and is the most westernised of UAE cities evidenced by the 100,000 Britons who live there out of a total population of just over one million.

The property market has developed because of:

- a fast growing economy;
- subdued inflation;
- strong employment opportunities;
- a very high demand for properties from investors and expatriates;
- the relaxing of the law allowing foreign freehold ownership of property.

More than 80 per cent of Dubai's inhabitants are foreign nationals, who work in the country under short-term contracts that are generally for one year. At current growth rates the economy needs more workers, which in turn increases the demand for rental property. Dubai's population growth is one of the highest in the world and it's projected to double to two million residents over the next few years.

While the demand for property still remains high, there has been little supply over the past four years, which has put a squeeze on rental demand and prices. Rents have risen by an average of 38 per cent in 2005 and this, together with new property rights for foreigners, has encouraged many to buy rather than rent. However, in November 2005, rental price increases were capped at 15 per cent until the end of 2006. The government is bridging the gap between the current shortage of supply and the completion of the huge amount of new property in late 2006 and 2007.

Research suggests that 85 per cent of off-plan apartments and 50 per cent of off-plan villas were bought in 2004 by speculators, most of whom intend to sell before completion. Some of the off-plan units are reported already to have been resold up to five times to other investors, despite delivery being a number of years away. Those investors have made a sizeable profit as property prices have risen up to 100 per cent before completion.

Supply and demand is the key concept in economics and property investing. So far, the see-saw favoured the high demand side allowing investors to make good profits, but supply is increasing fast. A huge number of large-scale residential building developments have been started which will release a massive number of units onto the market in the next few years, but even with the projected increase in population over the next four to five years it remains uncertain as to whether the demand will be sufficient to absorb this huge supply. It seems likely that the market and prices will cool as the mass of new developments comes on stream.

Property hotspots

It's fair to say that the whole city of Dubai could be viewed as a hotspot, and after considering the opportunities it presents, it's easy to see why it's such an attractive option for jet-to-let investors. The cost of property is generally cheap in comparison to Europe and the UK. Apartments in the less upmarket locations can be as little as $60,000 and villas are available for around $150,000. The majority of properties are bought off-plan, with continual construction of new apartment buildings ensuring a steady supply of opportunities.

In addition to Dubai's land reclamation projects at Dubai Waterfront, The World archipelago and the three Palm islands of Jumeira, Jebel Ali and Deira (the largest man-made offshore structures in the world), new developments planned include **International City** with its wide range of different architectural features and **Golf Towers**, which will be particularly appealing to the golfing fraternity. **Dubailand** will be the biggest theme park with 45 different projects plus 8,000 properties with a broad range of prices, starting as low as $55,000.

Some of the more expensive apartments in the new **Sports City** development (scheduled for completion in 2008) are currently selling from $100,000 to $500,000. At the high end of the market are apartments within the world's tallest tower, the **Burj Dubai**. Prices go up to $700,000 and are set to increase during the construction phase. In **Marina Terrace**, this figure rises to $1 million, with **Jumeirah Beach** highest at a maximum price of around $1.8 million, while properties on the three Palm projects and in The World command prices from $10 to $38 million.

The buying process

The new law introduced in February 2006 has made it possible for foreigners to own the freehold title to property but only in specially selected areas. Non-residents are permitted to buy plots through a contract with one of three developers owned by the Dubai government – Emaar, Nakheel and Dubai Real Estate.

Purchasing a property in Dubai is a lot simpler than it may seem at first glance. A buyer is required to sign an agreement with a developer to pay the property price with all transaction costs. The developer then submits a letter to the Dubai Lands and Properties Department on behalf of the buyer, stating that all payments have been completed. Only after this letter has been accepted will the property be registered in the buyer's name. This purchase transaction will likely involve a deposit payment on signing the contract and the balance on completion. If you trade the contract before completion (i.e. sell the property), the developer is likely to charge a fee, so make sure that you know how much this is likely to be before signing the contract.

The majority of British investors in Dubai invest off-plan. In essence, the contract for sale outlines the terms and conditions of the agreement and in particular details what you have bought, when it will be ready, at what price and how you will pay. Clearly, in a fast growing market such as this, many speculators have made a considerable amount of money by following the principles of gearing in rising markets.

The alternative to this is the resale market, which is growing considerably. You can find properties in Dubai on the internet and through newspaper advertisements which are often being sold by speculators who bought off-plan some time ago. If you have your heart set on a holiday home in Dubai, then this may be a route to research, as investors who are keen to sell may be prepared to negotiate on the price. After some research on the market, you will find yourself in a strong negotiating position, particularly if the property has been on the resale market for some time.

Transaction costs

The following transaction costs are typical:

- **Mortgages** – presently local lenders are charging around one to two per cent of the total value of the loan as a processing fee.

- **Legal fees** – usually about two per cent.

- **Taxes** – when the Dubai Lands Department registers the title, buyers will pay a tax that is equivalent to 1.5 per cent of the purchase price of the property and if you have a mortgage, you will pay 0.25 per cent of the value of the loan.

Annual costs

There are no annual property taxes in Dubai, but service charges and maintenance costs can come up to one per cent of the property price.

Taxes

Dubai is virtually tax free. There is no income, withholding or Capital Gains Tax and, with the exception of banks and oil companies, no Corporation Tax is payable by companies. The taxes imposed in Dubai include import duties (mostly at rates up to ten per cent), a five per cent residential tax assessed on rental value, and a five per cent tax on hotel services and entertainment.

Dubai contains a number of economic 'free zones', with various economic incentives to encourage investment and commercial development.

Summary

Strengths

- Presently a stable political system.

- No tax.

- No annual property taxes.

- Cultural tolerance.

- Large international community.

- English widely spoken.

- Relatively low prices.

- All-year-round climate.

- Low interest rates.

- All-year-round climate for short-term lets.

- Growing population and requirement for accommodation which has a positive effect on rents and prices.

Weaknesses

- Not a democracy.
- Poor public transport.
- Flying time from UK (six hours).
- Human rights issues.
- Potential oversupply of property.
- The resale market is yet to be tested.
- It can be too hot in the summer!

Opportunities

- Development of Dubai as a regional centre for business and finance.
- Development of world-class tourist facilities.
- Opportunity to relocate any business interests due to the favourable tax regime.
- Huge choice of good quality property.

Threats

- Terrorism.
- Islamic fundamentalism.
- Oversupply of property as expansion continues unchecked.
- Is the rental demand sufficient for the number of properties and do expats buy or rent?
- Change of leadership/government in the country; will this make a difference to how westerners are accepted?

Comment

Dubai is very much flavour of the month and what is happening there is truly amazing and a real testament to the vision, foresight and energy of the rulers. It's a happening place and I'm convinced that Dubai will achieve its goal of being a regional hub for business and tourism.

Speculators have made big money in Dubai as apartments have changed hands three or four times before construction – it has the feel of the Klondike Gold Rush of the late 19th century.

Like all of the countries featured in *The Jet-to-Let Bible*, you have to conduct your own due diligence and research and not be influenced by glossy marketing brochures and the prospect of making big money.

Good profits can be made by the savvy investor now and in the future, but like all investments which are 'hot' and potentially speculative, just make sure that you are not the one holding the parcel when the music stops.

Facts at a glance

Geography	
Population	UAE: 2,602,713 (2006 estimate) Dubai: 1,070,779 (2004 estimate)
Language	Arabic
Ethnic groups	Emirati Arabs, other Arabs, Iranians, South Asians, East Asians, Europeans, Americans
Local currency	UAE Dirham divided into 100 Fils

Political system	
Political structure	Federation of seven emirates with hereditary monarchs
Head of State for UAE	President Sheikh Khalifa bin Zayed bin Sultan Al Nahayan

Prime Minister and Head of State for Dubai	Sheikh Mohammed bin Rashid Al Maktoum

Economy, UAE

Unemployment rate in 2001	2.4%
Unemployment rate, February 2006	N/A
Inflation rate in 2005	4.5%
Inflation rate, February 2006	N/A
Interest rate in Dirham, March 2006	4.19%
GDP growth in 2005	6.5%
GDP growth forecast for 2006	6.4%
GDP per capita (income per person) in 2005	$29,100

Taxation

Income Tax	0%
Corporation Tax	0%
Capital Gains Tax	0%

Corruption statistics

Corruption rate	6.2
Corruption rank	30th

Industry and technology

Major industries	Petroleum and petrochemicals Aluminium Construction materials Tourism

The Dubai property market

Hotspots	City of Dubai

Property taxes (transactions)

Processing fees	1–2%
Legal fees	2%
Land registration	1.5%
Total costs	3–5%

Property taxes (annual)

Annual taxes	0%
Maintenance costs	Vary

Mortgage

LTV	60–80%
Currency	US dollar and UAE Dirham
Maximum term	25 years
Current interest rate	6.00–6.95%

Investor resources

Embassies

British Embassy in the UAE

22 Khalid bin Al Waleed Street
PO Box 248
Abu Dhabi

Tel: +971 2610 1100
Fax: +971 2610 1586
Website: www.britishembassy.gov.uk

UAE Embassy in the UK

30 Princes Gate
London SW7 1PT

Tel: 020 7581 1281
Fax: 020 7581 9616
Website: www.uaeembassyuk.net

Useful websites

Central Bank of the UAE
www.centralbank.ae

Dubai News
www.dubai.com

National Bank of Dubai
www.nbd.com

Tourism in Dubai
www.dubaitourism.ae

UAE Federal Government Portal
www.government.ae

UAE News
www.uaeinteract.com

The Eastern European 8: the Czech Republic, Estonia, Hungary, Latvia, Lithuania, Poland, Slovakia & Slovenia

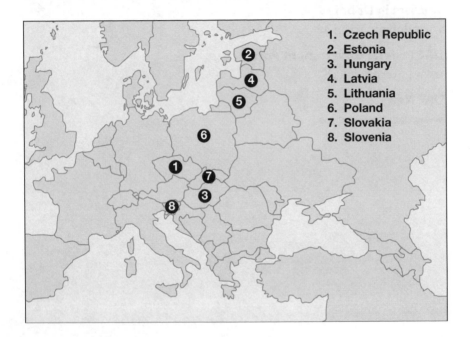

1. Czech Republic
2. Estonia
3. Hungary
4. Latvia
5. Lithuania
6. Poland
7. Slovakia
8. Slovenia

The Eastern European 8 consists of Czech Republic, Estonia, Hungary, Latvia, Lithuania, Poland, Slovakia and Slovenia. These countries, with Cyprus and Malta, joined the European Union (EU) on 1 May 2004. EU accession has increased the viability of these countries for overseas property investors as these countries leave behind the last echoes of Communism to become enterprising political democracies.

The Czech Republic

The story so far...

The Czech Republic is one of the most stable countries in Eastern Europe. Communist rule came to an end in 1989 and in 1993, the country of Czechoslovakia was split into the independent nation states of the Czech Republic and Slovakia. A recession in the late 1990s slowed the country's economic growth, but foreign direct investment (FDI) and EU exports have since helped to make it one of the most successful post-Communist states in Eastern Europe.

Where is it?

The Czech Republic has borders with Poland to the north and Germany to the north-west. The country also shares borders with Slovakia to the east and Austria to the south. The Czech Republic is divided into two geographic and cultural regions, Bohemia and Moravia, which have a combined territory of 78,866km².

What is the weather like?

Summers are moderately warm with temperatures rising during July and August. The weather in the spring is usually changeable and can swap from sun to snow very quickly and spring and summer are the wettest seasons. Winters are generally cold and wet, sometimes with snowfall and temperatures below freezing point.

Prague

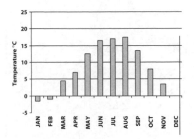 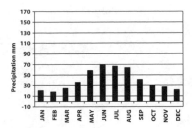

Language

The Czech Republic has an estimated population of 10,241,138, mainly consisting of Czechs (90.4 per cent), Moravians, Poles and Slovaks. The official language is Czech, spoken by the majority of the population, but other spoken languages include Polish, Hungarian, German and English.

Currency

The currency in the Czech Republic is the Ceska Koruna or Czech Crown (CZK), divided into 100 Halers. The Czech Republic is presently forecast to adopt the euro on 1 January 2010.

Politics

The Czech Republic is a parliamentary democracy, with a President as Head of State. In 2003, Václav Klaus was elected President of the Czech Republic and continues to serve in this post. Klaus leads the right-wing

Civic Democratic Party and previously served as a Prime Minister until 1997. He launched ambitious economic reforms, notably through privatisation and a pro-western foreign policy.

Following the 2002 parliamentary elections, the centre-left parties gained a small majority, forming a coalition government. The main parties are the Czech Socialist Party (CSSD) and the Civic Democratic Party (ODS). The Czech Republic's Prime Minister is Jirí Paroubek, elected in 2005.

Economy

After a period of political and economic crisis that ended in the separation of the Czech and Slovak Republics, the Czech government went ahead with a series of economic reforms. The country soon gained a standing as one of the most steady and prosperous of the post-Communist states.

Manufacturing is the main source of economic activity, most notably in the production of cars. Other industries that contribute significantly to the Czech economy include iron and steel, electronics and chemicals.

The Czech Republic continues to attract companies looking for less expensive labour than in the other more mature Western economies such as Germany. Companies such as Toyota, Peugeot, Skoda and Bosch have all capitalised on using an Eastern European labour force to get work done to the same standard at lower costs. More recently, Hyundai has announced plans for a €1 billion car plant to be built in the Moravia-Silesia region which will produce 300,000 cars each year and employ 2,000 people. This will be the biggest foreign investment in the history of the Czech Republic and it's estimated that it will boost its gross domestic product (GDP) by an impressive 1.3 per cent. At this point, the final agreement has yet to be signed, but even plans on this scale illustrate that large and successful companies are attracted to the opportunities present in the country.

Economic indicators

Economic growth

The European Commission reports that real GDP in Czech Republic is expected to grow by 4.4 per cent in 2006, after growing at 6.0 per cent in 2005. Real growth statistics for the past six years are presented in the table below.

Year	2000	2001	2002	2003	2004	2005
Real growth of GDP (%)	3.9	2.6	1.5	3.7	4.0	6.0

Source: Eurostat, the Statistical Office of the European Communities

The Czech Republic's GDP per capita is €17,100 according to 2005 estimates.

Inflation

The annual inflation rate was 1.6 per cent in 2005 and this was caused mainly by an increase in fuel and gas prices.

Interest rates

Central Bank interest rates are two per cent (March 2006) and Czech rates are expected to remain below the European Central Bank (ECB) rate for the next 12 months.

Unemployment

Unemployment has not changed much over the last five years and still remains at nearly eight per cent. Serious structural problems remain in the labour market, such as continuing long-term unemployment and marked regional differences in employment opportunities.

Unemployment rate (percentage unemployed)

2000	2001	2002	2003	2004	2005
8.7	8.0	7.3	7.8	8.3	7.9

Source: Eurostat, the Statistical Office of the European Communities

Foreign direct investment (FDI)

The introduction of financial incentives in the late 1990s has encouraged a substantial inflow of FDI and throughout the pre-EU period, the country received more FDI per capita than any of the other Eastern European 8 countries. The government has moved quickly to modernise the economy and adopt EU standard practices, which continues to be rewarded by foreign companies having the confidence to invest considerable sums of money.

The highest percentage of FDI goes into financial and manufacturing sectors, in industries such as car manufacturing, software development, engineering products and electronic goods.

Foreign direct investment in the Czech Republic (€ million)

1999	2000	2001	2002	2003	2004	2005
5,932.8	5,403.5	6,296.0	9,012.4	1,862.7	3,595.5	5,233.2

Source: Czech National Bank

The property market

Czech property prices have risen constantly since 1991, but they are still lower than in Western Europe. This gap in prices will shrink dramatically as the Czech Republic becomes wealthier.

Despite the property boom, foreigners currently represent only about one to two per cent of buying activity in the property sector. Demand from investors at this stage is not affecting the whole market, particularly outside of the capital Prague.

The property market is also fuelled by increasing tourism. The number of arrivals to the Czech Republic is expected to double by 2010 to reach 14 million visitors per annum. Growth is expected to be stimulated by EU membership, the development of the regions, the rise of low-cost air travel and growing demand for short breaks. Currently, 90 per cent of tourists visit only Prague, but this percentage is expected to fall due to growing interest in other parts of the country.

Property hotspots

As it's the capital city, it's unsurprising that **Prague** is the Czech Republic's prime jet-to-let investment destination. Economic activity in Prague is high and the city has almost no unemployment. It's also the top Czech tourist destination and property prices reflected these factors when they rose by 15 per cent last year. Prices and rents are higher in the centre of Prague and fall the further out you go. Prices in the city centre are in the region of €18,00 to €4,000 per square metre falling to €1,000 to €2,400 per square metre in outlying districts.

Brno is the country's second largest city and an ever-growing European business hub, making new-build apartments the investor's first choice. As an example, a two-bedroom apartment currently costs in the region of €60,000–75,000. Brno and several other Czech towns have beautiful rural houses and ski-chalets which offer opportunities as live-and-let investments. Property prices are cheaper than Prague and rental yields can be in double digits.

Transaction costs

Buying a property in the Czech Republic is fairly straightforward. There are certain restrictions on foreign ownership and, unless the buyers have permanent residency in the country, foreign nationals can only buy a property if they establish a limited liability company (known as an SRO in the Czech Republic). Foreigners are still not permitted to buy forest or agricultural land and these restrictions will remain in force until 2009.

When choosing a property, the buyer should check whether it's being sold with private or collective ownership, which usually applies to apartments in old-style blocks that date from Communist times. Ideally, the property would be sold with private ownership, free of any loans, but your lawyer should confirm this before you make an offer.

When signing the preliminary contract the buyer pays a deposit which is usually around 10–20 per cent of the total price. The rest of the payment is made when signing the final contract and the buyer then becomes the legal owner after the contract and relevant documentation have been lodged with the Land Registry. This process can take up to several months, so it's normal for a buyer to leave the completion monies in either a notarial or escrow account until the purchase is legalised and completed.

The overall expenses are as follows:

- **Transfer Tax** is charged at a rate of three per cent of the sale price of the property or the usual market price, depending on which figure is higher. It's paid by the seller, but the buyer becomes liable for this tax in the event that the seller doesn't pay.

- **Legal expenses** vary – typical costs are up to €2,000 including the incorporation of an SRO.

- **Notary fees** are in the region of €300–400.

- **Estate agents' fees** come to three to six per cent.

You should allow up to eight per cent of the purchase price for taxes and fees.

Annual costs

At the moment, annual tax rates are low, but they may rise in the future.

- **Property Tax** is charged on an annual basis depending on the value of the property. It's calculated by special evaluation rules which depend on the use of the property, where it's located and several other factors. For a large two-bedroom apartment the annual amount should not exceed €50.

- **Land Tax** is imposed on plots of land entered in the Land Register and is payable by the owner.

Taxes

Income Tax

Individual Income Tax rates in 2006:

Tax	Annual tax base (CZK)
15%	0–109,200
20%	109,201–218,400
25%	218,401–331,200
32%	331,201 and over

Corporation Tax

Corporation Tax is charged at a rate of 24 per cent.

Capital Gains Tax

Capital gains are taxed as income for companies and individuals. Individuals are exempt from the sale of a main residence which has been held for at least two years.

Facts at a glance

Geography	
Population (2005 estimate)	10,241,138
Language	Czech
Ethnic groups	Czech (90.4%). Minority groups include Moravians, Poles and Slovaks, which form the largest ethnic minorities
Local currency	Ceska Koruna or Czech Crown divided into 100 Halers

Political system	
Political structure	Parliamentary democracy
President	Václav Klaus
Prime Minister	Jirí Paroubek
Main parties	Civic Democratic Party (ODS) Socialist Party (CSSD)

Economy	
Unemployment rate in 2005	7.9%
Unemployment rate, February 2006	7.7%
Inflation rate in 2005	1.6%
Inflation rate, February 2006	2.4%

Interest rate, March 2006	2.0%
GDP growth in 2005	6.0%
GDP growth forecast for 2006	4.4%
GDP per capita (income per person) in 2005	€17,100

Taxation

Income Tax	15–32%
Corporation Tax	24%
Capital Gains Tax	Taxed as income

Corruption statistics

Corruption rate	4.3
Corruption rank	47th

Industry and technology

Major industries	Machinery and equipment Motor vehicles Glass

The Czech property market

Hotspots	Prague, Brno

Property taxes (transactions)

Transfer Tax	3%
Notary fees	€300–400
Estate agents' fees	3–6%
Legal fees	€2,000
Total fees	8%

Property taxes (annual)

Property Tax	Negligible
Land Tax	Negligible

Mortgage	
LTV	50–85%
Term	5–25 years
Currency	Czech Koruna only
Current interest rate	3.5–5.0%

Investor resources

Embassies

British Embassy in the Czech Republic

Thunovska 14
118 00 Prague 1
Czech Republic

Tel: +420 257 402 111
Fax: +402 257 402 296
Website: www.britain.cz

Embassy of the Czech Republic in the UK

26–30 Kensington Palace Gardens
London W8 4QY

Tel: 020 7243 1115
Fax: 020 7727 9654
Website: www.mzv.cz/wwwo/?zu=london

Useful websites

Czech National Bank
www.cnb.cz

Czech Statistical Office
www.czso.cz

Invest in Czech Republic
www.czechinvest.org

Tourism in Czech Republic
www.czechtourism.com

Estonia

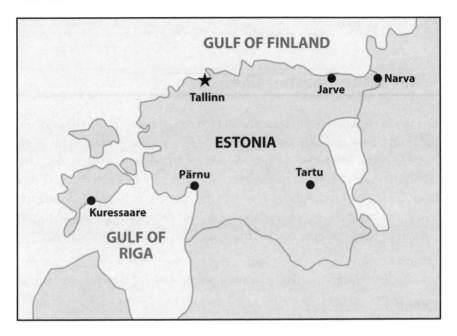

The story so far...

Estonia became a sovereign state in 1918, but after occupation by German forces from 1941 to 1944 it was again annexed by the Soviet Union in the aftermath of the Second World War.

In 1989, Estonians, Latvians and Lithuanians joined hands in a human chain that ran from Tallinn through Riga to Vilnius. This was a symbol of the desire for independence in the Baltics which was finally granted in 1991 and the fall of the USSR is still celebrated as a holiday in Estonia. Since then, the Baltic States have sought closer ties with the West, implemented economic reforms, including privatisation, while keeping inflation and unemployment relatively under control.

Where is it?

The Republic of Estonia borders Latvia to the south and Russia to the east. The country is separated from Finland in the north by the Gulf of Finland.

The Estonian coastline is 3,794km long and the country has more than 1,500 islands, with Saaremaa and Hiiumaa being the largest. Estonia has 45,226km² of territory.

What is the weather like?

Estonia is slightly colder than the surrounding countries because of its proximity to the Baltic Sea. The climate is relatively mild with high humidity and persistent winds. Summers are warm and winters are relatively mild compared to the average for countries located across this latitude. It rains throughout the year but rainfall is heaviest in August. Snow is usual in the winter and the cover lasts for approximately 80 to 100 days from the beginning of December through to the end of March.

Estonia has long hours of daylight in the summer (the longest summer day lasts up to 19 hours), and dark winters when daylight lasts just six hours.

Tallinn

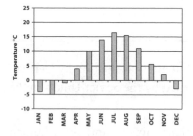 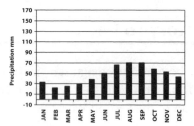

Language

Estonia has an estimated population of 1.33 million people consisting mainly of ethnic Estonian (68 per cent) and Slavic minorities, divided into Russian (26 per cent), Ukrainian (two per cent) and Belarus (one per cent). The country's official language is Estonian, spoken by 68 per cent of the population. The ethnic minorities predominantly speak Russian and Finnish, while English and German are also widely spoken and understood as second languages.

Currency

The Estonian currency is the Kroon (EEK) divided into 100 Cents. Estonia is aiming to adopt the euro in January 2007, although this date may be later due to Estonia not fulfilling the economic criteria set by the European Union (EU). The Kroon is pegged to the euro at EEK 15.646: € 1.

Politics

Estonia is a democratic parliamentary republic. The current government coalition is made up of the liberal right-wing Reform Party, the centre-left Centre Party and the conservative People's Union. Estonia's current President is Arnold Rüütel, elected in 2001. The current Prime Minister is Andrus Ansip, elected in 2005.

After independence in 1991, the Estonian government created the circumstances for rapid economic growth by instigating radical political and economic reforms. This paid off and Estonia quickly became a stable country.

Estonia is known for having the world's first electronic government and conducts its proceedings using a web-based system. Almost everything administratively is accessible online, making it one of the most open governments in the world. Voting via the internet is also something that has been tried in local elections and is set to allow much of the population to vote electronically in the national elections that will follow.

Economy

The newly independent Estonia has accepted and pursued the vision of a free market economy. Estonia abolished all barriers to trade and also fully opened the economy to foreign investment, ensuring that foreign and domestic investors were treated the same. Additionally, the Estonian government launched a radical privatisation programme and other effective measures included the introduction of its own currency and a flat-rate Income Tax. Following this Estonia's gross domestic product (GDP) grew a massive 11.4 per cent in 1997!

Estonia's economic development continued from 2000 onwards, with GDP growing at an astonishing rate. The modern Estonian economy has relatively low inflation, low levels of unemployment and strong FDI. Estonia has been referred to in the press as the Hong Kong of Europe. In 2005, the Global Growth Competitive Index placed Estonia 20th of 104 countries, above any other Eastern European country and, ironically, above Hong Kong!

Economic indicators

Economic growth

Estonia's economy continues to grow at a remarkable rate. The European Commission reports that Estonia's GDP is expected to grow by 7.2 per cent in 2006 after achieving an impressive 9.8 per cent in 2005. Estonia's GDP per capita is €13,000, according to a 2005 estimate.

Year	2000	2001	2002	2003	2004	2005
Real growth of GDP (%)	7.9	6.5	7.2	6.7	7.8	9.8

Source: Eurostat, the Statistical Office of the European Communities

Inflation

Inflation increased to 4.1 per cent in 2005, caused mainly by an increase in fuel prices, transport, clothing and housing costs, but it's forecast to fall to just over three per cent by the end of 2006.

Interest rates

The interest rate in March 2006 is 2.9 per cent.

Unemployment

Unemployment rose to its highest in 2000, but since then it has been progressively falling. Unfortunately, this is hampered by high levels of regional unemployment, especially in the north, although in 2005 unemployment decreased throughout the country and reached its lowest level since 1993.

Unemployment rate (percentage unemployed)

2000	2001	2002	2003	2004	2005
12.5	11.8	9.5	10.2	9.2	7.9

Source: Eurostat, the Statistical Office of the European Communities

Foreign direct investment (FDI)

Estonia recently became one of the leaders in Central and Eastern Europe in terms of FDI per capita. There have been speedy advances in privatisation and in stabilising and reshaping its economy. Other advantages include a stable currency, liberal economic policies, free trade and an excellent and improving climate for business.

Companies that are partly or fully owned by foreigners account for 33 per cent of Estonian GDP and over 50 per cent of the country's exports. Foreign investment is forecast to increase further.

Foreign direct investment in Estonia (€ million)

1999	2000	2001	2002	2003	2004
284.2	424.6	602.6	306.7	822.2	837.9

Source: Estonian National Bank

The property market

Property prices have been rising by an average of 15 per cent since 1995 and peaked in the run-up to EU membership. However, according to a report from the Royal Institute of Chartered Surveyors (RICS), property prices in Estonia grew 28 per cent in 2005, which was faster than anywhere else in the whole of the EU.

The demand for new-build apartments remains strong and the bulk of developments continue to sell off-plan. Property prices are forecast to continue rising by five to ten per cent per annum for the next five to ten years.

Property hotspots

Tallinn is the medieval capital of Estonia, a key harbour and a centre of business and commerce. It receives 81 per cent of all of the country's FDI and is the focus for the majority of jet-to-let investors. Property prices in Tallinn rose by 153 per cent between 1998 and 2004 and in the last two years they have risen by 50 per cent in the most popular districts. Property in Estonia is still cheaper than the EU average and the neighbouring Baltic state of Latvia.

The rental market remains strong around Tallinn and while outlying apartments mainly attract local families or students as tenants, those in the centre are mainly tenanted by the growing number of foreign corporate or diplomatic workers. Other investment options to consider include coastal properties and **Pärnu** continues to appeal with increased local interest and new projects planned to develop holiday homes and leisure activities. Prices on the coast are not much cheaper than Tallinn.

Transaction costs

There are no restrictions on foreign ownership in Estonia. The ownership of land can be transferred to a foreigner or a foreign company providing you have permission from the County Governor.

The process of buying a property is well established and straightforward. Buying off-plan houses and apartments is the most common method of buying a property. The alternative of old Soviet-style apartments have high renovation costs in order to bring them up to modern standards.

When buying off-plan, the developers normally require a non-refundable deposit of 10–20 per cent of the price at the time the preliminary contract is signed. The construction period is usually 12–18 months. The final balance is payable on completion.

Transaction costs are relatively low. There are no transfer taxes or stamp duties in Estonia. Notaries, rather than solicitors, typically oversee the transfer of ownership.

Purchase expenses are:

- **Registration fee:** When new-build apartments are purchased, there is a fee of up to 0.5 per cent of the transaction value to register the property at the Land Registry.

- **Notary fees** are based on the price of the property and on average are about 0.5–1.0 per cent of the purchase price.

- **Estate agents' fees** are almost always included in the sales price of the property. There is no standard commission, but they often range between three and seven per cent and are normally split between the buyer and the seller.

- **Legal fees** will cost in the region of £150–£300, depending on the length of the contract.

- **Other additional expenses** may include a translation of the contract and you should allow around £70 for this.

Total costs come to about four to six per cent of the purchase price.

Annual costs

The cost of living in Estonia remains lower than the European average but has been rising steadily. Annual operating costs for running a property are summarised below:

- **Land Tax.** The local authority decides the rate of Land Tax, which varies from 0.1 to 2.5 per cent of the value.

- **Maintenance costs** cover heating, utilities and maintenance of communal areas and vary according to the type of property.

Taxes

Income Tax
A flat rate of 23 per cent is charged on income earned in 2006.

Corporation Tax
The standard rate of Corporation Tax is 23 per cent in 2006.

It's important to note that the flat rate of Income and Corporation Tax will be reduced to 22 per cent in 2007, 21 per cent in 2008 and to 20 per cent in 2009.

Capital Gains Tax
In most cases, capital gains in Estonia are taxed as income for individuals and companies. Individuals are exempt from Capital Gains Tax on the sale of their main residence.

Facts at a glance

Geography	
Population (2005 estimate)	1,332,893
Language	Estonian
Ethnic groups	Estonian (67.9%). Ethnic minority groups include Russian (25.6%), Ukrainian (2.1%) and Belarus (1.3%)
Local currency	Kroon (EEK) divided into 100 Cents

Political system	
Political structure	Democratic parliamentary republic
President	Arnold Rüütel
Prime Minister	Andrus Ansip

Main parties	Estonian Centre Party
	Estonian Reform Party

Economy

Unemployment rate in 2005	7.9%
Unemployment rate, February 2006	5.9%
Inflation rate in 2005	4.1%
Inflation rate, February 2006	4.5%
Interest rate, March 2006	2.9%
GDP growth in 2005	9.8%
GDP growth forecast for 2006	7.2%
GDP per capita (income per person) in 2005	€13,000

Taxation

Income Tax	23%
Corporation Tax	23%
Capital Gains Tax	Taxed as income

Corruption statistics

Corruption rate	6.4
Corruption rank	27th

Industry and technology

Major industries	Engineering
	Electronics
	Wood and wood products
	Information technology

The Estonian property market

Hotspots	Tallinn, Pärnu

Property taxes (transactions)

Registration fee	0.5%
Notary fees	0.5–1%
Estate agents' fees	3–7%
Legal expenses	£150–300
Total fees	4–6%

Property taxes (annual)

Land Tax	0.1–2.5%

Mortgage

LTV	70–85%
Term	Up to 30 years
Currency	Euros, Estonian Kroons and US dollars
Current interest rate	3.5–4.5% in euros

Investor resources

Embassies

British Embassy in Estonia
Wismari 6
10136 Tallinn, Estonia

Tel: +372 667 4700
Fax: +372 667 4756
Website: www.britishembassy.gov.uk/estonia

Estonian Embassy in the UK
16 Hyde Park Gate
London SW7 5DG

Tel: 020 7589 3428
Fax: 020 7589 3430
Website: www.estonia.gov.uk

Useful websites

Bank of Estonia
www.eestipank.info

Estonian Statistics
www.stat.ee

Invest in Estonia
www.investinestonia.com

Tourism in Estonia
www.visitestonia.com
www.tourism.ee

Hungary

The story so far...

Hungary gained independence in 1918 following the collapse of the Austro-Hungarian Empire. In the Second World War Hungary fought alongside Germany and after defeat, it became part of the Soviet bloc.

Hungary's transition to a Western-style democracy was the first and the smoothest of the former Communist states and the Republic of Hungary was established in 1989. Since then, the country has made considerable progress in terms of political democracy and economic growth, successfully taking control of inflation and unemployment to become a leading destination for foreign investment in Eastern Europe. Hungary joined NATO in 1999 and the European Union (EU) in 2004.

Where is it?

Hungary has borders with Slovakia in the north, Ukraine in the north-east, Romania in the east, Croatia, Serbia and Montenegro in the south, Slovenia in the south-east and Austria in the east. The total territory is 93,030km².

What is the weather like?

Summer or winters may differ significantly from one year to the next. Summers tend to be warm from June to August and winters are cold and with lots of snow. Spring and early summer are the wettest seasons with regular thunderstorms.

Budapest

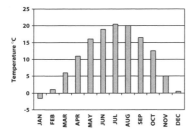 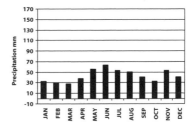

Language

Hungary has an estimated population of just over 10 million people, consisting mainly of ethnic Hungarians (92 per cent). Other groups include Germans, Roma, Slovak and Romanians. The official language is Hungarian, spoken by 94 per cent of the population with German as the most common second language, although English is becoming popular.

Currency

The currency is the Forint (HUF), which is equal to 100 Filler. Hungary is forecast to adopt the euro in January 2010. The Forint is pegged to the euro at HUF 282.36: € 1.

Politics

Politics is dominated by the centre-right Hungarian Civic Party (also known as Fidesz) and the centre-left Hungarian Socialist Party (MSZP).

Hungary is a parliamentary democracy. The present coalition government consists of the liberal Alliance of Free Democrats and Hungarian Socialist Party. László Sólyom is the President of Hungary, elected in 2005. The current Prime Minister is Ferenc Gyurcsány, elected in 2004.

Economy

Hungary has completed the transformation from being state run to a free market economy fairly quickly. The economy has been comprehensively liberalised due to a systematic and successful policy of privatisation, with a flow of high levels of foreign direct investment (FDI) and the creation of a wide-ranging set of commercial laws.

The country swapped trading partners in the early 1990s from its post-Soviet neighbours to the West. This was not without some initial pain but has proven successful in the long run. Hungary's main exports to the EU are high-quality manufactured products, such as cars and electrical goods.

Economic indicators

Economic growth

The European Commission reports that the real gross domestic product (GDP) in Hungary is expected to grow by 3.9 per cent in 2006. Hungary's GDP per capita was €14,500 in 2005. Economic growth has been steady over the last five years.

Year	2000	2001	2002	2003	2004	2005
Real growth of GDP (%)	5.2	3.8	3.5	2.9	4.2	4.3

Source: Eurostat, the Statistical Office of the European Communities

Inflation

Inflation was 3.5 per cent in 2005, the lowest achieved by Hungary throughout the transition period. Inflation was typically driven by high oil and producer prices.

Interest rates

The National Bank of Hungary's base rate in March 2006 was six per cent.

Unemployment

Unemployment in Hungary is below the EU average but started rising in 2005. The government has implemented a series of job creation initiatives in order to boost employment opportunities and has achieved some successes, particularly in reducing youth unemployment.

Unemployment rate (percentage unemployed)

2000	2001	2002	2003	2004	2005
6.3	5.6	5.6	5.8	6.0	7.2

Source: Eurostat, the Statistical Office of the European Communities

Foreign direct investment (FDI)

Since transforming to a market economy, Hungary has attracted a steady flow of FDI. Currently, foreign firms control 90 per cent of telecommunications, 66 per cent of manufacturing and 60 per cent of the energy sector.

The attractiveness of the country as a destination for FDI is enhanced by a low 16 per cent Corporation Tax and tax exemptions for some foreign investors. The high-tech sector has benefited from increasing FDI as the number of research and development companies relocating to Hungary has grown.

Foreign direct investment in Hungary (€ million)

1999	2000	2001	2002	2003	2004
3,106.3	2,998.4	4,390.7	3,185.1	1,909.0	2,948.0

Source: Bank of Hungary

The property market

Alongside the Czech Republic and Slovenia, Hungary is one of the most developed of the new European countries. The Hungarian property market is continually expanding, fuelled by high domestic demand, a growing number of jet-to-let investors and a dynamic expanding economy. Government subsidies for housing play a key role in promoting home ownership. As a result, Hungary has one of the highest levels of property ownership in Europe at 95 per cent.

Property prices grew 15–20 per cent between 2003 and 2005 and are forecast to grow at an annual rate of ten per cent until 2010, when Hungary is expected to adopt the euro.

Rental demand is strongest for studios and one- or two-bedroom apartments in central Budapest. Hungarians can also afford to buy and rent these properties, which provides an alternative market to the corporate, business or expatriate tenant. The expected average rental yields are five to seven per cent.

Property hotspots

Budapest, the capital, is a popular tourist destination and prosperous commercial centre that is also rich in architecture and heritage. For the typical jet-to-let property investor, this city offers a great entry point into the Hungarian property market, where prices are currently rising at an average annual rate of 15 per cent. Budapest is home to 20 per cent of Hungary's population and it's where the majority of business activities take place.

The most popular jet-to-let strategy in Budapest is buying new developments off-plan and either selling them on completion or letting them to the local market. Another option is to renovate older properties in central locations to let or sell them when they are completed. You will need to do lots of research on local suppliers, builders and surveyors as well as have the time to keep an eye on the project.

Every corner of Hungary can be reached by car from Budapest within two hours. Commentators are predicting that other major Hungarian towns and the countryside will follow the lead of Budapest and develop their own strong and dynamic jet-to-let markets.

Transaction costs

Foreign nationals can purchase any type of property freehold apart from agricultural land and the process of buying a property is relatively simple. If a foreign national is buying multiple properties as a private individual, then he must get a permit from the local Administration Office. This is an easy process, and takes two to three months to obtain, costing €350–€400.

Alternatively, incorporating a Hungarian company avoids the need to obtain a permit and allows investors to purchase as many properties as they wish.

In the Hungarian system it's a lawyer rather than a notary who acts as a representative of both parties. The lawyer prepares the preliminary contract, the buyer pays a ten per cent deposit and the remaining balance is paid on signing the contract.

If you buy an off-plan property, you will be required to make stage payments throughout the building process.

The transaction costs are:

- **Purchase Tax (stamp duty)** is calculated on a progressive rate between two and ten per cent, depending on the value and type of the project purchased. You are advised to take professional advice on which category your property is in before committing to the investment.

- **Legal fees** are about 1–1.5 per cent of the purchase price.

- **Notary fees** vary but usually come to one to two per cent of the purchase value.

- **Estate agents' fees** are three to five per cent of the purchase price.

Total purchase costs amount to about eight to ten per cent of the purchase price.

Annual costs

This is a tax imposed by a local authority on land and buildings.

- **Buildings** – to an upper limit of HUF 900 per square metre per annum, or 1.5 per cent of the market price.

- **Land** – to an upper limit of HUF 200 per square metre per annum, or 1.5 per cent of the market price.

- **Communal charges** come to approximately €350 per year, depending on the size of the property.

Taxes

Income Tax

Individual Income Tax rate in 2006:

Tax	Annual tax base (HUF)
18%	1,500,000
36%	1,500,001 and over

Corporation Tax

The rate of Corporation Tax is 16 per cent.

Capital Gains Tax

Capital gains of companies are generally taxed as income. The Capital Gains Tax rate for individuals is 25 per cent.

Facts at a glance

Geography

Population (2005 estimate)	10,006,835
Language	Hungarian
Ethnic groups	92.3% of ethnic Hungarians. Other ethnic minority communities include Germans, Roma, Slovak and Romanians
Local currency	Forint divided into 100 Filler

Political system

Political structure	Parliamentary democracy
President	László Sólyom
Prime Minister	Ferenc Gyurcsány
Main parties	Hungarian Civic Party (Fidesz) Hungarian Socialist Party (MSZP)

Economy

Unemployment rate in 2005	7.2%
Unemployment rate, February 2006	7.6%
Inflation rate in 2005	3.5%
Inflation rate, February 2006	2.3%
Interest rate, March 2006	6.0%
GDP growth in 2005	4.3%
GDP growth forecast for 2006	3.9%
GDP per capita (income per person) in 2005	€14,500

Taxation

Income Tax	18–36%
Corporation Tax	16%

Capital Gains Tax	25%

Corruption statistics

Corruption rate	5.0
Corruption rank	40th

Industry and technology

Major industries	Mining Metallurgy Construction materials Chemicals

The Hungarian property market

Hotspots	Budapest

Property taxes (transactions)

Stamp duty	Progressive rate from 2 to 10%
Notary fees	1–2%
Estate agents' fees	3–5%
Legal expenses	1–1.5%
Total fees	8–10%

Property taxes (annual)

Property Tax	Buildings – to an upper limit of HUF 900 per square metre per annum, or 1.5% of the market price Land – to an upper limit of HUF 200 per square metre per annum, or 1.5% of the market price Communal charges come to approximately €350 per year, depending on the size of the property

Mortgage	
LTV	50–70%
Term	1–20 years
Currency	Euro, pound sterling and Hungarian Forint
Current interest rate	4–6% in euros

Investor resources

Embassies

British Embassy in Hungary

1051 Budapest
Harmincad utca 6

Tel: +36 1266 2888
Fax: +36 1266 0907
Website: www.britishembassy.hu

Embassy of the Republic of Hungary in the UK

35B Eaton Place
London SW1X 8BY

Tel: 020 7201 3466
Fax: 020 7235 8630
Website: http://dspace.dial.pipex.com/huemblon/front.htm

Useful websites

Bank of Hungary
www.mnb.hu

Hungarian Central Statistical Office
http://portal.ksh.hu

Invest in Hungary
http://www.itdh.hu

Tourism in Hungary
www.hungarytourism.hu

Latvia

The story so far...

Latvia's strategic location on the Baltic coast led the country to be ruled by many peoples including the Germans, Poles, Swedes and Russians. It became a self-governing nation at the end of the First World War, but was annexed by the Soviet Union along with Estonia and Lithuania in 1940 as a result of a 'non-aggression' pact between Germany and the Soviet Union. Latvia gained independence in 1991 following the fall of Communism and has developed strong links with Western Europe. Latvia is now a successful member of the European Union (EU).

Where is it?

The Republic of Latvia borders Estonia to the north, Russia and Belarus to the east, Lithuania to the south with the Baltic Sea to the west. The coastline is 531km long and the country has a total area of 64,589km².

What is the weather like?

Latvia has long days in the summer and short days in the winter, with generally mild weather. The winter months bring snow that can remain until March, while rain is persistent and at its heaviest in the summer.

Riga

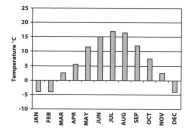 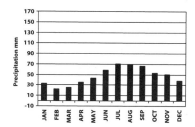

Language

Latvia has an estimated population of 2.3 million people, consisting of ethnic Latvians (58 per cent) and Slavic ethnic minorities including Russian (29 per cent), Belarusian (four per cent), Ukrainian (three per cent) and Polish (three per cent). The official language is Latvian, spoken by 58 per cent of the population. Russian is the most widespread minority language and English and German are also spoken as second languages.

Currency

The Latvian currency is the Lat (LVL), divided into 100 Santims. Latvia is set to adopt the euro on 1 January 2008, although this will possibly be delayed if the strict economic criteria are not met. The Lat is pegged to the euro at LVL 0.702: € 1.

Politics

Since gaining independence, Latvian politics has been undermined by frequent changes of government and cabinet reshuffles. Coalitions were unstable with many collapsing at early stages in their political lives. However, Latvia gained relative political stability in 1999 when politically independent Vaira Vike-Freiberga became President. Dr Vaira Vike-Freiberga is a well-respected academic, known for her energetic pursuit of EU and NATO membership and she remains the most popular politician in Latvia after re-election in 2003.

The Republic of Latvia is a parliamentary democracy. The present right-wing coalition government comprises the Conservative People's Party, the Union of Greens and Farmers, the First Party and the New Era Party. Aigars Kalvitis is the current Prime Minister, elected in 2004.

Economy

Latvia's economic reform has been steady and somewhat cautious. The unstable political situation in the 1990s limited the ability and mandate of the government to make the necessary reforms to enable the country to adopt a market economy.

The economy recovered in 2000, pushed by strong exports to the EU. Since then, annual economic growth has accelerated to its current level of over seven per cent, which is the highest growth rate in the EU. The amount of foreign investment has been growing, output is increasing and business confidence continues to pick up.

Economic indicators

Economic growth

The International Monetary Fund (IMF) notes that Latvia's economy has been one of the best performing among the EU accession countries. The European Commission reports that Latvia's gross domestic product (GDP) is expected to grow by 7.7 per cent in 2006. Real GDP grew by a whopping 10.2 per cent in 2005 and it reached 8.3 per cent in 2004. Real growth has been robust over the last five years See the table below.

Year	2000	2001	2002	2003	2004	2005
Real growth of GDP (%)	6.9	8.0	6.4	7.2	8.3	10.2

Source: Eurostat, the Statistical Office of the European Communities

Latvia's GDP per capita is €10,900, according to a 2005 estimate. Despite the highest GDP growth levels, Latvia's GDP per capita is still the lowest among the EU-25 countries.

Inflation

Those investors considering Latvia as a potential jet-to-let destination are advised to keep an eye on the rising inflation. It reached 6.9 per cent in 2005 – the highest since 1997.

Interest rates

Latvia's interest rates have been consistently declining. The short-term rate in March 2006 is 3.96 per cent.

Unemployment

Unemployment continues to fall gradually, reaching historically low levels, but remains higher than the EU average. Long-term unemployment has been cut by 50 per cent over the last five years.

Unemployment rate (percentage unemployed)

2000	2001	2002	2003	2004	2005
13.7	12.9	12.6	10.4	9.8	9.0

Source: Eurostat, the Statistical Office of the European Communities

Foreign direct investment (FDI)

Latvia's accession to the EU has improved its already friendly business climate. The country has managed to attract large sums of FDI, which is one of the powerful forces behind Latvia's great economic growth. In 2005, FDI accounted for about five per cent of GDP.

Foreign direct investment in Latvia (€ million)

1999	2000	2001	2002	2003	2004	2005
291.2	359.8	118.6	224.9	240.8	542.5	507.9

Source: Bank of Latvia

The property market

Latvia is one of the best performers in the EU and its economy is growing at a remarkable pace. Latvia has the highest real growth rate in Europe, low interest rates, a stable currency and a competitive mortgage sector.

Latvia's economic development has fuelled the property market. Since 1998 residential property prices have risen on average by 300 per cent, or 15–20 per cent per annum, and are expected to continue rising at this rate for the next ten years.

Currently, Latvians have one of the lowest GDP per capita rates in the EU, but this will soon change with the robust performance of the economy. Latvian banks are recording a record number of loans, but mortgages only account for 4.6 per cent of yearly GDP. Compared to the EU average of 48 per cent, mortgage lending has some room to grow! A developing mortgage market, increased local and jet-to-let demand for properties and still quite moderate property price levels suggest that Latvia has the potential to offer good medium- to long-term property investment opportunities. Prices are also supported by a shortage of modern properties creating the jet-to-let ideal of a market where demand exceeds supply and supply cannot expand sufficiently to absorb that demand.

Property hotspots

Riga is the capital of Latvia. It's also the region's largest transport hub, has a rapidly growing financial and commercial sector, and is a centre for tourism. Property prices, especially for apartments, have been increasing by 30 per cent annually over the last two years, but the market still represents good value when compared to other European capitals. Local demand for property remains high and presently this exceeds supply, which is a key consideration for jet-to-let investors.

Apartments represent the most flexible investment, although there are other options available such as town houses. When choosing an area, take into account that the majority of new development projects are in **Riga** and the surrounding area. The property markets in some other coastal towns are starting to develop, including places such as **Jurmala** and **Liepaja**, but presently Riga is the favoured jet-to-let target and worth further research.

Transaction costs

There are no restrictions on EU citizens purchasing apartments in Latvia, but there are some restrictions when buying land. To buy land you must establish a local company, which takes up to ten working days at a cost of around £800.

The property buying process is very straightforward. You pay a non-refundable deposit of 10–15 per cent when signing the preliminary contract. The remaining balance must be paid on completion. Normally, there are no stage payments, which is another benefit for jet-to-let investors.

The transaction costs are:

- **Purchase Tax (stamp duty)** is two per cent and is paid in order to register the property with the Land Registry.

- **Notary fees** are fixed between €300 and €450.

- **Legal costs** are between €250 and €400.

- **Estate agents' fees** come to about five per cent of the purchase price. They are normally paid by both the buyer and the seller.

Transaction costs associated with a property purchase amount to approximately four to five per cent of the purchase price.

Annual costs

- **Property Tax** is 1.5 per cent annually of the cadastral value (i.e. an administrative value which is used as a base or a point of reference for tax) of the land and buildings on it. The cadastral value is determined by the council and will be equal to or less than the market value of the property.

- **Maintenance costs** vary depending on the type of property.

Taxes

Income Tax
The standard Income Tax rate is a flat rate of 25 per cent.

Corporation Tax
The standard flat rate of Corporation Tax is 15 per cent.

Please note that the Latvian government is considering reducing Corporation Tax to 12.5 per cent in July 2006.

Capital Gains Tax
Capital gains in Latvia are generally treated as income for individuals and companies. Individuals are exempt from Capital Gains Tax on the sale of property if the property has been held for at least 12 months.

Facts at a glance

Geography	
Population (2005 estimate)	2,290,237
Language	Latvian
Ethnic groups	57.7% of ethnic Latvians. Ethnic minority groups include Russian, Belarusian, Ukrainian and Polish

Local currency	Lat divided into 100 Santims

Political system

Political structure	Parliamentary democracy
President	Vaira Vike-Freiberga
Prime Minister	Aigars Kalvitis
Main parties	New Era Party
	People's Party

Economy

Unemployment rate in 2005	9.0%
Unemployment rate, February 2006	8.0%
Inflation rate in 2005	6.9%
Inflation rate, February 2006	7.0%
Interest rate, March 2006	3.96%
GDP growth in 2005	10.2%
GDP growth forecast for 2006	7.7%
GDP per capita (income per person) in 2005	€10,900

Taxation

Income Tax	25%
Corporation Tax	15%
Capital Gains Tax	Taxed as income

Corruption statistics

Corruption rate	4.2
Corruption rank	51st

Industry and technology

Major industries	Electronics
	Synthetic fibres
	Pharmaceuticals

The Latvian property market

Hotspots	Riga, Jurmala, Liepaja

Property taxes (transactions)

Stamp duty	2%
Notary fees	€300–450
Estate agents' fees	5%
Legal fees	€250–500
Total fees	4–5%

Property taxes (annual)

Cadastral Tax	1.5%

Mortgage

LTV	85%
Term	Up to 40 years
Currency	US dollars, Latvian Lats and euros
Current interest rate	3.5–4.5% in euros

Investor resources

Embassies

British Embassy in Latvia

5 Alunana Street
Riga LV-1010, Latvia

Tel: +371 777 4700
Fax: +371 777 4707
Website: www.britain.lv

Latvian Embassy in the UK

45 Nottingham Place
London W1M 3FE

Tel: 020 7312 0040
Fax: 020 7312 0042
Website: http://latvia.embassyhomepage.com

Useful websites

Bank of Latvia
www.bank.lv

Invest in Latvia
www.liaa.gov.lv/eng/invest

The Latvian Institute
www.li.lv

Statistics of Latvia
www.csb.lv/Satr/aorg.htm

Tourism in Latvia
http://latviatourism.lv

Lithuania

The story so far...

Lithuania was a significant power in the Middle Ages and subsequently part of Poland. By the end of the 18th century the majority of the country came under the Russian Empire until it declared independence in 1918, which it retained until annexed by the Soviet Union in 1940. It later came under German occupation and was reoccupied by the Soviet Union in 1945. The establishment of the independent state of Lithuania in 1990 brought 50 years of Communist rule to an end.

Since then, Lithuania and the other Baltic countries have sought closer political and economic ties with the West. Lithuania has actively pursued privatisation of major industries while keeping inflation and unemployment under control. Estonia, Latvia and Lithuania are now referred to as the Baltic Tigers and since 2001 their economies have consistently averaged seven per cent growth per annum.

Where is it?

The Republic of Lithuania shares borders with Latvia to the north, Belarus to the south-east, Poland to the south and Russia to the south-west, as well as a Baltic coastline to the west. The country has a total territory of 65,303km².

What is the weather like?

The weather in Lithuania is similar to that of the other Baltic States with wet moderate summers and winters with regular rainfall and snow.

Vilnius

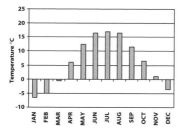 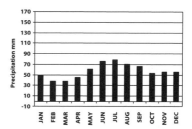

Language

Lithuania has an estimated population of 3.6 million people, consisting of mainly ethnic Lithuanians (83.4 per cent) and two ethnic minorities – Polish (6.7 per cent) and Russian (6.3 per cent). The official language is Lithuanian, spoken by 82 per cent of the population. English is widely spoken as a second language.

Currency

The Litas (LTL) is the Lithuanian currency and is equal to 100 Centas. Lithuania is forecast to adopt the euro on 1 January 2007, making it one of the first new accession countries to do so. This is dependent on meeting strict economic terms set by the European Union (EU). The Litas is pegged to the euro at LTL 3.4582: € 1.

Politics

The Republic of Lithuania is a parliamentary democracy. The present centre-left government coalition is made of the Social Democratic Party, the New Union, the Farmers and New Democracy Union and the Labour Party. Algirdas Mykolas Brazauskas, a former President of Lithuania, has served as Prime Minister since 2001. Since 1991, political control has swung between the Conservatives and the Democratic Labour Party of Lithuania. The current centre-left coalition, formed in 2001, has actively pursued policies of economic reform and membership of both NATO and the EU. President Rolandas Paksas, formerly Lithuania's Prime Minister, was impeached by parliament in 2004 on corruption charges. He was replaced by the current President Valdas Adamkus.

Economy

In the 1990s, the majority of Lithuania's trading partners were former Soviet states, but the Russian economic crisis of 1998 prompted a recession in Lithuania which forced a shift in economic focus towards the West. Firm fiscal policies, large-scale privatisation (especially in the financial sector) and foreign direct investment (FDI) put Lithuania on the way to economic recovery and expansion.

Economic growth levels have been strong since 2001, driven by private sector spending and exports. Services have expanded rapidly since Lithuania's independence and now account for 60 per cent of its gross domestic product (GDP). Modern Lithuania is growing at a fast pace with low inflation, but unemployment remains a problem, especially in the rural areas.

Lithuania's economy has performed robustly and it continues to sustain strong economic growth. The country received €1.521 million between 2004 and 2006 for regional development. The Lithuanian government is currently focused on improving the country's business environment and attracting more FDI, but it's some way short of the achievements of both Estonia and Latvia.

Vilnius is the economic heart of Lithuania and one of the largest financial centres in the Baltic region. It generates approximately 35 per cent of

Lithuanian GDP, even though it has only 15 per cent of the country's population.

Economic indicators

Economic growth

The European Commission reports that Lithuania's GDP is expected to grow by 6.2 per cent in 2006. Real growth has been robust over the last five years and Lithuania's GDP per capita was €11,900 in 2005. The per capita GDP in Vilnius was approximately €26,100 in 2005, above the EU average.

Year	2000	2001	2002	2003	2004	2005
Real growth of GDP (%)	3.9	6.4	6.8	9.7	6.7	7.4

Source: Eurostat, the Statistical Office of the European Communities

Inflation

According to the European Commission, annual inflation was 2.7 per cent in 2005 due to increased costs of healthcare, energy, transport and food.

Interest rates

The Central Bank short-term rate in March 2006 was 2.81 per cent.

Unemployment

Unemployment has halved in the last five years, mostly due to a growing economy and more employment opportunities. Long-term unemployment has been steadily declining, but it still accounts for more than 50 per cent of all of those without jobs.

Unemployment rate (percentage unemployed)

2000	2001	2002	2003	2004	2005
16.4	16.4	13.5	12.7	10.9	8.2

Source: Eurostat, the Statistical Office of the European Communities

Foreign direct investment (FDI)

Lithuania is an attractive investment country with a large and diversified economy, investment laws that conform to EU standards and low Corporation Tax. It needs to attract more FDI in order to maintain its competitiveness, although large inflows of capital from EU funding should provide a boost to the economy.

Foreign direct investment in Lithuania (€ million)

1999	2000	2001	2002	2003	2004	2005
456.6	412.3	498.8	771.7	159.9	623.0	806.9

Source: Bank of Lithuania

The property market

Lithuania is known for its strong economy and low inflation. It has good jet-to-let investment potential as property prices continue rising at over 15–20 per cent annually. This is driven by a continually increasing demand for high-quality apartments and houses.

Demand for modern properties remains high while supply is low and Lithuania has one of the lowest numbers of dwellings per 1,000 inhabitants. Nearly 25 per cent of all properties were built before the 1960s, and around 90 per cent of these are in a bad condition and are in need of some renovation. New-build apartments are especially in high demand.

Lithuania has the highest level of homeownership in Europe, which, combined with a reported shortage of quality new-builds, is great news for the off-plan investor selling on completion into a market with a strong culture of buying rather than renting. For this strategy to work, plenty of research is needed into the needs and wants of the local market.

The rental market is slowing as people are more interested in buying than renting. The supply of rental properties currently exceeds demand, although there is still a demand for town houses and cottages.

Property hotspots

The capital **Vilnius** is the administrative and economic centre of Lithuania. The medieval old town was listed as a UNESCO World Heritage site in 1994 due to the wealth of historic buildings. A new purpose-built city centre is being created north of the Neris River which will be the main business district.

Property prices are growing at 30 per cent a year and demand for high-quality new-build one- and two-bedroom apartments is very strong. Prices continue to appreciate and many off-plan developments have been selling very quickly.

As the market develops, you might also want to consider **Kaunas**, the second city, or the seaside resort of **Klaipeda**.

Transaction costs

There are no restrictions on the purchase of property in Lithuania. EU citizens can buy buildings, land or apartments. Agricultural land can also be purchased, but there are some special requirements. Complex regulations and procedures continue to be obstacles for jet-to-let investors, especially as the right of ownership of buildings is separated from the right of ownership of land. In Lithuania, the State continues to own much of the agricultural land.

Transaction costs are:

- There is no **stamp duty** or transfer taxes.

- **Notary fees** are about 0.5–1.0 per cent of the purchase price.

- **Legal fees** range from €500 to €650.

- **Estate agents' fees** are from three to seven per cent.

Overall transaction costs are about three to five per cent of the purchase price (less estate agents fees if they are not paid by the seller).

Annual costs

- **Property Tax** is one per cent of the building value.

- **Land Tax** amounts to 1.5 per cent of the value of the land and is paid by the landowner.

Taxes

Income Tax

The standard Income Tax rate is a flat rate of 33 per cent. There is a reduced 15 per cent rate applicable to certain types of income, including income earned from rent or the sale of property.

Please note that the Lithuanian government is considering reducing the current rate of 33 per cent to 30 per cent in 2006, 27 per cent in 2007 and 24 per cent in 2008.

Corporation Tax

The standard rate of Corporation Tax is 15 per cent.

Capital Gains Tax

Resident companies are taxed at a Corporate Tax rate. Non-residents (both individuals and companies) pay a flat rate of ten per cent on capital gains. Capital gained by residents on the sale of property owned for more than three years is exempt from tax.

Facts at a glance

Geography	
Population (2005 estimate)	3,596,617
Language	Lithuanian
Ethnic groups	83.4% of ethnic Lithuanian.

	Ethnic minority groups include Polish and Russian
Local currency	Litas divided into 100 Centas

Political system

Political structure	Parliamentary democracy
President	Valdas Adamkus
Prime Minister	Algirdas Brazauskas
Main parties	Labour Party Social Democratic Party

Economy

Unemployment rate in 2005	8.2%
Unemployment rate, February 2006	6.6%
Inflation rate in 2005	2.7%
Inflation rate, February 2006	3.4%
Interest rate, March 2006	2.81%
GDP growth in 2005	7.4%
GDP growth forecast for 2006	6.2%
GDP per capita (income per person) in 2005	€11,900

Taxation

Income Tax	33%
Corporation Tax	15%
Capital Gains Tax	10%

Corruption statistics

Corruption rate	4.8
Corruption rank	44th

Industry and technology

Major industries	Shipbuilding

Agricultural machinery
Electronic components

The Lithuanian property market

Hotspots	Vilnius, Kaunas, Klaipeda

Property taxes (transactions)

Transfer Tax	n/a
Notary fees	0.5–1%
Estate agents' fees	3–7%
Legal fees	€500–650
Total fees	3–5%

Property taxes (annual)

Property Tax	1%
Land Tax	0.5%

Mortgage

LTV	70–80%
Term	Up to 30 years
Currency	Euro, US dollars and Litas
Current interest rate	3–5% in euros

Investor resources

Embassies

British Embassy in Lithuania

Antakalnio 2
Vilnius LT-10308, Lithuania

Tel: +370 5 246 2900
Fax: +370 5 246 2901
Website: www.britishembassy.gov.uk/lithuania

Lithuanian Embassy in the UK

84 Gloucester Place
London W1U 6AU

Tel: +20 7486 6401/2
Fax: +20 7486 6403
Website: http://lithuania.embassyhomepage.com

Useful websites

Bank of Lithuania
www.lb.lt

Invest in Lithuania
www.lda.lt

Lithuanian Department of Statistics
www.std.lt

Tourism in Lithuania
www.tourism.lt

Poland

The story so far...

Poland was one of the largest and most powerful countries in the 16th century but has had a troubled history since. Invaded and occupied by German troops at the beginning of the Second World War, Poland suffered cruel losses, losing the highest percentage of its citizens (six million) of all the combatant nations and 20 per cent of its pre-war territory. It became a satellite nation of the Soviet Union until the Solidarity party, led by Lech Walesa, won elections in 1989, the beginning of a period of lasting democracy in Poland. The country joined the European Union (EU) in May 2004.

Where is it?

The Republic of Poland is the largest of all the Eastern European 8 countries. Its neighbours are Germany to the west, the Czech Republic and Slovakia to the south, Ukraine and Belarus to the east, and Lithuania and

Russia to the north. Poland also has a coastline to the Baltic Sea in the north, which is 491km long. The country's total territory is 312,685km².

What is the weather like?

The climate in north-west Poland is slightly different to the rest of the country. The winters in these regions are humid and mild, while summers are wet and relatively cool. The rest of Poland has colder winters and hotter, drier summers. It snows on average 50 days a year with snow cover remaining in the Carpathian and Sudetan Mountains.

Warsaw

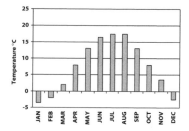
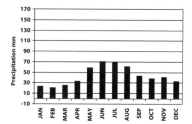

Language

Poland has an estimated population of 38.6 million people, consisting largely of Poles (96.7 per cent). The official language is Polish, spoken by 97.8 per cent. Small numbers of people in Poland also speak Russian, Ukrainian, German and English.

Currency

The currency in Poland is the Zloty (PLN), divided into 100 Groszy. Under the terms of accession to the European Union (EU), all new member state countries are expected to adopt the euro at some future stage. Poland is the only member which as yet has no target date to adopt the euro.

Politics

The political situation of the 1990s can be summarised by the dominance of the left-wing coalition between socialist and social democratic parties. During this time, Poland continued with its programme of free market reforms and achieved impressive economic growth. In 1999, the coalition became a party under the banner of the Social Democratic Alliance (SLD). However, in 2004, SLD's Prime Minister Leszek Miller and his cabinet resigned due to many corruption scandals and the party's popularity has since waned. The 2005 parliamentary elections were won by two centre-right parties: Law and Justice and Citizens Platform. The expected coalition between the two parties has failed, and even though they are both centre-right, they are in political opposition to each other.

Poland is a democratic republic. The current main party is the Conservative centre-right Law and Justice, which presently holds power with a minority government. Lech Kaczynski was elected as President in 2005. The Prime Minister is Kazimierz Marcinkiewicz, elected in 2005.

Economy

Poland was the first former Communist-planned economy in Eastern Europe to end its recession and return to economic growth. Since 1992, the Polish economy has enjoyed a strong recovery, driven by significant expansion in the private sector. This was achieved through large-scale privatisation and the restructuring of old outdated industries.

However, Poland's economic growth has slowed since 2001, but it's now recovering with the help of strong exports and growing domestic demand. The gross domestic product (GDP) forecast for 2006 is over four per cent and the economy is also benefiting from large inflows of foreign direct investment (FDI).

The agricultural sector remains very important, employing 16 per cent of the population. Poland's biggest challenge remains high unemployment, which reached 17.9 per cent in 2005 (higher than in any other EU country).

Economic indicators

Economic growth

GDP growth has been moderate over the last six years as shown in the table below. The European Commission reports that Poland's GDP is expected to grow by 4.3 per cent in 2006, having reached 4.2 per cent in the final quarter of 2005. Poland's GDP per capita in 2005 was €11,600.

Year	2000	2001	2002	2003	2004	2005
Real growth of GDP (%)	4.0	1.0	1.4	3.8	5.4	2.6

Source: Eurostat, the Statistical Office of the European Communities

Inflation

Annual inflation in Poland was 2.2 per cent in 2005, caused by increases in the price of oil, fuel and food.

Interest rates

The Polish Central Bank cut its key policy rate to 4.00 per cent in March 2006. Interest rates are expected to drop further to 3.75 per cent during 2006.

Unemployment

Poland struggles with exceptionally high levels of unemployment, currently the highest in the EU. Unemployment started growing in the late 1990s due to an economic recession and the continuing restructuring of the economy. The rate of increase has slowed in the last few years due to a recovery in the economy. Unemployment is highest in rural areas and among the oldest, youngest and least educated workers.

Unemployment rate (percentage of unemployed)

2000	2001	2002	2003	2004	2005
16.4	18.5	19.8	19.2	18.8	17.9

Source: Eurostat, the Statistical Office of the European Communities

Foreign direct investment (FDI)

Poland attracts large sums of FDI. The country has the largest market in Central Europe, with a diverse industrial base and an investment-friendly attitude. The majority of investment is in the manufacturing sector (42 per cent) and financial services (23 per cent). FDI accounted for almost five per cent of GDP in 2004. The largest foreign investors in Poland are France Telecom, Fiat, Daewoo, HVB and Citibank.

Foreign direct investment in Poland (€ million)

1999	2000	2001	2002	2003	2004	2005
6,824	10,334	6,372	4,371	4,067	10,279	6,132

Source: Bank of Poland

The property market

The property market in Poland has expanded significantly since joining the EU in 2004. Poland is experiencing classic multiplier effects as a result of FDI, although at a slower rate than some other new entrant EU countries. Factories, manufacturing plants and services relocating to Poland have provided new employment opportunities and have created greater wealth. This is reflected in the upward pressure on property prices. New jobs create demand for rented accommodation and, as a result, jet-to-let investors can expect yields of eight to ten per cent, depending on the location of the property.

The economy continues to grow at a steady rate, but Poland still struggles with extremely high levels of unemployment making the choice of location even more important for the jet-to-let investor. Property prices are growing in the main cities where jobs can be found more easily.

The property market is forecast to maintain a steady rate of growth as demand exceeds supply. The Institute for City Development (IRM) estimates that the market currently has a shortfall of around 1.4 million properties. To meet this demand, 300,000 units a year need to be constructed, which is significantly greater than the present rate of construction at 90,000 units. In June 2005 alone, building and construction output grew by 30 per cent on the previous year, according to Poland's Central Statistical Office.

Prices remain low, but have been gradually rising – up by 17 per cent in 2004. Foreign investors choose mainly new-build or renovated properties in Warsaw and Krakow, although other regional towns have started to look attractive for investors.

Property hotspots

Warsaw is the main industrial and commercial centre of Poland. It's a relatively small capital city and only five per cent of the nation's population live there. However, as the city expands in line with the economy, the demand for labour should increase, which will lead to migration from rural areas to the city. The number of Poles moving to Warsaw is expected to double over the next 15 years, providing solid jet-to-let investment opportunities as properties are constructed to meet the increased demand. Prices for new-build properties increased by ten to 15 per cent in 2005 depending on location.

Krakow is one of the most beautiful cities in Poland and is the cultural and educational centre of the country. Unlike Warsaw, the property market in Krakow is supported by tourism, which is growing each year, aided by the arrival of low-cost airlines. The population is rising and demand for new off-plan properties is intense, outstripping supply by 40 per cent in some areas. Property prices rose by 27 per cent in 2005.

Apart from the big cities, Poland has much more to offer – **ski resorts, mountains and the Baltic coast beaches**. Property prices in the coastal towns of the TriCity area (also called the Triple City or **Trójmiasto**, consisting of **Gdansk**, **Gdynia** and **Sopot**) increased by 28 per cent in 2005.

Transaction costs

The process of buying property is relatively simple. The buyer pays a deposit, usually 20 per cent on signing the preliminary contract. The remainder is paid at the final contract meeting where the seller must provide documents ensuring that there are no debts secured on the house.

As always, an independent lawyer will cut through the maze for you. The transaction costs are:

- **Transfer Tax (stamp duty)** is paid on the transfer of ownership and is two per cent of the market value of the property.
- **Notary fees** are two to three per cent of the purchase price.
- One per cent in **legal fees** and two per cent in court **registration fees**.
- **Estate agents' fees** are about five per cent. These are normally paid by the seller.

Total costs come to about eight to ten per cent of the purchase price.

Annual costs

Real Estate Tax is paid annually by the registered owner of the land. The rate of tax is determined by the local authorities.

Taxes

Income Tax
Individual Income Tax rates in 2006:

Tax	Annual tax base (PLN)
19%	0–37,023
30%	37,024–74,028
40%	74,029 and over

Corporation Tax
The standard rate of Corporation Tax is 19 per cent.

Capital Gains Tax
Capital gains are taxed as income for companies and individuals. Individuals pay ten per cent tax on the sale of the property. Properties owned for more than five years are exempt from tax.

Facts at a glance

Geography

Population (2005 estimate)	38,635,144
Language	Polish
Ethnic groups	96.7% of ethnic Polish. Ethnic minority groups include Ukrainian and German
Local currency	Zloty divided into 100 Groszy

Political system

Political structure	Democratic republic
President	Lech Kaczynski
Prime Minister	Kazimierz Marcinkiewicz
Main parties	Law and Justice Citizens Platform

Economy

Unemployment rate in 2005	17.7%
Unemployment rate, February 2006	17.0%
Inflation rate in 2005	2.2%
Inflation rate, February 2006	0.9%
Interest rate, March 2006	4.0%
GDP growth in 2005	2.6%
GDP growth forecast for 2006	4.3%
GDP per capita (income per person) in 2005	€11,600

Taxation

Income Tax	19–40%
Corporation Tax	19%

Capital Gains Tax	10%

Corruption statistics

Corruption rate	3.4
Corruption rank	70th

Industry and technology

Major industries	Iron and steel Coal mining Food processing

The Polish property market

Hotspots	Warsaw, Krakow, TriCity (Gdansk, Gdynia and Sopot), Wroclaw

Property taxes (transactions)

Transfer Tax	2%
Notary fees	2–3%
Estate agents' fees	5%
Legal fees	3%
Total fees	8–10%

Property taxes (annual)

Property Tax	Varies from region to region

Mortgage

LTV	60–80%
Term	4–35 years
Currency	Swiss Francs, US dollars, euros, Polish Zloty and British pounds
Current interest rate	3–6% in euros

Investor resources

Embassies

British Embassy in Poland

Warsaw Corporate Centre
ul. E. Plater 28, 00-688 Warsaw

Tel: +48 22 311 00 00
Fax: +48 22 311 03 11
Website: www.britishembassy.pl

Polish Embassy in the UK

47 Portland Place
London W1N 3AG

Tel: 0870 774 2700
Fax: 020 7291 3575
Website: http://poland.embassyhomepage.com/poland_embassy_
london_united_kingdom.htm

Useful websites

Bank of Poland

www.nbp.pl

Central Statistical Office of Poland

www.stat.gov.pl

Invest in Poland

www.paiz.gov.pl

Tourism in Poland

www.polandtour.org

Slovakia

The story so far...

Having formed part of the Ottoman and then the Austro-Hungarian Empires, Czechoslovakia was founded in 1918. The threats perceived with the rise of Nazi Germany caused Slovakia to declare independence in 1939 and the new Slovak Republic became an ally of Germany during the Second World War. The Republic of Czechoslovakia was re-established in 1945 and the Communist party took over the government in 1948. The Soviet Union invaded Czechoslovakia in 1968 after calls and protests in favour of a more free society.

Communist rule came to an end in Czechoslovakia in 1989 during a peaceful revolution followed by a peaceful divorce in 1993, which gave birth to the two new nation states of Slovakia and the Czech Republic.

A successful policy of privatisation began to move state-owned companies into the private sector and encouraged foreign investment. The transition to a market economy initially created economic hardship, but after a recession in the 1990s, the Slovak economy has grown rapidly due to sound macro-economic management and reforms. Economic change and reform has given foreign investors confidence and the economy has continued to exceed expectations since 2000.

Where is it?

The Slovak Republic borders Poland in the north, Ukraine in the east, Hungary in the south, and Austria and the Czech Republic in the west. Its total area is 49,035km².

What is the weather like?

The weather in Slovakia is similar to that of the Czech Republic. Generally, the summers are relatively warm and the winters are cold and wet.

Bratislava

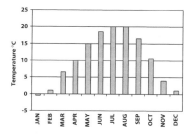
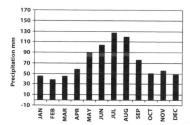

Language

Slovakia has an estimated population of 5.43 million, consisting of ethnic Slovaks (85.8 per cent) with Hungarians making up the largest ethnic minority (9.7 per cent). The official language is Slovak, spoken by 83.9 per cent of the population. Hungarian is widely spoken (by 10.7 per cent of the population) and German is the most common second language, with some English also spoken.

Currency

The Slovak currency is the Slovenska Koruna or Slovak Crown (SKK), divided into 100 Haliers. It's predicted that Slovakia will adopt the euro on 1 January 2009. The Slovak Koruna is pegged to the euro at SKK 38.455: € 1.

Politics

Politics in independent Slovakia was greatly influenced by Vladimir Meciar, who was Prime Minister from 1992 to 1998, and who with Václav Klaus agreed to separate Czechoslovakia and create two independent states.

The Slovak Republic is a parliamentary democracy. The current government is a centre-right coalition made up of the Slovak Democratic and Christian Union, the Party of the Hungarian Coalition, the Christian Democratic Movement and the Alliance of the New Citizen. The key policies of the coalition are fighting corruption, attracting foreign investment and modernising social services while maintaining a worthwhile contribution to NATO and the European Union (EU).

The President of Slovakia is Ivan Gasparovic, elected in 2004. Mikulás Dzurinda is serving his second term as Prime Minister having been elected in 1998.

Economy

Slovakia's transition into a market economy was a slow and difficult process. During the transitional period in the 1990s, the economy performed fairly well, but eventually went into recession. Growth stagnated while the budget deficit and unemployment climbed to high levels.

A new government changed this by overhauling the tax and social welfare systems and working hard to attract new FDI. The economy rebounded into growth, averaging over four per cent per annum, indicating that Slovakia's economy has recovered and is developing swiftly.

Slovakia is now one of the most attractive FDI destinations with low flat-rate taxes and various incentives for investors. Inflation is moderate, but unemployment at 16.4 per cent still remains at a disappointingly high level.

Economic indicators

Economic growth

Slovakia's economy has steadily grown since 2000. The European Commission reports that the real gross domestic product (GDP) in Slovakia is expected to grow by 5.5 per cent in 2006 and further in 2007.

Slovakia's GDP per capita is €12,700 according to the 2005 estimate.

Year	2000	2001	2002	2003	2004	2005
Real growth of GDP (%)	2.0	3.8	4.6	4.5	5.5	6.0

Source: Eurostat, the Statistical Office of the European Communities

Inflation

Inflation fell from 12.0 per cent in 2000 to 3.3 per cent in 2002, rising again in 2003–2004 due to increases in taxes and regulated prices. The annual rate of inflation fell further to 2.8 per cent in 2005 – the lowest rate in Slovakia's history.

Interest rates

After a continual decline since September 2002, the Slovak Central Bank raised its key interest rate by 0.5 per cent to 3.5 per cent in March 2006. More interest rate rises are expected this year.

Unemployment

Slovakia's high rate of unemployment – the second highest in the EU – remains a problem. Like Poland, regional differences account for some of this, particularly where Communist-style working practices and industries have been replaced by the private sector On the positive side, the labour market started showing signs of improvement in 2005 and unemployment was 15.8 per cent in February 2006, which is a small improvement.

Unemployment rate (percentage unemployed)

2000	2001	2002	2003	2004	2005
18.7	19.4	18.7	17.5	18.2	16.4

Source: Eurostat, the Statistical Office of the European Communities

Foreign direct investment (FDI)

Slovakia has considerably reformed its legal system in order to attract more FDI and now is one of the most appealing investment options in Europe. According to the World Bank, Slovakia had the fastest changing business environment in the world in 2004, and comparisons are being made with Ireland's economic miracle in the 1990s.

With its flat-rate tax of 19 per cent, Slovakia now has one of the lowest tax burdens in the EU. Its solid industrial base attracts FDI into a diverse range of sectors, such as electro-technology, automotive, engineering, IT and services. It has recently attracted some top car makers, beating its larger northern neighbour, the Czech Republic, for major motor vehicle investment. Slovakia is now the world's largest car manufacturer (per capita) and further plants are planned to be built in 2006–2007. Major companies manufacturing in Slovakia include Peugeot-Citroën, Kia Motors, Ford Motor, Hyundai and Volkswagen.

Foreign direct investment in Slovakia (€ million)

1999	2000	2001	2002	2003	2004	2005
474.2	2,379.8	2,049.1	5,023.1	743.3	1,088.7	1,595.4

Source: Bank of Slovakia

The property market

The property market in Slovakia is considered to be a few years behind the Czech Republic and Hungary. Prices are cheaper than many of the other new

EU members, which are at a more advanced stage in the property market cycle.

Demand from the local Slovak population is strong and growing. The development of Slovakia's property market follows the typical Eastern European trend of economic growth, followed by the liberalisation of financial services (including the mortgage market) and supply side issues leading to a price squeeze and rising prices.

The mortgage market in Slovakia is developing and as cheaper mortgages become more readily available, property prices will be pushed higher. Many Slovaks are now using mortgages to buy property and this trend is set to grow as Slovaks generally prefer to buy rather than rent.

There is a shortage of good quality property in Slovakia and in particular Bratislava. Construction levels are one of the lowest in Europe, although the government estimates that 50,000 new properties need to be built to meet current needs. Consequently, house prices will continue to rise as demand outstrips supply in the short to medium term.

Property prices are rising at 10–15 per cent annually (over 20 per cent in some of Bratislava's districts) and rental returns are between eight and ten per cent. Property prices are forecast to continue rising at current levels.

Property hotspots

Bratislava, the capital city, is a popular jet-to-let choice for property investors as it's possibly the most undervalued EU capital. Property prices have been rising 15–20 per cent and a similar level of growth is forecast to continue for a few years yet, fuelled by the huge demand from locals for quality properties. Demand is strongest for new-build or pre-war apartments in the city centre with price rises ranging from five to 20 per cent depending on the location.

Bratislava is also only an hour by car from Vienna, the capital of Austria, and property prices there are more than double those available in the Slovak capital. A new motorway connecting these two cities should be completed by 2007, which will reduce the journey to only 30 minutes. This major reduction in travelling time will have a positive substitution effect on the property market in Bratislava. Bratislava is also well served by low-cost airlines from many UK cities and is also only 40km from Vienna airport.

Other cities experiencing growing property prices are **Trnava** and **Zilina**, due to high levels of FDI and good rental returns. Also, do consider **Trencin** and **Nitra** for further research.

Transaction costs

The buying process is fairly simple. On signing the preliminary contract, the buyer pays a 10–20 per cent deposit. If you are purchasing an off-plan property, then a series of stage payments will follow as construction progresses. Once all fees and taxes have been paid, the property will be registered at the Land Registry and you become the legal owner.

The expenses are:

- **Property Transfer Tax** was abolished on 1 January 2005.
- **Lawyers' fees** are usually around €500.
- **Notary fees** come to around €150.
- **Estate agents' fees** are in the range of three to five per cent and are normally split between the seller and buyer.

Total costs come to three to five per cent of the purchase price.

Annual costs

Property Tax is paid by owners of buildings, flats and land. This depends on the size, location and the type of buildings, flats and land. For a large two-bedroom apartment the annual amount should not exceed €40.

Taxes

Income Tax
Income Tax is paid at a flat rate of 19 per cent.

Corporation Tax
The standard rate of Corporation Tax is 19 per cent.

Capital Gains Tax
Capital gains are taxed as income for both companies and individuals. Exemptions apply to the sale of a property used as an individual's permanent address for the last two years and property that was owned for at least five years prior to sale.

Facts at a glance

Geography	
Population (2005 estimate)	5,431,363
Language	Slovak
Ethnic groups	85.8% of Slovaks. The largest ethnic minority group is Hungarians
Local currency	Slovenska Koruna or Slovak Crown divided into 100 Haliers

Political system	
Political structure	Parliamentary democracy
President	Ivan Gasparovic
Prime Minister	Mikulás Dzurinda
Main parties	Slovak Democratic and Christian Union

Economy	
Unemployment rate in 2005	16.4%
Unemployment rate, February 2006	15.8%
Inflation rate in 2005	2.8%
Inflation rate, February 2006	4.3%

Interest rate, March 2006	3.5%
GDP growth in 2005	6.0%
GDP growth forecast for 2006	5.5%
GDP per capita (income per person) in 2005	€12,700

Taxation

Income Tax	19%
Corporation Tax	19%
Capital Gains Tax	Taxed as income

Corruption statistics

Corruption rate	4.3
Corruption rank	47th

Industry and technology

Major industries	Metal and metal products Transport vehicles Electrical and optical apparatus

The Slovak property market

Hotspots	Bratislava, Trnava and Zilina

Property taxes (transactions)

Notary fees	€150
Estate agents' fees	3–5%
Legal fees	€500
Total fees	3–5%

Property taxes (annual)

Property Tax	Negligible

Mortgage

LTV	70%

Term	4–30 years
Currency	Euros and Slovak Koruna
Current interest rate	4–6%

Investor resources

Embassies

British Embassy in the Republic of Slovakia

Panská 16

811 01 Bratislava, Slovak Republic

Tel: +421 2 5998 2000

Fax: +421 2 5998 2269

Website: www.britemb.sk

Embassy of Slovakia in the UK

25 Kensington Palace Gardens

London W8 4QY

Tel: 020 7313 6470

Fax: 020 7313 6481

Website: www.slovakembassy.co.uk

Useful websites

Central Statistical Office of Poland

www.statistics.sk

Invest in Slovakia

www.sario.sk

National Bank of Slovakia

www.nbs.sk

Tourism in Slovakia

www.sacr.sk

Slovenia

The story so far...

From the 14th century, most of Slovenia formed part of the Austro-Hungarian Empire and, following its collapse in 1918, the Slovenes joined the Croats and Serbs to form a new state which became Yugoslavia in 1929. Occupied by German, Italian and Hungarian armies during the Second World War, Yugoslavia was liberated by the Soviets, who established the Communist Federal People's Republic of Yugoslavia (FPRY). This comprised the present-day independent states of Slovenia, Croatia, Macedonia, Serbia and Montenegro, and Bosnia and Herzegovina. Present-day Slovenia gained independence from the FPRY in 1991. Slovenia joined the European Union (EU) in May 2004.

Where is it?

Slovenia is in South-Eastern Europe with 46.6km of coastline to the Adriatic Sea in the south-west. Slovenia borders Austria to the north,

Hungary to the north-west, Croatia to the south and east and Italy to the west. The country's total area is 20,273km².

What is the weather like?

Slovenia's climate varies across the country. The north-west has an Alpine climate with lots of rain, moderate summers and cold winters. The Adriatic coast has a pleasant sub-Mediterranean climate with warm weather throughout the year and mild winters, while inland and the eastern parts of Slovenia have a typical Eastern European climate, with hot summers and cold winters. Slovenia gets most of its rain in the spring and autumn.

Ljubljana

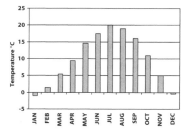 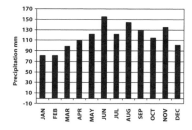

Language

Slovenia has an estimated population of just over two million people, consisting of ethnic Slovenes (83.1 per cent). The ethnic minorities are mainly ex-Yugoslav nationals, such as Serbs, Croats, Bosnians and ethnic Italians and Hungarians. The official languages are Slovenian, Italian and Hungarian.

Currency

The Slovenian currency is the Tolar (SIT), which is worth 100 Stotin. Slovenia is scheduled to adopt the euro on 1 January 2007 and is likely to achieve that target and become the first of the new 2004 EU entrants to adopt the single currency. The Slovenian Tolar is pegged to the euro at SIT 239.640: € 1.

Politics

Unlike some other former republics of Yugoslavia, Slovenia avoided much of the fighting that beset the Balkans during the 1990s. The country has made good progress towards developing a market economy and has a stable democratic political system.

The current government coalition comprises four parties: the Slovenian Democratic Party, the New Slovenia Christian People's Party, the Slovenian People's Party and the Democratic Party of Pensioners of Slovenia. Janez Drnovsek, from a centre-left party called Liberal Democracy of Slovenia, was Prime Minister in 1992–2002. He now serves as President of Slovenia until 2007. The current Prime Minister is Janez Jansa, elected in 2004.

Economy

Slovenia is one of the top economic performers of the countries that joined the EU in 2004. As part of the Yugoslav Republic, it accounted for 20 per cent of total GDP and 33 per cent of exports. Now Slovenia enjoys the highest standard of living and the highest GDP per capita of the ten new member states of the EU.

Privatisations in the banking, telecommunications and utility sectors stimulated growth and foreign direct investment (FDI) is expected to increase over the next few years as restrictions on foreign investment are slowly abolished. Slovenia's economy is highly dependent on trade and is focused mainly towards the EU.

Economic growth reached 4.2 per cent in 2005 after a relatively slow performance in 2003 (2.7 per cent) and is forecast to remain strong. Slovenia is growing at a robust pace, with low inflation and low unemployment and is almost certain to meet the necessary criteria to adopt the euro in 2007. This said, Slovenia continues to face economic challenges with relatively high taxes, an inflexible labour market and much of the economy still under state control. In 2005, the government put plans in place to address these issues.

Economic indicators

Economic growth

The European Commission reports that real GDP in Slovenia is expected to grow by 4.0 per cent in 2006, after growing 4.2 per cent in 2004 and in 2005. GDP per capita was €18,900 in 2005.

Year	2000	2001	2002	2003	2004	2005
Real growth of GDP (%)	4.1	2.7	3.5	2.6	4.2	4.2

Source: Eurostat, the Statistical Office of the European Communities

Inflation

Inflation, at 3.6 per cent in 2004, fell to 2.5 per cent in 2005.

Interest rates

The interest rate in March 2006 was 3.5 per cent.

Unemployment

Unemployment in Slovenia is the lowest among the Eastern European 8 and is lower than the EU average. The labour market is strong and employment growth is steady.

Unemployment rate (percentage unemployed)

2000	2001	2002	2003	2004	2005
6.6	5.8	6.1	6.5	6.0	6.3

Source: Eurostat, the Statistical Office of the European Communities

Foreign direct investment (FDI)

Slovenia was initially slow to attract FDI, and had one of the lowest FDI per capita rates in the EU. However, the present government is committed to attracting more overseas investment and has introduced a number of policies.

Between 2004 and 2006 Slovenia received EU structural aid of €433 million for projects such as motorways. The country will attract higher amounts of FDI in the future, contributing to the multiplier effects which positively impact the national property market.

The greatest proportion of FDI goes into manufacturing, financial services, trade and tourism.

Foreign direct investment in Slovenia (€ million)

1999	2000	2001	2002	2003	2004
2,675.0	3,109.8	2,952.4	3,922.9	5,131.0	5,556.7

Source: Bank of Slovenia

The property market

The Slovenian property market has performed well in the last couple of years. It's supported by local demand, as well as by jet-to-let investors, who can now purchase properties relatively hassle free after Slovenian entry into the EU. Foreigners are attracted by Slovenia's economy, overall stability and its eye-catching natural beauty.

The number of jet-to-let investors in Slovenia is still relatively insignificant with the British being the main foreign buyers (29 per cent), followed by Germans and Austrians. The lack of mortgage finance for foreigners, hence the inability for investors to gear their portfolios with local funds, has kept a brake on the market so far, but this situation is likely to change in the future.

Slovenia is set to adopt the euro by 2007, which will give a further boost to its property market. The country's attractive landscape and geographical diversity are also attracting a large number of tourists. The inflow of British holidaymakers alone has increased by 17 per cent during 2005. The rental market is also expected to remain healthy supported by a growing economy and an increasingly robust tourist industry.

The overall prospects for the Slovenian property market are positive.

Property hotspots

Ljubljana is the political and commercial heart of the country. Property prices rose 32 per cent last year, initially in the city centre, followed by the suburbs. Property and rental demand is strongest for older historical houses in the city centre and for modern new-build apartments. Cheap flights bringing jet-to-let investors, as well as tourists from Europe, have been a factor in the growth of property prices, not just in Ljubljana but throughout the country.

The rental market is well established in Ljubljana, particularly around the main tourist areas. Elsewhere, the market for property in Slovenia is still relatively immature but growing.

Jet-to-let investors are presently concentrating their efforts on buying properties in the tourist areas rather than in the capital. Property prices in the western coastal region of **Primorska**, which is very popular for adventure sports, and the Alpine region of **Gorenjska** with the ski resorts of the Julian mountains increased up to 30 per cent. British and Irish investors are the prime movers in the Gorenjska region, where the ski resort **Kranjska Gora** is the most popular, followed by the picturesque towns of **Bled** and **Bohinj**.

Rural properties are popular in the area of **Pomurje** in the north-east, offering stunning countryside with vineyards on the hills and the region's main attraction of thermal health resorts. Again, this region is in great demand from British, Austrian and German investors so competition is high.

Transaction costs

There are no restrictions for EU citizens buying property in Slovenia. For non-EU citizens there is an option to incorporate a company in order to purchase property.

In most cases, buying property in Slovenia is straightforward and uncomplicated. Offers are usually made by a lawyer, who often acts on behalf of both the vendor and the purchaser. The buyer is required to pay ten per cent deposit. Foreign buyers will need to apply for an EMSO number (a unique identification number that Slovenian citizens receive at birth), which is usually provided within two working days. The estate agent or a lawyer will be able to help you to obtain an EMSO.

The transaction costs are:

- **Land registration costs** are payable to the Land Registry. This fee is about €150.

- **Notary fees** come to approximately €300.

- **Legal fees** are about €500.

- **Estate agents' fees** amount to two to four per cent of the property purchase price.

- **A translation fee** is around €200.

Overall costs will come to about five per cent of the purchase price.

Annual costs

- **Property Tax** is paid annually. The tax rate varies depending on the property size.

- **Public utility costs** (apartment communal charges) on average come to €20 per month.

Taxes

Income Tax
Income Tax is paid at a progressive rate of 16–50 per cent as of 2005.

Corporation Tax
The rate of Corporation Tax is 25 per cent.

Capital Gains Tax
Capital gains of companies are taxed as income. Individuals are taxed at progressive Income Tax rates.

Facts at a glance

Geography	
Population (2005 estimate)	2,011,070
Language	Slovenian
Ethnic groups	83.1% of ethnic Slovenians. Ethnic minority groups include mainly ex-Yugoslav Serbs, Croats and Bosnians
Local currency	Tolar divided into 100 Stotin

Political system	
Political structure	Parliamentary republic
President	Janez Drnovsek
Prime Minister	Janez Jansa
Main parties	Slovenian Democratic Party Liberal Democracy of Slovenia

Economy	
Unemployment rate in 2005	6.3%
Unemployment rate, February 2006	N/A
Inflation rate in 2005	2.5%
Inflation rate, February 2006	2.3%
Interest rate, March 2006	3.5%
GDP growth in 2005	4.2%
GDP growth forecast for 2006	4.0%
GDP per capita (income per person) in 2005	€18,900

Taxation	
Income Tax	16–50%
Corporation Tax	25%

Capital Gains Tax	Taxed as income

Corruption statistics

Corruption rate	6.1
Corruption rank	30th

Industry and technology

Major industries	Lead and zinc smelting Wood products Chemicals

The Slovenian property market

Hotspots	Ljubljana

Property taxes (transactions)

Land registration costs	€150
Notary fees	€300
Estate agents' fees	2–4%
Legal fees	€500
Total fees	About 5%

Property taxes (annual)

Property Tax	Varies

Mortgage

Mortgage availability	Mortgages are currently not available to foreign buyers

Investor resources

Embassies

British Embassy in Slovenia
Trg republike 3
1000 Ljubljana, Slovenia

Tel: +386 1 200 3919
Fax: +386 1 425 0174
Website: www.britishembassy.gov.uk/slovenia

Slovenian Embassy in the UK

10 Little College Street
London SW1P 3SJ

Tel: 020 7222 5400
Fax: 020 7222 5277
Website: http://slovenia.embassyhomepage.com

Useful websites

Bank of Slovenia

www.bsi.si

Invest in Slovenia

www.investslovenia.org

Statistical Office of the Republic of Slovenia

www.stat.si

Tourism in Slovenia

www.slovenia-tourism.si

Summary

In the first part of this book, I examined how economic factors drive property markets and how a top down approach to jet-to-let investment will pay handsome dividends over the medium to long term.

The story of the Eastern European 8 (EE8) is one of rapidly expanding economies leading to greater wealth within a framework of political democracy driving property prices upwards as demand exceeds supply. This will continue, in my view, for some years and well into the next decade of the 21st century.

However, the EE8 is not a single homogeneous property market. Some countries will outperform others and within countries particular cities and regions will also outperform and underperform the market. What is certain is that the astute investor who uses the tools and techniques discussed in chapters 1–10 of this book will be able to identify the countries and areas in which to invest in order to maximise returns. Look to see where the FDI is being invested and where the jobs are being created. Wealth creation drives property markets and this is the story of the EE8.

Indicative property prices in the EE8

	Houses 2-bedroom	3-bedroom	Apartments 1-bedroom	2-bedroom
Czech Republic				
Prague	€200,000–240,000	€220,000–250,000	€70,000–90,000	€110,000–130,000
Brno	€50,000–70,000	€80,000–90,000	€40,000–50,000	€70,000–90,000
Estonia				
Tallinn	€130,000–160,000	€210,000–230,000	€80,000–100,000	€120,000–150,000
Hungary				
Budapest	€100,000–120,000	€160,000–190,000	€80,000–100,000	€110,000–150,000
Latvia				
Riga	€90,000–110,000	€180,000–210,000	€80,000–100,000	€100,000–130,000
Lithuania				
Vilnius	€110,000–130,000	€140,000–160,000	€30,000–50,000	€50,000–60,000
Poland				
Warsaw	€90,000–120,000	€150,000–170,000	€60,000–80,000	€90,000–110,000
Gdansk	€70,000–90,000	€110,000–140,000	€30,000–50,000	€55,000–75,000
Slovakia				
Bratislava	€120,000–150,000	€170,000–190,000	€40,000–60,000	€60,000–80,000
Slovenia				
Ljubljana	€200,000–230,000	€260,000–290,000	€90,000–110,000	€140,000–160,000

USA – Florida

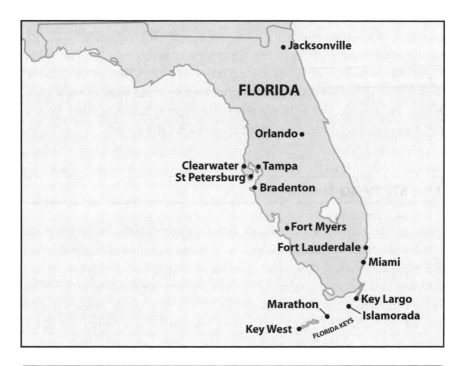

Why invest in Florida?

Florida continues to be one of the most popular locations for jet-to-let property investors. Whether you are looking for somewhere to retire, a second home or a live-and-let option, Florida has something for everyone. Over 1.5 million people from the UK visit Florida every year. In 2005, 18,500 Britons made their home in the US, and this mass exodus is expected to top 250,000 by the end of the decade. Investors and home buyers are attracted to the sunshine, high quality of life and value for money in property.

Florida has long been a popular year-round holiday destination for people of all ages, so it's not surprising that it has become one of the major jet-to-let hotspots. In addition to the climate, Florida also benefits from cheap flights and a multitude of leisure activities that make it increasingly popular with tourists and, as a result, investors achieve good all-year-round rental returns. Florida has a high standard of living and the locals speak English, which for many Britons is a major attraction, particularly in retirement.

The demand for property in Florida is high and is driven by both local and jet-to-let investors. It's estimated that more than 1,000 new residents move to Florida every day. Average property prices in Florida grew by over 25 per cent in 2005, which ranks it second in the US for capital growth. It's unlikely that the market in 2006 will perform as robustly as last year as the effect of a sustained rise in interest rates begins to kick in, but the demand in Florida will remain strong. With prices predicted to cool, Florida looks more like a medium- to long-term investment, which should be the timeframe that jet-to-let investors have in mind at the start.

The story so far...

Prior to the arrival of the British and European colonists, Florida was inhabited by various Indian tribes. The Spanish conquerors first arrived in 1513 and established their rule. Spain was not the only European nation that found Florida attractive; both France and England were eager to exploit the wealth of North America. Control of parts of Florida passed among the Spanish, British and Americans until Spain finally ceded the territory to the United States (US) in 1821.

Florida became the 27th State of the US in March 1845. After becoming one of the founding members of the Confederate States during the Civil War in 1861, full representation in congress was restored in 1868.

The expansion of the railroads across America made Florida into a popular tourist destination in the late 19th century, and the improved transport links helped to open up much of the state to visitors. This expansion continued into the 20th century, with the Florida Land Boom in the 1920s that led to properties in Miami and Palm Beach being snapped up by investors.

After the Second World War, a newly improved motorway system made travelling to Florida easier and the state also proved to be a popular retirement destination for many Americans.

Where is it?

Florida is situated mostly on a large peninsula in the south-east of mainland USA. It has a coastline with the Gulf of Mexico to the west and is bordered by the Atlantic Ocean to the south and to the east. It borders Georgia to the north and Alabama to the north-west. The state covers 65,758m² in total.

Florida is flat with a rolling landscape to its highest point in the north-west. The state has three main regions: the Atlantic Coastal Plain, the East Gulf Coastal Plain and the Florida Uplands. Thousands of small islands, known as the Florida Keys, stretch along 150 miles of coral reef below the southern tip of Florida.

About 77 per cent of Florida's population live in coastal areas. The coastline is 1,350 miles long and consists of the Atlantic coast, 580 miles of shoreline, and the Gulf coast, 770 miles long.

What is the weather like?

Florida averages 300 days of sunshine a year. The dry season is during autumn and winter when temperatures stay around 25°C and the humidity is tolerable. The spring and especially the summers (the wet season) are hot and humid with temperatures exceeding 32°C and humidity rising to nearly 100 per cent.

A good umbrella is essential! It rains almost every day in most months (less during the winter), but showers are generally short and the sun usually reappears quickly. Severe weather is a common occurrence in Florida, with the hurricane season lasting from August through to late October. During these months, fierce tropical storms can bring high winds and relentless rainfalls. Thunderstorms are common from late spring to early autumn, occur unexpectedly and can often be heavy.

Orlando/Davenport/Kissimmee

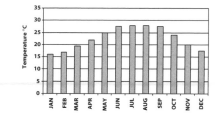 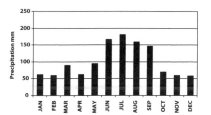

Miami

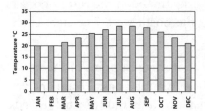
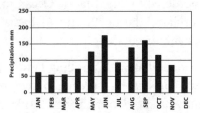

Key Largo

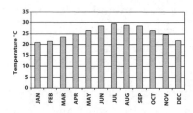
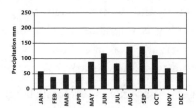

Key West

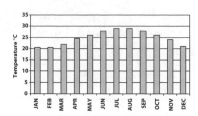
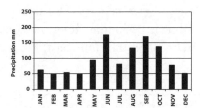

Clearwater/St. Petersburg/Bradenton

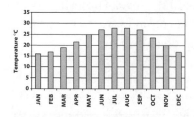
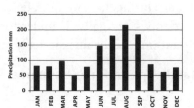

Language

Florida's official language is English. Currently, 77 per cent of the population speak English as their first language and 17 per cent speak Spanish. Florida is America's fourth most populous state with almost 18 million people.

Currency

The official currency of the US is the dollar (US) divided into 100 cents.

Politics

The US is a federal republic which operates as a presidential democracy. There are three levels of government: federal, state and local. The US has a party system, with the two largest political parties, Republican and Democratic, holding most of the elected offices. The current President of the US is George W. Bush, who has held the position since 2000.

Despite the fact that the state is approximately evenly split between the two parties, the Republicans control the governorship and most other state-wide elected offices. The Governor is the chief executive of the Government of the State of Florida, and serves as chairman of the Cabinet. Jeb Bush, brother of the president, is the current Governor and has held this position since 1998.

Administratively, Florida is divided into 67 counties.

Economy

Florida has one of the most advanced and diverse economies in the US. The state has a sophisticated service sector with trade and tourism being the main forces behind economic growth. Florida is one of the most business-friendly states in the country and leads in job creation with more than 33 per cent of all employment opportunities created in the US in the last five years.

The wealth is on the coast in Florida along with the majority of the state's population and income. There has been powerful economic growth since 2001 and it is expected to continue developing at the same pace throughout 2006. Florida's overall economy is the fastest growing among the ten largest states in the US. If Florida was an independent country, it would have the 20th largest economy in the world.

Florida leads the south-east in farming, producing about 75 per cent of American oranges and supplying 40 per cent of the world's orange juice. By contrast, Florida has one of the highest rates of business formation in the US and has managed to successfully develop its high-tech industry. Growth has been especially strong in business services, trade, transportation, aerospace, tourism, education, healthcare, construction and property (real estate).

Economic indicators

Economic growth

Despite hurricanes and high energy prices, the US economy grew at a steady 3.5 per cent in 2005 and the average national gross domestic product (GDP) per capita amounted to $42,122. The economic growth that the US enjoyed in 2005 is forecast to continue in 2006.

In 2005, Florida's Gross State Product (GSP is the state version of GDP) was $638 billion, which ranked it as the fourth wealthiest state in the US. Florida's high population makes the numbers less impressive when you look at the income per person, which was $33,219 (rank 23rd). Florida's real GSP grew by 6.6 per cent in 2005 and 2006 is expected to be another year of robust economic growth as GSP is expected to increase by 4.6 per cent.

Inflation

The US economy was on 'inflation watch' in 2005 and it's still the main concern of the policy makers at the Federal Reserve who determine interest rates. Inflation was triggered by the surge in prices of crude oil and natural gas and the strong economic performance of the US economy in general. The annual rate of inflation was 3.4 per cent in 2005. *The Economist* poll forecasts that inflation will be annualised at 2.9 per cent in 2006.

Interest rates

From early 2001 to mid 2003 the Federal Reserve lowered interest rates 13 times, from 6.25 to one per cent, in order to prevent a recession. Consequently, the property market expanded significantly in this falling interest rate environment.

Since then, interest rates have been rising by a quarter-point at each policy meeting since June 2004. On 28 March 2006, the Federal Reserve raised interest rates to 4.75 per cent.

The steady rise in interest rates may have a much-needed cooling effect on the property market, not just in Florida, but in the US as a whole. As the economy expands, analysts are consistently raising their expectations of where and when US interest rates will peak in this interest rate cycle. Wherever it is, the rising costs of borrowing will have an effect on the demand for property and consequently on prices in the short term.

Unemployment

The chart below represents the annual average rates of unemployment for Florida and the US and illustrates how the state has outperformed the national average between 2000 and 2005.

Unemployment for Florida compared to the US national figures

	2000	2001	2002	2003	2004	2005
Florida	3.8	4.6	5.7	5.3	4.8	3.8
US	4.0	4.7	5.8	6.0	5.5	5.1

Source: US Department of Labor

Foreign direct investment (FDI)

Florida has established itself as one of the leading FDI states in the US benefiting from a diverse economy, a strong knowledge base, modern infrastructure and low state taxes. The main inflow of investment capital is from Western European countries (primarily Netherlands, Germany and the UK), which in any year account for more than 50 per cent of all foreign holdings in Florida. More than 33 per cent of all FDI goes into manufacturing, while property and wholesale trade sectors receive about 15 per cent each.

The latest FDI data available is for 2003. Total holdings by foreign-owned firms reached $29,452, ranking Florida tenth among all US states. These companies employed 248,900 locals.

Foreign direct investment in Florida (million US dollars)

2000	2001	2002	2003
28,021	30,520	28,662	29,452

Source: Enterprise Florida, Inc., Marketing and Information Department

Economic summary

The US economy is strong with solid growth, low inflation and high employment. This is reflected in the more localised economy of Florida, which has local GDP, which most small countries would be proud of and ranks its economy as 20th in the world. Looking forward, the short-term blip may be interest rates which are reflecting the growth in the economy and some external factors, such as the high cost of oil and gas. However, the signs at present appear to favour a cooling of the market rather than a crash and as long as the economic fundamentals remain buoyant, then investors in this market have a good medium- to long-term outlook for property prices and rents.

So, what is the catch?

There are a number of issues worth thinking about before investing in Florida.

Hurricanes

Hurricanes are inevitable in Florida. However, tropical storms and hurricanes have recently increased in number and intensity. In 2004, four hurricanes struck Florida within six weeks, causing damage of $42 billion. Last year's hurricanes were even stronger and more destructive. Out of four hurricanes that struck Florida in 2005, three were classified as Category 5 (the most powerful on the five-step Saffir-Simpson scale of hurricane intensity) in the Atlantic region.

The unfortunate events and the sad loss of life and livelihoods illustrate the devastating impact these natural events have on the local population, towns and cities. Insurance costs rise and the people wait with bated breath for the start of the next hurricane season and what it will bring.

A jet-to-let investor looking at investing in Florida must consider hurricanes and their impact when making an analysis of potential investment areas.

Terrorism and homeland security

It's not unreasonable to expect that after the tragic events of 9/11 that the US government would review and enhance its border security. This is also happening in the UK and in Europe. With advanced security such as visas, biometrics, finger printing and whatever else might be on the cards, will the delays and sheer hassle factor of visiting the US put potential travellers off and instead cause a substitution effect which could reduce the demand for rental accommodation? At this moment it doesn't appear to be too serious an issue, but it's one that you must bear in mind when looking at future risk.

The property market

The US property market has expanded significantly over the last five years and Florida was among the best performers growing by over 100 per cent. Furthermore, throughout 2005, property prices have increased by over 25 per cent outperforming the national market, which grew by 13 per cent.

Florida's property market is driven by retirees, second home owners and investors – a fact unlikely to change in the near future. The huge tourist industry provides a ready supply of tenants throughout the season. 1.5 million British holidaymakers travel to Florida each year and over 50,000 of these have bought holiday homes and investment properties. The British love affair with Florida is continuing to grow as traditional investors still see Florida as a solid long-term investment.

About 77 per cent of Florida's population live in its coastal counties where the average value of property has increased almost 50 per cent more than inland. For this reason, properties in central Florida are becoming more and more popular. British and European investors are also finding US properties more affordable due to the weaker dollar compared with sterling and the euro, although in recent months the pendulum has swung back away from sterling. As US interest rates have recently climbed above those in the UK for the first time since 2001, the effect on the USD/GBP exchange rate may move back in favour of the US.

With rising interest rates, the jet-to-let investor has to consider what the effect will be on the property market. Many analysts fear that property prices have peaked in this cycle and with mortgage payments increasing, it may force a crash on the US property market. The evidence presently suggests that the US market has started showing signs of cooling but no signs of crashing.

Tourism

Florida is predominantly a service-based economy and tourism is its biggest industry. The number of tourists has been steadily rising since 2001 and reached 85 million in 2005 with revenues of $62 billion and employment within the sector of 944,500 workers. One dollar in every seven spent by overseas tourists in the US is spent in Florida. By 2010 it's estimated that 97 million tourists will visit Florida, generating $103–136 billion in economic output.

It's also worth noting that Florida is mainly a domestic tourist market. The number of visitors from the EU (excluding the UK) dropped between 1999–2004 and the US in general is facing increasing competition from the Caribbean and Central America. Despite this, the US remains the world's third most popular destination for travellers and tourists and with $74.5

billion revenue it leads the rest of the world in terms of tourist sector revenues.

Property hotspots

Cities

Orlando is 45 minutes from some of Florida's most popular tourist attractions, including Disney World and Sea World, and is also a thriving business and commercial centre. The city has developed into a tourist hotspot attracting millions of visitors each year. The establishment in 1971 of Disney World helped to put Orlando firmly on the tourist map and ever since it has been attracting holidaymakers by the thousands.

Although last year demand slowed for a time as a result of the hurricanes, the property market bounced back and continues to remain strong. Despite strong growth, property prices in Orlando remain below the state and national averages and generally offer good value. A two-bedroom house in Orlando can be bought for $230,000 and will let for around $750 a week. It's worth bearing in mind that the closer you are to Disney World the higher are the prices and you can expect to pay anything up to $750,000 for a four-bedroom house close to the resort.

Orlando is a good jet-to-let investment with high rental returns due to the strong demand for Disney World and the other attractions. It's important, however, to ensure that the property is in the correct rental zone for what you are trying to achieve. You could possibly be limited by restrictions on how long you can rent your property and to whom, so you need to check before you invest.

The expansion of Disney World has led to **Davenport** becoming a popular target area for both investors and home buyers. It has a number of quality leisure facilities which are being improved as more people go to the area. Resort communities are popular as are the quality golf courses which are close by.

Davenport is an emerging property market and prices are expected to rise over the next few years. Currently, a two-bedroom apartment will cost about $150,000, while you can expect to pay approximately $250,000 for three bedrooms. These popular gated resort complexes have pools, health clubs, spas and clubhouses and provide a very attractive rental prospect. You would expect to get around $700 per week for a three-bedroom apartment.

Davenport provides an excellent opportunity for the jet-to-let investor. Demand and prices for rental property will remain strong over the next few years and, as with Orlando, the rental market is virtually 365 days a year.

Kissimmee in south Orlando is ideal for those looking for a retreat from the hustle and bustle of Disney World. Tourism accounts for about 40 per cent of the jobs in the city and its closeness to the theme parks results in year-round rental demand.

A new three-bedroom house can be bought for under $250,000 rising by another $100,000 for a larger house with an additional bedroom.

Islands and coastal

The **Florida Keys** consist of more than 800 islands covering over 1,000 square miles. The Keys consist of five main areas: Key Largo, Islamorada, Marathon, Key West and Layton. The Keys earn much of their income from visitors who enjoy the chilled-out lifestyle. Property prices have risen strongly over the past few years and the high demand ensures a fast moving and liquid market. Although the Keys are a popular destination, there are comparatively few European retirees or second home owners, which may be due in part to the relatively high cost of living.

Key Largo is the largest of the islands at around 30 miles long. At the lower end of the market, bungalows start at around $500,000. A five-bedroom property in Key Largo can set you back nearly $3 million. Properties on the waterfront are more expensive, and at the higher end of the market you can pay up to $6 million.

At the southern end of the Lower Keys lies the town of **Key West** with its upmarket, trendy cafes and restaurants, where seafood is the speciality. Key West has become the chosen location for an increasing number of tourists and second home buyers alike and, as a result, property prices have increased steadily. Two-bedroom apartments and bungalows start at about $425,000. There have been reports of a slowdown in the market because prices have risen to such an extent that they have priced out people who wish to live there.

The **Gulf Coast** has become known as one of the commercial and business centres of Florida, due to its combination of low costs, sound infrastructure and highly skilled labour.

Clearwater is one of the Gulf Coast's liveliest and most popular resorts, attracting more than a million visitors every year. A two-bedroom apartment in Clearwater costs up to $200,000, but in the most exclusive areas a condo can sell for anything up to $2 million. You will find lower-priced properties in the suburbs which in terms of rental yield will be more favourable for a jet-to-let investor.

St Petersburg sits on the edge of Tampa Bay, surrounded by lively resorts and suburbs. While St Petersburg is very popular with tourists, it's quieter than some of the Gulf's other resorts. It's home to an assortment of shops and restaurants but the city's central focus is its pier. St Petersburg's weather and low unemployment supports the property market. Areas of historical importance, such as **Kenwood** and **Crescent Lake**, have seen property prices rise by 300 per cent in the last few years. The rental market in St Petersburg primarily consists of longer-term lets and houses in this area can still be purchased for under $200,000.

Fort Myers is situated on the south of the Gulf Coast and has one of the strongest rental markets in Florida. Property prices are increasing but they still offer good value. A three-bedroom apartment will cost you approximately $400,000, while you can expect to pay upward of $2 million for a five-bedroom house.

Bradenton, home to some great beaches, is regarded as one of Florida's major property hotspots. The average property price rose by 24 per cent in 2004 and the county's population has grown significantly in the last three years increasing the demand for property even further.

Property prices in **Miami** are somewhat higher than the rest of Florida, and areas such as **South Miami Beach**, **Bal Harbour** and **Biscayne Bay** are particularly expensive, with annual capital growth up to 20 per cent. At the cheaper end property can be found in **North Miami Beach**, where a two-bedroom apartment will cost in the region of $180,000. Miami is worth further research if you want exposure to the US residential lettings market as long-term lets are more common in this part of Florida.

South Beach is a 12-mile-long island next to the city of Miami. South Beach is regarded as one of Miami's most desirable resorts, although this was not always the case. In the 1980s, it had crime and drugs problems, but transformed itself into a trendy and stylish area. As a result, property is expensive and a two-bedroom townhouse can set you back around $1 million. The demand for property in this area is high and doesn't tend to stay on the market for very long. South Beach is one of the only areas in Miami that has a short-term rental market as most Miami locations are geared towards long-term lets. Rental prospects in South Beach are good and demand is high.

The buying process

Unlike the UK, each county in Florida has its own laws. Although the conveyancing process is somewhat similar to that in England and Wales, you will find that certain restrictions which may apply in one county may be different from the next.

Once you have found your jet-to-let property, you should have any documents relating to the purchase checked by your lawyer. When you sign the contract, you are likely to be asked to pay a preliminary deposit, typically of ten per cent of the purchase price for US residents and 20–30 per cent for non-residents.

Once the contract has been signed, there is usually a two- to three-week period for all the searches and other checks to be processed.

If the results are unsatisfactory, you can pull out of the contract without any penalty, provided that protective clauses have been inserted into the contract by your lawyer. It's sensible to have a survey conducted if the property is a resale and an independent valuation if you are buying a new-build or off-plan.

Transaction costs

Below is an outline of the expenses you can expect to pay on your purchase:

- **Documentary Stamp Tax (Transfer Tax)** is due on documents that transfer an interest in the property. The rate of tax depends on the location and type of property but generally it's $0.70 per $100.

- **Legal fees:** The cost of these services will depend on whether you use a title company (most Americans buying in Florida do) or a local lawyer. Title companies charge a set fee from $150 to $300, while lawyers' fees would be about $600.

- There are no **estate agents' fees** for buyers.

- **Mortgage fees** amount to three to four per cent of the mortgage and may include the following: mortgage application fee, documentary stamps, Intangible Tax, title insurance, etc.

As a general guide, when buying property in Florida, you should allow two per cent of the purchase price for closing costs if you don't require a US mortgage, and five per cent if you do.

Other important costs to consider include the survey, valuation if instructed, and insurance premium, which may be quite high if you live in the flood zone or on the coast, where you will be vulnerable to hurricane activity.

Annual costs

- **Ad Valorem (Property) Tax** is an annual tax based on the taxable value of the property. Ad Valorem payments are calculated per thousand dollars and usually range from one to two per cent of the property value.

- **Non-Ad Valorem (Council Taxes)** are based on factors such as square footage or number of units. Local authorities are responsible for setting the Non-Ad Valorem assessments and rates differ between counties.

Taxes

Taxation in the US is complex and involves payments to different levels of government: federal, state and local.

Income Tax
US federal Income Tax
Federal Income Tax is levied on the taxable income of US residents and non-

residents. Federal Income Tax is a progressive tax and the filing status is tied to taxpayers' marital status. Here we look at tax rates for a single individual.

Single taxpayer Income Tax rates 2006

Tax rate	Annual tax base (US dollars)
10%	$0–7,550
15%	$7,551–30,650
25%	$30,651–74,200
28%	$74,201–154,800
33%	$154,801–336,550
35%	Over $336,551

Florida State Income Tax

The good news is that the State of Florida doesn't impose personal Income Tax.

Corporation Tax

Federal corporate Income Tax rates 2006

Taxable income in US dollars	Tax rate
$0–50,000	15%
$50,000–75,000	25%
$75,000–100,000	34%
$100,000–335,000	39%
$335,000–10,000,000	34%
$10,000,000–15,000,000	35%
$15,000,000–18,333,333	38%
Above $18,333,333	35%

In addition to federal taxes, states also impose Corporation Tax. Florida's Corporation Tax is a flat rate of 5.5 per cent.

Capital Gains Tax

The tax rate that applies to capital gains depends on how long the individual or company holds an asset. Short-term capital gains are investments held for one year or less. These are taxed as ordinary income at the standard rate. The rates for long-term capital gains are lower and vary according to the seller's Income Tax band, the type of asset sold, and how long the seller held it. Rates vary between five and 15 per cent.

Please note that there is an exemption from Capital Gains Tax of $250,000 ($500,000 for a married couple filing jointly) of gains on the sale of property if the owner used it as the main residence for two of the five years before the date of sale.

Intangible Tax imposed by Florida (similar to Wealth Tax)

Residents of Florida, corporations and persons doing business in Florida are liable for Intangible Tax. Intangible Tax is assessed on properties, stocks, bonds and loans. The first $250,000 of total taxable assets is exempt. Assets above $250,000 are taxed at $0.50 per thousand dollars of value.

Summary

Strengths

- Value for money property.

- Direct flights from the UK.

- English-speaking.

- Worldwide demand for property.

- Strong retirement market.

- High-quality, world-class leisure facilities.

- All-year-round season.

- Strong rental prospects.

- Mature political democracy.

- Strong state economy.

- High job growth.

- Stable property market.

- Low crime rate.

- No restrictions on foreign ownership.

- Large British interest.

Weaknesses

- Hurricanes and damage to property.

- High insurance costs.

- Competition from hotel industry for rentals.

- Competition from the many other owners of properties for rentals.

- Package tour versus private rentals in a high-demand destination.

- The property market may be at the top of the cycle.

- Flying time.

- Visa and other security measures may decrease demand for holidays for foreigners.

- High cost of healthcare has encouraged US retirees to look at other alternatives for retirement, such as Panama.

Opportunities

- Perennially popular with holidaymakers, expats and the retired.

- Lifestyle investment – 'live-and-let' – huge leisure industry and good quality of life.

Threats

- Hurricanes may become more severe with climate change.

- Steadily rising interest rates.

- Competition from the Caribbean and Central America.

Facts at a glance

Geography

Population (2005 estimate)	17,789,864
Language	English
Ethnic groups	The principal ethnic group is White of European origin. Next is: African American (14.6%), Hispanic (16.8%), Asians and Pacific Islanders (3%) and Native Americans (0.3%)
Local currency	US dollar divided into 100 cents

Political system

Political structure for the USA	Federal Republic
President of the USA	George W. Bush
Political structure of the State of Florida	Democratic Republic
Governor of Florida	Jeb Bush
Main parties	Republicans Democrats

Economy

Unemployment rate in 2005	3.8%
Unemployment rate, February 2006	3.2%
Inflation rate in 2005	3.4%
Inflation rate, February 2006	3.4%
Interest rate, March 2006	4.75%
GDP growth in 2005	3.5%
GDP growth forecast for 2006	3.3%
GDP per capita in 2005	$42,122

Florida GSP growth in 2005 (gross state product)	6.6%
Florida GSP growth forecast for 2006	4.6%
Gross state per capita in 2005	$33,219

Taxation

Federal Income Tax	10–35%
State Income Tax	0%
Corporation Tax	Federal Income Tax plus 5.5%
Capital Gains Tax	Federal Income Tax rate for short-term gains 5–15% for long-term gains
Intangible Tax (similar to Wealth Tax)	$0.50 per $1,000 of value

US corruption statistics

Corruption rate	7.6
Corruption rank	17th

The Floridian property market

Hotspots	Inland Cities: Orlando, Davenport, Kissimmee Islands and Coastal: Miami, Florida Keys

Property taxes (transactions)

Documentary Stamp Tax (Transfer Tax)	On general $0.70 per $100
Legal fees	Title company's charge: $150–300 Lawyer's charge: $600
Estate agents' fees	Buyers don't normally pay these fees. There can be a fee of $250 if a buyer's agent is hired

Mortgage fees	3–4%
Total fees	Average 2–5%

Property taxes (annual)	
Ad Valorem (Property) Tax	Ranges 1–2%
Non-Ad Valorem (Council Tax)	Varies within regions

Mortgage	
Maximum percentage of the purchase price	70–80% for non-US residents Up to 90% for the US residents
Term	Up to 30 years
Currency	US dollar, UK pound sterling and euros
Current interest rate	Varies around 6.21%

Investor resources

Embassies

British Embassy in the United States of America
Website: www.britainusa.com

Embassy of the United States of America in the UK

24 Grosvenor Square
London W1A 1AE

Tel: 020 7499 9000
Fax: 020 7408 8020
Website: www.usembassy.org.uk

Useful websites

Business in Florida
www.businessflorida.com

The Official Portal of the State of Florida
http://myflorida.com

State of Florida Information Resources
www.stateofflorida.com

Tourism in Florida
www.visitflorida.com

US Department of Commerce
www.bea.gov

US Department of Labour
http://stats.bls.gov/eag/eag.fl.htm

France

As a place to buy a jet-to-let property, holiday home or permanent residence, it's hard to find somewhere better than France. It's one of the most economically developed countries in the world, and has a long-established property market. The beautiful French countryside and exceptionally high standard of living are particularly appealing, along with its cultural attractions that are second to none.

France is still a major jet-to-let investment country and is an ideal investment location for new and experienced investors.

Why invest in France?

Despite growing competition from low-cost holiday destinations, France is still the world's number one tourist destination. Its close proximity to the UK and all-year availability of budget airline tickets make it easy to escape there for a weekend. The country is home to some of the world's finest and most cosmopolitan cities including the capital, Paris, which is the centre of French government, tourism, art, music and architecture. Tourists continue to be enticed by all parts of the country.

The property market in France is more stable than the UK market, with houses steadily appreciating in value rather than rapid jumps in price before falling. The average house price inflation was highest between 1999 and 2004, growing 10–15 per cent per annum, which has recently slowed to ten per cent in 2005.

Overseas investors are continuing to help the French property market grow and according to the Office of National Statistics, France is second only to Spain as Briton's most favoured country to own a second home. Of all the UK residents with second homes overseas, 20 per cent have chosen to invest here.

Recent statistics reveal a growth in demand for new-build properties, most noticeably for new-build apartments, which are fast becoming the hottest choice for British investors in France.

The story so far...

France has a long history that has seen considerable shifts in the country's influence on global affairs. The French Revolution led to the establishment of the First Republic in 1792 and in 1799, Napoleon Bonaparte proclaimed himself Emperor. During the following years, France expanded through military operations and became the leading force in mainland Europe. In the years after Napoleon's defeat by Wellington at Waterloo in 1815, the monarchy was reinstated, then after defeat by the Prussian Army in 1870, a Third Republic was formed.

France participated in the two world wars and lost a significant number of soldiers and civilians in both conflicts. France was occupied for four years until it was liberated after the Allied landings in Normandy in 1944. Further conflicts in Indochina and Algeria resulted in more losses to its empire, with France's status as a global power being further eroded. The Fifth Republic, the current constitution of France, was created in 1958 introducing a more robust presidential style of government.

The post-war need to bring about economic integration and political stability led to the signing of the Treaty of Rome by France, Belgium, Germany, Italy, Luxembourg and the Netherlands. This established the European Economic Community in March 1957, which was the beginning of the European Union (EU).

Where is it?

France borders Belgium and Luxembourg to the north-east, Germany, Switzerland and Italy to the east and has the Mediterranean to the south. To the south-west are Spain and Andorra and to the west is the Bay of Biscay and the Atlantic Ocean.

The country has stunning scenery, from the Alps and Pyrenees to the Loire valley, Rhône and Dordogne and the countryside in Normandy and on the Atlantic coast. France has a total area of 547,030km^2 and 3,427km of coastline, including 644km on Corsica.

What is the weather like?

There are three types of climate in France, which are oceanic, continental and the Mediterranean. The oceanic climate in the north-west has a small range in temperature, extreme humidity and modest rainfall averaging 35 inches (900 millimetres) a year.

The continental climate covers Eastern and Central France and has warmer summers and colder winters than areas farther west while the Mediterranean climate in the south is for many people ideal, with cool winters and hot, sunny summers.

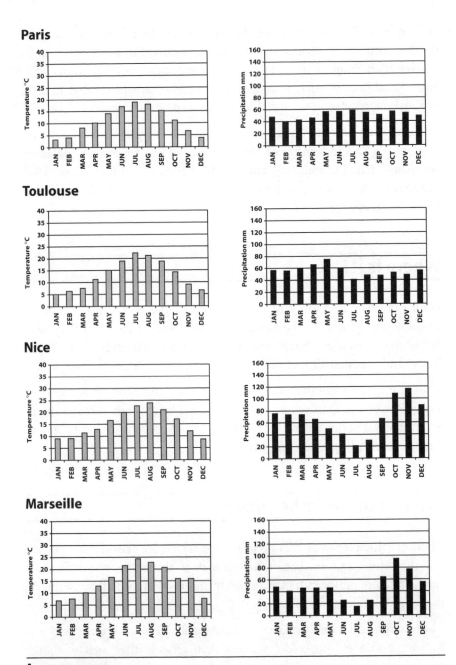

Paris

Toulouse

Nice

Marseille

Language

France has a population of over 60 million people and French is the national language. A high level of immigration, especially from France's ex-colonies, has given France a multi-cultural society with German, Arabic, Spanish and English being spoken as second languages along with regional variations of French.

Currency

The official currency is the euro (EUR) divided into 100 cents.

Politics

France is a semi-presidential democratic republic with a political system that is based on the constitution of 1958. Following the 2002 parliamentary elections, the main ruling parties are the Union for a Popular Movement (UMP) and the Socialist Party (PS). The current president of France is Jacques Chirac (UMP), who was re-elected in May 2002. Dominique de Villepin is the Prime Minister, appointed in May 2005.

France is made up of 26 regions, divided into 100 departments. The departments are administrative units of France, similar to British counties. 22 of these regions and 96 of the departments are in mainland France. The remaining four are Martinique, Guadeloupe, La Réunion and French Guiana.

Economy

France is Europe's third largest economy, but, like other countries in the Eurozone, economic performance has been relatively sluggish in recent years. Economic growth fell from 4.2 per cent in 2000 to its lowest level since of 0.5 per cent in 2003. One of the main reasons behind France's poor performance is a continued decline in consumer spending, which accounts for over half of the French economy.

France has a growing services sector which provides 76 per cent of the country's gross domestic product (GDP). The government retains extensive ownership of the railway, electricity, aircraft and telecommunication industries, but it has been slowly relaxing its control since the early 1990s. Industry generates just over 21 per cent of GDP and more than 80 per cent of export earnings and even though agriculture only accounts for 2.5 per cent of GDP, France is still the EU's foremost agricultural producer and sixth largest in the world.

The French agricultural sector is dependent on EU funding from the Common Agricultural Policy (CAP). France is the main recipient of these subsidies and it currently receives €9 billion per year (22 per cent of the total funds in 2004).

Economic indicators

Economic growth

In 2005, the economy grew by 1.5 per cent and GDP per capita was €25,500. In the second half of last year, France had some encouraging increases in consumer demand, exports and new business start-ups. Increasing consumer confidence and continuing high levels of activity in the property market are likely to push GDP growth close to 1.9 per cent in 2006 and France's main trading partners, Germany and Italy, are also showing mild signs of recovery, which is likely to provide a boost to trade.

Inflation

Inflation in France has traditionally been low and in 2005 was 1.9 per cent, but it's forecast to rise above two per cent in 2006.

Interest rates

France is a part of the Eurozone so its monetary policy is regulated by the European Central Bank. Interest rates were at a flat two per cent from June 2003 until the benchmark was increased to 2.25 per cent in December 2005, and to 2.50 per cent in March 2006.

Unemployment

Unemployment has been a persistent problem for the French economy. The rate has not significantly changed in the last five years; moreover, other data suggest that it has not changed in the past 15 years!

Unemployment rate (percentage unemployed)

2000	**2001**	**2002**	**2003**	**2004**	**2005**
9.1	8.4	8.9	9.5	9.6	9.5

Source: Eurostat, the Statistical Office of the European Communities

In 2006 and 2007, employment opportunities are forecast to increase as a result of improvements in corporate profitability and a brighter economic outlook. However, there remain whole sections of the adult population without work. A massive 63 per cent of 55–64-year-olds are unemployed, which is one of the worst figures among the Organisation for Economic Co-operation and Development (OECD) countries. The latest youth unemployment rate of 23 per cent is among Europe's highest and this reaches 40 per cent in areas with a high immigrant population.

The French government has recently attempted to pass legislation to make the employment market more flexible for the French youth in order to create conditions for more employment opportunities. This led to riots and the government decided against moving forward with this much-needed reform. Until the creation of a more liberalised labour market, continued high levels of unemployment, particularly among the young, will remain.

Foreign direct investment (FDI)

France is one of the biggest sources of FDI in the whole of Europe, but both outward and inward investment have considerably reduced in the last few years. Inflows of foreign investment almost halved in 2004, falling from about €38 billion to just under €20 billion. The US, Germany, Italy and the UK are the main foreign investors in France.

Foreign direct investment in France (€ million)

2000	**2001**	**2002**	**2003**	**2004**	**2005 (estimate)**
46,900	56,400	52,100	37,700	19,600	43,022

Source: Bank of France

Economic summary

France's economy continues to underperform, growing by just 1.5 per cent in 2005. This can be accounted for by a fall in exports which led to lower industrial output.

There are three main issues that will have a significant effect on all areas of the French economy, including the property market:

- **Interest rates** – the European Central Bank (ECB) is continuing to tighten monetary policy, leading to concerns for job creation and business investment. In addition to this, higher mortgage costs may have a negative impact on activity in the property market.

- **Consumer confidence** – the factor of high unemployment means that consumers save more because of financial insecurity. In order to reduce unemployment, changes in government policy are required to increase consumer spending, but this will only happen when there are clear signs of a revival.

- **Labour costs and flexibility** – French competitiveness has been reduced by high labour costs and a highly inflexible labour market. Measures designed to tackle these issues have been unpopular, but without action France will continue to lose out to cheaper, more flexible competitors in Europe and beyond.

What does this mean for the property investor?

In essence, France is a first-world country with a strong economic base and a well-established property market which points to a track record of solid and consistent returns for the jet-to-let investor.

Like many other countries which have a combination of tourist, retiree and home grown demand, the French property market is not homogeneous. Supply and demand for second homes will continue to grow as foreigners who move to France are not deterred by higher European interest rates or high unemployment. Likewise, rentals to holidaymakers will continue as long as France remains the world's favourite tourist destination.

The aspect that will be affected by the economic outlook and high unemployment is the more traditional buy-to-let route in the large cities. If you are after high capital growth in the medium term, then you may be better off looking elsewhere as in terms of opportunity cost, the emerging markets in Eastern Europe fare better when adopting this strategy.

So, what is the catch?

France currently faces a number of serious social issues, threatening the country and its society. Unemployment and immigration are the government's top priorities, but little progress has been achieved to date on either of these.

Unemployment

High unemployment remains one of the most serious issues facing France today reaching 10.2 per cent in May 2005, but since it has started to decline. It remains high among some groups, especially in the areas with a high number of immigrants. It's also a continuing problem for the youth and protests by students in March this year led to rioting. The Prime Minister has implemented a number of successful reforms to confront this issue, but the presidential elections will take place in 2007, meaning that some of the more bold measures may be scrapped.

Immigration

The issue of immigration has recently hit the headlines again in France. After the deaths of two teenagers of African descent in October 2005, youths rioted in the more deprived suburbs of Paris. Rioting spread to other places across the country and continued for 20 nights, leading to one death, 8,973 burnt-out cars and 2,888 arrests.

France has Europe's biggest immigrant population and an estimated 15 per cent of the total population are either immigrants or children of immigrants. Some have blamed the riots on the failure of the French government and society to integrate the second and third generations of the newcomers. The immigrant-born population faces racial discrimination, high unemployment and lives in the more deprived areas.

Far-right politics

Front National is an extreme right-wing political party founded in 1972 and gaining in popularity. The party leader, Jean-Marie Le Pen, came second after the first round of the presidential election in 2002, but was defeated by Jacques Chirac. Many fear that the party may gain political capital from the recent riots as Front National's stance opposes immigration and seeks greater independence from the EU.

Birth rate and ageing population

France has one of the highest birth rates in Europe as well as one of the highest life expectancies in the world. The birth rate has stayed at the same level for the last five years and was 12.15 births to 1,000 of population in 2005. The life expectancy for women has reached 83 years, the highest in the EU, and for men it's 75.5 years. Such increases in the birth rate and life expectancy will put pressure on government welfare spending as the size of the dependent population increases.

The property market

Property prices have grown by 87 per cent between 1997 and 2005 according to *The Economist*. Despite increasing competition from low-cost destinations, it's predicted that the French property market will remain strong. In part, this is due to it being the tourist capital of the world with over 75 million tourists visiting France every year – about 22 million more than the next most popular, Spain.

As in many other European countries, more people rent property than buy it, so opportunities for long-term jet-to-let properties are there, but choosing the right property and location is crucial. The Alps and French Riviera offer short-term jet-to-let opportunities for holidaymakers, although property prices in the major tourist resorts reflect the high demand from nationals and foreigners alike.

The increasingly popular leaseback scheme, which lets you lease your property back to a property management company for up to 12 years, is worth researching. The most obvious benefit of this is that the French government will offset the VAT (known as 'TVA' in France) of the purchase price and the rental income. This usually applies to new-build properties. In effect, you get a rebate that amounts to 19.6 per cent, unless you sell before the end of the lease period.

Tourism

France remains the world's number one tourist destination and has maintained its leading position for several years. Tourism provides €25.6 million and accounts for about 6.5 per cent of GDP.

Property hotspots

Cities

Paris is a major attraction for property investors and tourists alike and the city is famous for its culture, food, fashion and architecture. There is a clear opportunity to let to the expanding city break market, as well as the student population, corporate employees, diplomats and local Parisians.

Paris is divided into 20 districts ('arrondissements') that spiral out from the central district in the heart of the city. These regions vary from the popular tourist sites to wealthy areas such as the seventh and 16th arrondissements, where house prices are significantly more expensive.

The average price of a property in Paris is above €400,000, although you can still buy studio apartments for less than €100,000. Both prices and rents are strong, as is the liquidity of this market.

Away from the capital, there are several other French cities that provide similarly good investment opportunities and would be worth further research, such as **Lyon** in the heart of a region with a strong heritage, an excellent integrated transport system and vineyards a short drive away. Short-term lets are in demand from visiting tourists attracted by the area's reputation for fine wines and food, while long-term rental opportunities exist to service the local demand.

Toulouse is home to the second largest student population in France and it's also an attractive destination for tourists in search of a weekend break. A small apartment in the suburbs can be found for €75,000 and general living costs are average for the rest of the country,

Another city to consider is **Nantes**, birthplace of Jules Verne, as it's relatively close to the Atlantic Coast. There is less competition and lower prices compared with Paris, and its population of over half a million people (of which 35 per cent are under 25 and around ten per cent are students at the university) allows for opportunities to let to the local population.

Ski

France has some of the biggest and best ski resorts in Europe and in recent years has seen a dramatic increase in the price of properties in the major areas such as the Alps. Demand is still high, although French slopes are facing competition from countries such as Bulgaria in terms of attracting skiers, but lower airfares, a short flight time and perceived higher-quality skiing make it a very strong candidate for long-term investment. The average price of a three-bedroom property in the Alps is about €400,000. Weekly rents range from €500 to over €1,000, depending on the season.

There are also a number of ski resorts located in the French **Pyrenees** along the Spanish border including the village of **Bareges**, which has the largest skiing area in this region.

Coastal resorts

Coastal properties on the **French Riviera** have become increasingly expensive due to strong house price inflation and excessive demand. The most widely available properties are apartments and villas, but the cost has been driven upwards thanks to the ever-present factor of 'location, location, location'.

Prices in **St Tropez** and **Cannes** are particularly steep, but the places themselves continue to be popular destinations so as a jet-to-let location it has the potential for excellent returns.

Nice can be a cheaper alternative than the nearby resorts and works well as a base from which to see the surrounding areas. Nice is a haven of culture, with more museums and galleries than any French city outside of the capital, numerous festivals, and the mixture of architecture that makes the city a colourful destination.

You can find a relatively spacious villa on the French Riviera for just under €500,000. Rents for an average two- to three- bedroom villa range from €700 to over €1,300 per week depending on the season.

Rural

Dordogne in the south-west has been one of the most popular areas with British, Dutch and German buyers for years and the area boasts some truly beautiful scenery. Prices here are high, particularly in the south, driven up by high demand from locals and foreign buyers alike. Typical buyers are families and retirees and demand has been further boosted by new low-cost airline routes.

One noteworthy area of France that still offers reasonable prices, year-round mild weather and beautiful scenery is the province of **Languedoc**, an area with one of the fastest growing property markets in the country. Languedoc has the ideal blend of everything, from busy cities to quiet villages and coasts. With a rapidly growing British expatriate community and prices rising elsewhere, Languedoc is worth some further research. Like Spain, prices are lower inland.

Other rural destinations include the **Normandy** and **Brittany** regions, which are both less expensive and easier to reach from the UK via the main ferry ports in northern France.

Transaction costs

There are no restrictions on foreign ownership of property in France. One of the differences you will encounter compared to purchasing property in the UK is the role of the notary, an officer of the state who prepares the title deeds, records that the deed has been signed in his presence and understood by the parties concerned. It's highly advisable for buyers to instruct an independent lawyer for advice.

Upon a sale being negotiated, an initial legal contract is prepared and signed by both parties. On signing the preliminary contract, the buyer must pay a non-refundable ten per cent deposit. After this, the notary starts the legal process and will choose a date for signing the final contract. The remainder of the balance, including legal fees, will be due on completion.

The expenses on a purchase are:

- **Legal fees** are charged by the notary and include the following: Transfer Tax, notary fees and a charge for mortgage security. Overall, the legal fees will come to eight to ten per cent of the purchase price for older properties and three to four per cent for new-build properties.

  The breakdown of legal fees reveals that Transfer Tax is five to seven per cent for resale properties and less than one per cent for new-builds; notary fees are up to two to three per cent; and if you require a mortgage, there is a charge for mortgage security of one to two per cent.

- **Estate agents' fees** can be as high as five to ten per cent and it varies between the seller or buyer paying the fees or the fees can be equally split.

- **Solicitors' fees** are approximately one to two per cent.

- **The mortgage arrangement fee** of one per cent is payable to the mortgage provider.

Buyers should expect to pay in total between 12 and 15 per cent of the purchase price for estate agents' legal and purchasing fees. A growing number of agents are offering all-inclusive sales prices, but it's important to clarify early on exactly what is included.

Annual costs

There are two principal taxes on residential property in France, which are collected by the local authorities of the region. These include:

- **Property Tax** ('Taxe Foncière') is paid by the owner.

- **Municipal Tax** ('Taxe d'Habitation') is paid by the tenant or the owner.

- **Wealth Tax** is paid on all French assets. Its rates vary from 0.55 to 1.8 per cent.

Taxes

France has one of the highest tax burdens in Europe and also one of the most complex taxation systems, so it's strongly advisable that you and your professional advisors conduct a thorough research of taxation rules.

The major taxes in France are summarised below:

Income Tax
Income Tax rates for 2006:

Tax	Annual tax base (euro)
0%	4,412
6.83%	4,413–8,676
19.14%	8,677–15,273
28.26%	15,274–24,730
37.38%	24,731–40,240
42.62%	40,241–49,623
48.09%	Over 49,624

Under the proposed reforms announced in the 2006 budget, from 2007 the new bands will range from 5.5 per cent to a maximum of 40 per cent, replacing the current range of 6.83 per cent to 48.09 per cent. There will also be a 60 per cent ceiling on the total amount of tax paid by any one person, including Income Tax, Wealth Tax and local taxes.

Corporation Tax

The standard rate of Corporation Tax is 33.33 per cent.

Capital Gains Tax

The rate for French residents is 27 per cent (including 11 per cent solidarity Contribution Tax, which is a form of National Insurance contribution).

The tax rate for non-residents in France, but residents of the EU, is 16 per cent. Non-EU residents are taxed at 33.33 per cent.

On the sale of property, ten per cent of the gain is exempted for each complete year of ownership after five years, giving a total exemption after 15 years. You are exempt from Capital Gains Tax on the sale of your principal private residence.

Wealth Tax

A Wealth Tax is levied in France each year on individuals with a total net wealth exceeding €720,000. The tax rate is progressive and varies between 0.55 and 1.80 per cent. For non-residents, wealth is assessed on the basis of their assets in France.

Summary

Strengths

- Political democracy.
- Stable economy.
- Member of the EU.
- Very strong tourist industry.
- Established property market with tried and tested resale and lettings.
- Large cities with opportunities for traditional buy-to-let model.
- Cheaper annual running costs than the UK.
- Strong opportunities for rental/resale.
- Close to the UK with sea, air and rail links.

- Leaseback property schemes.

- France will not go out of fashion.

- Blue chip property investment country for long-term capital growth and income.

Weaknesses

- Competition from other owners of properties for rentals.

- Very high taxation which includes a Wealth Tax.

- Inheritance laws can be an issue and you should take professional advice on how you and your heirs may be affected.

- High unemployment.

- Inflexible labour market.

- Tensions in large urban areas due to immigration.

Opportunities

- Established tourist market promises secure investment returns.

- All-year direct routes from UK and other countries – including budget airlines.

- Development of inland property.

- Renovation of rural properties for selling or letting is a fantastic opportunity.

Threats

- Government not reforming the economy.

- Increasing tax burden.

- Property prices peaking in certain areas.

Facts at a glance

Geography	
Population	60,656,178
Language	French
Ethnic groups	French represent 91% of the population. The remaining groups include North African, Indochinese, and Basque minorities
Local currency	Euro divided into 100 cents

Political system	
Political structure	Democratic republic based on a semi-presidential system
President	Jacques Chirac
Prime Minister	Dominique de Villepin
Main parties	Union for a Popular Movement (UMP) Socialist Party (PS)

Economy	
Unemployment rate in 2005	9.5%
Unemployment rate, February 2006	9.1%
Inflation rate in 2005	1.9%
Inflation rate, February 2006	2.0%
Interest rate, March 2006	2.5%
GDP growth in 2005	1.5%
GDP growth forecast for 2006	1.9%
GDP per capita (income per person) in 2005	€25,500

Taxation

Income Tax	0–48.09%
Corporation Tax	33.33% or 34.43% depending on income
Capital Gains Tax	27%, 16% or 33.3% depending on your residential status
Wealth Tax	0.55–1.8%

Corruption statistics

Corruption rate	7.5
Corruption rank	18th

Industry and technology

Major industries	Telecommunications Automobile Aerospace Textiles and luxury products Tourism

The French property market

Hotspots	Cities: Paris, Montpellier, Marseille, Lyon, Toulouse, Bordeaux and Nantes Ski: the Alps, Pyrenees Coastal Resorts: St Tropez, Nice and Cannes Rural: Dordogne, Brittany, Loire Valley, Languedoc and Provence

Property taxes (transactions)

Legal fees	10% on resale properties and 4% on new-builds
Estate agents' fees	5–10%
Solicitors' fees	1–2%
Mortgage registration fees	1%

Total fees	Average 12–15%

Property taxes (annual)	
Property Tax	Varies significantly across the regions
'Council Tax'	Varies significantly across the regions

Mortgage	
LTV	85% for non-residents 100% for French residents
Term	Up to 25 years
Currency	Euro and other major currencies
Current interest rate	Varies between 2.9 and 4.5%

Investor resources

Embassies

British Embassy in France
35, rue du Faubourg St Honoré
75383 Paris Cedex 08

Tel: +33 (0)1 44 51 31 00
Fax: +33 (0)1 44 51 41 27
Website: www.britishembassy.gov.uk

French Embassy in the UK
58 Knightsbridge
London SW1X 7JT

Tel: 020 7073 1000
Website: www.ambafrance-uk.org

Useful websites

All about France
www.france.com

Bank of France
www.banque-france.fr

French National Institute of Statistics and Economic Studies
www.insee.fr

Invest in France
www.investinfrance.org

Tourism in France
www.francetourism.com

Germany

Rich in history and culture, and with cities that have a very high standard of living, Germany has a lot of potential for the jet-to-let property investor.

Why invest in Germany?

Germany should be viewed as an opportunity for investment rather than a certainty. Even after having a near-stagnant economy and flat property market for the last decade, it's very unlikely that Germany, as one of the largest economies on the planet, will fall off the map entirely. Instead, analysts predict that the election of a new grand coalition government, the sale of public housing and a boost from hosting the FIFA World Cup this year will see resurgence in the German economy soon. The jury is still out and, at this stage, a lot needs to change before things start to look more promising for jet-to-let investors.

The story so far...

Germany played a key role in 20th century history. The country was defeated in both World Wars, which led to its occupation and division into East and West. Since the end of the Second World War, Germany has undergone enormous social, political and economic change and established itself as the dominant economic powerhouse in Europe.

The most significant event of recent times has been the reunification of the country in 1989. The Berlin Wall came down ending 44 years of imposed separation but, ironically, this has been an obstacle for subsequent development of modern, united, Germany. The area that was formerly East Germany has struggled to catch up with the more developed West even after an extensive programme of modernisation accounting for the transfer from West to East of an estimated €1 trillion to date since reunification.

West Germany was one of the founding members of the European Union (EU) and modern Germany remains a committed member. The country joined NATO in 1955.

Where is it?

Germany has borders with its neighbours Denmark in the north, Poland and the Czech Republic in the east. Austria and Switzerland lie to the south, France and Luxembourg in the south-west and Belgium and the Netherlands in the north-west. Germany shares more borders with other countries than any other country in Europe.

Germany stretches from coastline along the North Sea in the north-west and the Baltic Sea in the north to high mountains of the Alps in the south. Germany has a total area of 357,021km² and 2,389km of coastline.

What is the weather like?

The climate is moderate without extreme cold or hot periods. Most of Germany is situated in the cool west wind zone with damp westerly winds from the North Sea so the climate in north-west and coastal Germany is oceanic, characterised by relatively mild weather. The rest of the country has a continental climate, with variations in temperature throughout the seasons, leading to warmer summers and colder winters.

Berlin

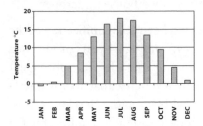
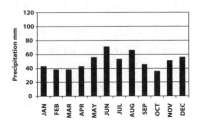

Frankfurt

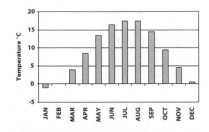
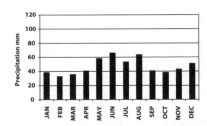

Munich

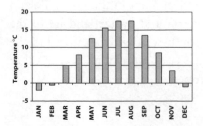
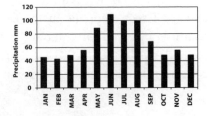

Hamburg

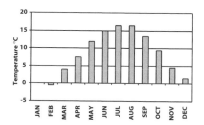
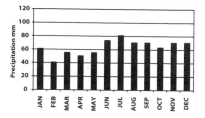

Language

Germany has a population of around 82 million, of which 92 per cent are German. The remainder of the population is 2.4 per cent Turkish and six per cent from other groups. The official language is German, which is spoken by over 95 per cent of the population and English is widely spoken as a second language.

Currency

The official currency is the euro (EUR) divided into 100 cents.

Politics

Germany is a federal parliamentary republic, with the Chancellor acting as the head of government. The Chancellor is traditionally a candidate of the party with the most seats in parliament, supported by a coalition of two or more parties with a majority.

The most recent elections took place in 2005 and a Grand Coalition government was formed with the main ruling party being the Social Democratic Party of Germany (SPD) in coalition with the Christian Democratic Union (CDU) and the Christian Social Union of Bavaria (CSU). Angela Merkel (CDU) was elected as the Chancellor of Germany.

As a federal republic, Germany is divided into 16 states which are further subdivided into 439 districts.

Economy

The German economy is the largest in Europe and one of the largest in the world. It operates under a social market economy, which brought about miraculous economic progress since the war ended in 1945. There are some concepts that are central to the social market, which strives to keep a balance between high growth, low inflation, low unemployment, good working conditions and effective social welfare.

As a result, modern Germany has an exceptionally high standard of living and a generous welfare system. The country's economy is based on a strong industrial sector and Germany has long established itself as one of the world's largest and most advanced manufacturers.

The services sector, including banking, insurance, transportation and tourism, has grown steadily over recent years and now contributes the largest share of its gross domestic product (GDP), which was 66.5 per cent in 2005.

The German economy has recently spent several years in near stagnation and has been one of the slowest growing economies in Europe over the past decade. This slow growth has been accompanied by high levels of unemployment and a marked lack of business confidence.

Nobody predicted that the long-awaited reunification of Germany would mark the start of a period of economic stagnation. The continuing integration of the Eastern economy remains an expensive long-term process and this economic setback, along with the failure to adjust to modern business requirements, has meant that Germany has become a less attractive place to invest in. This is particularly noticeable when compared with cheaper and more flexible labour markets over the borders in neighbouring Poland and the Czech Republic.

Economic indicators

Economic growth

The economy grew at an average yearly rate of 1.2 per cent from 2000 to 2005. In 2005, it grew by just 1.1 per cent, while the GDP per capita in the same year was €25,300. The European Commission forecasts an increase in activity and forecasts economic growth of 1.5 per cent in 2006. This growth will be export driven as foreign trade has recently received a significant boost from a more favourable euro/dollar exchange rate.

Inflation

Inflation is traditionally low in Germany and in 2005 year-on-year inflation grew by 1.9 per cent. The forecast for 2006 is 1.6 per cent and this is based on a predicted decline in oil prices, but continuing political tensions in the Middle East currently give them little room to fall.

Interest rates

Germany is a part of the Eurozone so its monetary policy is regulated by the European Central Bank. Interest rates remained at a flat two per cent since June 2003 until the benchmark was increased to 2.25 per cent in December 2005 and to 2.50 per cent in March 2006.

Unemployment

Unemployment is both a cause and a symptom of the latest economic slowdown. The threat of relocating manufacturing companies to Eastern Europe has forced employees in Germany to work longer hours or to accept pay cuts. The wide-ranging social welfare system and a high tax burden has reduced the motivation to work, and high labour costs and inflexible employment laws, combined with weak demand, have reduced the number of job opportunities.

Unemployment rate (percentage unemployed)

2000	2001	2002	2003	2004	2005
7.2	7.4	8.2	9.0	9.5	9.5

Source: Eurostat, the Statistical Office of the European Communities

Recent data confirm that the percentage of long-term unemployed is about 52 per cent of the total, which is one of the highest rates in the EU. There are some positive signs of a recovery in the labour market as employment growth has started to stabilise. The jobs created by stronger exports and the wealth and confidence which has resulted has led to a gradual pick-up in domestic demand.

Foreign direct investment (FDI)

When looking at the figures, FDI in Germany seems sporadic and reflects uncertainty in the current economic climate. The major foreign investors are the USA, Japan and Switzerland and FDI inflows are widely distributed across various economic sectors, such as software, business services, automotive components and electronics. The German government continues directing investment to the east of the country where it's most needed, and offers incentives and grants to promote this policy.

Germany is one of the largest investors abroad, but the amount of money invested has decreased significantly since 2003. It invested €16.8 billion in other countries in 2005.

Foreign direct investment in Germany (€ million)

2000	2001	2002	2003	2004	2005
215,209	29,518	56,871	25,873	-12,172	26,264

Source: Deutsche Bundesbank (German Central Bank)

Economic summary

German workers are on average paid more per hour than Americans, although they produce 13 per cent less (*sources: Capital Economics; BLS*). There lies one of the problems of the German economy, namely labour cost, flexibility, mobility and the reduction of skills in the long-term unemployed. Reform is key and one of the reasons for Angela Merkel being elected was to push this through, but the reality seems to have fallen short of this for now.

Attitudes towards investing and business sentiment are rising in Germany, but until the German people's attitude shifts away from saving money and moves towards spending it on goods and services, then it's up to the export market to continue driving the economy. With rising Eurozone rates and also a strengthening currency, the validity and duration of any German economic revival is still unclear.

What does this mean for the property investor?

German property has lost value in real terms and in opportunity terms for investors over the last ten years. Analysts don't foresee the market situation reversing very quickly and a boom in property prices in the short term is unlikely. This is because of sluggish growth, high unemployment, rising interest rates and a culture that has a tendency towards renting rather than purchasing property. High transaction costs and a lack of competitive loans and mortgages add weight to the idea that a rapid improvement is some time away.

So, what is the catch?

Although Germany's social market economic system has helped it to build one of the largest economies in the world, the country continues to suffer from several key social problems that could act as major obstacles to recovery.

Reunification

The reunification of Germany in 1990 was without doubt a positive event for the German people and the geo-political climate in Europe, but the logistical implications have presented the country with a number of problems. The economic divides that existed when the East of the country was much poorer than the West continue to persist in 2006. There are also prejudices held towards Easterners, and bitterness regarding the financial cost of reunification, which has not been helped by the weak economic performance of recent years.

Unemployment

High levels of unemployment remain one of the most crucial social issues to resolve in modern Germany. The unemployment figure for 2005 was 9.5

per cent, but, despite this, Germans are not in favour of labour reforms to rectify the situation, such as longer working hours, and they seem to prefer the 'job for life' culture. The new Chancellor is expected to propose several new policies that will affect the labour market in an attempt to address the issue, but it has been necessary to scale down many of her more radical plans to appease the current coalition government.

Low birth rate and ageing population

Germany has one of the lowest birth rates in Europe, and one of the highest life expectancies. Birth rates have plummeted to around 8.3 per 1,000 of population in 2005 from 11.4 in 1990, with average life expectancy for men being 76 and 81 for women. This represents a key shift in demographics that will cause further strains on Germany's ability to provide social welfare in the future.

Corruption

According to Transparency International, the 2005 German Corruption Perception Index (CPI) is ranked 16th with a score of 8.2 ahead of the US, France, Belgium, Japan and Spain. This indicates that Germany is virtually a corruption-free country from a business perspective, which should be encouraging for potential investors.

The property market

The German property market has experienced negligible growth over the past 15 years due to the economic slowdown. However, attitudes towards home ownership among most German citizens, who have traditionally rented, may be changing as banks and large corporations begin to sell off significant numbers of apartments to overseas investors. This reduces costs as the investors go on to sell the properties to tenants, but opinion is divided as to whether this will act as a significant catalyst for growth in the property market.

The German property market continued to stagnate in 2005, with property prices remaining flat along with the level of housing loans. The prospects for 2006 don't look too promising, although there is plenty of media coverage and marketing activity talking the market up!

Tourism

Germany is ranked ninth in the world by the number of tourist arrivals, with over 20 million visitors last year. These contributed to a 5.8 per cent rise in revenue from tourism of €14.1 billion.

Germany is expected to benefit immensely from hosting the FIFA World Cup in 2006 with an estimated attendance of over ten million fans from around the globe. This is fantastic news for the short term, but the real gain is the global exposure that Germany will receive for up to a month during the championship.

Property hotspots

If you want to invest in jet-to-let property in Germany, then it's the bigger cities that should be investigated first. Rural properties in the German countryside are also an option for investors, but those seeking sun, sea and sand will find little of any of these things here. Investing in Germany is about long-term tenants and the traditional buy-to-let model.

Cities

Berlin, the capital city, has a population of around 3.4 million people. It remains debatable as to whether Berlin is a good investment in terms of opportunity cost, but with economic recovery possible, letting prospects can only improve. In all of the major cities and suburbs, apartments are popular as there is often a shortage of land for housing. For a capital city, Berlin is cheap as a two-bedroom apartment in the city can be purchased for €95,000 and rental income from this averages around €600 per month.

The city has a rich cultural life and is at the centre of reunified Germany, but the property market can be erratic due to comparatively low demand from other buyers. This aside, with low prices and the possibility that Germany will regain its economic prowess, this city might be just the sort of speculative investment that could pay off in the future.

Frankfurt is an attractive jet-to-let option. The standard of living is excellent, with Frankfurt ranked top in Germany and a very respectable eleventh in the world, with a strong financial services market attracting international executives, city financiers and merchant bankers. Frankfurt is the economic centre of Germany and is home to hundreds of banks and financial institutions, including the Bundesbank and, since 1998, the European Central Bank. It's a modern international and cosmopolitan city, with just under 30 per cent of its residents coming from overseas.

Munich is one of the drivers of the German economy and is home to the corporate headquarters of many successful multi-national companies, such as insurance company Allianz, BMW, defence contractor EADS, Siemens and the German headquarters of Microsoft. The city also has the second largest airport in Germany after Frankfurt.

When considered alongside the rest of Germany, higher returns are more likely in these dynamic and vibrant cities. In a future economic resurgence, these locations will maintain their pivotal position and the business opportunities that arise will provide a boost that will increase property prices and rental income.

Compared to other European cities with similar standards of living, such as Geneva and Vienna, prices in potential German hotspots are very inexpensive. It would seem, at least to the more optimistic investor, that if there is a good time to invest in German property, it would be now. Other cities with the highest rental levels that feature highly for their standard of living are **Stuttgart**, **Hamburg**, **Düsseldorf** and **Cologne**.

Rural

At least 75 per cent of German houses have been built since the Second World War, although traditional village homes can still be found in rural areas. There are many properties in the former East Germany which need modernisation. The **Rhine** and **Mosel** valleys are popular destinations for those seeking a rural lifestyle alternative to the bustling cities. The **Black Forest** is also a favourite choice for those who find their element in a more nature-orientated holiday destination.

Transaction costs

There are no restrictions on foreign ownership of property in Germany. A lawyer who specialises in conveyancing can conduct the legal work on your behalf and you must pay the following transaction costs:

- **Purchase Tax** is 3.5 per cent of the price. This is payable four weeks after the notary deed has been signed by the buyer and seller.

- **Notary fees** are around 1.2–1.5 per cent of the purchase price, plus any translation fees.

- **Estate agents' fees** vary across the country. They are usually around five to six per cent plus VAT and would normally be divided between the buyer and the seller.

- **Registration fees** are between 0.8 and 1.2 per cent.

- If financing is required, there may also be some fees payable to the bank and additional notary and registration fees for the mortgage.

On average, the total fees to take into account on top of the purchase price are approximately 10–12 per cent.

Annual costs

- **Property Tax** – This is annually levied on all residential property by local authorities. It tends to vary between different cities and regions, but, as a guide, it's between €150 and €300 per apartment per year. It would be slightly higher for a house and the figure is also dependent on the size of the property.

- **'Council Tax'** – Additional costs for refuse collection, water, common areas, maintenance and the like add up to about €0.5–2 per square metre per month.

Taxes

The German taxation system was overhauled in 2000 with the intention of boosting the country's economic competitiveness. Even after these changes, Germany has one of the most complex taxation systems in Europe.

The major taxation rules for Germany are outlined below:

Income Tax
Individual Income Tax rates for 2006:

Tax	Tax base (€)
0%	Up to 7,664
15%	7,665–52,151
42%	52,152 and over

As of 1 January 2007, for high-income individuals with income exceeding €250,000, the highest tax bracket will increase from 42 per cent to 45 per cent.

Corporation Tax
The basic federal Corporation Tax rate in Germany currently stands at 25 per cent.

Capital Gains Tax
A capital gain in Germany is treated as income and is therefore taxable at the Income Tax rate for both an individual and a company. There is an exemption on the sale of a private property that has been owned for over ten years.

Summary

Strengths

- Political democracy.
- EU member.
- Mature and stable judiciary and legal framework.

- Modern infrastructure.

- Little/low corruption levels.

- Strong industrial producer.

- World beating manufacturing brands.

- Large long-term rental markets in urban centres and also the possibility of short lets in Berlin.

- High living standards.

Weaknesses

- The present government doesn't have sufficient political power to implement radical reform necessary for economic growth.

- Weak economy.

- High savings ratio which inhibits a consumer-led recovery.

- Labour market rigidity.

- Rental culture.

- Mortgage market.

- Rising interest rates.

- High transaction costs for an investor.

- Relatively complex taxation system and high rates.

Opportunities

- 'Bottom fishing' – is this the bottom of the property market?

- Reform leading to strong economic growth.

- Liberalisation of the mortgage market?

- Berlin property prices on a square metre basis are rock bottom.

- FIFA World Cup 2006 will provide global exposure which may increase awareness of investment opportunities in general.

Threats

- Continued economic slowdown.

- 'Bottom fishing' too early and a continued real fall in prices thus making an opportunity loss.

- When will interest rates peak?

- Further relocation of manufacturing to Eastern Europe.

Facts at a glance

Geography	
Population (2005 estimate)	82,431,390
Language	German
Ethnic groups	92% German. Minority groups include Turkish, Greek, Italian, Polish and other
Local currency	Euro divided into 100 cents

Political system	
Political structure	Federal republic with parliamentary system
Chancellor	Angela Merkel
Main parties	A coalition between Christian Democratic Union (CDU)/ Christian Social Union (CSU) and Social Democratic Party (SPD)

Economy	
Unemployment rate in 2005	9.5%
Unemployment rate, February 2006	8.9%

Inflation rate in 2005	1.9%
Inflation rate, February 2006	2.1%
Interest rate, March 2006	2.5%
GDP growth in 2005	1.1%
GDP growth forecast for 2006	1.5%
GDP per capita (income per person) in 2005	€25,300

Taxation

Income Tax	15–42%
Corporation Tax	25%
Capital Gains Tax	Taxed as income

Corruption statistics

Corruption rate	8.2
Corruption rank	16th

Industry and technology

Major industries	Iron Cement Steel Chemicals Automotive

The German property market

The most popular destinations in which to invest	Berlin, Frankfurt, Munich, Stuttgart, Hamburg, Düsseldorf and Cologne

Property taxes (transactions)

Transfer Tax	3.5%
Notary fees	1.2–1.5%
Estate agents' fees	5–6% plus VAT
Registration fees	0.8–1.2%

Total fees	Average 10–12%

Property taxes (annual)	
Property Tax	Varies. Normally is around 1% of rateable value
'Council Tax'	€0.5–2 per square metre per month

Mortgage	
LTV	70%
Term	30 years
Currency	Euro
Current interest rate	Varies between 4.90 and 6.15%

Investor resources

Embassies

British Embassy in the Federal Republic of Germany
Wilhelmstrasse 70–71
10117 Berlin

Tel: +49 (0)30 204 570
Fax: +49 (0)30 204 57 594
Website: www.britischebotschaft.de/en

Embassy of the Federal Republic of Germany in the UK
23 Belgrave Square
London SW1X 8PZ

Tel: 020 7824 1300
Fax: 020 7824 1449
Website: www.german-embassy.org.uk

Useful websites

Deutsche Bundesbank (German Central Bank)
www.bundesbank.de

Expatriate Resource

www.howtogermany.com

Federal Statistics Office of Germany

www.destatis.de

Invest in Germany

www.invest-in-germany.de

A Manual for Germany

www.handbuch-deutschland.de

Tourism in Germany

www.germany-tourism.de

Greece

Why invest in Greece?

Sunshine on every day of the year and an extremely relaxed lifestyle has helped Greece to become a popular destination for tourists and investors. It's one of the most beautiful countries in the world, with a varied and scenic landscape and one of the richest histories in Europe. Greece was the third most popular destination for British holidaymakers in 2005.

Greece offers a good variety of properties for jet-to-let investors, second home buyers and retirees. Greece is tipped to become a new hotspot among the more traditional EU-15 markets, and Athens and the Greek islands look set to benefit from this most.

The story so far...

In 1829, Greece gained independence from the Ottoman Empire and went on to add neighbouring islands and territories to the area it controlled. Greece was invaded by Mussolini's Italy in 1940 and was subsequently occupied by Germany from 1941 until it was liberated by the Allies in 1944.

Following the Second World War, fighting continued in a civil war between Communists and royalist supporters of the king, with the former being defeated in 1949. In 1974, democratic elections and a referendum created a parliamentary republic and abolished the monarchy. Greece joined the European Community in 1981 and became the 12th member of the Eurozone in 2001.

Tensions continue to exist between Greece and Turkey over Cyprus and the established borders in the Aegean Sea, but relations have improved somewhat in recent years.

Where is it?

Greece is located in Southern Europe on the tip of the Balkan Peninsula. It borders Bulgaria, the Former Yugoslav Republic of Macedonia and Albania to the north and Turkey to the east. Also to the east is the Aegean Sea, with the Ionian and Mediterranean Sea to the west and south.

Mainland Greece consists of a mountainous peninsula extending 500km into the Mediterranean Sea. It consists of 3,000 islands, of which only about 150 are inhabited. The mainland and the islands have a combined coastline of some 13,676km.

What is the weather like?

Greece has a Mediterranean climate with subtropical summers in the lowlands, although the mountainous areas are much cooler and often covered with snow for much of the winter. Winters are mild in the lowlands. Most rainfall in Greece occurs between November and March and there is often no rain in June, July and August. On average, the sun shines for over eight hours a day.

Athens

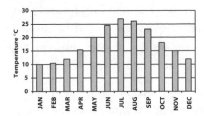

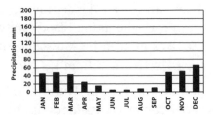

Crete

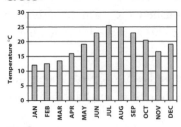

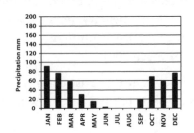

Corfu

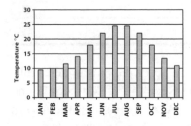

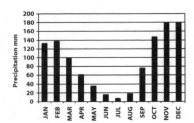

Rhodes

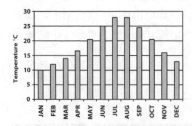

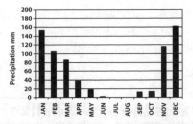

Halkidiki

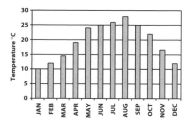

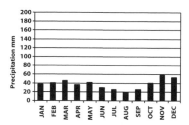

Language

The official language is Greek, which is spoken by 98 per cent of the 10.7 million inhabitants. The largest minority language is Macedonian, spoken by only 1.8 per cent of the population and English is widely spoken as a second language.

Currency

The currency in Greece is the euro (EUR) divided into 100 cents.

Politics

Greece is a parliamentary-based democratic republic. The main parties at the moment are the centre-right New Democracy (ND) and the Panhellenic Socialist Movement (PASOK). Karolos Papoulias is the President of Greece, who has held office since 2005. The Prime Minister is Kostas Karamanlis, who was elected the year before.

Administratively, Greece is divided into 13 peripheries (regional districts) – nine on the mainland and four island groups. The peripheries are further subdivided into 51 prefectures

Economy

Greece has been successful in diversifying its economy from one which is agriculture-based to one that is increasingly industrialised and service-oriented. Services account for over 71 per cent of its gross domestic product (GDP), dominated by tourism. Greece is also the world's leader in shipping.

Greece has benefited considerably from joining the Eurozone with lower interest rates leading to a boost in the economy and strong growth rates. Growth has been sustained at a time when some countries of the Eurozone are in a sharp economic slowdown.

Despite this economic growth, Greece is still one of the poorest countries in the old EU-15. It's a major beneficiary of funding from the European Union (EU), which accounts for 3.3 per cent of GDP. Since 2000, the European Council has allocated €25 billion to Greece, which helped fund some major public investments and development projects. This has improved the standard of living in poorer regions. The allocation of funds for 2007–2013 is yet to be finalised, but transfers to Greece are expected to fall by up to 50 per cent as EU aid is diverted to the ten new member states that joined the EU in May 2004.

The Greek government intends to privatise several state-owned companies as at the moment the state controls 55 per cent of the economy, which is the highest level in the EU. This privatisation should provide a catalyst for further reform of the economy.

Greece's main economic challenge for 2006 is the effective reduction of its budget deficit to meet the Eurozone target of three per cent of GDP. Spending on the Olympic Games left Greece with a large deficit of 6.1 per cent of GDP in 2004, which has since been reduced to 4.6 per cent in 2005. The 2006 budget is planning to reduce the deficit to just 2.6 per cent of GDP by the end of the year.

Economic indicators

Economic growth

The European Commission reports that GDP grew by 3.7 per cent in 2005 with current GDP per capita estimated at €19,400. The economy has slowed after growing at 4.7 per cent in 2004, mainly as a result of the slump in investment activity following the Olympic Games. The forecast for 2006 is a growth of 3.4 per cent.

GDP averaged over 4.2 per cent from 2000 to 2005, which is well above the EU average of 1.5 per cent. This is a strong performance relative to Greece's peers and this looks promising for future development of the economy.

Inflation

The European Commission reports that inflation rose by 3.5 per cent in 2005 (the EU-25 average rate was 2.2 per cent), driven by a surge in world oil prices, indirect taxes and high wage growth. Inflation is forecast to stay just below three per cent throughout 2006.

Interest rates

Greece is part of the Eurozone and therefore its monetary policy is regulated by the European Central Bank. Interest rates increased to 2.25 per cent in December 2005 and then to 2.50 per cent in March 2006.

Unemployment

The level of unemployment in Greece is above the EU average, but the jobless rate has started falling recently as the country has achieved sustained economic growth.

Unemployment affects significantly more Greek women than men. In 2005, the jobless rate among women was 15.2 per cent, compared to only 5.6 per cent for men and the country also has a very high youth unemployment rate with over 25 per cent of all registered unemployed being under the age of 25.

Unemployment rate (percentage unemployed)

2000	2001	2002	2003	2004	2005
11.3	10.8	10.3	9.7	10.5	9.8

Source: Eurostat, the Statistical Office of the European Communities

Foreign direct investment (FDI)

FDI in Greece decreased substantially after 2001 and peaked again in 2004, driven by the Olympic Games. Although it's an investment-friendly country, it still has a number of limitations. The government has only just begun liberalising the telecommunications and energy sectors, but it has plans to promote business, reduce red tape and allow the introduction of investment incentives as a priority. These measures should provide a welcome boost to future foreign investment. The real effect will be determined by the pace of government reforms and the extent to which the tiger economies of Eastern Europe affect investments in the traditional EU-15.

Foreign direct investment in Greece (€ million)

2000	2001	2002	2003	2004	2005
1202.8	1776.1	53.4	585.9	1088.4	212.3

Source: Bank of Greece

Economic summary

Greece has experienced stable economic growth for each of the last five years and appears to be well situated for further growth this year. Employment growth is strong and inflation is still restrained. The ongoing reforms in restructuring the economy are expected to minimise bureaucracy, which will create a more investment-friendly location. These reforms will contribute to further accelerated growth.

What does this mean for the property investor?

Property investment in Greece is supported by the continued economic growth and an expanding services sector. Infrastructure investment in Greek cities, particularly Athens, has encouraged business and corporations and provides a target market for longer-term rentals.

The Greek islands rely on tourism, which is still running as strong as ever. The second home market is expanding along with the demand for quality properties for the growing band of European and British retirees.

For a medium- to long-term jet-to-let strategy, Greece and its islands will provide a solid and stable investment return.

So, what is the catch?

Unemployment

The Greek economy is still challenged by high unemployment, particularly among young people and women. More than 50 per cent of all registered unemployed have been out of work for more than a year.

Low birth rate and ageing population

Greece has a very low birth rate compared to other European countries. In 2005, the birth rate was just 9.7 births per 1,000 of population. Life expectancy for men is 76 and for women is 81. This shift towards an older population will cause a strain on welfare provision which has to be paid from somewhere, which usually means by taxation or other government receipts.

Corruption

According to Transparency International, Greece scored 4.3 points and was ranked 47th, alongside the Czech Republic and Slovakia.

The property market

In the last few years the Greek property market has not performed to its clear potential and there are a number of reasons which have led to that. Transaction costs were very high, making Greece less attractive to the jet-to-let investor and second home buyer. In addition to this, competition in the tourist market is strong and a number of alternatives, such as Cyprus, Bulgaria and Turkey, have emerged in that region. Finally, Greece's major cities are still known for their poor infrastructure.

Change is in the air

The Olympic Games in 2004 had a major impact on infrastructure spending and propelled Greece onto the world stage. A number of projects were completed around the country and particularly in Athens, which had a much-needed boost in tourism. Furthermore, the build-up to the Games contributed significantly to the relatively strong performance of the Greek economy in the earlier years.

The government has introduced several reforms to maintain the post-Olympic development trend and to create a more liberal, free-market economy. A major change in the purchasing process was introduced in January 2006, which effectively substitutes the Transfer Tax for 19 per cent VAT on new-build and off-plan properties. The new legislation is complex and unclear so it remains to be seen what effect this will have on the property market as a whole.

The majority of jet-to-let investment in Greece is currently centred on the retirement, second home and holiday home markets. Following the Olympics, however, investors have started taking a lot more interest in residential and commercial opportunities in large Greek cities such as Athens.

Residential properties for sale in Greece along the coast and on the islands are presently cheaper than similar properties in countries such as Spain or France, which makes Greece potentially more attractive to new entrants in the overseas property market.

Greece offers investors a property market at a different stage in the cycle. It's still relatively undiscovered and it certainly is not as sophisticated or developed as the Spanish property scene. It's expected that property prices in Greece will continue to rise at an estimated growth rate of near to ten per cent per annum.

Tourism

Tourism is the most important service industry in Greece and has a major impact on the Greek economy. An estimated 13.5 million tourists visited the country in 2005 and this number is predicted to continue to rise.

The 2004 Olympic Games increased confidence about the future of tourism. Many tourism-related infrastructure projects have transformed Greece into a year-round destination. According to the World Travel and Tourism Council, the total tourism revenues in Greece were €28.6 billion in 2005 and are forecast to increase by over five per cent per annum over the next ten years. This sector currently contributes 16 per cent of national GDP and 18 per cent of all jobs.

The majority of tourists are from the UK and Germany, although there has been an increase in the number of arrivals from as far away as the United States and Australia.

Property hotspots

Cities

Athens is the capital of Greece and is considered by many as the cradle of European civilisation. As such, the city benefits from several millennia of history and is an attractive destination for tourists and investors alike.

Visitor numbers have continued to rise and combined with the infrastructure improvements have boosted the demand for property. Property prices in Athens have grown by over 60 per cent in the last five years compared to a national house price inflation (HPI) of 55 per cent in the same timeframe. Analysts expect the property market in Athens to remain strong in the next few years, which presents an opportunity for the astute investor looking to target locals to let to, along with the growing number of corporate tenants and expats.

The strong student population in the city offers an alternative market as does the considerable demand for short-break accommodation for visiting tourists who prefer to do their own thing in preference to going on a package tour. The low-cost airline EasyJet, for instance, flies to Athens, increasing the opportunities for catering to the weekend-break market. Being a large city, the majority of properties available for purchase are apartments in new developments. As an example, a one-bedroom apartment in Athens will cost €70,000 to €80,000.

Islands and coastal

Crete is Greece's largest and most southerly island, and perhaps the most beautiful. The island is easily accessible from the rest of the world, with two international airports located at Heraklion and Chania, as well as a third at Sitia in the east with direct charter flights in the summer. Crete also has a well-developed road network and regular sea routes that connect the island with mainland Greece, the Aegean Islands and Cyprus. The wonderful climate, low cost of living and very low crime rate make an attractive combination that will appeal to those looking to buy a second home or for somewhere to retire.

Over the last few years the number of people investing in Crete has boomed, with 80 per cent of foreign houseowners being from the UK. The island's growing popularity as an investment location has pushed up prices to the extent that they are now double what they were a few years ago and are still rising steadily along with stronger rental prospects.

The majority of British property-owners in Crete are currently based in western Crete near **Chania**, which is less populated than the rest of the island. The Venetian port, waterfront restaurants and narrow shopping streets come together to create a beautiful setting. There is a wide selection of property available in the region and demand is strong, but for now you can still purchase a two-bedroom apartment for under €100,000.

Agios Nikolaos is one of the more developed towns in Crete, but it has retained its traditional character and, as a result, it has become very popular with tourists. For this reason, property here can be difficult to obtain and is more expensive than some of the other areas of the island.

Just north of Agios Nikolaos is **Elounda**, which has the perfect blend of mountains and sea, lending it a more tranquil setting. Elounda is known worldwide for its luxury spa resorts and also offers some seriously challenging golf courses.

Sitia is an area in eastern Crete which appears to have growing potential as a jet-to-let investment hotspot following the recent expansion of the airport. Now it looks set to become increasingly popular and the combination of traditional tavernas and harbour makes the perfect location for short-term lets with strong potential for strong capital growth. You can pay between €125,000 and €140,000 for a two-bedroom apartment in the Sitia region, but jet-to-let properties in eastern Crete have higher average rental returns than those in the west. Currently, there is little competition as relatively few investors have tuned into the rental market in eastern Crete, but this is unlikely to stay the case for long.

In south-east Crete is **Makris Yialos**, a small fishing village which has grown to become a bustling tourist resort. A golf course is scheduled for completion this year which will have an impact on tourist numbers, the types of people visiting and so will open up the area to winter golf tourism.

Corfu is the second largest Greek Ionian island and is one of Greece's top holiday destinations. Corfu has a lot to offer, such as stunning scenery and fascinating archaeological sites. Many foreign investors have chosen to make Corfu their home to benefit from the relaxed and healthy environment and low crime rate.

Property prices on Corfu are currently increasing at a rate of ten per cent per annum. Like in Crete, strict planning regulations prevent the development of high-density or high-rise buildings like those found in some parts of Spain. This is important for the jet-to-let investor as it means that a 20-storey tower will not eventually block your much-treasured sea view. In addition to this, the supply of property is restricted, which supports and encourages property price inflation as demand expands.

On the western coast of Corfu is the town of **Lakones**, which attracts an influx of tourists in summer but has still managed to retain its traditional character. A little further along the coast lies **Glyfada**, which has a great beach, good selection of bars and tavernas and Aqualand, a huge water park. All of these things make this a perfect location for families, and investors thinking of buying property in this area would have little trouble letting it during the peak season. You can expect to pay up to €170,000 for a two-bedroom house and €250,000 for a three-bedroom depending on the property's location.

Property prices on another of the Greek islands, **Rhodes**, are increasing on average by 15 per cent a year. Purchasing a property has the potential for great returns and as Rhodes is considered to have the best weather in the whole of Greece, a shortage of short-term tenants is unlikely.

There is a downside, and that is that property in Rhodes is more expensive than Crete. The average price of a house in Rhodes is €200,000 and at the top end of the market you might pay €400,000 for a five-bedroom house with a pool and a garden near the beach. With this in mind, renovation projects are an attractive option, and it's still possible to pick up a derelict house for as little as €60,000. Rhodes, unlike the rest of Greece, has an established Land Registry system.

At present there are only charter flights direct to Rhodes from the UK, but scheduled flights are expected to commence soon, which is a positive indicator for property investors and tourists. If you are planning to invest in Rhodes in the future, now is the time to begin your research as prices are forecast to rise significantly over the next few years.

Finally, **Halkidiki** is another destination worthy of further investigation. The three-fingered peninsula has beautiful white sandy beaches, clear waters and nicely varied scenery and the tourist facilities have been well designed. The frequent festivals attract many visitors each year, leading in turn to a higher demand for accommodation during these events. The nightlife is well developed and the city of Thessaloniki – Greece's second city with a huge student population – is close by. It's possible to find a three-bedroom house in Halkidiki for under €150,000, and a two-bedroom flat or apartment can be snapped for under €80,000.

The buying process

All EU citizens have equal rights concerning the purchase or sale of property in Greece. There are a few restrictions for foreign property buyers in border regions close to Turkey regarding security, but there are plenty of estate agents and lawyers available to assist with the buying process around the major coastal resorts and on the most popular Greek islands.

It's as important in Greece as anywhere to instruct an independent local English-speaking lawyer who is experienced in property law and conveyancing. The lawyer is responsible for conducting searches ensuring that the vendor has the legal right to sell you the property as well as to ensure that the property is free of any charges and claims. The lawyer also ensures that all property taxes owing by the vendor have been paid in full. In areas that do not yet have a Land Registry, ownership of property is based on the local Registry of Mortgages.

The next step in the buying process is to obtain a Tax Registration Number (AFM), which is necessary when dealing with the Greek Tax authorities and this is issued on the spot at Tax Offices, free of charge.

On signing a preliminary purchase agreement, you are required to pay a ten per cent deposit. Once the preliminary purchase contract has been signed in front of a notary, your lawyer can carry out the required searches. When the searches and survey have been completed, the final contract is signed in the public notary's office in the presence of both parties.

Transaction costs

When purchasing property in Greece, it's important to be aware that while the buying process is straightforward, it's also expensive. Therefore, you will need to include all additional fees and charges in your estimated purchase costs.

According to the new tax law of January 2006, transaction costs vary depending on when the building permit was issued for your particular property. If the building permit was issued prior to January 2006, then:

- **Transfer** or **Purchase Tax** ranges from nine per cent to 11 per cent. There may also be an additional two per cent for urban properties;

- **Notary fees**, **lawyers' fees** and **land registration fees** will overall total 2.5 per cent.

If the building permit was issued after January 2006 (new-builds), then:

- **notary fees**, **lawyers' fees** and **land registration fees** will total 2.5 per cent; **but**

- **VAT** at a standard rate of 19 per cent is added to the cost of the property in place of the Transfer Tax.

Note: At the time of going to print, the tax legislation relating to new-build property remains unclear and complex and the overall impact of the abolition of Transfer Tax and the introduction of VAT still needs clarification.

Apart from these costs, you may be partially or wholly liable for the estate agent's fees, although it's generally the seller's responsibility.

Annual costs

- **Local Municipal Tax:** This tax ranges from 0.025 to 0.035 per cent on the objective value of the property and is incorporated into the electricity bill.

- **Yearly Property Tax:** Owners of property pay a yearly Property Tax only if the objective value of their ownership(s) exceeds the amount of €243,600. The tax amounts to 0.3–0.8 per cent of the objective value of the property.

Taxes

The major taxes in Greece are summarised below:

Income Tax
As of January 2005, Income Tax rates ranges from 5 to 40 per cent.

Tax	Annual tax base (€)
0%	11,000
15%	11,001–13,000
30%	13,001–23,000
40%	23,001 and over

The Greek government is considering introducing a flat-rate 25 per cent Income-Tax band for both individual and corporate earnings. If it's approved, it will become law in January 2007.

Corporation Tax
The standard rate of Corporation Tax is 29 per cent as of January 2006. This rate is set to be reduced to 25 per cent on income earned in 2007.

Capital Gains Tax
A capital gain in Greece is added to income and is taxable at the same rate as regular income for both an individual and a company.

On a sale of property, the Capital Gains Tax is calculated on a sliding scale based on the length of time the person has owned the property and the property's value (20 per cent if the property has been held for 0–5 years, ten per cent for 5–15 years, five per cent for 15–25 years and 0 after that).

Summary

Strengths

- Political democracy.

- An EU member.

- Consistent economic growth.

- Strong tourist market and demand for second homes, retirement homes and rentals.

- Long tourist season.

- Stable and emerging property market at the same time.

- Great beaches.

- Beautiful scenery.

- Good infrastructure in Athens due to 2004 Olympics investment.

- Low crime rate.

- Low-cost flights.

- Huge variety of property and locations available.

- Relatively cheap coastal properties.

- No restrictions on foreign ownership.

- Large British interest.

- Large European interest.

- Cultural and business centre of Athens.

Weaknesses

- Competition from hotel industry for rentals.

- High unemployment and rigidity of the labour market.

- Ageing population.

- High levels of corruption.

- Falling FDI.

- High transaction costs.

Opportunities

- Although the Greek property market is clearly not 'emerging' as such, compared to countries like Spain, it's now showing signs of a sustained period of catch-up.

- More low-cost airline routes will open up the islands.

- Continually popular with holidaymakers, expats and retirees.

- Lifestyle investment for 'live-and-let' with a huge leisure industry and good quality of life.

- Renovation projects in the hills and the mountains offer fantastic money-making opportunities.

- Joint venture development projects (i.e. developing with a business partner) also have the potential for success.

Threats

- The relatively underdeveloped economy may suffer from rising EU interest rates.

- Possible overheating of the property market in some areas.

- Cheaper locations opening up in Bulgaria and Turkey.

Facts at a glance

Geography

Population (2005 estimate)	10,668,354
Language	Greek
Ethnic groups	Not recognised by government
Local currency	Euro divided into 100 cents

Political system

Political structure	Parliamentary democracy
President	Karolos Papoulias
Prime Minister	Kostas Karamanlis
Main party	New Democracy (ND) Panhellenic Socialist Movement (PASOK)

Economy

Unemployment rate in 2005	9.8%
Unemployment rate, fourth quarter 2005	9.7%
Inflation rate in 2005	3.5%
Inflation rate, February 2006	3.1%
Interest rate, March 2006	2.5%
GDP growth in 2005	3.7%
GDP growth forecast for 2006	3.4%
GDP per capita (income per person) in 2005	€19,600

Taxation

Income Tax	15–40%
Corporation Tax	29% in 2006
Capital Gains Tax	Gains are taxed as income

Corruption statistics

Corruption rate	4.3
Corruption rank	47th

Industry and technology

Major industries (contribution to GDP)	Tourism Textiles Chemicals

The Greek property market

Hotspots	Greek islands: Crete, Corfu and Rhodes Mainland: Halkidiki and Athens

Property taxes (transactions)

Notary fees, land registration fees, legal fees	Around 2.5%
Transfer Tax (on properties whose building permit was issued prior January 2006 only)	9 –11% (extra 2% applies on urban properties)
VAT (on properties whose building permit was issued after January 2006 only)	19%
Overall costs	15–20%

Property taxes (annual)

Local Municipality Tax	0.025–0.035%
Yearly Property Tax	0.3–0.8%

Mortgage

Maximum percentage of the purchase price	80% (up to 100% in some cases)
Term	Up to 30 years
Currency	Euros, US dollars and pound sterling

Current interest rate	Ranges between 3.90 and 4.45%

Investor resources

Embassies

British Embassy in Greece
1 Ploutarchou Street
106 75 Athens, Greece

Tel: +30 210 727 2600
Fax: +30 210 727 2723
Website: www.british-embassy.gr

Greek Embassy in the UK
1A Holland Park
London W11 3TP

Tel: 020 7221 6467
Fax: 020 7243 3202
Website: www.greekembassy.org.uk

Useful websites

Bank of Greece
www.bankofgreece.gr

Essential Information about Greece
www.ellada.com

Hellenic Centre for Investment
www.elke.gr

Invest in Greece
www.invgr.com

National Statistical Service of Greece
www.statistics.gr

Tourism in Greece
www.gnto.gr
www.greek-tourism.gr

Italy

Fending off competition from cheaper destinations such as Bulgaria and Turkey, Italy remains one of the most popular destinations for holidays and second homes in the world, thanks to its unique combination of culture, climate, cuisine and countryside.

Why invest in Italy?

Italy was one of the first European countries to attract significant numbers of tourists from the UK in the original package holiday era of the 1960s and 1970s. The recent boom in low-cost airline routes around Europe has provided a welcome boost to the Italian tourism industry, making northern and central areas not only easy to reach, but also very affordable. Flight times are also attractive and many destinations are now well within a three-hour flight from the UK.

Italy can offer you a sound jet-to-let investment opportunity provided you choose the right area. Investing in Italy is not a way to get rich quick, but with sound research, analysis and planning, you can find opportunities to make solid profits over the medium to long term. Italy is very unlikely to go out of fashion as some of the cheaper emerging markets may do.

The story so far...

Italy has a rich history and its influence from Roman times has dominated European history. More recently in the 20th century Mussolini's Fascist government joined an alliance with Germany in 1922, a disastrous choice which led to the country's defeat by the Allies in the Second World War. The Italian Republic was born in 1946 after a referendum which ousted the monarchy, and a new constitution was adopted two years later. It's a founding member of the European Union (EU), and a member of the United Nations, NATO and the G8.

Where is it?

Italy is in Southern Europe. It comprises the familiar 'boot'-shaped peninsula and two large islands in the Mediterranean Sea, Sicily and Sardinia. Italy shares its northern border with France, Switzerland, Austria and Slovenia, while San Marino and the Vatican City are independent within Italian territory and Campione d'Italia is an Italian enclave in Switzerland. The country's total area is 301,230km^2 and it has 7,600km of coastline.

What is the weather like?

Italy's climate is Alpine in the north, but the weather varies considerably depending on the geographical features of different regions. The winter is very cold in the Alps, cold and foggy in the Apennines, warm on the Liguria coast, the Neapolitan coast and Sicily. The summer is hot and dry, but the temperature is cooled on the coast by sea breezes.

Rome

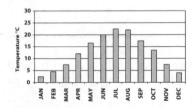 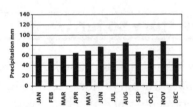

Venice

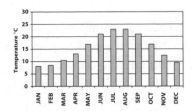 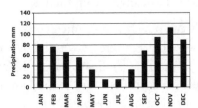

Florence

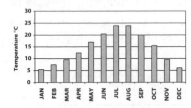 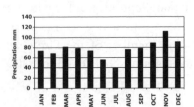

Milan

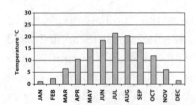 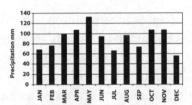

Tuscany

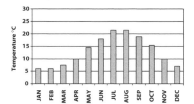

Sardinia

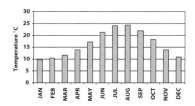

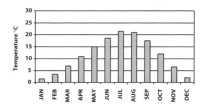

Turin

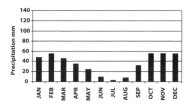

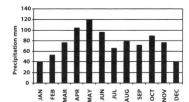

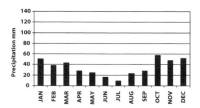

Language

The official language is Italian. The country has a total population of over 58 million people, consisting of Italians along with small communities of German, French, Slovene, Albanian and Greek descent.

Currency

The official currency is the euro (EUR) divided into 100 cents.

Politics

Italy is a parliamentary democratic republic which has two political alliances: centre-right House of Freedoms and centre-left Olive Tree. Each political alliance is a coalition of a number of political parties. The major political party of the House of Freedoms' alliance is Forza Italia, while the majority of Olive Tree members are made up of left-wing democrats. The current President is Carlo Azeglio Ciampi, elected in 1999. Romano Prodi is the Prime Minister, after narrowly beating his predecessor, Silvio Berlusconi, in the April 2006 election.

Administratively, Italy is divided into 20 regions. The regions are then subdivided into provinces.

Economy

Presently, the Italian economy is in the doldrums as economic growth has slowed and stopped. Within the Eurozone, only Germany has grown more slowly than Italy.

Lack of growth is due in part to a loss of competitiveness. Prior to the adoption of the euro, Italian governments had the option to devalue the currency to make exports more competitive internationally. Italy can no longer do this as a result of the adoption of the single currency. Additionally, interest rates are set by the ECB in Frankfurt for the Eurozone as a whole and it has been argued that the rate is too high for countries such as Italy and Germany but too low for countries such as Ireland, all of which are at different stages in the economic cycle.

Furthermore, manufacturing plants have relocated to countries within the single market where labour costs are cheaper and the workforce is more flexible. This pattern is repeated across the countries of Old Europe, where companies find it more profitable to base their manufacturing operations in countries such as the Czech Republic and Slovakia.

Recent polls, particularly by *The Economist*, suggest that Italy will return to growth in 2006. With an election out of the way, the new government with a finely balanced majority will have its work cut out to force through the reforms necessary to generate solid economic growth.

Economic indicators

Economic growth

Economic growth averaged 1.2 per cent between 2000 and 2005, but in 2005 the country grew by a disappointing 0.1 per cent in real terms. Its gross domestic product (GDP) per capita was €24,200.

The forecast for 2006 looks slightly more promising as the European Commission projects GDP growth of 1.5 per cent. The Italian economy started showing signs of recovery in the latter half of 2005, when employment growth triggered a rise in consumer spending.

Inflation

Inflation grew by 2.2 per cent in 2005, largely due to a surge in energy prices. It's expected to remain above two per cent in 2006.

Interest rates

Italy is part of the Eurozone, and its monetary policy is regulated by the European Central Bank. Interest rates increased to 2.25 per cent in December 2005 and to 2.50 per cent in March 2006.

Unemployment

Unemployment has been falling for the last couple of years and currently stands below the European Union (EU) average. The services sector is providing the majority of new jobs.

Unemployment rate (percentage unemployed)

2000	2001	2002	2003	2004	2005
10.1	9.1	8.6	8.4	8.0	7.7

Source: Eurostat, the Statistical Office of the European Communities

Despite a small reduction in the rate of unemployment, there are still some serious structural problems in the labour market, and the large north/south divide in job opportunities and the number of long-term unemployed is evidence of this.

In the last quarter of 2005, the jobless rate was 4.5 per cent in the north, 6.7 per cent in central Italy, and in the south there was a sharp decline to 14.2 per cent.

Foreign direct investment (FDI)

Unlike other European countries, Italy has managed to maintain a relatively constant level of foreign investment during the last six years.

Foreign direct investment in Italy (€ million)

2000	2001	2002	2003	2004	2005
14,517	16,618	15,455	14,544	13,542	12,720

Source: Bank of Italy

Italy enjoys a favourable international reputation for its sophisticated product brands (e.g. Versace, Dolce & Gabbana, Ferrari, Maserati and Alfa Romeo), excellent manufacturing base and high quality of production and finish. Its major FDI sources are Spain, UK and the US and the main sectors which benefit are textiles, financial services, IT and software.

Economic summary

All is not well with the Italian economy, which is suffering as a result of membership of the Eurozone and a lack of competitiveness. Reforms are necessary, particularly in the labour market, but with the recent election results it's debatable whether the newly appointed Signor Prodi has the majority to push policies forward.

Fierce competition from Eastern Europe is clearly having a detrimental effect on Italian manufacturing and it remains to be seen how well opportunities can be exploited in the services sector.

What does this mean for the property investor?

Italy is not an emerging property market, although it's fair to say that in pockets in the south, some markets are still very much undiscovered. Property investors can take comfort in the fact that the Italian economy's poor performance is not having an effect on the short-term rental market in the locations that Europeans flock to during the spring and summer. Renting to locals is a very different issue and the strength of that market clearly lies in the large cities, predominantly in the industrialised and more commercial north of the country.

So, what is the catch?

Regional disparity

Italy remains divided into an industrialised, economically developed north and a less developed south reliant on agriculture. To illustrate this, analysts have pointed out that if southern Italy was given independence overnight, it would be the poorest country in the EU-25 in terms of GDP per capita or income per person.

The EU and Italian government have invested heavily in these areas but it has had little effect. The black economy and organised crime appear to be the main beneficiaries according to some reports.

Ageing population

Life expectancy for men is 77 years and for women is 83 years; the population aged 65 and over will rise by 44 per cent between 2005 and 2050. When the decline of over 30 per cent in the working age population is combined with Italy's low birth rate (8.89 births per 1,000 population), the effect will be a huge increase in the dependency ratio, from 32 per cent in 2005 to 67 per cent by 2050. In 2004, Italy was one of four EU-25 countries where the proportion of the population aged 65 and over exceeded the proportion aged under 16. The implications of an ageing population are more pronounced than in many other countries and this trend will be responsible for putting an increased strain on public finances.

Corruption

Italy's score was 5.0 points in the Transparency International Corruption Perception Index (CPI) and was ranked 40th, alongside Hungary and South Korea. This is one of the worst performances among the EU-15.

The property market

For many years, Italy was ignored by jet-to-let investors, as it was not seen as a country to make money from property. However, in recent years, jet-to-let property investors have begun to realise Italy's investment potential and how best to unlock it.

Property prices in Italy have risen steadily for a number of years, but at fairly modest rates. Prices rose by about six per cent in 2004 following an eight per cent rise in 2003. Perhaps unsurprising is the fact that price growth has been concentrated in the more dynamic cities and regions such as Rome and Milan.

Italy has always been and remains a solid long-term investment. Property prices appreciate steadily while rental demand remains high. According to *The Economist*, property prices appreciated 69 per cent between 1997 and 2005. In 2005, Italy experienced a four per cent average rise in property prices and the forecast for 2006 suggests a near-flat rate.

Renovation projects

Low-cost airlines flying to regional airports in Italy have brought other property markets to the attention of those investors who are attracted to period properties. These can still be bought at low prices which makes renovation a profitable option. The Italian government offers grants for renovation projects in order to entice the overseas property investor and this approach seems to be working.

Italy is different to many of the other popular jet-to-let locations covered in this section of the book. Here, there is the culture, history, class and food to attract high-net-worth individuals to the countryside and the coast and will continue to do so, regardless of the economic outlook for the country. A jet-to-let investment in Italy will perform well over the medium to long term.

Tourism

Italy is the world's fifth most popular tourist destination with over 37 million arrivals spending €28.7 billion in 2005. People from other EU states make up the largest numbers of tourists and those coming from the UK, Scandinavia and Eastern Europe have risen.

Italy's most popular sites to visit are the ruins of Pompeii, Rome, Tuscany, Sicily, the coastline of the Adriatic Sea and the Alps. The Italian cities of Venice, Florence, Milan, Pisa and Naples are as popular as ever.

Italy's enduring appeal provides a cushion from the fashion-led and often fickle tourist market. Given its history, beauty and weather, Italy is not prone to being affected by some of the uncertainties that other tourist destinations may have and repeat tourism provides strong support to the industry.

Property hotspots

Cities

Properties in tourist-centred cities attract a premium and are more expensive than the rest of Italy. Top of the list is the capital, **Rome**, where prices vary considerably from district to district. In cheaper areas, a two-bedroom apartment will cost about 300,000, but for an identical property overlooking the Coliseum, you will pay twice as much. This is no surprise, as the supply of property overlooking the Coliseum is highly 'inelastic'.

Rome has a lot to offer the jet-to-let investor and the tourist alike, making short-term lets an attractive option. The city is one of the oldest in the world and is a magnet for visitors from around the globe. With the advent of low-cost flights to Ciampino Airport, it can be cheaper to fly to Rome than to get a train from Runcorn to Reading. Summer is a particularly busy time for visitors, although rental prospects are good all year round and long-term rentals from the local population and students are also a viable option.

There are several other cities across Italy that make good jet-to-let destinations. Famous for its canals, gondolas, architecture and romance, **Venice** is one of the most visited of all Italian cities. While it can be expensive, the tourist trade is bustling, guaranteeing rental income between spring and autumn which, on a two-bedroom apartment, could be as much as €1,000 per week. Apartment prices vary, but on average you should expect to pay over €400,000 for a two-bedroom apartment in Venice.

Another top destination for the Italy-bound tourist is **Florence**, the regional capital of Tuscany. Again, property prices are far from cheap, but the high volume of visitors for most of the year pretty much ensures that rental apartments are rarely empty.

In complete contrast is the city of **Milan**, Italy's business capital famous for its fashion and nightlife. Letting to the local population is a viable option, though as with many other Italian cities, short-term lets can provide sufficient rental income to cover costs and then some.

Verona is also popular, especially with those in search of a weekend away. Among other things, the city has its own airport and well-preserved artistic heritage as well as a wealth of archaeological sights and narrow streets to explore. Venice's annual two-month opera festival is also a major attraction.

Rural

The Italian countryside is some of the most beautiful in Europe. The most popular place to invest in jet-to-let property is **Tuscany**. Property in Central Tuscany is in high demand and, as a result, reflects this with higher relative prices. This said, it's possible to pick up a smaller property at a reasonable price if you look carefully enough. North Tuscany, around Lucca, can be better value as it still remains relatively undiscovered where a two-bedroom house can be found for around €250,000 while a one-bedroom can be found for under €150,000. It's possible to get a weekly rent for around €550–650, depending on the location. Although properties in the region may initially seem expensive there is never a shortage of people wishing to rent them for family holidays and short breaks.

Umbria, next to Tuscany, is a cheaper alternative. It has many great features, but, most importantly, it's in a location that allows visitors to explore neighbouring areas, such as Tuscany, Lazio and Romagna. It's a good place to invest in, and although the region's main airport Perugia is not a low-cost airline destination yet, Pisa and Ancona are within easy reach. Property is generally more expensive in the tourist towns of **Assisi** and **Orvieto**, while prices are more reasonable in the more rugged region around **Citta di Castello** and **Umbertide**. Also worth considering is the area around **Lake Trasimeno**, where you can pick up a two-bedroom apartment for less than €100,000.

The Italian lakes are growing in popularity, after recently losing out to the likes of Tuscany and the Côte d'Azur. The region consists of six lakes that lie close to the Swiss border in Lombardy. It's the largest lakes, Garda, Maggiore and Como, that attract the most attention from visitors and second home buyers.

Lake Como, which is just half an hour's drive from Milan, is by far the most popular, especially with British jet-to-let investors and second home buyers, who make up 15 per cent of the market. A two-bedroom apartment near the strip between Menaggio and Como can be purchased for around €200,000 and would let for up to €600 a week.

Lake Maggiore is the second largest lake in Italy, stretching between Lombardy and Piemonte reaching into the Alps, and property is slightly cheaper than Lake Como. It's a good idea to look for the lesser known lakes, such as **Ledro**, which is just 15 minutes from Garda, as well as **Lake Idro** and further south, **Liguria** is still very relatively cheap.

Abruzzo is located on Italy's long and narrow peninsula and is sparsely populated with vast unspoilt countryside. Abruzzo is often overlooked by investors, but it offers a taste of the genuine article of Italy, with the majority of tourists here themselves being of Italian origin and are attracted by the allure of beautiful scenery and food. There are plenty of old farms for sale and small village properties requiring refurbishment. Jet-to-let investors should keep an eye on this region as prices are low in comparison with other places in Italy, but with flight connections increasing at the local Perscara airport and intense media interest in the

UK, prices may well be set to rise. A one-bedroom apartment could be found for €90,000 while renovation projects can be purchased very cheaply, and in some cases for as little as €30,000.

Coastal and islands

Despite its climate and stunning coastlines, **Puglia**, in the far south of Italy, has never been recognised as a fashionable region of Italy so property prices are relatively cheap. Accessibility is an issue that has restricted development in this part of Italy, but this is continually improving. Both of the region's two closest airports, Bari and Brindisi, receive regular direct flights from the UK and Puglia is just an hour's drive from the airport. The new routes opened by low-cost airlines mean that demand for rental property here is set to soar. At the moment, depending on location, you can find four-bedroom houses for under €250,000.

The Mediterranean island of **Sardinia** has a lot to offer, from quiet coves and beaches through to nature reserves, mountaintop ruins and a clear blue sea. Property prices vary considerably in Sardinia with resorts on the north being among the most exclusive in the Mediterranean.

While property in Sardinia may not be ideal for all buyers, it's generally a good investment prospect as the island is becoming more and more popular with tourists and second home buyers. Airline connections are improving each year and the higher demand from people visiting the island will be matched by the need for accommodation. A jet-to-let investment here could quite easily pay dividends over the medium to long term.

Ski

There is no shortage of ski resorts in Italy thanks to the country's geography. The best facilities are in the north of the country in the Alpine region. **Turin**, location of the recent Winter Olympics, has an airport attracting budget airlines which supply tourists to its fantastic ski resorts. Notable ski resorts include **Sauze d'Oulx**, **Bardonecchia** and the more developed **Sestriere**.

On the other side of Italy is the Dolomite mountain range with the popular resorts of **Madonna di Campiglio** and **Cortina d'Ampezzo**.

Other destinations in the region include **Breuil-Cervinia**, the beautiful spa town **St Vincent** and **Pila**. With property in places as beautiful as this, you might find yourself wanting to stay there permanently!

The buying process

There are no restrictions on foreigners buying property in Italy and the buying process is straightforward. Italy has a reputation for being highly regulated, conservative and for doing things in a fixed way, but even so it's very important to employ a local English-speaking lawyer.

Once you've found your property, you make an official offer to purchase. As a gesture of good faith, this will normally include putting down a deposit, ranging from two to five per cent. The next step is the signing of the preliminary contract, which will usually be conditional upon satisfactory surveys and the buyer being able to secure a mortgage, if required. At this stage the buyer also pays an additional deposit of 10–20 per cent.

A few points have to be made here. The responsibilities of an Italian surveyor, 'gerometra', are different to those in the UK. The gerometra partially acts primarily as an architect, but also as a surveyor with the main responsibility of establishing the planning status of the property and its boundaries. The preliminary contract is usually drawn up by an estate agent and this is normal practice in Italy.

Following this, the notary then checks the title deeds, planning consents and other documents relating to the purchase. Once this has been successfully completed, the buyer and seller meet to sign the final contract. For completion, the buyer will need to have a tax code and the balance of the price with all taxes is paid. The notary then issues a certified copy of the deed of sale and registers the original document with the Land Registry, to show you as the legal owner of the property.

Transaction costs

The transaction costs are as follows:

- **Real Estate Tax** is three per cent of the property value.

- **Local Tax** ranges from 0.4–0.8 per cent of the cadastral value (i.e. an administrative value which is used as a base or a point of reference for tax) of the property.

- **Legal fees** are one to two per cent of the sales value of the property.

- **Registration Tax/stamp duty** is charged instead of VAT on resale properties and comes to three to seven per cent of the property value.

- **Notary fees** are fixed by law on a sliding scale. As a general guide, allow one per cent of the declared price.

- **Estate agents' fees** are three to six per cent and are normally split between the buyer and seller.

- Apart from that, allow funds for the **surveyor's fees** and connection to the water, electricity and gas mains if required.

Overall transaction costs can be as high as 15 per cent of the purchase price.

Annual costs

- **Community Tax** is paid by anyone who owns property or land in Italy. It's levied at between 0.4 and 1.2 per cent of a property's cadastral value, the actual rate being decided by the local authority depending on the size of the property, location, class and category.

- **Local Tax** covers locally supplied services, such as rubbish collection, street cleaning, etc. The tax rate varies from region to region.

Taxes

The major taxation rules in Italy are outlined below:

Income Tax

Tax	Annual tax base (€)
23%	Up to 26,000
33%	26,001–33,500
39%	33,501–100,000
43%	Over 100,001

Corporation Tax

The standard rate of Corporation Tax in Italy is 33 per cent.

Capital Gains Tax

The rules on Capital Gains Tax are complex so you should take specialist advice, but generally the tax is 12.5 per cent.

Summary

Strengths

- Political democracy.

- Stable economy.

- A member of the EU.

- Strong tourist industry.

- World-class culture.

- Higher end of the tourist market attracting greater revenues.

- Strong repeat business tourist market.

- Established property market.

- Strong opportunities for rental/resale.

- Low-cost airline routes.

Weaknesses

- Competition from other owners of properties for rentals.
- High taxation.
- High transaction costs.
- Persistent and high unemployment.
- Sluggish economy.
- Regional imbalances in wealth creation.
- Inflexible labour market.
- Ageing population.

Opportunities

- Established tourist market promises secure investment returns.
- All-year direct routes from UK and other countries, including budget airlines.
- Development of inland property.
- Growing market in the south for second homes and holiday rentals.
- Renovating older properties for resale or letting.

Threats

- Government not reforming the economy.
- Increasing tax burden.
- Property prices peaking in certain areas.
- Corruption in places.

Facts at a glance

Geography

Population (2005 estimate)	58,133,509
Language	Italian
Ethnic groups	Mainly ethnic Italians and small communities of Italians from German, French, Slovene, Albanian and Greek descent
Local currency	Euro divided into 100 cents

Political system

Political structure	Parliamentary republic
President	Carlo Azeglio Ciampi
Prime Minister	Romano Prodi
Main parties	Forza Italia Left-wing democrats

Economy

Unemployment rate in 2005	7.7%
Unemployment rate, December 2005	7.7%
Inflation rate in 2005	2.2%
Inflation rate, February 2006	2.2%
Interest rate, March 2006	2.5%
GDP growth in 2005	0.1%
GDP growth forecast for 2006	1.5%
GDP per capita (income per person) in 2005	€24,200

Taxation

Income Tax	23–43%
Corporation Tax	33%

Capital Gains Tax	12.5%

Corruption statistics

Corruption rate	5.0
Corruption rank	40th

Industry and technology

Major industries	Precision machinery Motor vehicles Pharmaceuticals Fashion and clothing Tourism

The Italian property market

Hotspots	Cities: Rome, Venice, Florence and Milan Rural: Tuscany and Umbria Coastal and islands: Sardinia, Puglia, Amalfi coast and the Italian lakes Ski: Turin

Property taxes (transactions)

Real Estate Tax	3%
Local Tax	0.4–0.8%
Solicitors' fees	1–2%
Stamp duty	3–7% (resale properties only)
Notary's fees	About 1%
Estate agents' fees	3–6%
Total fees	15%

Property taxes (annual)

Community Tax	0.4–1.2%
Local Tax	Varies
Maintenance costs	€800–1,100

Mortgage	
LTV	85%
Term	5 to 30 years
Currency	Euros
Current interest rate	3.93–4.45%

Investor resources

Embassies

British Embassy in Italy

Via XX Settembre 80
I-00187 ROMA RM

Tel: +39 06 4220 0001
Fax: +39 06 4220 2334
Website: www.britishembassy.gov.uk

Italian Embassy in the UK

14 Three Kings Yard
London W1K 4EH

Tel: 020 7312 2200
Fax: 020 7312 2230
Website: http://wwp.londonw1.com/embassy/italy-embassy.htm

Useful websites

All about Italy

www.allaboutitaly.com

Bank of Italy

www.bancaditalia.it

Institute of Statistics in Italy

www.istat.it

Invest in Italy

www.investinitaly.com

Tourism in Italy

www.italiantourism.com

Morocco

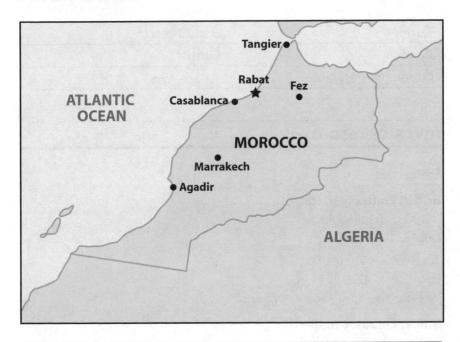

Why invest in Morocco?

Morocco is one of the fastest rising stars among jet-to-let investors. Located in North Africa, but at points less than ten miles from mainland Spain, the country benefits from both a fantastic climate and a unique cultural mix. Its geographical position puts it within easy reach of UK airports, but far enough away to give this exotic place some serious jet-to-let potential.

The story so far...

For 12 centuries Morocco succeeded in holding onto its independence, even during most of the colonial period. However, in 1912, France took control of most Moroccan territory while a small part in the north was occupied by Spain.

After gaining independence from France in 1956, the country went on to regain control over Spanish-occupied areas, leading eventually to a military conflict. Some of the Spanish-ruled area was retaken, but to this day Spain continues to occupy the small enclaves of Ceuta and Melilla in the north.

The 1990s brought an era of modernisation and liberalisation for Morocco and included empowering the regional governments and establishing non-governmental organisations. Recent key events were the establishment of a bi-cameral legislative body in 1997 and the signature of free-trade agreements with the US and European Union (EU) in 2004, leading to significant opportunities for economic growth.

Where is it?

Morocco is in the north-west corner of Africa. It has a long coastline of approximately 1,835km facing the Mediterranean Sea on the north and the Atlantic Ocean on the west. The country shares borders with Algeria and an area of Western Sahara. Morocco has a total area of 446,550km².

What is the weather like?

The climate is one of the main attractions for visitors to Morocco. It's extremely varied with temperatures over 40°C in the summer and not dropping below 15°C in the winter. As a result, Morocco is a fantastic place to live or visit throughout the year.

Rabat

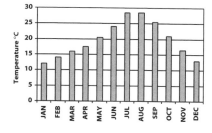
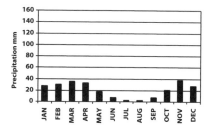

Marrakech

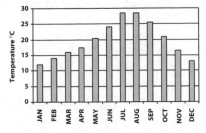
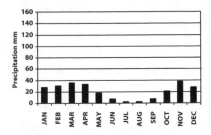

Casablanca

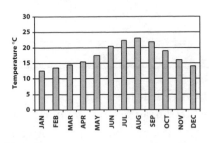
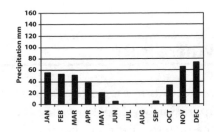

Tangier

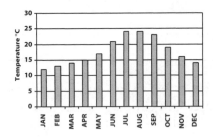
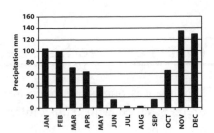

Language

Arabic is the main language and is spoken by 75 per cent of the population. French is often used for government and business and as a second language by the better educated, and Spanish is spoken in the cities in the north. Berber dialects are also spoken but by less than 25 per cent of the population.

Currency

The currency used in Morocco is the Moroccan Dirham (MAD). This is divided into 100 centimes. The Moroccan Dirham is pegged to a number of currencies, chiefly the euro at a rate of MAD 10 to € 1.

Politics

The Kingdom of Morocco is a constitutional monarchy and the current ruler is King Mohammed VI, who came to the throne in 1999. The current Prime Minister is Driss Jettou, appointed in October 2002. The main political parties include the Socialist Union of Popular Forces and the Independence Party.

Administratively, the country is divided into 37 provinces and two municipalities.

Economy

Economic indicators

Economic growth

In 2005, the economy grew by 1.6 per cent and its gross domestic product (GDP) per capita was $4,300 (€3,400). The economy has been stable with good growth averaging 3.6 per cent between 2000 and 2005. The economy is expected to recover to more robust levels in 2006 and is forecast to grow by a further 5.7 per cent in 2006 (*source: Economist Intelligence Unit*).

Inflation

Over the past decade, Morocco has managed to keep inflation under control. The annual rate of inflation reached 2.1 per cent in 2005. The forecast for 2006 is 2.8 per cent.

Interest rates

Continually low inflation has allowed a substantial reduction of interest rates. Short-term interest rates were 2.3 per cent in March 2006.

Unemployment

Unemployment is a serious economic and social problem for Morocco. Unemployment is highest among women and young adults and is also significantly higher in urban areas than in the countryside. There is pressure in the textile sector, traditionally a major employer in Morocco, which continues to face strong competition from China. Nevertheless, the economy has managed to sustain relatively robust employment growth in sectors such as commerce, agriculture, construction and the public sector.

Unemployment rate (percentage unemployed)

2000	2001	2002	2003	2004	2005 (estimate)
13.6	12.5	11.6	11.4	10.8	10.5

Source: Central Bank of Morocco

Foreign direct investment (FDI)

Morocco is an attractive location for foreign investors. According to a report by the European Investment Bank (EIB), in 2003 and 2004 Morocco received more foreign investment than any other country in Africa and the Middle East. The Moroccan government has instigated significant reforms designed to improve foreign trade and encourage investment. Relatively cheap labour and the free-trade agreements with the United States and the EU have attracted many new foreign companies.

The main investor countries are France, USA and Spain and the key industries benefiting from FDI are tourism, light manufacturing, retail and construction.

Foreign direct investment in Morocco (million US dollars)

2000	2001	2002	2003
1,175.3	2,955.3	564.2	2,497.4

Source: www.state.gov

Economic summary

Morocco is an emerging economy, is macro-economically stable and has very low levels of inflation. Growth, however, has not been strong enough to reduce poverty and high urban unemployment.

In total, 22 per cent of the country's GDP is derived from agriculture, 36 per cent from industry and 43 per cent from services. The strongest industry in Morocco is phosphate mining, which makes a significant contribution to national income. However, the country remains over-dependent on agriculture, but the government is sensibly developing other sectors in order to diversify its economy.

In 2004, Morocco began a process of market reform and privatisation. It's a major step forward as reforms should boost FDI and trade as well as attract multi-national corporations leading to a growth in employment opportunities.

The economic outlook for Morocco is bright as the country emerges from the early stages of economic development. The government continues to pursue its policies to tackle poverty and unemployment, improve education and raise the standard of living for its people.

So, what is the catch?

Poverty

Poverty continues to be a major problem and affects a significant proportion of the population. Some estimates suggest that as many as 20 per cent of the country's population lives in poverty.

Poor literacy rate

The literacy rate is poor with just 52 per cent of adults able to read and write and women being noticeably less literate than men. This limits the future employability and flexibility of the Moroccan labour force and, unless it's tackled, will have a detrimental effect on future economic growth and prosperity.

Corruption

Transparency International publishes a yearly corruption index (CPI). The 2005 index ranked Morocco in 78th place with a score of 3.2 along with China, Senegal, Sri Lanka and Suriname. This score is the worst performing among all the countries mentioned in this reference guide. Corruption in Morocco is a serious issue and potential investors must take it into account.

The property market

Morocco's year-round sunshine and close proximity to Europe have made it an increasingly popular target for jet-to-let property investors. The property market is still in its infancy, and for this reason it's often referred to as an emerging market. In recent years the country has experienced a flood of investors, keen to invest in property now that prices are still relatively low. The major cities of Morocco have recorded capital growth of over 30 per cent in the last few years.

Forecasts for the property market are upbeat as long-term economic indicators point to sustained economic growth. The property market is set to continue to grow at a brisk rate driven by the Kings Vision 2010 scheme.

This scheme will see $10 billion invested in the regeneration of the country with cash injected into infrastructure projects in order to encourage mass tourism. This should provide a stable base for jet-to-let investors to generate strong returns as the Moroccan economy grows and foreign interest in holiday and retirement property grows.

Morocco has become a favourite for golfers. A number of developments have been constructed around Morocco's 16 best golf courses in Marrakech, Rabat, Casablanca and Agadir to satisfy the demand from golfers for quality accommodation. All in all, Morocco has more than 30 golf courses and there are a growing number of tour operators offering tailor-made golfing holidays and breaks.

Unlike many emerging property markets, Morocco has a strong rental market, ideal for investors looking for a pure jet-to-let approach. A €100,000 two-bedroom apartment could be expected to generate a monthly rental income of €2,000 for the peak summer season months. Morocco has potential for a property investor looking for both income and growth over the medium to long term. Rental income is now exempt from tax for five years and no Capital Gains Tax is paid if the property is sold after ten years. This encouraging change in policy reinforces the view that the government is serious about achieving its targets for 2010.

Tourism

In 2005, 5.8 million tourists visited Morocco (a seven per cent annual increase) with income up 18 per cent to MAD 41.1 billion. The majority of arrivals came from France, Spain, the UK (an increase of 29 per cent year-on-year) and Germany. Morocco has set up a tourism strategy to attract ten million tourists by the year 2010.

Hotspots

Rabat is Morocco's capital city. It's home to the government and is more cosmopolitan than some of Morocco's other cities. It's also home to some of Morocco's best golf courses, which are a major attraction for many of the people who visit the area. Economic reforms have had a noticeably positive impact on the city's property market and in the last few years there has been exceptional growth.

Marrakech is in south-west Morocco at the foothills of the Atlas Mountains and it continues to be a favourite destination for travellers and traders alike. It's now attracting jet-to-let property investors, second home buyers and people seeking a new life in the sun. Local estate agents have reported increasing interest from British investors and Marrakech has become the country's hottest tourism and property investment location. People flock to Marrakech all year round ensuring a high demand for short-term rentals, which is encouraging for those looking to buy a property to let.

Marrakech has a hot, dry climate and it benefits from over 300 days of sunshine. The city has a broad appeal with a mixture of African, Spanish and French influences. With upmarket developments under construction, Marrakech looks set to continue attracting increasing attention from buyers and tourists in the coming years, with significant potential for jet-to-let investors as prices are about half of those for similar properties in Spain. The western-leaning Moroccan government is eager to promote investment from overseas and, as a consequence, property prices have risen by about 50 per cent in the last couple of years.

Riads are historic Moroccan homes set around a courtyard with traditional features, and there are plenty of them available in Marrakech as renovation projects. Interest in riads has been extremely high over the last couple of years and prices are starting to reflect that, but they are still comparatively low. In contrast, the most expensive part of Marrakech is the Palmeraie where many of the villas are owned by French nationals and can sell for anything between €1.5 million and €3 million. Somewhere in between both extremes of these properties are four-bedroom luxury villas with pools in locations near golf courses. These are currently selling for upwards of €550,000 with room for this to increase as demand for property rises.

One emerging hotspot is **Tangier**, located on the northern tip of Morocco. Tangier is Morocco's most cosmopolitan city and the mix of cultures means that it doesn't have an especially Moroccan feel to it. Today, the city is made up of the busy port, lively markets and its superb bay and beaches. Flight times from the UK are just two and a half hours making it even more of an accessible location for a jet-to-let property. In 2008, a new tunnel is planned to be built that will link Tangier to Gibraltar.

The tourist market in Tangier is very strong, mainly due to its easy access from the European mainland. There is a growing demand for long-term rental property, which is ideal for an investor looking for stable opportunities for income in this market. Prospects for short-term lets are encouraging and property prices in Tangier are on average 25 per cent of a similar property in Spain, giving an extra incentive to those who want to invest here. As such, a two-bedroom apartment close to the coast can be purchased for less than €70,000 and a small villa can be found for under €100,000.

Located on the western tip of Africa, **Casablanca** is the economic hub of modern Morocco. It's the capital in all but name and because of the various foreign influences that have left their mark here, it has a feel of a Southern-European city. Casablanca offers a variety of investment options ranging from recently renovated traditional houses to large villas and apartments. Although there is a good supply of hotels in Casablanca, they are almost always fully booked so apartments for short-term lets offer the jet-to-let investor an interesting opportunity. The number of people visiting Casablanca is expected to rise in the coming years and increasing property prices are forecast to reflect this.

The buying process

There are no restrictions imposed on foreign buyers of property in Morocco. The process of purchasing a property is relatively straightforward and is similar to that in many European countries.

Your first step will be to find a local estate agent, known locally as a 'simsaar'. It may also be necessary to use a translator, as these agents often speak very little English. Alternatively, you may choose to purchase through a property company based in the UK, which may make the process easier.

When you have found your property and the vendor or developer has accepted your offer, you may want to employ a local surveyor to perform a structural survey if necessary. An independent lawyer should then be appointed by you to formalise the agreement.

After these steps have been completed, the buyer pays a ten per cent deposit. It's important to note that the vendor can still sell to someone else if he offers a higher price, but you will be able to get your full deposit back. Gazumping is not just confined to the UK market!

Normally it takes six to eight weeks for searches to be completed and as some older properties may not have title deeds, the notary will create the official title deeds for you in return for an additional fee of one per cent.

Completion happens in the notary's office where all parties must be present. The buyer pays the remaining costs and taxes and the notary then prepares and signs all of the necessary documents to register the property.

Transaction costs

These expenses are outlined below:

- **Notary fees:** the public notary will usually charge one per cent of the purchase price.
- **Legal fees** are approximately one per cent.
- **Estate agents' fees** are usually around 2.5 per cent of the purchase price.
- **Land registration fees** are around 2.5 per cent.
- **Surveyor costs** are approximately MAD 2,500.

Total costs will be six to seven per cent of the purchase price.

Annual costs

Buyers are liable to pay the following annual taxes on their Moroccan property:

- **Property Tax** is paid at a progressive rate, which ranges from 0 to 30 per cent depending on the property value. The property owner is exempt from this tax for the first five years of ownership. The tax is based on the property's annual rental value. There is a 75 per cent discount if the home is your permanent or holiday home.
- **Property Rental Tax** is 13.5 per cent on the rental value of the property.
- **Refuse Collection Tax** is ten per cent of the property's annual rental value. The property owner is exempt from this tax for the first five years of ownership.

Taxes

The taxation system has recently been liberalised, but it's advisable to seek advice from a tax advisor who specialises in Morocco. Below are some major taxation rules:

Income Tax
Income Tax rates:

Tax	Annual tax base (MAD)
0%	0–18,000
13%	18,001–24,000
21%	24,001–36,000
35%	36,001–60,000
44%	Over 60,001

Corporation Tax
The tax rate applicable to corporations in Morocco is 35 per cent.

Capital Gains Tax
Capital Gains Tax is 20 per cent if the property is sold within five years of purchase. If the property is sold after five years but less than ten, then the rate is ten per cent on profits over MAD 1 million. After ten years of ownership, the property is exempt from Capital Gains Tax.

Summary

Strengths

- A stable monarchy.
- Increasing liberalisation.
- A special trading status with the EU and US.
- Consistent economic growth.
- Strong tourist market and demand for second homes, retirement homes and rentals.

- All-year-round tourist season.
- Stable and emerging property market at the same time.
- Great beaches.
- Beautiful scenery.
- Low-cost flights.
- A variety of property and locations available.
- Relatively cheap coastal properties.
- No restrictions on foreign ownership.
- Large French interest and growing British demand.
- Golf tourism is strong.
- Low property purchase costs.
- Low transaction costs.

Weaknesses

- Competition from hotel industry for rentals.
- High unemployment and rigidity of the labour market.
- Poverty is widespread.
- Education system is poor.
- Unlikely to attract large-scale service-focused industries.
- Already under pressure from low-cost labour markets, such as China.
- High dependency on agriculture which can be prone to drought.

Opportunities

- Growing popularity with holidaymakers and second home owners.
- Lifestyle investment or 'live-and-let'.

- The King's 2010 vision is having a significant effect on the property market.

- If the proposed tunnel from mainland Europe is built, it will have a major impact on tourism and trade.

- More low-cost carriers and cheaper airfares.

Threats

- Relatively underdeveloped economy.

- Competition from other low-cost property markets.

- Political stability is not presently an issue, but what may the future hold?

Facts at a glance

Geography	
Population (2005 estimate)	33,241,259
Language	Arabic
Ethnic groups	Arab-Berber 99.1%, other 0.7%, Jewish 0.2%
Local currency	Moroccan Dirham divided into 100 centimes

Political system	
Political structure	Constitutional monarchy
Monarch	King Mohammed VI
Prime Minister	Driss Jettou
Main parties	Socialist Union of Popular Forces Independence Party

Economy

Unemployment rate in 2005	10.5%
Unemployment rate, December 2005	10.5%
Inflation rate in 2005	2.1%
Inflation rate, March 2006	2.1%
Interest rate, March 2006	2.3%
GDP growth in 2005	1.6%
GDP growth forecast for 2006	5.7%
GDP per capita (income per person) in 2005	$4,300 (€3,400)

Taxation

Income Tax	0–44%
Corporation Tax	35%
Capital Gains Tax	20%

Corruption statistics

Corruption rate	3.2
Corruption rank	78th

Industry and technology

Major industries	Phosphate mining and processing
	Food processing
	Leather goods
	Textiles
	Construction
	Tourism

The Moroccan property market

Hotspots	Rabat
	Marrakech
	Tangier
	Casablanca

Property taxes (transactions)

Land Registry fees	2.5%
Notary fees	1%
Legal fees	1%
Estate agents' fees	2.5%
Total fees	6–7%

Property taxes (annual)

Property Tax	0–30% of annual rental value
Property Rental Tax	13.5% of annual rental value
Refuse Collection Tax	10% of annual rental value

Mortgage

LTV	70%
Term	Up to 15 years
Currency	Moroccan Dirham
Current interest rate	5.5–7.5%

Investor resources

Embassies

British Embassy in Morocco

17 Boulevard de la Tour Hassan
PO Box 45, Rabat

Tel: +212 (37) 238 600
Fax: +212 (37) 704 531
Website: www.britishembassy.gov.uk

Moroccan Embassy in the UK

49 Queen's Gate Gardens
London SW7 5NE

Tel: 020 7581 5001
Fax: 020 7225 3862
Website: http://morocco.embassyhomepage.com

Useful websites

Central Bank of Morocco – Bank Al-Maghrib
www.bkam.ma

Moroccan Government Information
www.mincom.gov.ma

Tourism
www.visitmorocco.com

Portugal

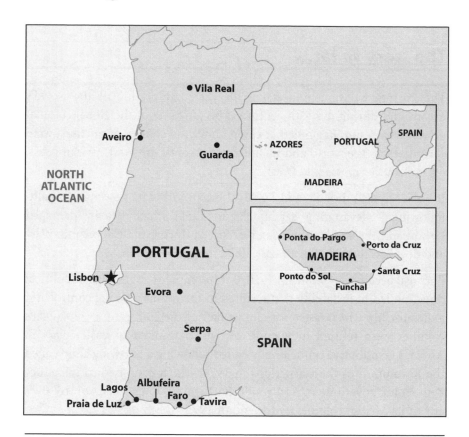

Why invest in Portugal?

Portugal has always been an extremely popular destination for British home buyers and retirees with a wonderful climate, beautiful scenery and good investment opportunities. With the property market possibly at the top of its present strong run in neighbouring Spain, investors are searching for an alternative. In effect, Portugal is benefiting from the strong house price inflation we have seen in Spain over the last five to eight years.

When thinking of Portugal, most people think of the Algarve. This region lies on the southern coast of Portugal and it has always had the largest number of developments targeted at overseas investors and second home buyers. The Algarve remains the most popular destination for buyers of all types, but improved road and budget air links mean there are new areas of interest that are opening up.

The story so far...

The Portuguese were pioneers in the early exploration of the world's oceans and during the 15th century it became one of the global colonial powers as a result. Regions that came under the control of Portugal were spread across the world and included the Azores, the West African coast, part of southern Asia and Brazil.

It wasn't to last, though, and Portugal began losing its power and wealth following a devastating earthquake in 1755, which heavily damaged Lisbon and the south. It was later occupied during the Napoleonic Wars and declined further after Brazil gained independence in 1822.

Portugal became a republic in 1910, but the subsequent change of political direction led to instability that resulted in the military taking control and a dictatorship which lasted for almost half of the 20th century. Portugal's colonies were refused independence, which resulted in costly wars in Africa. The military regime finally ended following a left-wing coup called the Revolution of the Carnations in 1974, which promised to introduce democratic government. As a result, Portugal no longer had control over any of its African colonies by the end of 1975.

Portugal was one of the founding members of NATO in 1949 and joined the European Union (EU) in 1986.

Where is it?

Mainland Portugal is on the Iberian Peninsula and is bordered by Spain in the north and east, with the Atlantic Ocean to the south and west. Portugal is divided into provinces, including the Atlantic islands of Madeira and the Azores. North Portugal is mountainous, and the Serra da Estrela is a popular area for skiing. Portugal has a total area of 92,391km^2, and 1,793km of coastline.

What is the weather like?

Portugal has a mild all-year-round climate with summers that are sunny, dry and clear. Southern Portugal is warmer and less humid than the rest of the country, with temperatures sometimes reaching as high as 40°C inland. Late autumn and winter are cool, wet and can be windy. Most of Portugal's rainfall occurs during the winter months when temperatures range from 5 to 10°C.

Lisbon

 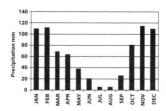

Algarve

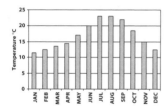 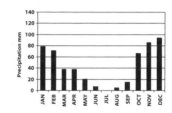

Madeira

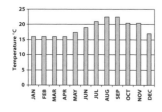 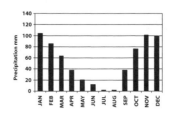

Azores

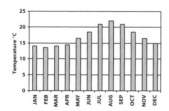 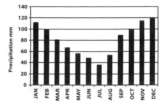

Language

Portuguese is the official language, spoken by the majority of the 10.6 million inhabitants. English is widely spoken as a second language.

Currency

The official currency is the euro, divided into 100 cents.

Politics

Portugal is a parliamentary democratic republic and the main parties are the Socialist Party (PS) and the Social Democratic Party (PSD). The current President is Aníbal Cavaco Silva, elected in 2006. José Sócrates (of the Socialist Party) is the Prime Minister, appointed in 2005.

The country is divided into 18 districts and two autonomous regions – the Azores and Madeira.

Economy

Portugal joined the EU in 1986 and since then its economy has become more reliant on the services sector. In 2005, services contributed 67 per cent of the country's gross domestic product (GDP). Over the past decade, governments have privatised many of the state-owned industries, which has led to the liberalisation of many key areas of the economy, including both the financial and telecommunications sectors.

Average income per person has grown from being just over half of the EU average upon accession in 1986, to around 72 per cent in 2004. Membership of the EU has allowed for stable economic growth, primarily through an increase in trade and radical improvements in the country's infrastructure.

Even after these improvements in the economy, Portugal is still the poorest of the EU-15 countries and the new members Slovenia and Cyprus already have a higher GDP per capita. Portugal has the advantage of low labour costs but it has increasingly lost out to even lower-cost producers across central Europe and Asia.

The outlook for Portugal's economy is not particularly bright. Like Spain and Greece, EU structural funds will most likely be significantly reduced from 2007, after the addition of the ten new member states. The Portuguese labour market reflects a poor standard of education among the workforce while rising unemployment presents a threat.

The government is pursuing unpopular measures to implement fiscal tightening, especially in the public sector, which costs the equivalent of 15 per cent of GDP in employees' salaries. The Portuguese government faces a series of tough choices in its efforts to further boost Portugal's economic competitiveness and bring it into line with the other EU countries.

Economic indicators

Economic growth

Portugal's GDP per capita in 2005 was €16,600 and real GDP grew by 0.4 per cent. Portuguese economic performance was slow from 2000 to 2005, with annual GDP growth averaging just 1.1 per cent. Economic development during this time was primarily as a result of EU structural funds.

Even now, there is little sign of any recovery soon. The European Commission forecasts a growth in GDP of 0.8 per cent in 2006, while exports and investment are expected to remain poor because of increased competition.

Inflation

Despite high inflation levels in the past, Portugal has managed to hold inflation at relatively low levels during the last five years. Annual inflation was 2.1 per cent in 2005, which was driven by increases in the rate of VAT and the surge in oil prices. Inflation is forecast to remain at the present level throughout this year.

Interest rates

Portugal is part of the Eurozone and therefore its monetary policy is regulated by the European Central Bank. Interest rates were increased to 2.25 per cent in December 2005, and then to the current level of 2.50 per cent in March 2006.

Unemployment

Unemployment in Portugal is below the European average and there was a sharp rise in unemployment in 2002 and early 2003. The rates of unemployment for the last five years are presented in the table below:

Unemployment rate (percentage unemployed)

2000	2001	2002	2003	2004	2005
4.1	4.0	5.0	6.3	6.7	7.4

Source: Eurostat, the Statistical Office of the European Communities

In 2006, unemployment has reached an 18-year high and is projected to continue rising. Job losses have been particularly high in manufacturing with international companies seeking cheaper labour elsewhere.

The Portuguese government introduced several reforms in order to increase the flexibility of the country's labour market, as well as promote investment in research and information technologies, which will improve Portugal's competitiveness.

Foreign direct investment (FDI)

Portugal is losing its attractiveness as an FDI destination and the gross level of FDI has reduced in the last few years. The EU remains the main foreign investor in Portugal with most of the funds being targeted at manufacturing, retail and property.

Foreign direct investment in Portugal (€ million)

2000	2001	2002	2003	2004	2005
7,200	7,000	1,912	7,614	1,906	2,504

Source: Bank of Portugal

Economic summary

The Portuguese economy is expected to grow at a very slow rate over the next few years. The country is to lose a considerable amount of EU funds and the FDI inflows have contracted meaning that Portugal will need to restructure its economy in order to increase its competitiveness in a global market.

The property market outside of Lisbon is dependent on tourism, second home owners and retirees. As long as Portugal's appeal is sustained in those markets, then the troubled economic situation will have only a negligible impact on the growing interest from overseas buyers. The property market in Lisbon is more geared towards business, commerce and government and so will be impacted by any positive or negative developments in the Portuguese economy.

So, what is the catch?

Rising unemployment and poorly educated workers

The rate of unemployment in Portugal is still below the EU average, but it has started rising, reaching seven-year highs of 7.5 per cent in the first quarter of 2005. Unemployment has almost stabilised since, but there is likely to be weakness for some time to come.

Portugal has the lowest level of salaries among the EU-15 nations and has the highest percentage of poorly educated workers among the EU-25. Only 20 per cent of Portuguese people complete secondary education and nearly 40 per cent of the students in higher education fail to go on and finish their degrees. Due to its failing educational system and over-regulated economy, Portugal is unable to replace its declining industries with high-tech alternatives that would generate greater profits and employment.

Low birth rate and ageing population

Portugal has a comparatively low birth rate compared with other European countries. The birth rate started to fall in the 1970s and has now reached 10.8 births per 1,000 of population in 2005. Portugal's total fertility rate is 1.47 children born per woman (2005 estimate), but a rate of 2.1 is needed to stop the population from reducing. Life expectancy for men is 74 and for women is 81 and the number of people aged 65 and over has more than doubled since 1960, causing a huge strain for the social welfare system.

Corruption

Portugal is ranked in the CPI index at 26th place with a score of 6.5. This is a relatively low rate of corruption, but it does rank the country behind the majority of other EU member states.

The property market

The property market in Portugal has remained stable for the last 20 years and it continues to offer a good prospect as a medium- to long-term investment. The market has remained buoyant and property prices have continued to rise to varying degrees across the country. This is particularly true in the Algarve, which has a very strong market and rising prices.

There is still capacity for growth in the property market as average prices are still cheaper than in nearby France and Spain. Property prices have appreciated at an annual rate of ten per cent from 2000, but this rate slowed to five to eight per cent in 2005. Unlike Spain, Portugal doesn't yet have an overdeveloped coastline, so it has further capacity to expand supply in line with demand.

With supply in the Algarve becoming short and prices still increasing, other Portuguese regions are becoming attractive to investors. These include Lisbon and central Portugal, both of which saw an increase in the number of tourists following the 2004 European Football Championship.

The Portuguese property market is varied and the jet-to-let investor has a wide choice, including off-plan, new-build, resale, land and renovation projects. New-build properties are the most popular sector of the market at the moment, particularly in the Algarve region and Lisbon.

Golf

Portugal is the number one country for golfers and, as a result, there has been an increase of 50 per cent in the number of golf developments over the past couple of years. There are around 20 courses along the coast of the Algarve all within an hour and a half of Faro Airport. With golf attracting so many visitors and so much money to the region, a number of other courses are planned and expected to be completed over the coming five years.

Tourism

Tourism has become increasingly important to the Portuguese economy as the number of visitors has grown and now contributes about eight per cent of its GDP. Over 11.6 million tourists visited Portugal in 2005, which is currently ranked 19th among world tourist destinations. Portugal is especially popular with British holidaymakers and in 2005 it was their eighth favourite destination in the world. The most popular regions for tourists are the Algarve, Lisbon and Madeira.

Portugal's infrastructure was modernised with the help of EU funds and the 2004 European Football Championship held across the country led to large-scale investment in Portugal's tourism infrastructure. This included a programme of road building around the major cities and an expansion of the three main international airports.

Property hotspots

City

Lisbon is Portugal's capital city, and its combination of diverse history and great climate have made it a very popular tourist destination. It's also Portugal's latest property hotspot, with a number of budget airlines opening up the city's accessibility from all areas of Europe and, in particular, the UK.

Lisbon had tended to be overlooked by jet-to-let investors, having gained a reputation as being run down, but since it has joined the EU the city has undergone a transformation which has included some cosmetic improvements as well as upgrades to drains and water supplies. This investment in the local infrastructure has made Lisbon a target of overseas investors.

Lisbon, like many of its European capital city counterparts, has benefited greatly from the jet-to-let phenomenon. There is still good value for money to be found here as the city offers a diverse choice of properties. Jet-to-let prospects are reasonable as there is both a short-term and long-term rental market. A two-bedroom period apartment will cost less than €190,000 and rents average just over €600 per week. At the other end of the market, a penthouse in one of the more exclusive areas will cost upwards of €270,000.

Lisbon doesn't yet compare that favourably to other European cities, although it's one of the cheapest capitals in Europe. The regeneration currently underway will further increase the city's profile and overall attractiveness to jet-to-let investors.

Coast

The Algarve is on Portugal's south coast and is the most popular region in the country for retirees, holidaymakers and property investors alike, many of which are attracted by the equivalent of almost 40 weeks of sunshine a year. There is a diverse range of property in the Algarve for the jet-to-let investor, ranging from fantastic luxury villas to modest apartments and town houses.

The Algarve has retained its charm, as it's not overdeveloped, unlike many of the coastal areas of Spain. There are strict planning regulations, particularly in relation to the protection of the coastline, which is a very positive constraint to overdevelopment.

The property market in the Algarve has been booming in recent years, with property prices still rising significantly. Even though this region is the most popular in Portugal, property prices here remain cheaper than those in similar regions of Spain and France. A mixture of cheap flights, increased marketing activity and a new motorway has opened up the entire Algarve to more overseas visitors.

In terms of individual areas to look at, the resorts of **Vale do Lobo** and **Quinta do Lago**, which are close to the airport and offer fantastic beaches, are at the top end of the market. These resorts are popular all year round, attracting holidaymakers in the summer and golfers in the winter, and therefore allow for a 365-day-a-year rental market. Demand for holiday lets in these resorts comes from people wanting to stay in luxurious villas on the coast, and returns are very attractive. A gross yield of eight per cent plus for the most popular areas is achievable.

The tourist capital of the Algarve is **Albufeira**, which attracts a broad range of people, from teenagers looking for fun to retirees (also looking for fun, but maybe in different places). Albufeira has a strong rentals market and the area is considered to be the best in the Algarve for those looking to purchase a property for investment purposes. One-bedroom apartments can be found from €90,000 upwards, while houses with several bedrooms and access to a communal pool are available from around €200,000.

The Via do Infante motorway, which runs between Faro and Lagos, has opened up the western region since it was completed in 2003. As a result, demand for property has increased in **Lagos**, where the average cost for a four-bedroom house is around €525,000. There is a strong market for holiday rentals in Lagos, and the resort is busy all year round, but more so between June and September.

The property market in the eastern end of the Algarve is less developed than the central and western regions, and property tends to be generally less expensive the further east you go. **Tavira** is particularly popular with British and European buyers and the international jet-to-let demand for property experienced further west and inland has yet to arrive. While large numbers of tourists visit Tavira, rentals are more seasonal. A two-bedroom apartment can be found for €150,000 and will let for €500 per week.

Islands

The island of **Madeira** is situated 600km from the North African coast, and the nine islands that make up the Azores are almost 1,500km from Lisbon.

Madeira's capital is **Funchal**, which is located on the island's southern coast. Funchal is a modern city and it's the destination for nine out of ten of Madeira's visitors. Its streets are lined with cafes and restaurants that look out on to bustling markets and pubs. Property in the city is centred around apartments and the Balancal golf development with an average two-bedroom property costing in the region of €260,000. The rental market is good, particularly for short-term lets during peak season, and during Christmas.

To the north of Funchal is the attractive town of **Santa Cruz**. Santa Cruz is close to the airport but has managed to maintain its appeal and the traditional lifestyle here remains unchanged. The majority of jet-to-let property can be found in Santa Cruz and the villages of **Canico** and **Gaula**. An average two-bedroom property costs around €250,000, although homes around the villages can be cheaper. The rental market is focused predominantly on short-term rentals for tourists and golfers.

Ponta do Sol is in western Madeira and is close to the resort of **Riberia Brava**. Property prices in this area are among the cheapest throughout the whole of Madeira, but high demand and low supply means that they can be difficult to find. Like Santa Cruz, the rental market in Ponta do Sol is completely dominated by short-term holiday lets, and is again popular with golfers. The holiday rentals market is strong and not limited to being seasonal.

The Azores are located closer to the African coast than the Portuguese mainland. At present, property prices in the Azores are very affordable, and a two-bedroom house can be purchased from €95,000. The rental market in the Azores is still rather weak, particularly for long-term lets, and returns can be low. Most holiday lets come from 40-somethings, although the islands are becoming more popular with families, a trend which is likely to continue to ensure growth in the islands' tourist market.

The buying process

There are no restrictions placed on foreign buyers purchasing property and the buying process in Portugal is fairly straightforward. There are some important differences to many other European countries, so it's advisable that you instruct a local English-speaking lawyer to act solely on your behalf to oversee the process.

Before purchasing, a non-Portuguese resident must obtain a Portuguese fiscal number ('Numero Fiscal do Contribuinte'). Applying for a fiscal number is a simple procedure and a local tax office will issue a number immediately. The cost for applying for a fiscal number is negligible.

Once a price has been agreed with the vendor, both parties sign a preliminary contract. This is a legally binding document stating the conditions of sale and it must be signed in the presence of a notary (who acts as a representative of state and is completely impartial). At this stage you will pay a deposit of between 10 and 30 per cent. Following this, your lawyer will conduct various checks to ensure that there are no outstanding mortgages or other debts liable against the property.

The completion takes place in the notary's office. Upon signing the final contract, the buyer must pay the notary fee, although the remaining balance and purchase tax (IMT) must be paid prior to the final date and the proof of payment must be shown to the notary. Once this has been done, the copy of the final contract is taken to the Land Registry and local tax offices for registering the property under the new owner's name.

Transaction costs

Below is a brief outline of the expenses you can expect to pay on your property purchase:

- **Property Transfer Tax**, also known as IMT ('Imposto Municipal sobre Transmissoes') is payable on a sliding scale up to eight per cent on all properties valued at more than €83,500. New-build properties are exempt from IMT and IMT on rural land is a flat rate of five per cent.

- **Notary fees**, which would include notary fees, administration costs and property registration fees, are on average 1.5–2.5 per cent of the value mentioned in the contract, but can vary from one area to another. The notary fees are slightly higher when you require a mortgage because there is an extra charge for mortgage security.

- **Legal fees** are normally between one and two per cent of the value, but this will depend on the complexity of the case and the person used to represent you.

Total fees will usually add up to approximately eight to ten per cent of the purchase price.

As in the UK, the buyer doesn't have to pay estate agents' fees, but laws governing property disclosure may not be as strict. The agent acts on behalf of the seller and is paid a commission once the property has been sold. If you sell the property, you will have to pay the estate agents' fees and in some cases this can be as much as ten per cent.

Annual costs

Portugal remains one of the cheapest EU-15 countries to live in, but it does depend on which region you are in as the Algarve differs greatly from other areas.

Municipal Property Tax or IMI ('Imposto Municipal sobre Imóveis') is an annual tax on immovable property, levied by the local authority and is based on the registered value. The rates vary according to the type of the property: the tax rate of 0.8 per cent is set on rural properties and the rates vary between 0.2 and 0.8 per cent on urban properties.

Taxes

The major taxes in Portugal are summarised below:

Income Tax

Individual Income Tax rates for 2006:

Tax	Annual tax base (€)
10.5%	Up to 4,350
13%	4,351–6,580
23.5%	6,581–16,316
34%	16,317–37,527
36.5%	37,528–54,387
40%	54,388–60,000
42%	Over 60,001

Corporation Tax

The standard rate of Corporation Tax is 25 per cent. Municipalities may levy a surcharge, meaning that the effective rate may total as much as 27.5 per cent.

Capital Gains Tax

All Portuguese residents have a capital gain added to their income and are taxed at the income marginal rate. 50 per cent of the gain is taxed as income and the other 50 per cent is exempt. Capital gains arising from the disposal of an individual's main residence are tax exempt and capital gains realised on the disposal of property by non-Portuguese residents are taxed at a flat rate of 25 per cent. Certain conditions apply, so do be aware of this when you are seeking legal advice.

Summary

Strengths

- Political democracy.

- Member of the EU.

- Strong tourism industry and demand for property rentals and second homes.

- Strong retirement community demand for property.

- Established property market, procedures and resale market.

- No restrictions on foreign ownership.

- Cheaper annual running costs than the UK.

- Short flying times for many Europeans.

- The arrival of no-frills low-cost airlines will continue to attract rental and sales demand.

- The all-year-round rental market created by the proliferation of golf courses.

- Weather.

- Beaches.

- Cultural and architectural delights of Lisbon.

Weaknesses

- Competition from hotel industry for rentals.

- Competition from the many other owners of properties for rentals.

- Low economic growth.

- Persistent unemployment.

- Persistent inflation.

- Poorly educated labour market.

- High estate agent fees for resale.

Opportunities

- Lifestyle investment – 'live-and-let'.

- Development of inland resorts.

- Renovation projects inland where property prices are relatively cheap and there is a growing demand for them from foreigners.

Threats

- Loss of EU funding.

- Risk of property market overheating on the Algarve.

- Competition for property sales (demand) from other emerging markets at a more favourable position in the market cycle for property investors.

- Competition from other markets for holidaymakers and lettings.

- The opening up of other low-cost airline routes to other countries which may be viewed as competitors, such as Bulgaria, Cyprus, Dubai and Turkey.

Facts at a glance

Geography	
Population (2005 estimate)	10,566,212
Language	Portuguese and Mirandese
Ethnic groups	In the north, there are traces of Celtic influence; in the south, Arab and Berber influence is considerable
Local currency	Euro, divided into 100 cents

Political system	
Political structure	Parliamentary republic
President	Aníbal Cavaco Silva
Prime Minister	José Sócrates
Main parties	Socialist Party and Social Democratic Party

Economy

Unemployment rate in 2005	7.6%
Unemployment rate, February 2006	7.7%
Inflation rate in 2005	2.1%
Inflation rate, February 2006	2.9%
Interest rate, March 2006	2.5%
GDP growth in 2005	0.4%
GDP growth forecast for 2006	0.8%
GDP per capita (income per person) in 2005	€16,600

Taxation

Income Tax	10.5–42%
Corporation Tax	25% (27.5% when municipal surcharge applies)
Capital Gains Tax	Gains are taxed as income. Rates vary on a sale of property according to your residential status

Corruption statistics

Corruption rate	6.5
Corruption rank	26th

Industry and technology

Major industries	Electronics
	Energy
	Automotive
	Chemicals

The Portuguese property market

Hotspots	Urban: Lisbon
	Regions: Algarve
	Islands: Madeira

Property taxes (transactions)	
Notary fees	1.5–2.5%
Legal fees	1–2%
Property Tax (IMT)	Sliding scale up to 8%
Total fees	Up to 8–10%

Property taxes (annual)	
Municipal Property Tax	0.2–0.8%

Mortgage	
LTV	80%
Term	5–30 years
Currency	Euro and other major currencies
Current interest rate	Varies; the typical rate is 3.4%

Investor resources

Embassies

British Embassy in Portugal

Rua de São Bernardo 33
1249-082 Lisbon

Tel: +351 21 392 4000
Fax: +351 21 392 4021
Website: www.britishembassy.gov.uk

Portuguese Embassy in the UK

11 Belgrave Square
London SW1X 8PP

Tel: 020 7235 5331
Fax: 020 7235 0739
Website: portugal.embassyhomepage.com

Useful websites

About Portugal

www.portugal.org

Bank of Portugal

www.bportugal.pt

Invest in Portugal

www.investinportugal.pt

Portuguese National Institute of Statistics

www.ine.pt

Tourism in Portugal

www.visitportugal.com

Spain

It's hard to find a British or national from the European Union (EU) who has not holidayed in Spain. It's second only to France as the world's most popular tourist destination, with an estimated 53 million tourists in 2004. The old favourite continues to fend off increasing competition from cheaper destinations such as Bulgaria and Turkey, and remains the most popular destination for UK residents searching for a break in the sun.

Why invest in Spain?

The Spanish property market continues to draw buyers taking advantage of low interest rates and accessible finance. The market is well established and has produced solid returns for jet-to-let investors for a number of years.

Interest rates remain low and property prices are increasing, although at a reduced rate compared to the past. Over the next few years, 150,000 properties will be built, mainly for foreign investors and second home buyers. So considerable are overseas buyers in the market that they now possess almost two million properties – approximately 800,000 are British owned and 460,000 Germans, 120,000 French and 100,000 Scandinavians also own property.

The story so far...

Spain has a rich and colourful past often characterised in film by swashbuckling adventurers sailing the seven seas in search of trade and bounty. The country first established itself as a global superpower in the late 15th century, following Columbus' discovery of the New World. Spanish influence started to weaken at the beginning of the 17th century, due largely to a lacklustre economy. Frequent wars weakened Spain further and by the late 1800s the country had lost most of its colonial possessions.

The 20th century brought a fierce Civil War which ended in 1939 with the victory of the nationalist forces led by General Franco and supported by Nazi Germany. Franco's dictatorship lasted four decades, but after his death in 1975, King Juan Carlos I took control over the country, leading Spain to democracy. Spain joined NATO in 1982 and the EU in 1986.

Where is it?

Spain is on the Iberian Peninsula in the south-west of Europe. Spain also comprises the Balearic Islands (Mallorca, Menorca, Ibiza and Formentera) in the Mediterranean Sea, the Canary Islands (Tenerife, Lanzarote, Gran Canaria, Fuerteventura, La Palma, La Gomera and El Hierro) in the Atlantic Ocean, and Ceuta and Melilla in North Africa.

In the north, mainland Spain borders France and Andorra with the Pyrenean Mountains acting as a natural boundary. In the south, the Strait of Gibraltar separates the country from North Africa. The Mediterranean is at the eastern and south-eastern coast of Spain from the French border to the Strait of Gibraltar. In the west, Spain borders the Atlantic Ocean on both sides of its border with Portugal.

What is the weather like?

Spain's geography ensures a varied climate. The majority of the country has a continental climate, which is defined by large swings in temperatures and low, variable rainfall. In parts of Spain, summer temperatures are in excess of 40°C. The south-east of the country has a Mediterranean climate, where the average temperature in the winter is 10°C and about 27°C in the summer.

Madrid

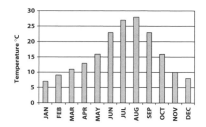
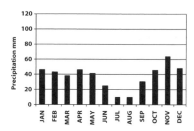

Barcelona and Costa Brava

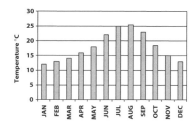
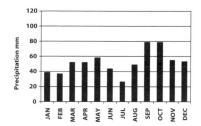

Costa del Sol

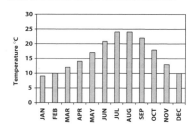
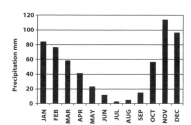

Costa Calida

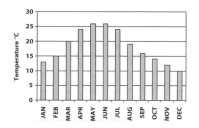
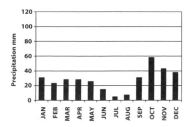

Costa Blanca

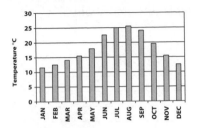

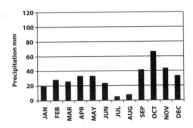

Balearic Islands

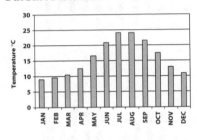

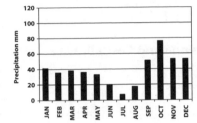

Canary Islands

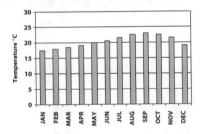

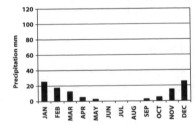

Language

Spain has an approximate population of over 40 million. The country's official language is Castilian Spanish spoken by 74 per cent of the population. Catalan is spoken by 17 per cent, seven per cent speak Galician and two per cent speak Basque. English and German are also spoken.

Currency

The currency in mainland Spain and its territories is the euro divided into 100 cents.

Politics

Spain is a parliamentary democracy and the current head of state is King Juan Carlos I. Spain's main political parties are the governing Spanish Socialist Workers' Party (PSOE) and the opposing Conservative People's Party (PP). The current President (comparable to Prime Minister) is José Luis Rodríguez Zapatero, elected in the 2004 parliamentary elections.

Spain is a Federation of Autonomous Communities and is administratively divided into 50 provinces.

Economy

The Spanish economy grew rapidly after entering the EU in 1986 and over the past decade, it has continued to maintain stable economic growth. The key factors responsible growth are:

- consumer spending;
- a property boom;
- falling unemployment;
- increased foreign direct investment (FDI); and
- EU funding.

In the last decade, Spain has been the largest beneficiary of EU structural aid, receiving almost €50 billion over the last five years. Although funding is secured until this year, further aid is in doubt due to the accession of ten new European states on 1 May 2004.

Economic indicators

Economic growth

In 2005, the economy grew by 3.4 per cent and its gross domestic product

(GDP) per capita was €23,000. Economic growth has averaged 3.5 per cent over the last five years and the European Commission forecasts growth of just under 3.2 per cent in 2006. The main engines of the economy are Madrid and Catalonia, with each producing about 20 per cent of GDP.

Inflation

Inflation increased by 3.4 per cent in 2005. Factors such as lack of competition in the utility and service sectors and the impact of high energy costs will continue to have an effect on prices.

Interest rates

As a member of the Eurozone, Spain's monetary policy is determined by the European Central Bank (ECB). Interest rates remained at two per cent from June 2003 until the benchmark was increased to 2.25 per cent in December 2005, followed by a further increase to 2.5 per cent in March 2006.

Unemployment

High unemployment in Spain is due in part to high social security taxes and a rigid labour market. Spain has the highest level of part-time employment within the EU, which has a damaging impact on permanent job creation and labour productivity.

Unemployment rate (percentage unemployed)

2000	2001	2002	2003	2004	2005
11.4	10.8	11.5	11.5	11.0	9.2

Source: Eurostat, the Statistical Office of the European Communities

In January 2006, unemployment reached its lowest level since 1979 at 8.4 per cent and is now close to the European area average of 8.3 per cent.

Foreign direct investment (FDI)

After Spain joined the EU in 1986, it received a significant boost in investment. With FDI of €112.9 billion between 1996 and 2001, Spain became the sixth largest recipient in Europe. The main investment targets are the services and industrial sectors.

Foreign direct investment in Spain (€ million)

2000	2001	2002	2003	2004	2005
38,291	34,741	41,666	22,971	13,480	15,130

Source: Bank of Spain

Economic summary

Spain and its economy have been major beneficiaries and a glowing tribute to the EU and its founding principle of spreading wealth and free trade throughout its member states. Anyone who has been there recently (and looking at the figures, that is a lot of us) will have noticed roads and other infrastructure projects which are superior to those found in the UK. Spain's income per person is now 95 per cent of the EU average.

The property market represents a significant proportion of GDP. This is a concern, as a sudden shift in sentiment, change in demand or perceived overvaluation will have distinct effects on the economy. Recently the European Central Bank (ECB) and others have argued that property prices are overvalued in some countries; Spain was cited as one of these.

Although the GDP figures are robust, there is still concern over the level of inflation and unemployment. With EU funds switching to the new members, a significant source of finance and investment will be difficult to replace, particularly in rural communities.

Off-plan risk

This poses a risk for investors entering this market in 2006, particularly those who are contemplating a geared off-plan investment, which is a rising market strategy.

What does this mean for the property investor?

It's only prudent to set out what an investment in Spanish property is not. It's not the sunnier equivalent of Poland, Slovakia or Slovenia or any other property investment which is based on rising wealth driving prices from low base levels to levels more akin to the EU average over time. Spain has been through a UK-style property boom. You are not investing at the bottom or even the middle of the market.

Timeframe and strategy

To a degree, risk is proportionate to time. If you invested in a property in Spain tomorrow, then history and economics would tell us that barring some form of catastrophe it will be worth more in real terms in ten years' time.

Spain has a growing supply of property and a growing competition for demand for property from other countries which were not around in investment terms a few years ago. There is a substitution effect going on with places such as Bulgaria, Dubai, Cyprus, Morocco, Turkey and other countries. Spain in 2006 is not a short-term investment, but it will be a solid performer over the long term.

So, what is the catch?

Unemployment

In the past decade Spain has been beset with high levels of unemployment which is particularly widespread among some groups, especially women and young adults. It's also alarming that the percentage of long-term unemployed is about 38 per cent of total unemployment in the country.

Inflation

Inflation above the EU average damages competitiveness by making goods and services more expensive. Inflation is fuelled by rigid markets in labour and services and these things combine to create a possible future negative effect on economic growth. Inflation in Spain in 2005 was 3.4 per cent and in March 2006 stood at 3.9 per cent.

Corruption

According to Transparency International, the 2005 Spanish Corruption Perception Index (CPI) is ranked 23rd with a score of 7.0. This suggests that Spain is a relatively corruption-free country.

It's worth noting that a new corruption scandal involving the mayor and several other officials in Marbella is presently being investigated after an alleged 30,000 homes were built illegally.

The market

There is an argument, supported by the ECB and the Central Bank of Spain, that property prices are overvalued and that supply of new property exceeds demand which, as we looked at in chapter 1–10, will affect prices.

The property market

Spain's property market is well established and has produced great returns for investors who entered the market in its early stages. Despite new property markets opening up in countries such as Turkey, Morocco and Bulgaria, and the continued popularity of old favourites such as France, Portugal and Italy, Spain is still by far the most popular destination for those in search of a holiday or a home in the sun.

Many investors are now questioning how long this trend can continue. Has the Spanish property market become overheated, or is there still potential for successful investment?

Tourism

The surge in tourism began in the 1950s when fewer than one million people visited Spain. Today, over 50 million people visit annually and in 2005, the country was the most popular destination for the British.

Tourism makes a strong contribution to the economy and over the next ten years, the sector is forecast to continue expanding from the current 70 billion to €157 billion.

Spain's most popular destination is Catalonia, with 25 per cent of the Spanish tourist market. The Canary Islands are in second place, followed by Andalucia and the Balearic Islands.

Property hotspots

Cities

Madrid is the capital of Spain. It's a truly international city with 100,000 foreigners making their homes here, attracted by the modern infrastructure and living costs which are cheap compared to other European capital city standards.

Two-bedroom apartments within the heart of the city can be found for just under €300,000, depending on their size and location. Prospects to let out property are as good as could be expected and, among other things, Madrid has a very large student population and high demand for rental property from corporate employees and expatriates. With this in mind, town houses are worth investigating, although properties further from the city centre will tend to produce better yields.

La Moraleja is the most elite suburb in Madrid, and is situated in the north-east of the city. Some of Madrid's highest-priced property can be found here and in some cases larger houses can go for €5 million. To the north-west of the city is a number of small towns, such as **Majadahonda** and **Las Rozas**, with contemporary developments that are significantly cheaper. Another area that is popular with English-speaking expatriates is **Charnartin**, which is just a short walk from the business district.

Demand for quality property, in the right location and at the right price, will continue to support the market and prove to be a profitable jet-to-let investment in this highly fashionable city.

Barcelona is Spain's most vibrant city, with modern up-to-date infrastructure and services, and some of the best health services in Europe. The property market in Barcelona has been rising steadily over the last ten years and presents the serious jet-to-let investor with a good long-term blue chip investment opportunity.

One of the most popular areas among investors is **Barceloneta**, which is one of the four districts in Barcelona's 'Old Town'. The area is popular with investors looking for short-term lets mainly to tourists. Most apartments in Barceloneta are small and therefore prices are still within reach for many buyers. Prices for studio apartments tend to start at €150,000, while an exclusive duplex apartment with four bedrooms can be found in the region of €850,000.

Born is another popular area with foreign investors with a great location, close to all of the city's main attractions and within walking distance of the Old Town. Born has experienced a sweeping revival in recent years and is now one of Barcelona's trendiest areas. The property market here looks certain to continue attracting investors and local professionals, but the high prices of property in the centre may force investors to look elsewhere at other less developed areas where prices remain lower. A good sized two-bedroom apartment here can be found for €225,000 or more, but because of the location it's unlikely that there will be many void periods, making it a sound investment.

The competition among investors is rising and, as a result, so has the supply of rental accommodation in Barcelona. Jet-to-let investors need to be aware that increased competition means that it takes a little more work to ensure that visitors don't stay elsewhere; for example, an increase in the number of hotel beds available in the city has led to a reduction in the occupancy rates of private rented accommodation, so marketing your property effectively becomes a cornerstone of your investment strategy.

Valencia is the third largest city in Spain and is on the Costa del Azahar. Valencia is a lively and cosmopolitan city with plenty to lure the astute property investor.

Property in Valencia is becoming popular with overseas investors and low-cost flights to the city make second homes easier to reach. This has also had a knock-on effect by boosting the demand for short-term accommodation as a result of the increase in the number of visitors.

Presently, a three-bedroom house in the west of Valencia can be bought for €150,000. Better deals can be found if you search further inland and those investors looking to get ahead of the crowd would do well to consider the coastal area to the north of the city. With planned golf developments and a new airport, there will be significantly added value to this area, which will encourage future capital growth and rental demand.

There is a high demand for rental property in Valencia making it an interesting prospect for those wanting a jet-to-let property.

Coastal and islands

The **Costa del Sol** continues to be popular with British and European retirees, second home owners and holidaymakers alike. The area has been at the forefront of the Spanish property market in terms of capital growth and property development. These rises have amounted to over 400 per cent in recent years and the sheer volume of jet-to-let investment means that there are now more foreigners living on the Costa del Sol than Spanish nationals.

Not unexpectedly, the property boom appears to be slowing down after such fantastic success. News from agents along the coast indicate a fall in demand for second homes for the first time in over six years. This suggests that rising prices and oversupply have driven those people looking for second homes to look elsewhere for more affordable property.

Costa del Sol has grown from a string of fishing villages and harbours, and it now spreads all the way from **Almeria** to Gibraltar. The more well-off retirees head for **Marbella** and the neighbouring marina of **Puerto Banus**. A two-bedroom house for sale in the more popular areas will sell for upwards of €250,000, but with enough research and investigation properties can be found for less without compromising on the location.

By contrast, the **Costa Brava** is one of the most cultural and captivating regions in Spain. It's also where you will find some of Spain's most popular towns and cities, such as **Barcelona** and **Girona**, which offer strong investment opportunities in both the short-break and short-let market as well as long-term rental prospects. This area is one of the most economically prosperous regions of Spain, producing almost 20 per cent of the country's GDP, and with virtually non-existent unemployment.

Over four million people visit the Costa Brava annually with the largest share coming from France, followed by Germany and then the UK. This area is also popular with Spanish people themselves, with over 33 per cent of Catalans visiting each year. Costa Brava also boasts some of the best golf courses in Europe, beaches, theatres, shopping, international restaurants and a lively nightlife. All of these factors combine to make the demand for property very high, whether for rental purposes or for second homes.

Costa Calida is on the south-east coast of the Iberian peninsular, stretching between the Costa Blanca and the Costa de Almeria.

Property prices have risen considerably on the Costa Calida in recent years. In **Murcia**, the capital of the region, prices have doubled in the last few years alone and on the coast, prices have increased by approximately 30 per cent.

The property market in this area of Spain is exciting and is outperforming many other coastal resorts in the country. Prices are offering better value than other more well-known areas (e.g. a three-bedroom house with a pool can currently be found for under €150,000), but getting in now would be the best plan as the region's popularity is expected to rise considerably soon, taking house prices up too. Murcia is one of the prime Spanish locations tipped by analysts to do well for investors in the medium to long term.

The **Costa Blanca** stretches 170 miles along Spain's east coast centred on Alicante and running from Valencia to La Manga in the south. The attractions of the Costa Blanca are clear, with more than 300 days of sunshine annually and a broad range of activities on offer for visitors.

House prices in the Costa Blanca are cheaper than those on the Costa del Sol. In Costa Blanca South, there is a lot of supply for under €150,000 on the coast and inland you can still find old properties in need of renovation for as little as €30,000. New developments stand out in Costa Blanca encompassing several new towns, such as **Santa Pola**, **Punta Prima** and **Cabo Roig**.

Resale properties in this area also offer good value, with villas from €200,000 and apartments for under €150,000. Prices in Costa Blanca North are higher as the property market is more established with fewer new-build options down to the fact that there is very little land available for large developments.

The delightful **Balearics** (which include Mallorca, Menorca, Ibiza and Formentera) are off the coast of Spain in the Mediterranean Sea. During the summer months the Balearics are full of life with tourists from across Europe after a variety of breaks.

Mallorca is the largest of the Balearic Islands, with more than six million visitors a year, which includes a massive influx of mostly British and German holidaymakers. Despite continued demand, there still remain many opportunities to buy good value properties across the island. A two-bedroom apartment will cost around €165,000 in the resort areas, but a lot less in the city of Palma. A villa on the island can be bought for about €325,000, although continued popularity means that prices are increasing all the time.

Menorca is more tranquil and relatively unspoilt and as a destination is ideal for anyone looking for a quieter location. The south of the island is slightly more developed to cater for the tourists and property buyers, and many beautiful villas can be found at considerably lower prices than the other islands.

Ibiza is the third largest of the Balearic Islands and it's still considered by many to be one of the top destinations in Europe to party. **San Antonio**, **Playa d'en Bossa**, **Santa Rafael** and **Ibiza Town** are popular and are within easy reach of the larger clubs. Whether you are looking for a year-round property investment or a holiday home, it's hard to go wrong with one of the most admired and revisited tourist destinations in Europe. Ibiza's year-round population is just 100,000, but there is a dramatic increase of residents in the summer due to seasonal workers and annual holidaymakers, and the demand for rental property becomes very high.

It seems as if the **Canary Islands** have always been a popular destination for UK tourists and their perennial popularity with UK and continental holidaymakers is undeniable. The islands have far more to offer than just sun and have proven their enduring appeal by attracting large numbers of visitors for many years. Even now, there is still good room for capital growth and income from property on each of the islands.

Demand for quality holiday accommodation in Spain's tropical paradise is very high to the extent that the Spanish government committed half of their entire 2005 tourism promotion budget to promoting the Canary and Balearic Islands, further increasing demand for accommodation. You can purchase a jet-to-let property on the Canaries' good potential, whether you choose to rent it out year-round in the short-let market or rent it out to generate a healthy income and then benefit from using it yourself for the rest of the year as a live-and-let investment.

Tenerife is the largest of the Canary Islands and it's the most developed in terms of infrastructure and industry. The beachfronts can be very lively, offering tourists all forms of entertainment. Properties away from the hustle and bustle of the coast are more peaceful but just as easy to let.

Gran Canaria is smaller than Tenerife and was the first of the Canary Islands to develop its tourism market. Now certain areas are in need of redevelopment or refurbishment, although some upmarket development projects are being constructed, serving to improve Gran Canaria's appeal to a more select market. As Gran Canaria is one of the most popular year-round holiday destinations, the demand for quality rental accommodation remains high. A three-bedroom villa is likely to cost the best part of €500,000 while a two-bedroom apartment can be found in the region of €125,000.

The property market on the island of **Lanzarote** is booming, with its unique attraction sustaining high demand and ensuring that property prices continue to rise sharply. Even though this is the case, you can still find a small apartment for less than €85,000.

Overall, buying a jet-to-let property on one of the Canary Islands can be a great investment and can give you the best of all worlds. The Canaries will be popular for a long time to come making investment here a relatively profitable, if unadventurous choice.

The buying process

There are no restrictions on foreign ownership of Spanish property. Foreigners have the same rights as Spaniards.

Once terms and conditions have been agreed with the vendor, a deposit of ten per cent of the purchase price is usually paid. The remaining 90 per cent is payable on the signing of the title deeds before a notary.

Transaction costs

If you are buying off-plan, the developer will usually require stage payments to be made as the construction progresses. These payments vary depending on the developer and the length of time to completion. Remember from chapters 1–10, it's sensible to invest as small an amount of cash as possible in order to drive the return on investment as high as possible. For this reason, you should negotiate with the development company to keep your deposits low over the lifetime of the build.

You also have to ask yourself whether off-plan geared investing is the best possible strategy in Spain in 2006.

Expenses include:

- **Transfer Tax** is six to seven per cent of the declared purchase value and it must be paid by buyers purchasing resale properties. If any deposit is paid before completion of the sale, it's not subjected to Transfer Tax.

  If a property is being sold for the first time, the IVA (the Spanish equivalent of VAT) of seven per cent is charged, plus an extra 0.5 to one per cent stamp duty. If any deposit is paid before completion of the sale, such deposit will be subject to IVA at the moment it's paid.

- **Notary fees** are generally between one and two per cent of the sale price. The appointed legal representative will represent both the buyer and the seller.

- **Land registration fees** are approximately one to 1.5 per cent of the purchase price of a property.

- **Municipal Tax** must be paid to the town hall when urban land is purchased. This tax varies from 10 to 40 per cent of the increase in the value of the property since its last sale.

- **Legal fees** normally come up to one to 1.5 per cent of the sale price, depending upon the complexity of the transaction.

The total purchase fees usually add up to eight to 12 per cent. This figure depends on variable factors, such as the location, and whether the property is a new-build or resale.

The buyer is liable to pay all the costs outlined above, but the seller is responsible for estate agents' fees of between five and ten per cent of the purchase price.

If you are buying from a non-resident in Spain, you pay the seller 95 per cent of the price and pay the other five per cent directly to the town hall, which serves as a guarantee against the non-resident seller's various Spanish tax liabilities.

Annual costs

The annual operating costs for a property are generally cheaper than in the UK. This will vary according to the type of property you buy, the area in which it's situated and the intended use.

- **Local Property Tax** ('Impuesto Sobre Bienes Inmuebles' (IBI)) is paid yearly to the town hall. The amount payable is calculated on the basis of the cadastral value. The percentage charged varies from area to area, and is roughly 0.5 per cent to one per cent.

- **Wealth Tax** is paid annually on the net value of all assets in Spain to the regional government. The rate varies from 0.2 to 2.5 per cent. This is payable regardless of whether you are resident in Spain.

- **Municipal Tax** (local mains drainage and refuse collection tax) is levied at 0.1–1.4 per cent of the cadastral value of your property – in practice between €200 and €800 per year, depending on the area.

- **Management or service charges** cover the costs of cleaning and maintaining communal areas, such as gardens, swimming pools and roads.

Taxes

Taxation is Spain is somewhat complicated. The major taxation rules for Spain are summarised below:

Income Tax

Income Tax rates for 2006:

Tax	Annual tax base (€)
15%	Up to 4,161.60
24%	4,161.61–14,357.52
28%	14,357.53–26,842.32
37%	26,842.33–46,818.00
45%	Over 46,818.01

Corporation Tax

Spain's standard corporate Income Tax rate is 35 per cent. The Spanish government plans a gradual reduction of the current Corporation Tax rate to 30 per cent by 2011.

Capital Gains Tax

Spanish residents have a capital gain added to their income and are taxed at the marginal rate. On the sale of a property, Spanish residents are subject to a 15 per cent Capital Gains Tax, provided that the property has been owned for more than one year prior to the sale. Any asset sales occurring in a period of less than a year are treated as income and subject to Income Tax. Non-residents are taxed at a flat rate of 35 per cent.

Wealth Tax

Spanish residents and non-residents alike are required to pay Wealth Tax on all capital assets. The tax rate is progressive and varies between 0.2 and 2.5 per cent.

Summary

Strengths

- Political democracy.
- A member of the EU.
- Consistent economic growth.

- Falling unemployment.

- Strong tourist industry and demand for property rentals and second homes.

- Strong retirement community demand for property.

- Established property market, procedures and resale market.

- No restrictions on foreign ownership.

- Cheaper annual running costs than the UK.

- Short flying times for many Europeans.

- No-frills low-cost airlines continue to attract rental and sales demand.

- All-year-round rental market created by the proliferation of golf courses.

- Weather.

- Beaches.

- Cultural and architectural delights of Madrid, Barcelona, Seville, Granada and Valencia, to name but a few.

Weaknesses

- Competition from hotel industry for rentals.

- Competition from the many other owners of properties for rentals.

- Persistent unemployment.

- Persistent inflation.

- Declining indigenous population.

- The opportunities for off-plan geared investments are not as strong as other alternatives.

Opportunities

- A growing number of distressed sellers will open opportunities for purchasing below market value.

- Properties which have been repossessed by the banks or are available for auction, which generally means making an offer through the use of a 'sealed bid'.

- Lifestyle investment – 'live-and-let'.

- Development of inland resorts.

- Renovation projects in the mountains, hills and villages where property prices are relatively cheap and there is a growing demand for them from foreigners.

Threats

- Loss of EU funding in 2006 and the negative effects on the Spanish economy.

- The risk of the property market overheating.

- Is the Spanish property market at the top and will you be buying in as other investors are leaving?

- Competition for property sales (demand) from other emerging markets at a more favourable position in the market cycle for property investors.

- Competition from other markets for holidaymakers and lettings.

- The opening up of other low-cost airline routes to other countries which may be viewed as competitors, such as Bulgaria, Cyprus, Dubai and Turkey.

- Potential oversupply of property.

- Recent cases of properties built illegally. (Therefore, do make sure that you get professional and competent legal advice, independent of the developer, when you are investing abroad.)

Facts at a glance

Geography

Population (2005 estimate)	40,341,462
Language	Castilian Spanish spoken by 74% of population. Catalan is spoken by 17%, 7% speak Galician and 2% speak Basque
Ethnic groups	Castilian (about 75%) Catalans (16%) Galicians (7%) Basques (2%)
Local currency	Euro, divided into 100 cents

Political system

Political structure	Parliamentary democracy
Monarch	King Juan Carlos I
President	José Luis Rodríguez Zapatero
Main parties	Spanish Socialist Workers' Party (PSOE) People's Party (PP)

Economy

Unemployment rate in 2005	9.2%
Unemployment rate, February 2006	8.7%
Inflation rate in 2005	3.4%
Inflation rate, March 2006	3.9%
Interest rate, March 2006	2.5%
GDP growth in 2005	3.4%
GDP growth forecast for 2006	3.2%
GDP per capita (income per person) in 2005	€23,000

Taxation

Income Tax	15–45%
Corporation Tax	35% for Spanish corporations 25% for non-resident ones
Capital Gains Tax	15% for Spanish residents 35% for non-residents
Wealth Tax	0.2–2.5%

Corruption statistics

Corruption rate	7.0
Corruption rank	23rd

Industry and technology

Major industries	Iron and steel Construction Motor vehicles Tourism

The Spanish property market

Hotspots	Urban: Madrid, Barcelona and Valencia Regions: Costa del Sol, Costa Brava, Costa Calida, Costa Blanca Islands: Balearic Islands and Canary Islands

Property taxes (transactions)

Transfer Tax	Applies to resale properties only at 6–7%
IVA (Spanish VAT)	Applies to newly built properties only at 7%
Stamp duty	Applies to newly built properties only at 0.5–1%
Notary fees	1–2%
Land registration fees	Approximately 1–1.5%

Municipal Tax	Applies to urban land only. Varies from 10 to 40% of the increase in the value of the property since its last sale
Legal fees	1–1.5%
Total fees	Average 8–12%

Property taxes (annual)

Local Property Tax	Varies from area to area but is roughly 0.5–1%
'Council Tax'	About €200 and €250 per year, depending on the area
Community fees	Vary and depend on a number of factors

Mortgage

LTV	50–70%
Term	5–30 years
Currency	Euros and other major currencies
Current interest rate	Varies between 2.9 and 4.5%

Investor resources

Embassies

British Embassy in Spain

C/ Fernando el Santo, 16
28010 Madrid

Tel: +91 700 8200
Fax: +91 700 8272
Website: www.ukinspain.com

Spanish Embassy in the UK

39 Chesham Place
London SW1X 8SB

Tel: 020 7235 5555
Fax: 020 7235 9905
Website: http://spain.embassyhomepage.com

Useful websites

Bank of Spain
www.bde.es

Invest in Spain
www.investinspain.org

Spanish National Statistics Institute
www.ine.es

Tourism in Spain
www.spain.info

Traveller's Guide to Spain
www.aboutspain.net

Turkey

Why invest in Turkey?

Turkey has recently become a hotspot destination for jet-to-let property investors, particularly among those buyers from the UK. As an emerging investor market, Turkey provides excellent value for money at a fraction of the cost of properties in traditional European markets, such as Spain and France.

Turkey is surrounded by the Aegean, Black, Mediterranean and Marmara seas and has attractive yet unspoilt coastal towns as well as resorts. The cost of living is low and travelling to Turkey is becoming easier and cheaper. With such an abundance of locations, from sea to mountains to cities, it's not difficult to see why Turkey is fast becoming one of the most popular emerging jet-to-let destinations.

The story so far...

Turkey has a very rich history. Its territories were conquered by the Persians, the Greeks under Alexander the Great, then the Romans and the Byzantines. The establishment of the Ottoman State in the 14th century brought Turkish dominance to South-Eastern Europe, the Middle East and parts of North Africa. The Ottoman Empire was the longest surviving empire that the world has ever known.

Turkey was on the losing side in the First World War, which led to the break-up of the empire and foreign occupation. In 1923, the Turkish Republic was proclaimed and Mustafa Kemal (Atatürk) was its founder and first president.

The political situation in Turkey during the latter part of the 20th century was at best unstable. In 1950, a multi-party parliamentary democracy was established, but the government became increasingly authoritarian, leading to the army staging a coup d'état in 1960 and a further revolt in 1971. Three years later, Turkish forces invaded Cyprus in order to prevent the island's possible unification with Greece after the failure of diplomatic efforts to resolve disputes between Turkish and Greek Cypriots.

Modern Turkey is very keen to join the European Union (EU) and wants to gain the political and economic stability that membership can bring. Turkey has recently amended some of its laws in order to conform to human rights legislation and to be more in line with Western ideas. The country is now governed by the Conservative Justice and Development Party.

Where is it?

Turkey is surrounded by the Aegean Sea to the west, Bulgaria, Greece and Sea of Marmara to the north-west, the Black Sea to the north, Georgia to the north-east, Armenia and Iran to the east and Iraq, Syria and the Mediterranean Sea to the south. The Turkish coastline is 7,200km long and the country's total territory is 780,580km^2.

Turkey is at a point where the three continents of Asia, Africa and Europe meet. The European portion of Turkey, known as the Eastern (or Turkish) Thrace, includes only three per cent of the total area and occupies the far south-eastern part of Europe. The majority of Turkey comprises the Asian territory of Anatolia, also known as Asia Minor, and this is a large mountainous peninsula.

What is the weather like?

The country has a diverse climate with some significant differences between regions and seasons. The Mediterranean region has hot and dry summers and mild rainy winters, but the Black Sea region is cooler with the heaviest rainfall in Turkey. While the coast has milder climates, inland Turkey experiences extremes of temperatures which make it very cold in winter and almost insufferably hot in summer. The hot summers have almost no rainfall, with high daytime temperatures and cool nights. Winters are cold with heavy snow.

Ankara

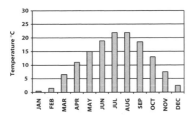 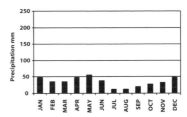

Istanbul

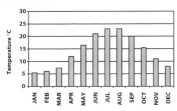 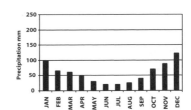

Bodrum/Kusadasi

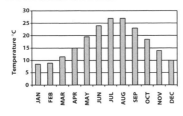 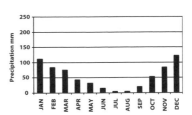

Marmaris

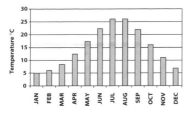 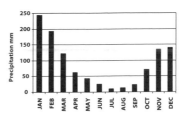

Antalya/Side

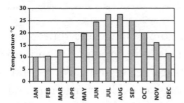
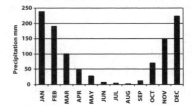

The language

The official language is Turkish, spoken by 90 per cent of the 69 million population. Other minority languages include Kurdish, spoken by six per cent of the population, Greek and Armenian. English and French are spoken as second languages.

Currency

Up until 31 December 2004 the Turkish Lira (TL) was the national currency. In 2005, the Turkish Lira was replaced by the new Turkish Lira (Yeni Turk Lirasi or YTL), at an exchange rate of one new Lira to 1,000,000 old. The YTL is divided into 100 Kurus.

Politics

Turkey is a secular parliamentary republic, founded on the principle of the division of powers into legislative, executive and judiciary. The main parties are the right-wing Conservative Justice and Development Party (AKP) and left-wing social-democratic Republican People's Party (CHP). The current President of Turkey is Ahmet Necdet Sezer, appointed in 2000 and the Prime Minister is Recep Tayyip Erdogan, elected in 2000.

Turkey has 81 administrative provinces and seven geographical regions.

A rocky road to European accession?

Turkey is a potential candidate to join the EU and has implemented a number of reforms in order to achieve closer integration with the EU. This included the abolition of the death penalty, reforms on human rights and greater freedom of speech. In response, the European Commission opened negotiations with Turkey in October 2005 on the country's possible membership. It will take some years to reach a conclusion on whether Turkey will actually join, or whether it will instead be granted a special trading status.

Economy

The Turkish economy has been noted for its numerous booms and busts over the years. However, the country has recently achieved macro-economic stability and inflation is now at a 30-year low.

The industrial sector was responsible for almost 30 per cent of Turkey's gross domestic product (GDP) in 2005. The country's major industries are textiles and clothing, but the automotive, metalworking, chemicals and pharmaceutical sectors are developing. The service sector is also continually expanding and now accounts for 58 per cent of GDP, largely due to tourism.

Despite the recent optimistic signs, Turkey continues to face many economic challenges that include a thriving black economy and unequal distribution of wealth. The complex legal system and high levels of bureaucracy also pose a burden.

In addition, the labour market is still far from being efficient and the spread of employment opportunities across the country is uneven, being focused mostly in the tourist areas and the cities.

Economic indicators

Economic growth

Last year, the economy grew by 7.4 per cent and GDP per capita was

€7,000. The European Commission forecasts a further 5.2 per cent growth in 2006. Forecasts for 2006 and 2007 also look good. Any fall in inflation will allow for a cut in interest rates and this will have a positive knock-on effect on both investment and consumer spending.

Inflation

Inflation fell to 7.7 per cent in 2005. This is remarkable when you consider that inflation averaged over 70 per cent between 1993 and 2001!

The Turkish Central Bank predicts that inflation will keep falling over the next 18 months despite a recent rise in energy costs. The government's inflation target is five per cent for this year and three per cent in 2007, although inflation in March 2006 is presently 8.2 per cent.

The dramatic fall in inflation and re-issue of the currency are a major success story for Turkey's economy and conveys an encouraging message to potential foreign investors.

Interest rates

Interest rates have remained high over the last 20 years, hitting 100 per cent in 1999. Compared to EU standards, short-term rates are still high at 13.5 per cent in March 2006. The Turkish Central Bank has announced that rates will remain at current levels during the first quarter of 2006, but are likely to fall later in the year.

Jet-to-let property investors do well to target countries in which interest rates are falling from high levels to low levels as a result of a shift in macro-economic management. This is not a reason in itself to invest in Turkey, but with other reforms in legal practices and mortgage finance, it's an interesting consideration and provides grounds for further in-depth research.

Unemployment

Turkey has relatively high rates of unemployment, which are comparable to France and Germany.

Unemployment rate (percentage unemployed)

2000	2001	2002	2003	2004	2005
6.5	8.3	10.3	10.5	10.3	10.3

Source: Eurostat, the Statistical Office of the European Communities

Unemployment is particularly high among the young population, reaching 22 per cent in the cities, which is highest among the less educated. Turkey has a problem with its education system, as less then 25 per cent of the workforce have completed secondary education and only ten per cent go on to get university degrees. This has serious implications for the economy and the type and quality of jobs which can be created as the skills are not present to allow for an increased diversification of the economy.

Foreign direct investment (FDI)

Turkey has attracted a growing amount of FDI, which has increased steadily and in parallel with the country's economic growth. There was a substantial inflow in 2005 of $9.65 billion, which is an increase of 239 per cent from the year before.

Foreign direct investment in Turkey (million US dollars)

2000	2001	2002	2003	2004	2005
982	3,352	1,137	1,752	2,847	9,650

Source: Bank of Turkey

A number of significant obstacles remain for foreign companies, which face unnecessary bureaucracy and a very weak legal system. As a result, FDI inflows have been less than those received by more investor-friendly countries, particularly in Eastern Europe.

So, what is the catch?

Corruption

Turkey is ranked at joint 65th place in the Transparency International table for perceived corruption levels, along with Peru, Panama, Mexico and Ghana, with a score of 3.5. This would suggest that corruption is significant in this country and Turkey has already seen a decline in the perceived level of corruption from the previous year's position at 77th.

Education

This is one key area that Turkey must improve to ensure that the country's labour force can operate and compete internationally. Statistics show that illiteracy continues to be a major concern which has serious implications for the labour market and diversification of the economy.

Human rights

Turkey has long attracted international concern about its commitment to democracy, human rights and freedom of speech.

Social inequality

Differences between income and social classes are deepening and may become a bigger issue in the future. According to the State Institute of Statistics from 2003, 29 per cent of the population live in poverty.

Earthquakes

The probability of an earthquake in Turkey is higher than in most other jet-to-let markets because of the country's proximity to the Ecemis fault line. As with property markets all over the world, a robust property insurance policy is a must to hedge such a risk.

The property market

The Turkish property market is in the early stages of a property boom, which has been triggered by a change in the law relating to foreign ownership. Growth was also accelerated by Turkey's decision in October 2005 to enter into accession talks with the EU.

Turkey is benefiting from a substitution effect as property values have risen significantly in traditional investment locations such as Spain, Italy and France. Home buyers and investors have substituted cheaper properties in the Eastern Mediterranean instead of the more expensive locations, hence fuelling the property market.

Turkey is experiencing 30–40 per cent house price inflation in certain regions and is still by far the cheapest market in Europe when comparing location, size and quality. This said, there are certain disadvantages that an investor must consider, such as a lack of mortgage finance (this is presently changing) and low income of the local population.

Being clear on your investment strategy is essential in order to succeed in this exciting but possibly unpredictable investment market. As with all property investments, location is key and picking a great spot means that in years to come it should pay dividends. This will become even clearer as the mortgage market opens up and property purchase becomes an option that is more accessible to the masses.

The future prospects for Turkey look promising, especially as the Turkish market appeals to a wide range of people, not just those looking at the country as a jet-to-let destination. With the recent announcement by EasyJet of routes to Istanbul from the UK, this is a country worth keeping a close eye on as the investment story unfolds. For those with an appetite for a little risk in their portfolios, Turkey warrants a closer look.

Tourism

Turkey continues to establish itself as a hotspot tourist destination and tourism accounts for almost 20 per cent of GDP.

A new record of 21 million tourists visited Turkey in 2005, compared with 17.5 million the year before. The target for 2006 is 26 million tourists with visitor numbers expected to grow by more than ten per cent for the next decade.

Property hotspots

Cities

Ankara became the Turkish capital with the declaration of the Turkish Republic in 1923. It then had a population of 30,000 compared to over four million people today.

Rental prospects in Ankara are reasonable, and opportunities are present to let to the city's student population and the growing number of tourists. The **Altindag** and **Cankaya** districts have a wealth of attractions that are high on many visitors' lists of places to see, so they are worthy of consideration if you are investing in the city. Many of the university departments are in **Kecioren**, making this area more popular for student and staff rentals.

Istanbul, often mistaken as the capital of Turkey, is beginning to broaden its appeal to the wider jet-to-let investor market. The demand for rental property comes from the 1.5 million visitors each year and the population of over ten million people in the greater Istanbul area.

In addition to the wealth of tourist attractions, Istanbul is a thriving educational, cultural, business and commercial centre. An improved infrastructure in the city has contributed to the growth in local investment and employment opportunities. After considerable growth in 2005, Istanbul's property market is forecast to have a strong 2006 and 2007.

The choice of properties available is not as varied in Ankara and Istanbul as on the coast and property prices are more expensive. As an example, you could find a three-bedroom apartment for €185,000. Rents average around €350–430 per week.

Coastal

Bodrum on the Aegean coast is a particularly beautiful town that has become very popular with tourists and property investors. With a multitude of interesting attractions for holidaymakers, Bodrum attracts tourists from all over the world. Property represents excellent value for money and prices compare favourably with many of Turkey's international competitors. It's not unusual to find four-bedroom villas in Bodrum on sale for under €215,000, and in more exclusive areas further down the peninsula, such as **Yalikayak**, prices can be closer to €300,000. A two-bedroom off-plan apartment can be bought for under €100,000.

Bodrum is very accessible with summer charter flights from major UK airports including Manchester, Cardiff and Birmingham, as well as London. The demand for property is particularly high during the summer months, making it a very viable jet-to-let rental prospect.

It's worth bearing in mind that the rental season in Turkey runs from June through to the end of October.

Marmaris is a popular tourist destination and centre of activity for those that enjoy yachting, benefiting from the revenue that comes with spending power of the boating fraternity. The town has grown into a substantial year-round resort with a wealth of bars and clubs and plenty of water sports activities. Despite these developments, Marmaris has managed to retain its charm and natural beauty.

Kusadasi is on the Aegean Sea in Western Turkey. The town is one of the country's top holiday hotspots, with dazzling sandy beaches, clear blue sea and great holiday amenities. The low-cost flights to Izmir and quick transfers to Kusadasi have helped to make the area more accessible and have brought further investment. Property prices in Kusadasi are cheaper than in other Turkish resorts and you can find a three-bedroom villa for around €100,000. A two-bedroom off-plan apartment currently costs in the region of €80,000, making this a popular and relatively cheap location.

Antalya, on Turkey's Southern Mediterranean coast, is an attractive resort, known as Turkey's very own capital of tourism. Antalya combines a historical charm with good modern facilities and its own airport. The resort's increasing popularity means that the demand for quality property is growing fast. A two-bedroom villa will cost in the region of €120,000 and the average price for a more spacious three-bedroom villa is about €190,000.

Side is on a peninsula flanked by two beaches and perfectly combines old- and new-world charm. Side has extensive tourist accommodation, shops, bars and restaurants and has become one of Turkey's most popular resorts. There are various types of property on offer and a modern three-bedroom villa can be found for €170,000.

Ski

Skiing may not immediately spring to mind when you think of investing in Turkey, but there are plenty of skiing centres scattered across the country. These include **Uludag**, south of Istanbul, **Kartalkaya** and **Palandoken**, the coldest and highest of all of Turkey's ski areas. Although the facilities are not as well developed as facilities in France or Italy, skiing in Turkey is becoming more popular.

The buying process

The buying process in Turkey is straightforward and the sale of property to overseas buyers depends on the concept of reciprocity. The UK and the Republic of Turkey have full reciprocity regarding property acquisition, as do other EU countries.

Foreigners can own up to a maximum of 2.5 hectares (25,000m²) of land and property. Upon application, the Council of Ministers may increase this to a maximum of 30 hectares (300,000m²) providing that this doesn't exceed a total of 0.5 per cent of the land area of the district in question. Foreigners are not allowed to buy property in the military and security zones of Turkey.

It cannot be overstated how important it is to instruct an independent local English-speaking lawyer. The many checks and searches that need to be conducted on a property must be done by a professional lawyer in order to reduce your risk and safeguard your interests.

After your offer is confirmed, your lawyer will draw up a preliminary contract. This is signed in the notary's office and upon signing it the buyer is required to pay a deposit of ten per cent of the purchase price. Next, both buyer and seller apply to the TAPU (Title Deeds) Office in order to proceed with the transfer of the title deed.

The title deeds searches include checks to ensure that the property is not in a military or security zone. This is just a formality, but, unfortunately for a jet-to-let investor, it can take up to three months.

When all searches have been satisfactorily completed, the buyer (or a lawyer acting with a Power of Attorney) and the seller sign the final contract in the Land Registry Office. The buyer pays the remaining balance to the seller. The buyer or his lawyer then attends a public notary office in order to confirm the transfer of the title deeds.

All of the final fees and taxes are paid on the receipt of the deeds.

Transaction costs

When purchasing a property in Turkey you need to allow for the following transaction costs:

- **Initial Purchase Tax:** 1.5 per cent of the declared purchase price.
- **Legal fees:** these are typically between £150 to £500. Allow £100 extra for translation costs.
- **Land registration fees:** approximately £450.
- **Public notary's fees:** approximately £90.
- **Utility connection fee:** approximately £200 to £350, depending on the type of property and location.
- **Estate agents' fees (fixed):** three per cent of the purchase price. Costs are normally split between the buyer and seller.

These expenses can amount to around five to six per cent of the purchase price.

Annual costs

- Annual property tax rates for different types of properties are:
  - **Land** – 0.3 per cent
  - **Buildings** – 0.2 per cent
  - **Residential buildings** – 0.1 per cent
  - **Fields** – 0.1 per cent

  Rates are twice as high in some metropolitan areas. New properties are exempt from this tax for five years.

- **Earthquake insurance:** depends on the property price and location (but it's required by law).

- If property is bought in a complex, there is an average **maintenance charge** of £170 to £750 depending on the property's size and location.

Taxes

Taxation in Turkey is relatively straightforward. Below we have outlined the major taxation rules.

Income Tax
Income Tax rates 2006:

Tax	Annual tax base (YTL)
15%	Up to 7,000
20%	7,001–18,000
27%	18,001–40,000
35%	Above 40,001

Corporation Tax
The tax rate applicable to corporations in Turkey is 30 per cent. The government proposes to reduce Turkey's Corporation Tax rate to 20 per cent in 2006, although this has not yet been approved.

Capital Gains Tax
In general, capital gains in Turkey, whether for an individual or for a company, is added to Income Tax. On the sale of property, individuals are exempt from this tax, provided that the property has been owned for more than five years prior to sale.

Summary

Strengths

- Political democracy.

- Improving economic management.

- Growing tourist market and demand for second homes, retirement homes and rentals.

- Good beaches.

- Beautiful scenery.

- Huge variety of property and locations available.

- Relatively cheap coastal properties.

- No restrictions on foreign ownership.

- Cultural and business centre of Istanbul.

- Low property transaction costs.

- Low cost of living.

- Labour costs low for renovation projects.

Weaknesses

- Competition from hotel industry for rentals.

- High unemployment and the rigidity of the labour market and increasing competition from China.

- High levels of corruption.

- High inflation.

- Low-value economy.

- Poorly educated workforce.

Opportunities

- Potential EU member.

- Emerging property market with growing demand.

- Liberalisation of financial services and greater access to mortgage finance will boost the market.

- Low-cost airline routes announced by EasyJet.
- Increasing popularity with holidaymakers and some retirees.

Threats

- Relatively underdeveloped economy.
- Possible overheating of the property market in some areas.
- In an earthquake zone.

Facts at a glance

Geography	
Population (estimate)	69.6 million
Language	The official language is Turkish, spoken by more than 90% of population. Other languages include Kurdish, Armenian, Greek and Arabic
Ethnic groups	80% Turkish and 20% Kurdish community
Local currency	New Turkish Lira divided into 100 Kurus

Political system	
Political structure	Secular parliamentary republic
President	Ahmet Necdet Sezer
Prime Minister	Recep Tayyip Erdogan
Main parties	Justice and Development Party (AKP) Republican People's Party (CHP)

Economy

Unemployment rate in 2005	10.3%
Unemployment rate, March 2006	11.2%
Inflation rate in 2005	7.7%
Inflation rate, February 2006	8.2%
Interest rate, March 2006	13.5%
GDP growth in 2005	7.4%
GDP growth forecast for 2006	5.2%
GDP per capita (income per person) in 2005	€7,000

Taxation

Income Tax	15–35%
Capital Gains Tax	Treated as income
Corporation Tax	30%

Corruption statistics

Corruption rate	3.5
Corruption rank	65th

Industry and technology

Major industries	Textiles and apparel Mining Construction Tourism

The Turkish property market

Hotspots	Coastal: Ankara and Istanbul Cities: Bodrum, Marmaris, Kusadasi, Antalya and Side Ski: Uludag

Property taxes (transactions)

Initial Purchase Tax	1.5%

Solicitors' fees	£150–500 plus £100 translation costs
Land registration fees	Approximately £450
Notary fees	£90
Utility connection fee	Approximately £200–350
Estate agents' fees	3%
Total fees	5–6%

Property taxes (annual)	
Annual Property Tax	0.3–0.6%
Earthquake insurance	Varies (required by law)
Community fees	£170–750

Mortgage	
Mortgage availability	Mortgages have not been available to foreign buyers, but this is rapidly changing

Investor resources

Embassies

British Embassy in Turkey

Sehit Ersan Caddesi 46/A
Cankaya 06680, Ankara

Tel: +90 312 455 3344
Fax: +90 312 455 3356
Website: www.britishembassy.gov.uk/servlet/Front?pagename=Open
Market/Xcelerate/ShowPage&c=Page&cid=1053446559682

Turkish Embassy in the UK

43 Belgrave Square
London SW1X 8PA

Tel: 020 7393 0202
Fax: 020 7393 0066
Website: http://turkey.embassyhomepage.com

Useful websites

Bank of Turkey
www.tcmb.gov.tr

The Statistical Institute of Turkey
www.die.gov.tr/ENGLISH/index.html

Tourism in Turkey
www.turkeytourism.com

Turkish Economy
www.turkisheconomy.org.uk

Appendices

Appendix 1: Economic data

Country	GDP Growth Rate, 2005	GDP Forecast, 2006	GDP Per Capita, 2005
Bulgaria	5.4%	4.3%	€7,500
Cyprus	3.8%	4.0%	€19,600
Czech Republic	6.0%	4.4%	€17,100
Dubai	6.5%	6.4%	$29,100 (€23,579)*
Estonia	9.8%	7.2%	€13,000
Florida	6.6%**	4.6%	$33,219 (€26,916)*
France	1.5%	1.9%	€25,500
Germany	1.1%	1.8%	€25,300
Greece	3.7%	3.4%	€19,600
Hungary	4.3%	3.9%	€14,500
Italy	0.1%	1.2%	€24,200
Latvia	10.2%	7.7%	€10,900
Lithuania	7.4%	6.2%	€11,900
Morocco	1.6%	5.7%	$4,300 (€3,484)*
Poland	2.6%	4.3%	€11,600
Portugal	0.4%	0.8%	€16,600
Slovakia	6.0%	5.5%	€12,700
Slovenia	4.2%	4.0%	€18,900
Spain	3.4%	3.2%	€23,000
Turkey	7.4%	5.2%	$7,000 (€5,672)*
United Kingdom	1.8%	2.3%	$27,100
USA	3.5%	3.3%	$42,122 (€34,130)*
EU-25	1.7%	2.2%	€24,800
Eurozone	1.5%	1.9%	€23,400

* Exchange rate 1 US dollar to €0.8103 as at 21 April 2006.

** The growth rate in Florida is calculated by using a Gross State Product (GSP), which is a similar concept to that of the Gross Domestic Product (GDP), but at the state level.

*** Exchange rate 1 pound sterling to €1.4436 as at 21 April 2006.

Appendix 1: Economic data (continued)

Country	Unemployment Rate, 2005	Unemployment Rate, Feb 2006	Interest Rate, March 2006
Bulgaria	9.9%	11.5%	2.28%
Cyprus	5.3%	5.2%	4.25%
Czech Republic	7.9%	7.7%	2.00%
Dubai	2.4% (2001 est)	N/A	4.19%
Estonia	7.9%	5.9%	2.90%
Florida	3.8%	3.2%	4.75%
France	9.5%	9.1%	2.50%
Germany	9.5%	8.9%	2.50%
Greece	9.8%	9.6% (Dec 2005)	2.50%
Hungary	7.2%	7.6%	6.00%
Italy	7.7%	7.7% (Dec 2005)	2.50%
Latvia	9.0%	8.0%	3.96%
Lithuania	8.2%	6.6%	2.81%
Morocco	10.5%	N/A	2.30%
Poland	17.7%	17.0%	4.00%
Portugal	7.6%	7.7%	2.50%
Slovakia	16.4%	15.8%	3.50%
Slovenia	6.3%	6.3% (Jan 2006)	3.50%
Spain	9.2%	8.7%	2.50%
Turkey	10.3%	N/A	13.50%
United Kingdom	4.7%	5.1%	4.50%
USA	5.1%	4.8%	4.75%
EU-25	8.7%	8.5%	2.50%
Eurozone	8.6%	8.2%	2.50%

* Exchange rate 1 US dollar to €0.8103 as at 21 April 2006.

** The growth rate in Florida is calculated by using a Gross State Product (GSP), which is a similar concept to that of the Gross Domestic Product (GDP), but at the state level.

*** Exchange rate 1 pound sterling to €1.4436 as at 21 April 2006.

Appendix 1: Economic data (continued)

Country	Inflation Rate, 2005	Inflation Rate, February 2006	FDI Inflow 2005, EUR Million
Bulgaria	5.0%	3.0%	€1,876
Cyprus	2.0%	2.3%	N/A
Czech Republic	1.6%	2.4%	€5,233
Dubai	4.5%	N/A	$11,300 (€9,156.1)*
Estonia	4.1%	4.5%	€837.9 (2004 est)
Florida	3.4%	3.6%	N/A
France	1.9%	2.0%	€43,022
Germany	1.9%	2.1%	€26,264
Greece	3.5%	3.1%	€212
Hungary	3.5%	2.3%	€2,948 (2004 est)
Italy	2.2%	2.2%	€12,720
Latvia	6.9%	7.0%	€508
Lithuania	2.7%	3.4%	€807
Morocco	2.1%	N/A	N/A
Poland	2.2%	0.9%	€6,132
Portugal	2.1%	2.9%	€2,504
Slovakia	2.8%	4.3%	€1,595
Slovenia	2.5%	2.3%	€5,556.7 (2004 est)
Spain	3.4%	4.1%	€15,130
Turkey	7.7%	8.2%	$9,650 (€7,819)*
United Kingdom	2.1%	2.0%	£90,500 (€130,647.9)***
USA	3.4%	3.6%	$116,813 million (€94,650.5)*
EU-25	2.2%	2.2%	N/A
Eurozone	2.2%	2.3%	N/A

* Exchange rate 1 US dollar to €0.8103 as at 21 April 2006.

** The growth rate in Florida is calculated by using a Gross State Product (GSP), which is a similar concept to that of the Gross Domestic Product (GDP), but at the state level.

*** Exchange rate 1 pound sterling to €1.4436 as at 21 April 2006.

Appendix 2: Taxation synopsis

Country	Income Tax	Corporation Tax	Capital Gains Tax (Individual)	Wealth Tax
Bulgaria	0-24%	15%	Taxed as income	Nil
Cyprus	20-30%	10%	20%	Nil
Czech Republic	15-32%	24%	Taxed as income	Nil
Dubai	Nil	Nil	Nil	Nil
Estonia	Flat rate of 23%	23%	Taxed as income	Nil
Florida	10-35%	Federal Corporation Rate (15-35%) +5.5%	5-15%	$0.5 per $1,000
France	0-48.09%	33.33%	16%	0.55-1.8%
Germany	0-42%	25%	Taxed as income	Nil
Greece	0-40%	29%	Taxed as income	Nil
Hungary	18-36%	16%	25%	Nil
Italy	23-43%	33%	12.5%	Nil
Latvia	Flat rate of 25%	15%	Taxed as income	Nil
Lithuania	Flat rate of 33%	15%	10%	Nil
Morocco	0-44%	35%	20%	Nil
Poland	19-40%	19%	10%	Nil
Portugal	10.5-42%	25-27%	25%	Nil
Slovakia	Flat rate of 19%	19%	Taxed as income	Nil
Slovenia	16-50%	25%	Taxed as income	Nil
Spain	15-45%	35%	35%	0.2-2.5%
Turkey	15-35%	30%	Taxed as income	Nil

Appendix 3: Transaction costs

Country	Total Transaction Costs
Bulgaria	8-10%
Cyprus	5-8%
Czech Republic	About 8%
Dubai	3-6%
Estonia	4-6%
Florida	2-5%
France	12-15%
Germany	10-12%
Greece	15-20%
Hungary	8-10%
Italy	15%
Latvia	4-5%
Lithuania	3-5%
Morocco	6-7%
Poland	8-10%
Portugal	8-10%
Slovakia	3-5%
Slovenia	About 5%
Spain	8-12%
Turkey	5-6%

Appendix 4: Holidaymaker's favourite destinations

A. British holidaymakers' top holiday destinations 2005

1. Spain
2. France
3. Greece
4. United States
5. Italy
6. Irish Republic
7. Netherlands
8. Portugal
9. Turkey
10. Cyprus
11. The Caribbean

Source: Association of British Travel Agents
www.abtamembers.org

B. World holidaymakers' top holiday destinations 2004

1. France
2. Spain
3. United States
4. China
5. Italy
6. United Kingdom
7. Hong Kong (China)
8. Mexico
9. Germany
10. Austria
11. Canada
12. Turkey
13. Malaysia
14. Ukraine
15. Poland
16. Greece
17. Hungary
18. Thailand
19. Portugal
20. Netherlands

Source: World Tourist Organisation
www.world-tourism.org

Appendix 5: Countries with expatriot residents drawing UK state pensions (2003)

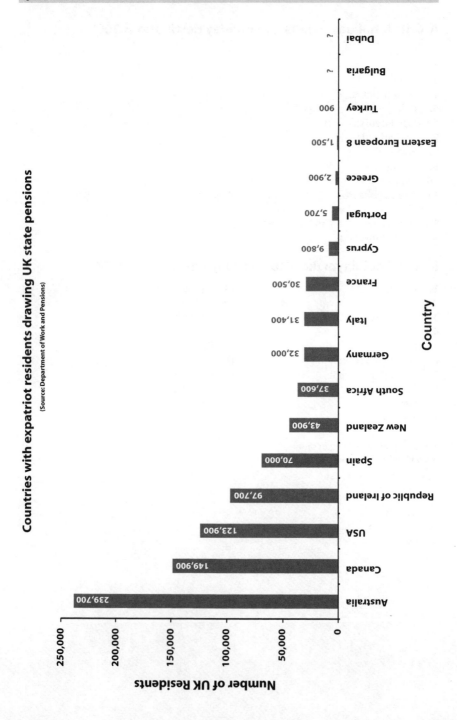

Countries with expatriot residents drawing UK state pensions

(Source: Department of Work and Pensions)

Country	Number of UK Residents
Dubai	~
Bulgaria	~
Turkey	900
Eastern European 8	1,500
Greece	2,900
Portugal	5,700
Cyprus	9,800
France	30,500
Italy	31,400
Germany	32,000
South Africa	37,600
New Zealand	43,900
Spain	70,000
Republic of Ireland	97,700
USA	123,900
Canada	149,900
Australia	239,700

Appendix 6: Low-cost airline routes from UK airports

EasyJet routes as at 18 April 2006 (Source: www.easyjet.com)

Aberdeen	London Luton	
Belfast Intl	Alicante	Liverpool
	Amsterdam	London Gatwick
	Berlin Schoenefeld	London Luton
	Bristol	London Stansted
	Edinburgh	Málaga
	Faro	Newcastle
	Geneva	Nice
	Glasgow	Palma (Mallorca)
	Inverness	Paris Charles de Gaulle
		Rome Ciampino
Bournemouth	Geneva	
Bristol	Alicante	Madrid
	Amsterdam	Mahon (Menorca)
	Barcelona	Málaga
	Belfast Intl	Marseille
	Berlin Schoenefeld	Murcia
	Budapest	Newcastle
	Edinburgh	Nice
	Faro	Palma (Mallorca)
	Geneva	Pisa (Tuscany)
	Glasgow	Prague
	Grenoble	Rijeka
	Hamburg	Rome Ciampino
	Inverness	Toulouse
	Krakow	Valencia
	La Rochelle	Venice Marco Polo
Doncaster/Sheffield	Geneva	
Edinburgh	Alicante	Geneva
	Amsterdam	London Gatwick
	Belfast Intl	London Luton
	Bristol	London Stansted
Glasgow	Alicante	London Luton
	Belfast Intl	London Stansted
	Berlin Schoenefeld	Málaga
	Bristol	Palma (Mallorca)

Appendix 6: Low-cost airline routes from UK airports (continued)

EasyJet routes as at 18 April 2006 (Source: www.easyjet.com)

Inverness	Belfast Intl	London Gatwick
	Bristol	London Luton

Liverpool	Alicante	Ibiza
	Amsterdam	Krakow
	Barcelona	Madrid
	Basel-Mulhouse	Mahon (Menorca)
	Belfast Intl	Málaga
	Berlin Schoenefeld	Marseille
	Cologne/Bonn	Nice
	Faro	Palma (Mallorca)
	Geneva	Paris Charles de Gaulle

London Gatwick	Alicante	Madrid
	Almeria	Mahon (Menorca)
	Amsterdam	Málaga
	Athens	Marrakech
	Barcelona	Milan Linate
	Belfast Intl	Milan Malpensa
	Berlin Schoenefeld	Murcia
	Budapest	Nice
	Cologne/Bonn	Olbia
	Cork	Palma (Mallorca)
	Edinburgh	Prague
	Faro	Rome Ciampino
	Geneva	Shannon
	Grenoble	Split
	Ibiza	Toulouse
	Inverness	Valencia
	Knock	Venice Marco Polo

London Luton	Aberdeen	Geneva
	Alicante	Glasgow
	Amsterdam	Grenoble
	Athens	Inverness
	Barcelona	Istanbul
	Basel-Mulhouse	Krakow
	Belfast Intl	Lisbon
	Berlin Schoenefeld	Madrid
	Bordeaux	Málaga
	Bratislava	Nice
	Bremen	Palma (Mallorca)
	Budapest	Paris Charles de Gaulle
	Cagliari (Sardinia)	Rijeka
	Dortmund	Rimini
	Edinburgh	Turin
	Faro	Warsaw

Appendix 6: Low-cost airline routes from UK airports (continued)

EasyJet routes as at 18 April 2006 (Source: www.easyjet.com)

London Stansted	Alicante	Ibiza
	Almeria	Ljubljana
	Amsterdam	Lyon
	Asturias	Málaga
	Barcelona	Munich
	Basel-Mulhouse	Naples
	Belfast Intl	Newcastle
	Bilbao	Nice
	Copenhagen	Palma (Mallorca)
	Edinburgh	Prague
	Faro	Tallinn
	Geneva	Valencia
	Glasgow	

Newcastle	Alicante	Ibiza
	Barcelona	London Stansted
	Belfast Intl	Málaga
	Berlin Schoenefeld	Nice
	Bristol	Palma (Mallorca)
	Budapest	Paris Charles de Gaulle
	Faro	Prague
	Geneva	Rome Ciampino

Nottingham East Midlands	Alicante
	Cologne/Bonn
	Faro
	Geneva
	Ibiza
	Málaga
	Prague
	Rome Ciampino
	Venice Marco Polo

Appendix 6: Low-cost airline routes from UK airports (continued)

Ryanair routes as at 18 June 2006 (Source: www.ryanair.com)

Aberdeen	Dublin
	Liverpool
Birmingham	Dublin
Blackpool	Dublin
	Girona (Barcelona)
	Stansted
Bournemouth	Dublin
	Girona (Barcelona)
	Glasgow (Prestwick)
	Pisa (Florence)
Bristol	Dublin
	Shannon
Cardiff	Dublin
Derry	East Midlands
	Liverpool
	London Stansted
Doncaster/Sheffield	Dublin
	Girona (Barcelona)
	Pisa (Florence)
Durham	Dublin

East Midlands	Bergerac	Lodz
	Berlin Schoenefeld	Murcia (Alicante)
	Carcassonne	Nantes (Brittany)
	Derry	Nîmes
	Dinard	Rome Ciampino
	Dublin	Shannon
	Girona (Barcelona)	Wroclaw
	Limoges	

Edinburgh	Dublin
Humberside	Dublin
Inverness	Liverpool
Leeds Bradford	Dublin

Liverpool	Aberdeen	Girona (Barcelona)
	Alghero (Sardinia)	Granada
	Ancona	Inverness
	Bergerac	Kaunas
	Carcassonne	Kerry
	Cork	Krakow
	Derry	Limoges
	Dublin	Milan (Bergamo)

Appendix 6: Low-cost airline routes from UK airports (continued)

Ryanair routes as at 18 June 2006 (Source: www.ryanair.com)

Liverpool (continued)	Murcia (Alicante)	Rome Ciampino
	Nîmes	Santander
	Oslo (Torp)	Santiago de Comp.
	Pisa (Florence)	Seville
	Porto	Shannon
	Poznan	Tampere
	Reus (Barcelona)	Venice (Treviso)
	Riga	Wroclaw

London Gatwick	Cork
	Dublin
	Knock-Ireland West
	Shannon

London Luton	Brest	Nîmes
	Dublin	Reus (Barcelona)
	Girona (Barcelona)	Rome Ciampino
	Knock-Ireland West	Shannon
	Milan (Bergamo)	Stockholm
	Murcia (Alicante)	

London Stansted	Aarhus	Genoa
	Alghero (Sardinia)	Girona (Barcelona)
	Almeria	Glasgow (Prestwick)
	Altenburg (Leipzig)	Gothenburg
	Ancona	Granada
	Balaton	Graz
	Bari	Grenoble Lyon
	Bergerac	Hamburg (Lubeck)
	Berlin Schoenefeld	Haugesund
	Biarritz	Jerez
	Blackpool	Karlsruhe-Baden
	Bologna	Kaunas
	Bratislava (Vienna)	Kerry
	Brindisi	Knock-Ireland West
	Brno	Krakow
	Bydgoszcz	La Rochelle
	Carcassonne	Lamezia
	Cork	Limoges
	Derry	Linz
	Dinard	Lodz
	Dublin	Malmo (Sturup)
	Düsseldorf (Weeze)	Milan (Bergamo)
	Eindhoven	Montpellier
	Esbjerg	Murcia (Alicante)
	Frankfurt (Hahn)	Nantes (Brittany)
	Friedrichshafen	Newquay
	Gdansk	Oslo (Torp)

Appendix 6: Low-cost airline routes from UK airports (continued)

Ryanair routes as at 18 June 2006 (Source: www.ryanair.com)

London Stansted (cont)	Palermo	Santiago de Comp.
	Parma	Seville
	Pau (Pyrenees)	Shannon
	Perpignan	Stockholm
	Pescara	Szczecin
	Pisa (Florence)	Tampere
	Poitiers	Toulon St Tropez
	Porto	Tours Loire Valley
	Poznan	Trieste
	Reus (Barcelona)	Turin
	Riga	Valencia
	Rodez	Valladolid
	Rome Ciampino	Venice (Treviso)
	Rzeszow	Verona (Brescia)
	St Etienne (Lyon)	Vitoria/Gasteiz
	Salzburg	Wroclaw
	Santander	Zaragoza (Pyrenees)
Manchester	Dublin	
	Shannon	
Newcastle	Dublin	
	Milan (Bergamo)	
	Oslo (Torp)	
Newquay	London Stansted	

Appendix 7: Exchange rates

A. Exchange rates as at 10 April 2006

		1 UK Pound Sterling
Bulgarian Lev	BGN	2.82
Cyprus Pound	CYP	0.83
Czech Koruna	CZK	41.43
Estonian Kroon	EEK	22.56
Euro	EUR	1.44
Hungarian Forint	HUF	386.74
Latvian Lat	LTV	1.01
Lithuanian Lita	LTL	4.98
Moroccan Dirham	MAD	15.83
Polish Zloty	PLN	5.73
Slovak Koruna	SKK	54.11
Slovenian Tolar	SIT	345.02
Turkish New Lira	TRY	2.34
UAE Dirham	AED	6.4
US Dollar	USD	1.74

Source: www.oanda.com

B. Exchange rates historical charts 2001–2006

British Pound to Bulgarian Lev

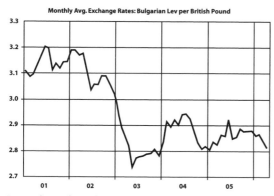

Monthly Avg. Exchange Rates: Bulgarian Lev per British Pound

Source: http://fx.sauder.ubc.ca

Appendix 7: Exchange rates (continued)

British Pound to Cyprus Pound

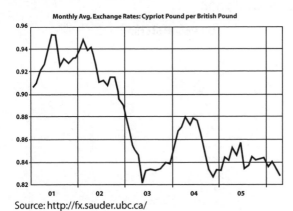

Source: http://fx.sauder.ubc.ca/

British Pound to Czech Koruna

Source: http://fx.sauder.ubc.ca/

British Pound to Estonian Kroon

Source: www.ozforex.com.au

Appendix 7: Exchange rates (continued)

British Pound to Euro

Source: http://fx.sauder.ubc.ca/

British Pound to Hungarian Forint

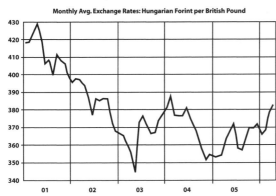

Source: http://fx.sauder.ubc.ca/

British Pound to Latvian Lat

Source: www.ozforex.com.au

Appendix 7: Exchange rates (continued)

British Pound to Lithuanian Lit

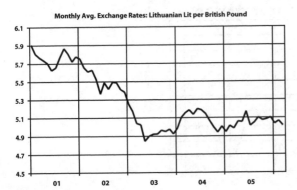

Source: http://fx.sauder.ubc.ca

British Pound to Moroccan Dirham

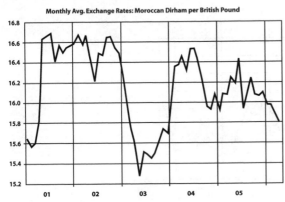

Source: http://fx.sauder.ubc.ca

British Pound to Polish Zloty

Source: http://fx.sauder.ubc.ca

Appendix 7: Exchange rates (continued)

British Pound to Slovak Koruna

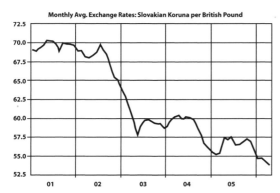

Source: http://fx.sauder.ubc.ca

British Pound to Slovenian Tolar (September 2003 till April 2006)

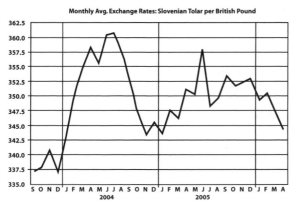

Source: http://fx.sauder.ubc.ca

British Pound to Turkish Lira

Source: http://fx.sauder.ubc.ca

Appendix 7: Exchange rates (continued)

British Pound to UAE Dirham

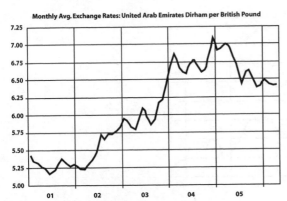

Source: http://fx.sauder.ubc.ca

British Pound to US Dollar

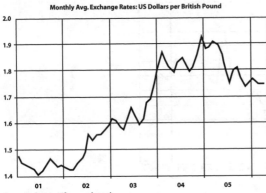

Source: http://fx.sauder.ubc.ca

Appendix 8: List of UK's double taxation treaties

1	Antigua and Barbuda	37	Indonesia	72	Philippines
2	Argentina	38	Ireland (Republic of)	**73**	**Poland**
3	Australia	39	Isle of Man	**74**	**Portugal**
4	Austria	40	Israel	75	Romania
5	Azerbaijan	**41**	**Italy**	76	Russian Federation
6	Bangladesh	42	Ivory Coast	77	St Kitts and Nevis
7	Barbados		(Côte d'Ivoire)	78	Sierra Leone
8	Belarus	43	Jamaica	79	Singapore
9	Belgium	44	Japan	**80**	**Slovak Republic**
10	Belize	45	Jersey		**(Slovakia)**
11	Bolivia	46	Kazakhstan	**81**	**Slovenia**
12	Botswana	47	Kenya	82	Solomon Islands
13	Brunei	48	Kiribati	83	South Africa
14	**Bulgaria**	49	Korea (Republic of)	84	Spain
15	Canada	50	Kuwait	85	Sri Lanka
16	China	**51**	**Latvia**	86	Sudan
17	Croatia	52	Lesotho	87	Swaziland
18	**Cyprus**	53	Luxembourg	88	Sweden
19	**Czech Republic**	54	Macedonia	89	Switzerland
20	Denmark	55	Malawi	90	Thailand
21	Egypt	56	Malaysia	91	Trinidad and Tobago
22	**Estonia**	57	Malta	92	Tunisia
23	Falkland Islands	58	Mauritius	**93**	**Turkey**
24	Fiji	59	Mexico	94	Tuvalu
25	Finland	60	Mongolia	95	Uganda
26	**France**	61	Montserrat	96	Ukraine
27	Gambia	**62**	**Morocco**	**97**	**United States of**
28	**Germany**	63	Myanmar (Burma)		**America**
29	Ghana	64	Namibia	98	Uzbekistan
30	**Greece**	65	Netherlands	99	Venezuela
31	Grenada	66	New Zealand	100	Vietnam
32	Guernsey	67	Nigeria	101	Yugoslavia
33	Guyana	68	Norway		(Federal Republic)
34	**Hungary**	69	Oman	102	Zambia
35	Iceland	70	Pakistan	103	Zimbabwe
36	India	71	Papua New Guinea		

Source: HM Revenue & Customs
www.hmrc.gov.uk

Appendix 9: Corruption synopsis

Transparency International CPI 2005

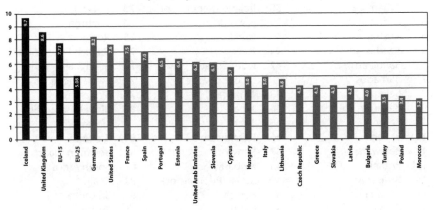

CPI Score relates to perceptions of the degree of corruption as seen by businesspeople and country analysts and ranges between 10 (highly clean) and 0 (highly corrupt).

Source: www.transparency.org

For a complete version of methodology, please go on www.transparency.org/policy_research/surveys_indices

Explanatory notes:

The Transparency International Corruption Perceptions Index (CPI) ranks countries in terms of the degree to which corruption is perceived to exist among public officials and politicians. It is a composite index, drawing on corruption-related data in expert surveys carried out by a variety of reputable institutions. It reflects the views of businesspeople and analysts from around the world, including experts who are locals in the countries evaluated.

The CPI focuses on corruption in the public sector and defines corruption as the abuse of public office for private gain. The surveys used in compiling the CPI ask questions that relate to the misuse of public power for private benefit, with a focus, for example, on bribe-taking by public officials in public procurement. The sources do not distinguish between administrative and political corruption or between petty and grand corruption.

The CPI 2005 draws on 16 different polls and surveys from 10 independent institutions. Transparency International strives to ensure that the sources used are of the highest quality and that the survey work is performed with complete integrity. To qualify, the data must be well documented and sufficient to permit a judgement on its reliability.

The institutions who provided data for the CPI 2005 are: Columbia University, Economist Intelligence Unit, Freedom House, Information International, International Institute for Management Development, Merchant International Group, Political and Economic Risk Consultancy, United Nations Economic Commission for Africa, World Economic Forum and World Markets Research Centre.

Appendix 10: EU Objective 1 areas

The eligible regions are:

- regions where the GDP per head is at or below 75% of the Community average;
- the thinly populated regions of Finland and Sweden (fewer than 8 people per sq. km);
- the outermost regions (French Overseas Departments, Canary Islands, Azores and Madeira).
- **Austria:** Burgenland
- **Czech Republic:** Strední Cechy, Jihozápad, Severozápad, Severovýhod, Jihovýchod, Strední Morava, Moravskoslezsko
- **Estonia:** Eesti
- **Finland:** East Finland, Central Finland (in part), North Finland (in part)
- **France:** Guadeloupe, Martinique, French Guiana, Réunion
- **Germany:** Brandenburg, Mecklenburg-Western Pomerania, Saxony, Saxony-Anhalt, Thuringia
- **Greece:** East Macedonia, Thrace, Central Macedonia, West Macedonia, Thessaly, Epirus, Ionian Islands, Western Greece, Continental Greece, Peloponnese, Attica, North Aegean, South Aegean, Crete (the whole of the Greek territory)
- **Hungary:** Közép-Magyarország, Közép-Dunántúl, Nyugat-Dunántúl, Dél-Dunántúl, Észak-Magyarország,Észak-Alföld, Dél-Alföld
- **Ireland:** Border, Midlands and Western
- **Italy:** Campania, Apulia, Basilicata, Calabria, Sicily, Sardinia
- **Latvia:** Latvija
- **Lithuania:** Lietuva
- **Malta:** Malta
- **Poland:** Dolnoslaskie, Kujawsko-Pomorskie, Lubelskie, Lubuskie, Lódzkie, Malopolskie, Mazowieckie, Opolskie, Podkarpackie, Podlaskie, Pomorskie, Slaskie, Swietokrzyskie, Warminsko-Mazurskie, Wielkopolskie, Zachodniopomorskie
- **Portugal:** North, Centre, Alentejo, Algarve, Azores, Madeira
- **Slovakia:** Západné Slovensko, Stredné Slovensko, Východné Slovensko
- **Slovenia:** Slovenija
- **Spain:** Galicia, Asturias Principality, Castile-Leon, Castile-La Mancha, Extremadura, Valencia, Andalucía, region of Murcia, Ceuta-Melilla, Canary Islands
- **Sweden:** North-Central Sweden (in part), Central Norrland (in part), Upper Norrland (in part)
- **United Kingdom:** South Yorkshire, West Wales & The Valleys, Cornwall & the Isles of Scilly, Merseyside

Source: http://europa.eu.int/comm/regional_policy/objective1/regions_en.htm

Appendix 11: Useful websites

In addition to the websites already mentioned at the back of each case study, you may find the following helpful:

- **BBC** www.bbc.co.uk

- **Bewarethesharks.com** www.bewarethesharks.com

- **Central Intelligence Agency (CIA), The** www.cia.gov/cia/publications/factbook

- **Country Analysis Resource, The** www.countryrisk.com

- **David Smith's (Economics Editor for Sunday Times)** www.economicsuk.com/blog

- **Department for Communities and Local Government** www.odpm.gov.uk

- **Economist, The** www.economist.com

- **Economist Intelligence Unit** www.eiu.com

- **European Central Bank (ECB)** www.ecb.int

- **European Union On-line, The** http://europa.eu.int

- **Eurostat (Statistical Office of the European Communities)** http://epp.eurostat.cec.eu.int

- **Federal Reserve** www.federalreserve.gov

- **Financial Times** http://news.ft.com/home/uk

- **International Monetary Fund (IMF)** www.imf.org

- **Investment News** www.moneyweek.com

- **OECD Observer** www.oecdobserver.org

- **Organisation for Economic Co-operation and Development (OECD)** www.oecd.org

- **Property Investor News** www.property-investor-news.com

- **Royal Institute of Chartered Surveyors (RICS), The** www.rics.org

- **Transparency International** www.transparency.org

- **UK Statistics** www.statistics.gov.uk

- **World Bank** www.worldbank.org

Glossary

Asset	Anything owned by an individual or a company that has a cash value. This includes property, savings, shares, bonds, jewellery, wine, furniture or other investments.
Bank of England	The Bank of England is the Central Bank of the United Kingdom and is responsible for issuing currency and government debt. In 1997, the government gave the Bank the power to set monetary policy and a committee (the Monetary Policy Committee) meets once a month to set interest rates.
Birth rate	The average number of births during a year per 1,000 inhabitants.
Budget deficit	The amount by which government spending exceeds government revenues for a given fiscal year. Such a deficit is financed by government borrowing.
Cadastral value	It's an administrative value which is used as a base or a point of reference for tax.
Capital gain	The profit (gain) from the sale of a capital asset, such as a property or a share.
Capital Gains Tax	A tax paid on the gains made from a sale of a capital asset, such as a property or a share.
Contract	A binding agreement between two or more parties that is enforceable by law.
Conveyancing	The legal process of transferring property ownership from one person or company to another.

Corporation Tax	Corporation Tax is a direct tax on the profits made by companies or associations.
Corruption	The practice of improper or unlawful conduct, and other means to gain dishonestly.
Democracy	Democracy is a political system in which power lies with the citizens, through a fair electoral process.
Double taxation treaty	Double taxation treaties between two countries ensure that tax on capital and income is not paid twice.
Economics	Economics studies the allocation of scarce resources to satisfy unlimited wants.
EU-25 & EU-15	The EU-25 is the collection of nations that form the European Union, after the accession of the ten new members in May 2004. The EU-15 is the term applied to the member states before the ten new states joined the European Union.
European Central Bank	The European Central Bank determines monetary policy for the participating member states in the European Monetary Union since 1 January 1999.
European Commission	The executive branch of the European Union which is responsible for applying the statutory regulations of the European Union.
Eurozone	The Eurozone is the set of European members that have adopted the common currency, the euro.
Exchange rate	The price of one currency expressed in terms of another currency.
Federal republic	A federal republic is a state in which powers of the central government are restricted and constituent parts retain some elements of self-government, such as the United States.
Federal Reserve	The Federal Reserve is the Central Bank of the United States which governs monetary policy.
Fiscal policy	A macro-economic policy pursued by the government to manage the economy through its spending and taxation powers. It's designed to affect the business cycle, maintain and attain price stability,

as well as sustain economic growth and full employment.

Foreign direct investment (FDI)	FDI refers to the amount of money invested in a country by companies owned in another country.
Free-trade agreement	A free-trade agreement is the absence of tariffs paid from one government to another in return for trading in each other's territory.
Freehold	A property where you own both the property and the land on which it's built.
GDP per capita	The GDP per capita is GDP divided by the total population of a country.
Gearing	A term used to describe the ratio of your own money versus money borrowed from a lender in an investment.
Gross domestic product (GDP)	GDP is the total value of goods and services produced in each country each year.
Gross yield	The income expressed as a percentage of the total cost of the property.
Hotspot	A jet-to-let hotspot is created when demand for property exceeds the available supply and prices are pushed higher, above the international average, by those wanting to buy *or* a jet-to-let hotspot is a country, region or city where economic factors are combining to increase long-term wealth, which will have a direct, positive effect on property prices and rents.
Illiquid	An asset that cannot be readily converted into cash through a sale or otherwise; the opposite of liquid.
Income Tax	Income Tax is a tax paid on income. It's paid by employees and people who are self-employed.
Inflation rate	The rate of increase in prices of goods and services expressed as a percentage. It's calculated on a monthly or annual basis.
Interest-only mortgage	With this type of mortgage the total loan remains constant throughout the term, while the monthly payments only pay the interest. When the mortgage

	term is complete the original capital borrowed needs to be repaid.
Interest rate	The amount of interest paid in addition to the loan, usually expressed as a percentage. Interest can be viewed as a fee from the provider of a loan for providing finance.
Jet-to-let	A generic term used to describe overseas property investment.
Jet-to-sell	Buying a property overseas with the express intention of selling it at a later date to take advantage of the increased price through appreciation. This is a particularly profitable strategy when done in rising markets, although it also encompasses renovation projects that are improved and sold for profit.
Leasehold	The right to possession and use of land for a fixed period of time. The lease is the agreement that creates this right.
Leverage	The use of borrowed capital to increase the return on a cash investment. For leverage to be profitable, the rate of return on the investment must be higher than the cost (interest) of the borrowed money. It can be interchanged for the term gearing.
Liquid	A term to describe the properties of cash or other assets that can be readily converted into cash (such as stocks and shares).
Literacy rate	The number of people in a country who can read or write to a set standard.
Live-and-let	Investing in a property with the intention of using it personally and renting it when unoccupied to create an income.
Loan to value (LTV)	The ratio of the amount of the mortgage as a percentage of the value of the property.
Monetary policy	The actions of a central bank to influence the cost of money and credit by affecting interest rates.

Monetary Policy Committee	A committee of the Bank of England which meets every month to decide the official interest rate in the UK and is independent of government.
Multiplier effect	In economics, a multiplier effect occurs when a change in investment or spending causes a disproportionate change in overall demand and greater wealth as a result.
Net yield	The income return on an investment after subtracting all expenses *or* net yield is gross yield after all costs.
Notary	A notary is a public officer who is legally empowered to draw up legal documents and witness signatures in accordance with specific state laws.
Off-plan	A property that is being purchased at the planning stage and is yet to be built. The investor therefore buys the property based on what he has seen on the architect's plans and drawings.
Price elasticity	Refers to price elasticity which is the ratio of the change of quantity demanded, or supplied, to a change in price.
Privatisation	Privatisation is the transfer of ownership of government enterprises to private individuals and businesses.
Real income	The purchasing power of your income. Effectively the amount of goods and services it will buy.
Repayment mortgage	With this type of mortgage the whole mortgage is repaid over a fixed period of time, referred to as the mortgage's term. Monthly payments include both interest and a proportion of the capital.
Republic	A state or nation in which power rests with its citizens and is exercised by representatives elected by them and responsible to them.
Return on investment (ROI)	A financial measure of the relative return from an investment, usually expressed as a percentage of earnings produced by an asset to the amount invested.

Stamp duty (or equivalent)	Stamp duty is a tax payable by the buyer of a property, calculated as a percentage of sales price. Countries have different rules and calculations.
Strategy	A long-term plan of action designed to achieve a particular goal.
Substitution effect	As the price of one good becomes more expensive, the substitution effect causes the consumer to substitute for a cheaper comparable good.
Supply and demand	In its simplest form, it is the economic theory that when supply exceeds demand, prices fall, and when demand exceeds supply, prices rise.
Surveyor	The person who is responsible for surveying the property. In the United Kingdom, he will usually be a member of the Royal Institute of Chartered Surveyors and will be a qualified expert in carrying out property inspections.
Tenant	An occupant of a property owned by another party. Tenants pay rent to the property's owner (landlord), sometimes through a letting agent or a separate individual.
Total fertility rate (TFR)	The average number of children expected to be born to a woman during her lifetime.
Unemployment rate	The number of people of working age without a job. This is expressed as a percentage of the working age population, which in the UK is between 16 and 65.

Index

This index covers all chapters (except end-of-chapter key points summaries), country studies and Appendices.